VALUES EDUCATION AND TECHNOLOGY

PETER C. EMBERLEY

Values Education and Technology: The Ideology of Dispossession

UNIVERSITY OF TORONTO PRESS

Toronto Buffalo London

© University of Toronto Press Incorporated 1995
Toronto Buffalo London
Printed in Canada

ISBN 0-8020-0423-7

Printed on acid-free paper

Toronto Studies in Education

Canadian Cataloguing in Publication Data

Emberley, Peter C. (Peter Christopher), 1956–
   Values education and technology : the ideology of dispossession

   (Toronto studies in education)
   Includes bibliographical references and index.
   ISBN 0-8020-0423-7

   1. Moral education.   2. Values – Study and teaching.
   I. Title.   II. Series.

   LC268.E52 1995   370.11'4   C94-932841-3

University of Toronto Press acknowledges the
financial assistance to its publishing program of the
Canada Council and the Ontario Arts Council.

This book has been published with the help of a grant from
the Canadian Federation for the Humanities, using funds
provided by the Social Sciences and Humanities
Research Council of Canada.

The original note sang of action, need, and terror; the overtone lulls us into a soft dilettante sleep.

Friedrich Nietzsche

We have been left with no words which ... summon out of uncertainty the good of which we may sense the dispossession.

George Grant

Contents

Acknowledgments

This study developed through a series of fortunate encounters and influences. I would like initially to thank the teachers who kindled and stoked my interest in politics and philosophy, Kim Campbell and Timothy Fuller, and my parents, who taught me why certain things are worth caring about. Without their enthusiasm and encouragement, I might never have embarked on the studies culminating in this book. Next, I must thank Barry Cooper, whose work and advice were constant companions while writing this study.

I am grateful to my colleague Tom Darby for the inspiration and stimulation provided in our many provocative hours of debate. And I wish to thank the graduate students – in particular Doug West, Herminio Teixeira, Philippe Azzie, and Peter Lindfield – who have endured my continuous preoccupations with the themes of this book and who contributed to their maturation. None of these should have to bear responsibility for the views expressed here; what errors and infelicities exist are of my own doing.

I am indebted, too, to the Calgary Institute for the Humanities for the resources they made available in my tenure as a post-doctoral fellow so many years ago; to the Challenge '85 program which permitted the Science Policy Research Centre in Ottawa to provide me with research assistants; and to Carleton University for research funds with which to complete this project.

Most particularly I dedicate this work to my wife, without whose support, critical commentary, humour, and patience it would not have been.

Spring 1994
Ottawa

VALUES EDUCATION AND TECHNOLOGY

Introduction

For over thirty years there have been major upheavals in and experimentation with the school curriculum and pedagogical technique. Values education is recurringly the most visible and most hotly contested area of reappraisal. For some, the schools – by promoting new values or new modes of re-evaluating old values – are seen to embark on an attack on the core of traditional morality. Others see the curriculum changes as merely making the practices and reasoning covered under the terms 'ethics' and 'morals' more explicit, consistent, and rational. Some embrace the new progressivism with enthusiasm and relief, and see the efforts in the schools as the most basic building block of social renewal.[1]

There are good reasons for reassessing the traditional school curriculum and particularly the part morality plays in it. The society in which traditional pedagogical theories and practices concerning morality were at home usually consisted of stable social forms and symbols belonging historically to that culture which played the dominant part in setting the tone of North American life. Speaking broadly, that culture was Anglo-Saxon and Protestant, and as such it held to, if even unconsciously, the ethos of European society. Schools could count on the tacit acceptance, even where there was hypocrisy and blunt violation, of a certain way of life, a distinct sensibility, and a code of unspoken taboos.

At least three reasons justify reassessment of the traditional curriculum. First, contemporary societies are increasingly polymorphic, their once-stable symbolic order challenged by ways of life, skills, and practices arising from a wide divergence of races, cultures, and religions. One cannot assume that the virtues and dispositions, the habits and unspoken codes, of the once-predominant culture are today held by most to be self-evidently good. With the extensive 'empowerment' of a great number of sectarian 'identities,' as the vernacular goes, the uncontested acceptance of a single vision of human order is something upon which we can no longer rely.

Second, the traditional sources of moral habits – the church, the family, the community – have come under such severe critical scrutiny, especially by social scientists, that representatives of these institutions have lost their will, in great part, to take on the responsibilities once associated with their moral authority. When the rituals, sensibilities, and customs – that is, the nascent intimations of moral order – of these institutions come to be seen by the intellectual vanguard as compulsive behaviour, or as masks of class-interest, or as reproducing inequitable social structures, then it is obvious that the school cannot continue, blindly and innocently, to build on these inherited foundations. It will have to resubstantiate those elements of the curriculum and pedagogical practice confirming the legitimacy of the ways of traditional institutions or align its own processes with the newly emerging order.

Finally, it cannot be denied that a general fragmentation of order has occurred in the past few decades so that now a vast profusion of images of right and just conduct emanate from an apparently infinite number of points in the social world: television, fundamentalist sects, the film industry, the courts, human rights commissions, popular music, and advocates for the environment and against drugs, violence, and nuclear power. No centre is sufficiently authoritative. No rational critique of one or another of these sources appears to carry much persuasive weight. We should not be surprised that students are more confused and disillusioned than ever and have a greater need for guidance in the midst of such conflicting and divergent options.

Major changes to laws, political forms, and educational institutions cannot, however, be undertaken lightly. The consequences to political order and personal existence are too significant to experiment unreflectively with such major areas of human life. Thus, a responsible assessment of those changes cannot be diverted by arguments which assume that the work is done when the immediate social effect is gauged or even when the minimal conditions of logical coherence have been demonstrated. Least of all should that assessment be mesmerized by fashionable doctrine or conformity to popular causes. Rather, if it is to be comprehensive, it must return to primary and elementary questions.

To date, while values education has been debated in a spirited and occasionally angry fashion, amidst charges of 'relativism,' 'secular humanism,' and 'behaviour-modification,' there has been no effort to assess it at the level where the programs imply a position regarding the fundamental relation that humans have to existence in all its dimensions. Nor has there been reflection on the comprehensive social and political implications which inevitably follow from adopting one or another metaphysical perspective or the perception of reality on which it is based. But a thorough consideration of the full meaning of proposals for change requires precisely such a wide-sweeping audit to uproot the historical and philosophical antecedents of the various models and to make clear how even undeclared and fragmentary principles implying commitments regarding questions of ground and core, substance and meaning, underscore a definite perception of reality and specific political and social effects.

Why such an audit is particularly important in evaluating the values education initiatives is because, unlike changes in the study of separate subject areas (history, physics, literature), the way students are stimulated to recognize human limit and possibility, to acknowledge others, and to give meaning to the course of their lives determines the terms of and even the nature of their participation in reality. When the coordinates of human judgment are established, what is at stake is the sense of existence itself.

The initiatives advanced by values education aimed at wide-sweeping changes to what was called the 'traditional' curriculum. Probing what it means to say that the schools must depart from a 'banking model' of schooling, or reject the 'bag of virtues' approach, or discontinue 'fostering the immorality of morality,' reveals that more was occurring in the educational reform than simply a search for a more effectual pedagogy or even for new measures of human doing. What was being rejected was the metaphysic of the traditional curriculum.

The experiential core of the old curriculum was based on obedience and commemoration. Each of these has a pedigree in Judaeo-Christian and Hellenic accounts of the mode of participation in reality. Each confers a distinct 'tonality' on the nature of that participation. Understanding that mode of participation explains the significance bestowed on recollection, on reverence, and on iconolatry. However crudely and bluntly notions of authority, respect, habituation, or honour were implemented, each was an implicit statement about what a human being is and what other humans are due. That statement invoked a sense that human life was driven by a desire for perfection and yet was harnessed by inevitable imperfection. Complex notions of consubstantiation, eternity, psychic sublimation and purification, and spiritual freedom under-lay the pedagogical practices of character-formation, story-telling, and memory-training.

The 'traditional curriculum,' as it was formed through the late Hel-lenic and Roman ages, and was further moulded through the Middle Ages, met opposition already in the fifteenth century. Thinkers of what is commonly recognized as the beginning of the modern age had grave reservations about the legacy of Athens and Rome. These moderns were less inclined to praise the practice of virtue than to celebrate the exercise of freedom and the unique power of expression of each person. Their Protestant Christianity led them to see education's objectives tied to worldly vocations and earthly consonance. The reforms in educational technique – self-discovery, interactive learning, the primacy of imagina-tion, and practical skills – spoke to a humanity born to creative exercise of freedom. But these notions of freedom and individual expression were rarely understood as without limits. They were as much tied to an order of reality, and to concrete forms of potentiality and actuality, as were the practices of the past. A person was a being within distinctive bounds, with particular determinations and with a structured potential-ity. The great modern programs of education – in Locke, Kant, and Hegel – combined a healthy balance of transcendence and practicality, freedom and order, individuality and community. The curriculum was grounded in a perception of intelligible order. It would be wrong to say that this meant a radical break from the 'traditional curriculum' for the modern curriculum, as it was developed in the three hundred years before our own century, sustained the most foundational characteristics of the education of antiquity.

To speak of 'empowered' individuals, 'proactive' behaviour, 'upgrad-ing' and 'downgrading' values, or 'being, not having,' however, is not a mere verbal refurbishing of the traditional curriculum. Nor do I believe that such language can be understood as a new variant on the modern *humanist* themes of spontaneous freedom and creative self-expression. One might say, instead, that behind this language lies a more radical expectation arising from the desire for a wholly new mode of valuation and from a radically novel construct of reality. From the healthy modern recognition of freedom has broken a dark and corrosive fragment whose spirit of relentless negativity is the subject of this book. That fragment defines our contemporary times and it threatens to undo the singular achievements of modernity and the residual ballast of tradition still informing the modern enterprise.

Modernity dismissed obedience and commemoration as routine behaviour, but the contemporary language of empowerment and 'decentring' goes further. What is in fact at stake is the interpretation of the structure of being itself. The wholesale rejection of every vestige of the old curriculum means denying two major metaphysical assumptions: that being manifests itself in images of finality, perfection, and order, and that the human intimation of such images coincides with the recognition of a permanent structure of tension or unrest in human existence. These denials were most thoroughly expressed by Nietzsche and it is our contemporary fate to live with the popular dissemination of Nietzsche's forceful rejection of everything which preceded him. Living under the shadow of Nietzsche's opposition to the metaphysical tradition is what I mean by 'contemporary.' The social and cultural forms defining our 'contemporary' times emerged from the *danse macabre* of the *fin-de-siècle* movement. The political form was struck when the realignments of nation-states began in 1945.

The educational field is not alone in raising questions concerning that metaphysic. One might say that an epochal transformation is at present occurring at all levels of discourse about human existence – in the natural sciences, philosophy, poetry, technology, economic and social analysis. It is a questioning driven by the idea that being *is* nothingness: instead of substance or form, at the source of all beings there is a vitalistic, generative abundance perpetually deferring completion or determinateness. This is a questioning impatient with metaphysical notions of matter, absolute space and time, trans-historical reality, the autonomous subject, natural laws, and moral principles. Having penetrated the educational field, that questioning has made the 'traditional curriculum' (to hypostatize what is in fact a plurality of historical programs) a 'problem.' Examining the language of values education reveals how the educational field is experimenting in aligning itself with the agendas of the leading spokesmen of progressive thinking today.

What does it signify when these spokesmen argue that, counter to the practice of the past, we must now think both 'globally' and 'locally,' 'holistically' and 'omni-dimensionally'? What is meant in saying that educators cannot be authoritative or make judgments, that the order of taxonomies, the tableaux of identities and differences, the parameters of origin and finitude, and the limits of foundation and image of perfection are no longer a meaningful way of making sense of reality? What is involved when things and stable identities, tradition and transcendence, are suddenly seen as anathema to the 'human'?

I have chosen the metaphor 'dispossession' to condense this sense of misgiving with and intolerance of the world of dense bodies, sequential time, enclosed space, finitude, and completion. In short, I am referring to a desire for dispossession of the stable aspect of beings. What links my chapters is a meditation on the centrality of 'possession' in Western consciousness. What I mean by possession runs the gamut of our relation of belongingness with things, to what is conveyed in speaking of 'self-possession,' to our notion of possessing truth. Ours is an age that now speaks of 'dispossession,' meaning a multiple cluster of disengagements: of objects, property, self-identity, and prescriptive principles. Some speak of the contemporary age as requiring an 'affirmative dissolution' of all those concrete phenomena which permitted relations of possession. It was my reading of Hegel's *On Christianity: Early Theological Writings*, and particularly his account of love and possession, and then my reflections on some of Heidegger's epigones (Sartre, Marcel, Mounier) which led me to understand how some could construe 'being' and 'having' as antithetical options.[2] By 'dispossession,' I wanted to convey the expectation which lies at the roots of the contemporary reappraisals, that we can denounce our possessive affinity towards being and see our existence as the experience of perpetual generative self-overcoming. A consideration of the roots of values education, in my mind, opens up the question of how we are to think about this new relation to being.

The question of metaphysics also lies at the core of the second term of my analysis – technology. We live in the midst of a technological dynamo of unprecedented power. Our lives depend, in decisive ways, on technologies steering our conceptions of potentiality and actuality, of birth and death, of pleasure and risk, of achievement and failure. Some would say that no area of human endeavour – war, culture, sex, politics, leisure, or play – is free of technology's touch or transfigurative influence. But nor are we sure any longer of where the human stands before this dynamo. When we think of nuclear energy, genetic splicing, space exploration, and toxic spills, the scale of the power involved seems to transcend human measure. The complexity of the system-linkages and knowledge-transfers which make these technologies possible is increasingly calling into question the continued viability of traditional theories of individual responsibility, agency, intentionality, and causality.[3]

The classic ethical teachings, particularly those of modernity, ran parallel to politico-legal conceptions of the sovereign individual, sequential and localizable action, and common-sense reasoning. Technological 'progress,' however, depends on overcoming i) the inefficiency of the idiosyncratic individual, ii) the context-specific (culture, craft) use of techniques, and iii) the concrete basis or contents of practical sense. Efficiency, technology's standard, is increased by aggregating skill-specializations, by systematizing discrete operations, and by fostering universalizable, instrumental procedures. In technology's most advanced form, as communications and information systems, the speed, scope, and ethereality of operations demote to near insignificance the part of individual initiative, non-instrumental goods, and concrete, situational modes of judgment in human life, leaving behind the evident experience of living associated with a body-oriented, materials-based, segmented culture. Individuation and fixed form, or contents and context, impede the fluidity of the revolving functionalities and circulating simulations of the new technological environment. That is why 'deskilling' has become the operative term of so much of contemporary education.

Many now wonder if technological development – the increasing mastery of nature and of contingency by systematization, optimalization, and rationalization – does not have its own momentum and a self-justifying logic. To some this logic appears to legislate its own agenda, its own timetable, and its own needs and to focus human purposiveness exclusively on efficient productivity and performance. Others speculate that technology, as a way of ordering the world and systematizing the everyday phenomena of human life, has permeated our existence to the point that it has simply become the 'ontology' of our age, so that even where we assume we are engaged in non-technological pursuits – the arts, politics, intellectual life, friendships, sexuality – the 'logic' and dynamism of technology are present.

Can a morality based on traditional, judicial categories of individual action and responsibility deal with the demands that technology poses? To what extent are the advanced technologies in place today, towards which we are diverting considerable resources and capital, still instrumental to our conceptions of truth, beauty, and goodness? Can we still hold on to what we have traditionally taken the 'human' to be?

When it was argued that schools had to take a position in the forefront of facilitating values awareness, for many of the proponents this was at one and the same time an opportunity to return to education its critical and detached perspective vis-à-vis the dominant power structure. Values education was a vehicle for addressing many of these questions. In 'values' was seen the vehicle for liberation, self-knowledge, and a gentler, more just communitarianism. Whether values education was seen as a way of 'humanizing' technology (attending to the 'human factor') or as providing an irrevocable measure of human worth in the face of a reductionist technology there was little doubt that values programs would prepare a student for a more thoughtful interaction with the technological system of means. The goals of values education were high: subjectivity rediscovered in contrast to objectifying technology; human bonding as opposed to social atomism; resoluteness and perspective rather than indifference or passive acceptance.

The aim of this study is to assess the extent to which values education has made true on this expectation. It is intended to be a philosophic exploration of the encounter between the phenomena which are covered under the terms 'values' and 'technology,' a reflection on how this encounter affects our possessive affinity to being, and finally a review of the dominant values education models.

It is not common to study values education from this perspective. One cannot expect that issues of ontology and questions concerning constructs of reality would have become topics of debate at the social inception of the values education programs. Moreover, modern liberal society, especially that of North America, has an impatience for foundational issues and is more inclined to proceed pragmatically and eclectically, experimenting by using one or another idea as a heuristic device until another more effective approach comes along. Even those who have proposed alternatives to the popular values education programs or who have criticized them wholesale have tended similarly to employ pragmatic and utilitarian arguments.

But failing to conduct the more comprehensive audit leads to insufficient recognition of the wide-sweeping implications that foundational transformations have. For it can be argued that program innovations – in law, politics, or education – even where they are in a provisional and transitional form, imply a metaphysic and these metaphysical principles, in turn, have a destiny enfolded within them. Resolutely denying the implications of the principles of that metaphysic, or creatively reconstructing theories to incorporate alternative principles, does not will those destinies away for, as George Grant perceptively noted, 'such destinies have a way of working themselves out – that is, of bringing forth from their principle everything which is implied in that principle.'[4] Since so much stands in the breach – public safety, common decency, human happiness – we cannot escape examining the innovative challenges to the traditional curriculum down to the roots.

While I cannot presume to achieve a full clarification of these roots, I hope by the end to have raised the sorts of questions and explored the sorts of themes which need to be advanced in the debates concerning values education. What is at issue in the term 'values,' and what is at stake in proceeding with values education, cannot be isolated from the full scope of human existence in all its dimensions. To ask 'how should values be taught?' or 'what values should students come to choose?' is to ask, at one and the same time, 'what is the structure of being?' 'what is the construct of reality expressing the human experience of being?' and 'what is the destiny of its logic?' My intent is not so much to analyse the nature or structure of 'morality' but, instead, as a prolegomenon to such work, to set out the conditions which must pertain if there is to be an answer to the question 'why be moral?' if one is to count on the persistence of moral understanding and action, and if moral zealotry is to be prevented. And as part of my inquiry I suggest what follows from projects seeking to produce values proceeding from conditions other than these.

I intend this study of values education to be a window to a consideration of the wider forces composing our present situation and foreseeable destiny. Educational practice and the debates surrounding the implementation of new programs seem to offer a kind of concentrated expression of the historical epoch in which one lives, for the education of the young has always been the arena of interventions, pedagogical techniques, and expectations in which a society presumes it has put forward its most intelligible and well-articulated self-interpretation. In educational practice, a society projects the ideal type of itself. It presents an image of that which it presumes it can become. And it is from how a society sees the perfection of itself that we can tell most about that society.

In chapter 1, I distinguish classic accounts of ethics and morals from the contemporary idea of values by examining the historical and philosophic contexts within which they were conceived. I also suggest how a concern with ethics or morality underlies the traditional curriculum and how values establish the agenda for the contemporary assault on the modern curriculum. In chapter 2, I present an account of human existence drawn from two contemporary writers, Hannah Arendt and Eric Voegelin, and focus specifically on their arguments that certain conditions must be met if the activity of politics and the life of reason are to continue to express our humanity most comprehensively. I have used these thinkers to develop a measure from which to judge contemporary practice because their thought has the virtue of comprehensively analysing the human condition, as well as warning of the errors of dispossession which jeopardize it, without returning to a dogmatic restatement of the metaphysics of antiquity. In chapters 3, 4, and 5 I examine the major models of values education by assessing their indebtedness to a major philosophic figure (Kant, Hegel, and Nietzsche respectively) and then by measuring these models against the principles developed in chapter 2. In chapter 6 I examine the nature of technological development, the consciousness formed in a technological society, and the novel forms of power which condition that consciousness and disrupt the conditions which in the past have prevented the baleful consequences of dispossession. In chapter 7, I offer some thoughts on what it has meant for the language of values and technological society to converge together and I consider the manner in which the values education project is a microcosm of the percolating possibilities and dangers manifest in the wider political and intellectual context. In a brief conclusion, I suggest some possibilities regarding the renewal of the 'traditional curriculum,' in line with its spirit, but not its letter.

1

Values and Values Education: Towards a New Regime

The persistent presence of a phenomenon can finally make us impervious to its significance. Where once it disturbed what was, and broke like a flash, beginning a whole new trajectory of effects, if that same phenomenon repeats its silent murmur, moment after moment, we take it as self-evident and as second-nature. The sleep of forgetfulness soon covers over the novelty that accompanied its birth.

It is nearly impossible to feel strange about identifying our mutual presence to one another with regards to what we permit ourselves to say and to do to another or with respect to visions of our own self-perfection as 'values.' We speak of 'Christian' values, of 'instrumental' and 'terminal' values, of 'human' or 'cultural' values, and we even now have mass-media targeting of 'consumer' values. What might once have been expressed by an understanding of 'ethics' or 'morals' is now, apparently more appropriately, conveyed as 'values.'

There are those, and they may even be in the majority, who would hold that what was expressed as ethics or morals in the past and now as values is one and the same thing. What is implied by such a contention is usually that language is a living phenomenon, its tokens changing with different circumstances, but that the underlying reality which either ethics, morals, or values signify is essentially the same. What we mean by 'values,' it is said, is equivalent to the language of ethics or morals: we are speaking of limits, of directives of human conduct, of ideals of self or social perfection. 'Values,' they say, simply gives a more positive or a more 'proactive' (to use the most recent vernacular) connotation to our efforts to compel or persuade others or ourselves to be what we can become.

I do not wish to counter this argument with the position that language constitutes the reality of what we can know and experience or say of it. Nor would I wish to put forward the historicist and nominalist claims, in their bald form, which deny the perseverance of a reality to which different words are simply attached. But while the contention of equivalence may be appropriate to how an individual or social group recognizes moral order, I would argue that at the level of collective meaning, and in terms of the intelligibility of contemporary society's self-interpretation, the transition to the term 'values' signifies a major shift both in what is now considered praiseworthy and blameworthy action and in how this assessment can be made. And my aim is to show that the language of 'values' opens us to rushing tides of an epochal transformation, that its meaning extends beyond individual or even group usage to involvement in the transforming forces of historical existence itself.

In setting out in this study the core of that language of values, I do not want to leave the impression that the present age, in my view, is not the site of multiple discourses, trajectories of power, rationalizations, and self-understandings. It is not my intention to argue that a single monolithic presence dominates us, or to deny that an infinite number of very sensible and viable judgments will always persevere in the midst of enormous social and intellectual alteration. But I see it as the task of a thinker to attempt to grasp the tentacles of the dominant public self-interpretation and to see how the preponderant resources of a society are brought to bear to sustain this regime of truth.

Nor will I deny that there is enormous confusion in the whole area, a confusion no more poignantly indicated than by those who speak of ancient Greek 'values' or 'Christian' values. Our task, in offering some clarity to the conceptual muddle, is to undo where the charm of simplicity has glossed over difference, and to again permit the intelligibility of alternative visions to manifest themselves. Clarity about these differences is a necessary prelude to an adequate interpretation of the logic of our own prevailing self-interpretation. We must lay ourselves under the primordial claim that language brings to bear on us, as it calls us to remember the experiential source from which it emerged.

I am suggesting that the meaningful existence within which ethics and morals ordered human desire, and the regime within which values are deployed, differ both in the image of reality which guarantees their intelligibility and in the institutional structures designed on their behalf to form human character. It may be that they each express the truth of some 'immutable essence' of human existence. But they are also historical constructs where politics and pedagogy collaborate to stimulate certain types of desires and passion, as well as motivational structures, behaviour, and attitudes, to incite certain forms of speech, to form particular forms of knowledge, to designate 'expert' overseers, and to organize controls to keep these all in place. The discourses of ethics, morals, and values, then, have a strategic place within a complex arrangement of knowledge and power, and each is a distinct modality of their interaction. The difference between ethics, morals, and values is not merely that each commands a different set of interdictions and prescriptions. Rather each operates within a separate construct of reality ordering the individual into a distinct regulative relation of desire and knowledge, thus establishing a specific tonality for how humans participate in reality. Each locates the relevant experiences differently; each delimits a unique sphere of intervention; each bestows a different status on the enunciable form of the ordering; and each problematizes pleasure differently.[1]

Ethics and Morals

The ancient Greeks ordered their actions by 'ethics.' The way of life that ethics enjoined is illustrated in Aristotle's work *The Nicomachean Ethics.* Aristotle articulates the intelligible structure of a concrete, but developing way of life. Human life is a process through which a person, following what disposes to please him, and taking his bearing from the particular circumstances and reputable opinions given to him first by habit and then through his political existence, is brought to pursue excellences whose increasing approximation to the highest good aligns him, happily, with the structure of reality itself. As reason increasingly forms the essence of his sense of pleasure, advantage, expedience, and use, such an ethical being acquires practical knowledge of the good, and in making the good life choiceworthy for its own sake, it can be said of him that he has made of his life a testimony to the pursuit of the beautiful, a life worthy of immortality. An ethical life composes all the practical dimensions of human existence into an exemplar of balance, uniting practicality with awe, concreteness with sound judgment, authority with choice. For Aristotle, 'ethics' is a symbol of the sum of the complex moments that go into making practical life an icon of the good.

This account must be understood neither as hedonism nor as situationism: pleasure for Aristotle is not static, nor are situations taken as merely episodic. Nor should Aristotle's portrait be understood either as conventionalism or as transcendentalism. If 'ethics' is 'political,' this means a way of life structured by an association itself striving to more closely actualize the good, where 'good' is simultaneously the object of rational inquiry. And if 'ethics' is a science of the good this means the comprehension of forms as they are apprehended in the particulars of everyday life. Finally, in so far as 'ethics' actualizes the beautiful, this is not licence to self-stylized affectation.

An aspect of Aristotle's work which is usually extracted from his study is his inventory of the virtues of the good human being (liberality, even-tempered spiritedness, truthfulness, friendliness, and so on) or the importance of habit and disposition in creating good judgment. But what is put forward by Aristotle is not simply a catalogue of praiseworthy character-traits, or a handbook of pedagogical techniques. One cannot read Aristotle's *Ethics*, or come to understand the dimensions of human existence articulated under the symbol 'ethics,' without first understanding the complex of interdependent elements within which the account of excellences or the formation of practical reason is elaborated. This complex implies a construct of reality and answers to the question regarding what the best life for a human is, within which expositions on character-formation, the place of the customary, the scope of voluntary choice, the role of tact, and the relation of justice to friendship are all components of an answer to the problem of human finitude and immortality. Since an understanding of ethics must take place within this complex, it is not possible to abstract one element and then another and formulate a teaching which is distinctively pertinent to an autonomous sphere of morality.

Ethics, Aristotle repeatedly intones, is a *praxis*, and unlike *techne* and *episteme*, which have to do with either those things wholly under our control, or knowledge of eternal things we cannot change, is an activity and a set of dispositions which have all the imprecision inevitably accompanying our complex participation in the structure of existence. That structure is composed of levels (organic, sentient, human passion, reason, divine principle) which are inherently discontinuous and ambivalent. Since ethics is not tied to an investigation into things which are always and everywhere, it cannot have the exactitude of mathematics, nor can it permit of demonstrable proof: 'for it is the mark of an educated mind,' Aristotle notes, 'to expect that amount of exactness in each kind which the nature of the particular subject admits' (*Ethics* 1.iii.4). As a *praxis*, it has neither a product nor a final end. Moreover, to complicate matters, the intelligible core of ethics which Aristotle wishes to exhibit is presentable only to those already habituated to a certain way of life, and thus of a certain character. Central to Aristotle's notion of polity is the experience of *pathos*, or commonly 'suffering' a dimension of existence (fear, grief, catharsis, truth, the divine), and his readers are assumed to share that common substance. Only then is Aristotle's account of ethics seen as admitting of reasonable justification. There is a continuous circularity to Aristotle's reasoning but this is because human life, unlike the models one could devise by abstracting some components of it, is one in which each of the elements is perpetually giving form to and deriving its substance from every other element.

These caveats aside, for analytic purposes, one can identify three topics whose convergence characterizes the distinctiveness of the 'ethical': the political, the teleological, and the cosmological.

First, acting and judging ethically develops and matures through general participation in a political regime. There are different ways to articulate the meaning of this. In one way, *poleis* are historical and cultural; the circumstances of their coming to be are contingent and yet those conditions compose a totality of conditions always already informing the tonality of human existence within them. The conventions and specific practices of historical and cultural association form a web of human meaning which is embodied in the exercise of reason and choice, in the assessment of praise and blame, and in the scope of voluntary and involuntary action.

The existence of this backdrop to action and judgment means not only that ethical activity always implies a context, but also that the place of such activity is always particular situations or circumstances, that the excellences are appropriate to the practices of cultural interaction, and that the first premise of judgment is always reputable opinion and the conclusion redeems the reasonableness of what is generally accepted. This judgment is always local and situated. One need not go so far as to say that ethics is historical sensibility, but the pre-modern assumption that one's circumstances (one's body, culture, fate, destiny) precede acts of reason and choice is central to Aristotle's meaning. This 'situatedness' implies both plurality within the *polis* and plurality in a world of *poleis*, a plurality characterized by varying visions of justice and the good.

Another way of understanding 'political' is to recognize Aristotle's principle that humans are naturally political, which is to say that essential characteristics of their humanness are actualized and completed by politics. Mere vitality or sentience is not sufficient, for humans are distinguished by capacities exceeding vegetative or organic existence. Only through topics raised in public debate, only in the passions and excellences associated with political power, and only by virtue of the opportunities to display public action before others are aptitudes forged which contribute to the actualization of a human's proper end. Pursuing honour, exhibiting righteous anger at injustice, sensing the appropriate occasion for action or speech, recognizing the irreducibility of plurality and the centrality of conciliatory speech, expressing loyalty, and appreciating the modalities of civic friendship 'naturally' condition the dispositional attitudes underlying ethics. Such opportunities and passions supply the motivation, tone, and object of ethical striving. A human being deprived of the *polis* cannot be just, cannot reason practically, nor can that human being be excellent because the talents informing each of these qualities are activated by political existence. Indeed, it is dubious whether such a human has a sufficient sense of the difference between the real and the apparent. In the *polis* reputable opinions and evidence of the sensible are debated and clarified; depriving oneself of these leaves one abandoned to private notions and phantasms.

In so far as being ethical aims at an existence where what is noble and beautiful is pursued for its own sake, thereby producing as much freedom from necessity as it is given to humans to have, it replicates at the microcosmic level the structure of the *polis*, whose strength and equipment are directed to actualizing the natural end of the *polis* – self-sufficiency. Nature and a situated practical know-how (*techne*) combine to produce this end: ethics entails action that is adapted to the arrangements of nature, but nature's deficiencies need to be corrected by human artfulness.

The second characteristic of Aristotle's account is that ethics is teleological. A cluster of interrelated notions is intended by this term. First, 'teleological' refers to Aristotle's understanding that ethical excellences, as qualities of character, are acquired by doing, and that an appreciation of the choiceworthiness of ethical performance is not the result of cognitive approval alone but rather is a product of a dispositional propensity formed by habit. Neither logical demonstration nor magisterial intonation of imperatives of conduct will achieve the required result. The formation of the type of character disposed to see what is noble or beautiful, comely or appropriate, is the consequence of a process of development that perfects and completes rudimentary forms of desire and passion by repetition and practice. Theoretical reason and logic are of little help here; only the drama of everyday life persuades (*Ethics* 10.ix.3–5). Habits, reinforced by coercion and praise –

where a legislative rule of the desires is necessary – and persuasion – where a constitutional rule of the passions is possible – establish the predilection to excellence, which eventually translates into rational apprehension of the principles of those excellences.

Next, 'teleological' refers to the fact that the object of ethics is the good and that the good is happiness. Ethics, for Aristotle, is not *sui generis*, and yet neither is it merely instrumental. Ethical activity is directed to an end beyond, though not distinct from, itself. It is not enough to be shown the reasonableness of ethical action. Nor is disposition, Aristotle says, enough; there must also be the inclination to manifest disposition in action. The desire for happiness supplies the motive just as suffering injustice supplies the disincentive to vicious conduct. Of course happiness is not merely the sentiment of personal satisfaction. The Greek *eudaemonia* attempts to capture the composure that comes from stability as the proper aspect of beings. Happiness is an assessment of 'living well' that extends over a whole lifetime, in a consideration of achievement in all dimensions of existence. Moreover, since happiness is the 'exercise of the soul's faculties in accordance with excellence' (1.vii.15), there can be no happiness for a human without the performance of ethical acts. This means that the excellences are not mere means; they are manifestations of the substance of happiness in qualities of character.

In addition, 'teleological' refers to the completed form in light of which all the components of ethical striving – habit, disposition, sense of advantage or expedience, choice, right, voluntariness – are educated. The understanding of what guides this development is an archetype of the good human, the magnanimous being. So important is the image of the human who most fully exemplifies ethical performance that Aristotle's work peaks in a discussion of the actions and desires of the human maximally enhanced by ethical practices, the person of great soul. That human being's sense of what constitutes use or expedience, depending as these do on character, sets the standard that underlies judgment of right action. The tone whereby the magnanimous being actuates the truth of existence in actions in concrete situations is the measure of ethics. His maturity is not marked by access to 'immutable truths' or by an ability to use discretionary judgment in applying universals to particulars, but by his exhibiting the amplitude of his participation in the process of reality in concrete actions. In so far as ethics is about character-formation, the great-souled person is the complete human type who actualizes (*entelecheia*) all of the potentiality (*dunamis*) that is given to individuals as human beings in the *polis*. His judgments and temper are paradigmatic for the cultivation of dispositions in those who are to be brought to ethical excellence. But one should not take Aristotle's *telos* of the most perfect being as the invocation of a new humanity, a transfiguration of human reality. The magnanimous human is 'mature' because he participates in the complexities of the world without expectation of a world-transfiguration. An education to ethical life is an act of *anamnesis*, or recollective recovery of the structure of being as it manifests itself most visibly in the actions of the magnanimous human.

Finally, being 'teleological,' ethics is about *phronesis*, or practical reason, the intellectual aptitude which makes a human being concerned with the good of a whole life. There are two features that characterize this faculty. The first links back to human situatedness. Phronesis is an aptitude which is less the mere application of universal or categorical principles to particular circumstances than a matter of assessing appropriateness, of judging *kata ton orthon logon*, or of using discretion. Because the things which concern judgment arise from a plurality of interpretations and from circumstances which change, there are no categorical guidelines. Only experience's gradual refinement of practical reason, through education, law, and public interaction, can ensure ethical astuteness. A repetition of practices and submission to the spiral of self-understanding arising from that produce the aptitude to 'see' the appropriate thing to do under the circumstances. This is why Aristotle hesitates in suggesting that the *Nicomachean Ethics* is a handbook by which to acquire ethical excellence, as if being ethical were merely a matter of cognitive clarity, or knowledge of right actions. It is more a 'sensing one's way' or 'knowing-how' for those already disposed to the noble, excellent, and beautiful and whose dispositions can be formed into qualities of character. To illustrate, Aristotle refers to the process whereby good is brought about as identifying the mean between the excess and the defect. He is borrowing a Pythagorean metaphor, associated with the tuning of a lyre, that relates knowing to acquiring the right 'pitch.'[2]

The second feature characterizing practical reason is its anticipation of what would be good in light of a whole human life. Such an assessment takes into account the full particulars of a usual existence – pleasure, health, children, honour, understanding, friendship, external prosperity, and leisure. The appropriate exercise of *phronesis* aims to strike a balance between them, acknowledging human participation at many levels in the structure of reality. Thus, *phronesis* is a faculty of attunement, or of participation, which aims at manifesting the truth of existence in the action of concrete circumstances.[3] The exercise of reason cannot be a matter of cognitive mastery or cunningness in achieving what is desired, wanted, or wished for. It is impossible, moreover, to conceive of a means/end logic governing the realm of ethics: there are no predetermined ends or goals posited prior to the exercise of *phronesis* or prior to the actions of a deliberate desire. While ethics is about reason and choice, it cannot be a reason understood as a method to reduce ambiguity to controllable order. Nor does ethics involve an autonomous act of legislation in attempting to free the human psyche from natural necessity. The urges and desires, judgments and informed opinions, form the core of ethics, though these must be understood as functions continuously under development in light of what is rationally good for human beings over a whole life. Reason, for Aristotle, is not an instrumental skill distinct from the personal, political, and spiritual dimensions of life.

The third major feature of Aristotle's account is that ethics is 'cosmological.' That is, the particulars of ethics correspond to both the structure of existence itself and the human effort to actualize that structure as the permanent foundation of human order. Thus, ethics is not simply a functional requirement for social life, or an instrument for more effective satisfaction of wants. There is a cosmological dimension to ethics: acting ethically recalls the structure of existence itself, and actualizes and perfects the human experience of it.

We can understand this point best by recalling Plato. At the heart of Aristotle's writings is the philosophic problem he adopts from Plato: how and under what conditions the precarious and contingent realm of becoming can manifest the ultimately real. Plato's answer leaves the realm of the practical in jeopardy: while most of his dialogues focus on the excellences of the soul – courage, piety, friendship, justice – and thus on those topics which fall within the domain of the 'ethical,' the Socratic teaching does not give much hope that a wholly reasoned account of those excellences is available. Socrates is most confident when he anticipates the results of philosophic inquiry on what is always and everywhere (*physis*) and when he outlines the beneficial effects that the life of such inquiry has on the human soul; he is least optimistic about bringing order and clarity to the opinions and judgments concerning the realm of things that come into and pass out of being (*tyche*). *Arete*, as the modality of human existence associated with temporal and finite things, does not, in Plato's work, appear to be a part of what is ultimately real and so no independent 'ethics' is proposed or even suggested.

Aristotle, in contrast, is more inclined to entertain the possibility that the ultimately real does appear in the everyday. This is partly because for him the reality of which it is possible to give a reasoned account is considerably more heterogeneous than that in Plato's work. It displays a far greater differentiation of beings and a more complex exchange of essence and finitude than Plato's tracking of the *logos* seems to allow. The things ethics orients humans within are neither wholly necessary nor entirely contingent, concerned neither with what is always the same, nor with what is always mutable. But, while intermediary, ethical practice serves to illuminate the core of a human's most profound desires. Aristotle, unlike Plato, marks out a distinct sphere of ethical activity, a sphere which has its own virtues, its own mode of judgment, and its own excellent human type. Of course, that does not mean that these can ever become the proper objects of theoretical cognition. However, nor are its phenomena merely transient and devoid of meaning. In ethical practices, there is a complex and paradoxical association of being and non-being, absoluteness and relativity, the eternal and becoming. Ethics is an 'in-between' realm in which transcendent reality can appear in practical activity, thus bestowing meaning and order within the realm of what undergoes change. For example, as already noted, for Aristotle, ethics begins with habituation. Such habituation is to archetypal actions. The habit is a shorthand version of the practical ontology evident in archetypal actions. This is because habit is not mere repetition of behaviour, but the deliberate enactment of a human's paradigmatic ways in the world, which through reiteration forms ethical substance in the psyche.

Ethical performance, for Aristotle, then has cosmogonic significance: to be ethical is to make the mundane important and meaningful. The magnanimous human makes of himself a microcosm of the order of the cosmos, and ethical action repeats the constitutive hierarchies of reality. This is why, in the context of a discussion of the happiness stemming from the ethical life, Aristotle writes: 'Considering human affairs, one must not ... consider man as he is and not consider what is mortal in mortal things, but think about them [only] to the extent that they have the possibility of immortalizing.' Ethical action is a type of immortalizing activity: to do beautiful and honourable acts is to align the psyche with its natural propensity to mirror the structure of reality. Ethics is the imperfect realization of transcendent perfection in the realm of practical activity. From this perspective, the 'doctrine of the mean' is not only a dogma symbolizing 'pitch,' to express the art of moderating the passions. It also sets out the structure of the political and spiritual balance of practicality and awe, order and difference, generality and particularity, wisdom and power.[4] The full import of the 'doctrine of the mean' is that it sets the tonality to ethics: rather than a project to surmount or control reality, striving to become more completely human is a matter of participation.

The last point which needs to be noted here, and which follows from the preceding, is that it cannot be forgotten that for Aristotle humans are not the best thing in the universe. A person's doings, even when refined by *phronesis* and sustained by rational principle, remain part of a realm which is transient, finite, and imperfect. Thus, these doings cannot answer to a human's most fundamental need, the questioning of what is and is no more, of his origin and of the whole. Ethical and political actions are not the highest form of excellence. Only by virtue of transcendence, of the pull towards an order of perfection, which composes the modulation of the intellectual and spiritual quest, do humans, as far as they are able, actualize something of the divine or godlike. The implication is that 'ethics' can only be a 'training-ground' for the formation of habits and tempers which activate and structure the life of intellectual questioning. A life of moderation, rather than continuous ethical self-control, is the closest approximation to the metaphysic of the world. The capacity for good judgment and excellence, living according to a rational principle, is possible only because of the ladder that connects humans to the eternal.

But Platonic or Aristotelian 'eternity' has no personal characteristics, nor does it concern itself wilfully with human affairs. No dynamic of command, rebellion, and consent informs the spirit of ethics. The origin of the 'moral,' by contrast, is in the articulation of a tension between the particular, rebellious 'will' and the general law legislated by a recognized supreme being. The distinctive inner experiences which come to be known as moral struggles centre on the problematic and ambiguous encounter which the individual has with its 'self,' a self resisting all efforts to be moulded by authoritative guidelines for it understands itself to be the exclusive source of meaning and order, and yet a self which must be brought to that image of perfection which it can become. For the distinctive tensions of *moral* life to have arisen as meaningful experiences required, on the one hand, the 'discovery' of an interior power in the psyche – the will – which, unlike reason and the passions, cannot be educated or persuaded for it is a faculty which tolerates no limits on its own activity, and, on the other, the existence of absolute interdictions stemming from an unimpeachable authority. The central moral task, once this tension is articulated, is to make the rebellious will come to recognize the logic of those interdictions as having the general form of its own activity. Acceptance of moral limit can then become an act of self-legislation.

The Stoic and early Christian account of the internal conflicts of the self, and yet its unique capacity for a free and spontaneous consent to the order by which it will live, establishes the will as the formative site of moral experience. The Stoic undertook a kind of mental 'gymnastic' of austerity and self-renunciation to distil his being (perceptual, intellectual, spiritual) into a single force: the will's power to assent or dissent to reality. As the magisterial first lines of Epictetus's *Enchiridion* read, 'There are things which are within our power, and there are things which are beyond our power ... the things within our power are by nature free, unrestricted, unhindered.'[5] While humans may be vulnerable and impotent amidst the personal and political circumstances of their existence, they can rule the 'impressions' they have of these 'outside things': 'The master threatens to chain me: "What say you? Chain me? My leg you will chain – yes, but not my will – no, not even Zeus can conquer that"' (ix). Thus, humans are 'fitted for command'; they are sovereigns who legislate how they will let reality appear to them: 'Men are disturbed not by things, but by the views which they take of things' (v). Moral assessment is, henceforth, not the result of the give-and-take of public deliberation, but the solitary activity of a will designating, and then legislating within, its own dominion.

Epictetus, then, is the first to fully recognize the omnipotence of the will. But Epictetus does not allow this recognition to derail into fantasy. Human willing takes place within acceptance of the fate (*heimarmene*) which harmonizes every part in the whole. 'Demand not,' he writes, 'that events should happen as you wish, but wish them to happen as they do happen, and you will go on well' (viii). That acceptance is the same as knowledge of the laws of the universe. And thus, 'All things serve and obey the [laws of the] universe ... Our body likewise obeys the same, in being sick and well, young and old, and passing through the other changes decreed. It is therefore reasonable that what depends on ourselves, that is our own understanding, should not be the only rebel' (lxxxi). The whole is a rational order, with whose universal laws humans must bring themselves into harmony. The exercises of delimitation that Epictetus recommends produce a distinctive moral domain structured not only by the power of command, but also by the responsiveness of obedience.[6]

Now, humans are vulnerable not only because of the world's transience. Even more so, human emotion and passion stand in the way of rationally aligning with, and yielding to, the metaphysical order. Virtue is, at its essence, 'self-mastery': to be virtuous requires a relation of the self to itself as obedience. Epictetus is strict regarding the danger of natural impulses and stricter still regarding their methodic control.[7] Since the desires lack self-direction, they must be legislated to and coerced: 'remember, now is the combat, now the Olympiad comes on, nor can it be put off' (l). No inclinations are in accord with nature; they must be subdued by an act of will. Thus, the Stoic 'keeps watch and guard on himself as his own enemy,' wary of the opposing self 'lying in wait for him' (xlviii). Where Aristotle ultimately gives primacy to moderation over continence, since moderation makes an individual more disposed to the spiritual tone that is necessary for contemplation, Epictetus establishes the supremacy of self-mastery within moral virtue as the expression of conformity to the universal law.

Yet, this does not mean unrelenting struggle: the Stoic aims at tranquillity, or even better, at invulnerability (*ataraxia*). By instituting a sphere of inner freedom the Stoic could procure a modicum of self-sufficiency: 'For no one is a slave whose will is free.'[8] The turn inward maximizes the distillation and concentration of power already undertaken by following the precepts of austerity and self-renunciation. With the goal of invulnerability, the internalization of the moral experience is perfected. Moral reasoning now has its own independent agenda.

While at the personal level such tranquillity answers the question regarding the best life, there is still the matter of living well with others. The highlight of the Stoic depiction of morality is the will's capacity to legislate a general form of reason to itself and thus to will its participation in a universal community based on moral law. Zeno's *Republic* presents the image of such a universal organization, a moral community erected on true knowledge of the laws of the cosmos and thus on a single immutable and immortal law. Every particular will has the ability to contract membership in that rational community, to consent to the higher will of the *logos spermatikos*. Now such membership is necessarily of a formal nature, positing a structure of universal justice that is devoid of particular ends, visions of the good, or embodied interests. But this is already prepared for in the Stoic understanding of judgment. In that account there is vacillation as to what constitutes the best kind of judgment: does it take its bearings from appropriate acts (*kathekon*) or from morally perfect acts (*katorthomata*)? In the final analysis, the Stoic aims towards the latter, away from the specific and contextual nature of appropriate acts toward the universalizable nature of moral intentions. The decisive issue of moral deliberation is directed less to what must be done than to how and why: the universality of intention overrides the specifics of content.

Universal in scope and solipsistic in method, Stoic morality appears deracinated and isolating. These two features do not, however, constitute the whole of the Stoic drama. At the same time, there is recognition of a natural benevolence, a *philostorgos*, or sense of endearment in human beings, which provides the substance of the bond in the universal community. Nonetheless, this is unlike Aristotle's 'agreeableness' and civic friendship, for these were predicated on the concrete particulars of a way of life and were compatible with the recognition of the essential differentiation of beings within the *polis*. Benevolence does not translate into the concrete duties towards family and nation, nor does it allow for different spheres of human striving. The model of Stoic imperturbability may be Socrates, but it is not Plato's Socrates who adapts speeches to souls and who speaks ironically because he knows human abilities differ. Benevolence is more a single-mindedness that finds a universal bond in humanity's common vulnerability. Yielding to truth means avoiding those occasions where particular wills agitate among one another. Pride, or the essential principle underlying Greek agonistic ethics, must be vanquished.

St Paul's account, while finding a similar solution to the truculent will in a higher, purified will (in this case, a covenantal commitment to the word of God), explores in greater depth the tortuous paths which precede the act of universal legislation. Moral life aims at the redemption of humanity's fallen nature and humans must suffer for the truth. In his letters, St Paul writes of the will's self-division and its paralysis ('for what I do is not what I want to do' – Rom. 7:18) and its recurring failures to follow through on the proper course of action. The inner struggle to will the good in the face of an equally forceful and recurring internal rebelliousness to do the opposite is where morality acquires its characteristic tone. In elucidating this tension, St Paul establishes the structure distinctive to morality: the struggling self's repeated cycle of excessive pride, self-mortification and guilt, flight from its own fallen nature, desire for redemption, and finally deliverance.

The last phase is accompanied by the righteousness that comes with certitude of faith. This is predicated on the act of conversion, a turning around from the impulses and passions natural to human beings (a 'mortification' of the 'flesh') towards a vision that purifies life of all that is transient and finite. That vision comes from the Gospels. To live the moral life is to commemorate the ways of that exemplary being, the half-human, half-god Christ, whose divine principle shows the direction of human transcendence (*Imitatio Christi*). The moral being is, as in the obedience that comes from faith (Rom. 1:5), a 'witness to Christ.'

Where the Greeks regulated acts and consequences by making ethical action appear for public judgment and put a premium on pride of performance which could be rewarded with political honours, the Pauline depiction of *morality* interiorizes the ordering of desire, focusing attention on the activity prior to action ('For what is seen is temporary, but what is unseen is eternal' – 2 Cor. 4:18). Under the order of morality, worldly appearance, and the mode of judgment appropriate to it (*phronesis*), is rendered deeply problematic, because Christian morality is compromised by publicity. Public excellences, therefore, are replaced by *virtues*, which, as the root word *virs* suggests, places the focus on the manly struggles and inner strength of the will (the truth 'dwelling within'). Moral determinations in the form of imperatives, resolutions, or duties must be arrived at through inner conviction and personal faith.

This is not to say that no human association results. To the contrary, morality puts a high premium on human sociability. The end of morality, after all, is a universal moral community. Unlike the Greek *polis*, though, where maintaining the differentiation of beings is paramount and civic friendship ensures a degree of tolerance, the Christian community is a single body of believers, suffering common anguish at the sight of unbelief. The spiritual bond by which this pentecostal community exists produces righteousness. This might make Christian society prone to the irascibility that comes from a too-pure dedication to virtue. Yet righteousness, as the example of Christ shows, has the social face of meekness or gentleness. Righteousness as meekness acquires its tonality through the ideal that the moral self is to become.

However, realization of the fickleness and transience of the self and its essential inability to be the pure phenomenon it has been ordered to be renders such activity fraught with self-doubt and recriminations of insincerity. The desire for certitude and steadfastness is inseparable from the moral life. As a consequence, a new set of practices for the self must accompany morality: exercises which, involving temptation and flight, test the will's resolve and sincerity. But no action can bring together the demands of temporal existence and the eternal message: Christian goodness is as much a conundrum as a statement concerning the principle of existence. The will's recurring paralysis and failure means that the image of perfection which it has been told it can become, the pure god/human, Christ, is never realizable.

The inner struggle is resolved not by a worldly assessment of what is appropriate, but by a love which brings to rest the torn heart and a divided world. It is the law 'written on their hearts, their consciences also bearing witness,' (Rom. 2:15) and unmerited grace which render this transfiguration. The 'good news' erupts into the darkness of the world, making possible the deliverance of the whole created universe (Rom. 8:19). The moral phenomena cannot be an expression of the impulses of natural existence (whether personal, social, or intellectual longings), as these display no nascent perfection. Instead, the impulses must be focused on a yet-to-be ideal whose possibility regulates the scope of self-renunciation. Love, as a unifying action, extends the inner experience of the will into the world. There it also unites divisions so that judgment need no longer turn on the prudent evaluation of shifting and complex circumstances. Instead, judgment is determined by an eternal promise, known less by its manifest contents than by its universal and unifying form. Neither naturally given propensities nor the practical judgment arising from political existence brings the self to seeing its moral substance in this form: grace corrects nature and the contingencies of circumstance, rendering order where none is apparent. That order, as both Stoics and Christians knew, meant citizenship in a world community, a cosmopolitanism of universal moral intent. Ecumenism and its accompanying imperial categories of law and sovereign legislation enter moral discourse. The aim is a universal moral community, since faith is comprehended as a ministry of reconciliation, inevitable when 'moral' phenomena are analysed under the category of the 'will.' After Christ there can be no more heroes, those exemplary beings who strove for superlative virtue. Now there can be only martyrs, those who give their life for the truth.

In the secularized, modern versions of this project, which find their consummate expression in Rousseau, Kant, and Hegel, the composition of the inner struggle changes from tension between one's immanent and transcendent existence to tension between one's particular self and the moral self one can become. Now, rather than willing the natural law of the *logos spermatikos* or reiterating the pure will expressed through the word of God, consciousness wills itself into a universal form of reasoning, making itself observe a rule of reason rising up from the structure of human development itself. The dynamic of power and obedience – solo struggle and consent – which underscores the idea of freedom as legislation remains, though the *telos* is now a regime of mutual recognition actualized in the state.

In this modern version, the social ideal replaces divine commandment, respect or civil manners replace love, a philosophy of history replaces grace. The cycle of sin, guilt, and deliverance remains though it is renamed and transfigured so as to highlight the correctable character of these moods: the secular cycle is one of alienation, self-consciousness, and science. The Stoic *heimarmene* or Christian providence is replaced by the assumption of a historical intelligence working with a purpose (the 'cunning of reason'), similarly overcoming divisiveness, but now immanently and with greater certainty. Substituting the flow of history for transcendental salvation means that archetypal recollection is replaced by remembrance of historical exemplars. There are still martyrs, though now they are revolutionary activists or exegetes of the revolutionary creed.

When the metaphysic of time as history dissipates, what remains for a time is a norm of universality based on statistical profiles and theories of normal distribution. Analysing these empirical facts is expected to produce evidence of a transcendental structure legitimating various social prescriptions. The tonality of this diminished project, while more limited in its expectations of perfection but more confident in its ability to control disorder and contingency, remains fairly much the same as that informing Stoic and Pauline morality. Virtue is attunement with universal laws; the acting power of virtue is strength of will; the will must overcome natural propensity to will rational action and to sustain its commitment to reproducing the general order.

Obviously there are great differences between ethics and morals evident in the way desires and temptations are problematized, regulatory passions and fears are invoked, and distinct images of the human who most fully maximizes the orderly life are elevated. These classic representations of how human desire is ordered do, however, share a common ground. There is an assumption in this heritage that to be what one can become requires *work*. To be human demands the task of transformation and thus the effort of negation. To be ethical and/or moral requires renouncing an undifferentiated immediacy to oneself and a re-presentation of oneself in the modality of otherness. Negation produces determinateness and constitutes limit or boundary. This is a type of work with a decisive beginning and end, guided by finalities which prescribe direction, continuity, and anticipated perfection.

Moreover, both ethical and moral work entail the repetition of certain actions and motivations taken to be paradigmatic. The representation of oneself as another takes place through an eternal archetype or historical exemplar, a Pericles or a Demosthenes, a St Francis or a St Anthony, a Danton or a Lenin. That model is taken to be the stable aspect of being in which what is shows itself in its most complete form. That model exists in *illus tempore*; it is the distillation of a unique event during which a hierophanic revelation occurs. In acting ethically or morally, one acts out the archetype or exemplar, thereby elevating oneself beyond the transience of desire and labour. While what is done in ethical or moral work has already been done, such work is not merely reiterating behaviour. It is more than a habit-formed replay of a remembered act. The work of ethical and moral action is an act of recovery of metaphysical import: the action, ritualistically, reconfirms the structure of the real, for in acting one becomes contemporary with the significant event. In recovering the event, one is opening oneself to the same hierophanic revelation. This is why recollection is so central to ethical and moral action. Recollection retrieves an *arche* (or source) so that, unlike in mere reminiscence, one is contemporary with the archetypal event. At that point, the psyche or body is an *axis mundi*, a point of intersection of everyday life with ultimate reality, of knowledge of both what is once and for all and what is the transience of the everyday. By repeating an exemplary action, one who acts ethically or morally establishes a link between existence and essence. This is why ethical and moral work is inseparable from narrative. Myths and legends, sagas and ballads, epics and chronicles, tell the story of exemplary men and women, paradigmatic actions, and archetypal experiences. To form one's character is an act of recollection, a re-possession which is an epiphany of reality.

Work which is understood to be metaphysically significant, as Mircea Eliade has shown, repeats the archetype of creation, the primordial event of transforming the inchoate into a cosmos by separation and differentiation.[9] Ethical or moral work is cosmogonic too, a symbolic repetition of creation's differentiations. But rather than beginning with nothing, such work is one of repair, attempting to retrieve the archetypal event to counter the corruption of time. Ethical and moral work retrieves phenomena presumed to have authority because, having been displayed during an event understood as hierophanic, they are assumed to have a durative and stabilizing character. Those phenomena include the properties or propensities, acts or commands, of the gods, of heroes, of nature, of ancestors, of a primeval event, or of historical tradition, any of which were made visible in the hierophantic event. The importance of enduringness explains the 'possessive' component present in the vocabulary of ethical and moral practice: proper, appropriate, comportment, behaving, beholden, and proportion. In ethical and moral work, the individual acts to reproduce in himself the substance presumed to have ultimate reality because it is constant and durable. To 'be' ethical or moral is to 'have' communion with what is taken to be ultimately real.

But the full possession of such substance is not possible. Ethical or moral work needs continuous re-enactment because the transience and finiteness of human desire recurringly render the achievement ambivalent and ambiguous. Ethical or moral action cannot cure the pain of existence in time. This is why ethical and moral work is essentially tragic. The prescribed actions and practices, while repeatable, ritualizable, and teachable, cannot invest existence with perfection. No ethical or moral work is completable. Like all ritual, it requires continuous re-enactment. Thus, paradoxically ethical and moral practices associate being with non-being, the absolute with relativity, the eternal with becoming. Human existence is a situation of unrest. Ethical or moral performance is only a fragile effort to make human existence meaningful. Ethical and moral acts both reveal and conceal the structure of the real, thus confirming the fundamental and irreducible mystery of human existence. Would hope or despair accompany this difficult work? Instilling and renewing the former, while combating the presumption and spiritual sloth of the latter, were the tasks of the traditional curriculum.

The 'Traditional Curriculum'

In important ways, I want to argue, this metaphysic is what underlies the so-called traditional curriculum. While the expression 'traditional curriculum' is in great part polemical (how could the educational proposals of Isocrates, Cicero, Quintilian, Plutarch, Augustine, Cassiodorus and Isidore, Robert Curzon, the Oratorians, Comenius, and the Port-Royal, just to illustrate, be held together?), there are, it is true, a number of prevalent practices recurring up to the time that modern reformers like Pestalozzi, Spencer, and Dewey undertook their radical overhaul of curriculum design as well as pedagogical practice. Contemporary advocates of values education, sustaining the progressivism of those reformers, focus on these practices as the 'flaws' of that curriculum: rote learning, memory drills, respect for rules and authority, acquisition of habits, obedience to prescribed conduct, the hierarchy of virtues, fixed and discrete topics of knowledge, recitation, emulation of human types, transmission of a heritage, accommodation to the given, and imitation of literary models. This traditional curriculum and pedagogy, the critics say, can be faulted for ineffectual methods, and irrelevant subjects, usage of which has petrified the educational process and produced docile and submissive students.

But what the values education advocates do not say explicitly is that in rejecting the instruments, practices, and learning models of the traditional curriculum there is more than mere 'effectiveness' at stake. The turn away from the traditional curriculum is root and branch. What they really mean is that the metaphysic underlying the traditional curriculum is no longer acceptable.

What is the rational core that justifies the traditional practices? If we are to take the traditional curriculum seriously as an option for forming an educated human being, we must rescue it from the charges of archaism and antiquarianism by first being clear as to its claim to be a rational account of human longing and then unfreezing its dogmatic doctrines and retrieving the formative experiences it identifies as needing education. The traditional curriculum and its pedagogical arts assumed that education meant preparing the student for encounter with the complexities of the world. The world, the student learned, was not one which could be radically transformed so as to relieve humans of the burdens of their existence. The 'truths' of existence to which he would be exposed in the topics of the curriculum, and whereby he would participate in the process of reality itself, were to be actuated in the reality of action in concrete situations. One might sum up the means by which this goal of the traditional curriculum is advanced as 'discipline by obedience, education through example.' Two assumptions explain those premises. First, that cognitive assent to rational principle can occur only if a specific psychic tonality has been formed, one that has been prepared for by certain dispositional habits. Second, that since what is most essentially 'human' manifests itself in 'types' whose completeness or perfection is paradigmatic for others, emulation instils a motive and a *telos* for human striving. In both cases, pedagogy will use 'icons' to guide the psyche and form it to the point where it can assent to reality. Those icons will appear as dogmatic or artificial constructs, but they are there only as a concentrated form of the spiritual tonality that is sought. For example, recalling the lives of heroes and emulating their actions is not yet courage, but disposes a person to that virtue. Or more profoundly, rote-drills are 'icons' of the process of *anamnesis*, forming the mind's recollective capacity to perceive unity in its existence. The means and ends of education, by this reckoning, must be distinguished: the amplitude and self-sufficiency of intellectual and spiritual sensitivity, which is the end, are in direct proportion to the stringency and discipline of the apprenticeship.

Two other principles structure the traditional curriculum: probability and *pathos*. The Platonic-Aristotelian roots are again evident. The manifold of things is taken as displaying a degree of differentiation which does not permit of certitude or reduction. It is a manifold which encompasses organic nature, sentient nature, the passions, and reason, each establishing a distinct vector in human action.[10] The somatic, political, intellectual, and divine dimensions of reality must all be addressed in a complete education. Humans are neither despiritualized bodies nor disembodied souls. As well, human affairs, taken to be transient and ultimately finite, are not taken as ultimate but their rhythms display sufficient regularity so as to permit of probable knowledge and understanding. Ability to appreciate the complexity and variability of human things requires a special kind of seeing: a capacity to discriminate among the diversity through which existence manifests itself, an aptitude to make distinctions and sense situations, and discretionary judgment. The maturity and self-control necessary to tolerate and hold apart the separate and multiplicitous elements of the manifold are a result of a training in division and subdivision, collection and re-collection, an intellectual talent Aristotle identified as *diaresis*.

Experiences that are 'suffered' by humans through a psyche that is open to truth, and which give human beings a common destiny, give substance to the distinctions by which the phenomena of the world are carved up. *Pathos* suggests that the formative human experiences, by virtue of which humans sense their commonality, are not willed constructs or accidental behavioural responses, but modes of participation in reality. The consequence of *pathos* is *homonoia*, the like-mindedness that is the spiritual substance constituting the bonds of a community. Pedagogy seeks to instil a sense of receptivity, reverence, and openness to the immutable structures of reality so that this bond can be manifested. Astuteness and obedience prepare the psyche to 'suffer' the decisive experiences establishing participation in reality. The erotic, transcending movement of speech, the civic friendship of public engagement, the discerning judgment that discriminates 'this' from 'that' – all ensure an openness to reality in all its manifold manner of being. The structures of reality they reveal give direction, structure, and purpose to choice, decision, and judgment. They moderate the assessment of possible action by awareness of what is not capable of being changed and of goals that cannot be fulfilled. Moral obtuseness and the rage of a *libido dominandi*, in contrast, like the fury which causes Xerxes to strike at the river, cause that same psyche to create for itself deformed constructs of reality. *Pathos* and probability identify the two poles between which the distinctive phenomena of human existence are actuated: commonality and singularity, authority and judgment. They testify to man's 'synthetic' nature, and speak to the need for a balance in the physical, moral, and intellectual elements of our being.

The sources of much of the traditional curriculum's particulars are Quintilian's *Institutio Oratoria*, Plutarch's *Peri Paidon Agoges* and *Lives*, and Cicero's *De Oratoria* whose influence casts a long shadow into the Middle Ages (the basis of the *trivium* and the *quadrivium*), the Renaissance, and the early modern era.[11] These are works whose focus on the rhetorical art and on the emulation of types forms the substance of the curriculum of the school of the *grammaticus*. The unity of that curriculum was based on a key principle: *recte loquendi scientiam et poetarum enarrationem* (the art of speaking correctly and interpreting the poets).[12] Coming to appreciate the scope of human possibility manifest in the *viva voce* and working with models of exemplary speech and action, the student would gradually acquire the aptitude of what Aristotle refers to as sensing what to do 'at the right time, on the right occasion, towards the right purpose and in the right manner' (*Nich. Eth.* 2.6.11). Knowledge of paradigmatic types and good judgment as to when these could be applied to particular cases formed the point of nearly the entire curriculum.

Such understanding, Quintilian, Plutarch, and Cicero understood, would not come spontaneously or easily. Rote-drills and memory exercises, conformity to ritualized forms of agreeableness, and acceptance of authoritative guidelines would etch formal structures in the mind. Such exercises would also dispose the student to the situated judgment needed to be culturally adept, while establishing the spiritual obedience required for intellectual assent to reality. Possessing pleasing manners, or agreeableness, could arise only through disposition, and this by habituation. Imitation of manners and rituals of conduct would eventually produce an understanding of the forms of civic friendship, and an appreciation of the necessity of these forms for political participation.

Obedience is respect for authority. Its value lies entirely in creating the appropriate attitude of yielding to the immutable order of reality, for obedience is not merely passive capitulation, but the growing insight into the goodness or reasonableness of what is commanded, a goodness or reasonableness not always rationally comprehended but vaguely sensed. Apprenticeship, Quintilian taught, involved learning by doing (*Institutio Oratoria*, 10.5.19–21). Habits of premeditation and improvisation, the talents necessary for speaking and judging well, were seen to be formed by imitation of styles. Instructors would offer prelections in which the paradigms to be imitated would be analysed. The student would be expected to repeat the same with other hypothetical themes. In the Middle Ages, the formal school schedule would consist of the lecture, the repetition, and the disputation: deduction of truth from accepted authorities – the collections of *Questiones* like Peter Lombard's *Sentences* – would be followed by the memorization of definitions, rules, and precepts by rote, and completed by exercises in applying them. The practice of declamation in rhetoric and peroration worked by the same principle. By accustoming himself to the manner of a Virgil, Horace, Ovid, Juvenal, or Catullus, the student would learn the best, in the hopes that the exemplary virtues of Virgil, Horace, Ovid, Juvenal, or Catullus would always form the *telos* of his own striving (*Institutio Oratoria* 10.2.25). Students would practise these skills by reiterating fables, expanding into moral essays the insights learned from proverbs, applying features of a class of situations to a particular case, emulating historical or mythological characters, and praising or refuting arguments. Sagas, legends, myths, and stories put forward the archetypal or exemplary character that would dispose the student's temper to discern and to discriminate between the beautiful and the ugly, the virtuous and the vicious, the important and the merely interesting. The figures of antiquity served as concrete types of ethical or moral principle.

It must not be thought that this curriculum lacked a hard core of reason. Imitation and emulation were not merely mechanical repetition. The assumption (Platonic in origin) was that using models of good speech and action, while not yet exemplifying goodness, disposed one to the good. To be like the good established an identity of psychic substance with the good. Imitation did not mean 'without understanding,' nor was understanding merely an act of 'sympathetic' bonding. A rigorous separating out and organization of topics, rules, and precepts structured the art of memory and speaking well. In *De Partitione Oratoria*, Cicero subdivides the preparation of speech into *inventio, dispositia, ele-*

cutio, memoria, and *pronuntiatio,* while organizing the oration itself into *exordium, narratio, divisio, confirmatio, confutatio,* and *peroratio,* each of which needed to be understood from the position of the principles from which they were derived.[13] Dividing and separating out the complex moments of human phenomena was justified, moreover, by the principle that education concerned cultivating distinct, natural potentialities of the soul. The virtues by this understanding pre-exist in tendencies of the psyche, and the teacher as 'midwife' would expose the relevant part of the psyche to the discipline of a specific subject. Memory-training, by illustration, proceeded by a rational elaboration of topics organized as 'commonplaces' (*topos koinos* or *locus communis*). These were a kind of locale in the imagination which 'spaced' understanding for effective retrieval and order.[14] The mapping of reality by 'commonplaces' established a structured firmament for organizing experience and facts, and even more importantly prepared the psyche for an anamnetic recovery of being. Memory drills were not intended to produce a mere mechanical repetition of knowledge, but to actuate the psychic capacity to retrieve the order and mystery of being within the order of personal time. The aim was to excite consciousness to the wonder of existence.[15] The panegyric, exemplum, encomium, and vituperation, for example, were rooted in commonplaces that retrieved the tension between virtue and vice. They were symbols of psychic attunement to the movement of being.

It should not be assumed that in specifically emphasizing those lessons which produce virtue, such writers as Plutarch and Cicero lacked acquaintance with, or tried to shield students from, the low, but solid shrewdness of common sense, self-interested conduct, and prudent calculations of convenience and utility. The aim in the classic curriculum was to display human life in all its diversity: in its petty motives and cunning ways, in its aspirations to noble existence and honour, in its evils and in its perfection. Life was displayed in unadorned breadth, so as to demonstrate how an educated mind must hold together, balance, and give what was due to a complex range of desires and aims. None of the modern discovery of the 'realism' of politics or the origins of human knowledge is absent in either the classic writings or the classic pedagogy. What is different, however, is that the ancients understood that the desires, in even their most elementary form, always already imply a natural development towards order and balance. It needed but an appropriate education to cause that development to occur.

In a decisive way this curriculum of 'discipline by obedience, education through example' is the child of the compilation of Aristotelian texts known as the *Organon*. It is faithful to the Aristotelian enumeration of topics, as well as the sequential development of the understanding appropriate to them. It adopts the principle of the essential and irreducible differentiation of beings and attempts to distinguish the modes of experience and science relevant to each. Aristotelian in origin, that curriculum also builds on the cardinal elements of the Platonic teaching: *anamnesis, pathos, homonoia*, the primordial claim of language, the primacy of politics, the dialectical ascent in speech. It adds to those elements Aristotle's understanding of the importance of *ethos, hexis*, and *phronesis, diaresis*, and *telos*. It is built on the principle that the soul is an entelechy, a living totality endowed with the tendency to actualize its own inherent potentialities. Specific subjects train distinct capacities of the soul, actualizing their germinal capacities. The aim of education is to have the psyche understand the rational order in the cosmos and to increasingly experience itself to be part of it. Quintilian and Cicero, Cassiodorus and Isidore, setting in place the substance of the *trivium* and the *quadrivium*, translate the Platonic-Aristotelian heritage into a workable pedagogy. Its practices of training the memory, emulating types, dividing and separating out topics, instilling habits, and engendering civic like-mindedness confirm the metaphysic of being that sees the 'human' as that which strives for, and comprehends its humanity in, finality, completeness, or perfection. This is a humanism, identifying humans as the beings who, in knowledge of their limits, nonetheless strive for transcendental perfection. It is a humanism with a definite sense of human limit, while at the same time identifying a determinate structure in reality, attentiveness to which will provide stable measures to guide and order human reason.

Moral habit or disposition, under this light, is seen as the prolegomenon to intellectual and spiritual striving: only a person sufficiently self-controlled and disposed to assent to the structure of reality could adequately undertake the intellectual task of questioning after the causes of things. Civic or political sense is recognized as the first necessary step in the ladder of ascent characterizing maturity. First, politics is about the security of the basic equipment of life, as Aristotle says. As he also makes evident, any amount of practicality and shrewdness, or capacity to compromise with the multiplicity of views which will be expressed, might be necessary where there are scarce resources, or where there are aggressions by those who hunger for power or feel themselves dishonoured, or where political mismanagement occurs. (*Politics* 5.2–3).

And no human situation, Aristotle reckoned, would be free of these. Cicero and Plutarch too understood the complexity of human passions characterizing everyday life. Theirs is a cosmos peopled by tyrants and lovers, citizens and poets, commanders and sons, gods and philosophers, and the student must, without shirking or denying any one constituent, come to see these as the dramatic forces of his own existence.

Second, political participation ensures the recognition of the concrete particulars of life that keep judgment and intellect from what Augustine would later call *imagio fornicatio*, or gross misconstructions of reality. Reputable opinion, common judgment, and the public exchange of opinions form the bulwark against unreason. Particular forms of human existence might be parochial or restrictive but that can be remedied. Contrary to the practice of the sophists, Quintilian, Cicero, and Plutarch understand that assertive disputation is not the proper instrument for educating for it fosters either dogmatism or scepticism where what is required is trust in the things of the common.

The 'traditional curriculum,' then, is innocent and devious, wide-sweeping and strict. It operates by a language of perfection and excellence, shrewdness and practical sense, final purposes and synthetic natures, coercive habituation and discipline by obedience. To use a Platonic language, it is a curriculum that combines poetry and mathematics – poetry to instil the erotic impulse towards transcendence and mathematics to temper the psyche and to sublimate its impulses by reasoned measure. Out of this education emerge the characteristic human phenomena: desire (both somatic and intellectual) aimed at beauty, political friendship (and its correlate political enmity), the deliberative passions attached to justice (anger, loyalty), intellectual and spiritual questioning, reverence for and wonder at being, and desire for the good. These varied impulses of human existence, often at odds, had to be mutually accommodated, while acknowledging that the structure of reality confers on human existence a tonality of unrest, tension, and ambiguity. To again use a Platonic language, humans, the beings who are self-moved, are situated in a field of tension structured by forces tending, on the one hand, towards limit, proportionality, and unity and, on the other, towards contingency, transience, and finitude. These forces emanate, Plato proposed, from two polar determinations, the unmoved One and the boundless infinite, or *apeiron*. The interplay of these forces means that human existence cannot be reduced to simple models of agency and action. Thus educational curricula cannot be construed on the assumption that reality is homogeneous and that human participation in reality can be without tension. This reductionism necessarily follows when, in the hands of an immature and unworldly educator, one pole is abstracted and the field of experience is no longer structured by tension. Then the psyche, Plato warned, no longer moves itself and it loses its distinctive capacity for measured thought and action.

One last issue must be raised. Reason and artifice, virtue and myth, and all the artifices of traditional pedagogy narrow the gap between nature's forces and chance, but they never close it. Sham educators will nonetheless proceed as if all contingency can be mastered. Conferring the status of truth on mere doctrine and denying that doctrine is a mere index of movement within the educative process is one extreme. Another extreme is the assumption that because one experiences movement in the psyche therefore everything is simply unstructured process. The centrality of judgment in the traditional curriculum was a bid to hold the two forces in balance, so that the tension and hence free self-movement of the psyche was preserved. Thought and action would then display a rhythm that united measure and dynamism. Judgment – the human faculty that discerns and discriminates among the particulars of a human life where things are not all necessary or all wholly contingent, neither always the same nor always mutable – once trained, maintains that balance. 'Judgment,' as Plutarch says, 'has need of chance.'[16] So long as human existence is understood as a field of tension, and education is understood as instilling a sense of balance amidst the forces of existence, responsible education required the techniques and aims of the 'traditional curriculum.'

The overthrow of that curriculum had its most influential spokesman in Francis Bacon, whose iconoclasm underlies nearly every progressive turn taken in modern education since the sixteenth century. Identifying the importance of Bacon is not to deny that publications of other modern thinkers' works were not also decisive watershed events: Erasmus's *The Liberal Education of Children*, Rabelais's *Life of the Great Gargantua*, and Descartes's *Discourse on Method* were major works of the new age. But Bacon's *New Organon* particularly heralds the decisive break from the Aristotelian legacy, and its import had a singular influence on two of the major architects of modern education: Comenius (the *Didactica Magna*) and Pestalozzi (*On Infants' Education*).[17] In *The New Organon*, Bacon puts forward a manifesto for the transformation of human consciousness fulfilling Machiavelli's call for an end to 'imaginary republics' and ancient wisdom by mastering fortune through method. Henceforth, human affairs would be less vulnerable to chance and circumstance. In the *New Organon*, Bacon razes the edifice of traditional learning to the ground so that man could 'begin the world anew.'[18] That task is performed by diagnosing the four 'species of idols beset[ting] the human mind' which impede the advancement of learning. The implications of that analysis constitute the basis of all subsequent critique, and the spirit of the empiricism he adopted forms the foundation for the thought of all his successors, even when this was in the name of rationalism, realism, or behaviouralism. In employing the term 'idols' Bacon meant to launch an offensive against every part of the traditional curriculum: the tonality of the soul it induced, its structure, and its topics; in short, the whole apparatus by which the classical and medieval framework had been applied. In his hands, reason would no longer take its bearing from the density and complexity of concrete human phenomena, but would rather seek an Archimedean point from which an 'objective' depiction of the world could proceed. Repudiation of the 'idols of the tribe' would eliminate all anthropomorphisms, thus jettisoning the primacy of the perspective of man in science: 'for man's sense is falsely asserted to be the standard of things.'[19] Believing that nature displayed either design or purpose, and thus was a model for man's own pursuit of ends, was a product of 'vanity' and 'error.' 'True induction,' Bacon wrote, shows that nature's motions show no tendency towards balance, or towards a more perfect or more complete state. Deconstructing the 'idols of the den' entails the removal of the constraints associated with embodied existence, each individual's historical singularity and each man's personal impressions. For, as Bacon observes, 'the spirit of man (according to its several dispositions) is variable, confused and, as it were, actuated by chance.'[20] The 'idols of the market' are those opinions, shrewd guesses, and unsubstantiated judgments which arise in the political intercourse of human beings and impede a direct encounter with facts. Orienting what can be known by words and definitions can only lead to 'vain and innumerable controversies.' Finally, exposing the 'idols of the theatre' was to reject the elements and axioms of philosophy and science, made inveterate by tradition. False trust in the world, captured by the momentariness of apparent evidence, and unfounded faith in the heritage of works had to be seen for what they were if there was to be advancement of learning. And thus would one have overcome 'two sorts of rovers, the one with frivolous disputation, confutations, and verbosities, the other with blind experiments and auricular traditions and impostures.'[21] With this, the deconstruction of ethics and morality could proceed.

The Advent of 'Values'

Before we turn to consider how this deconstruction became philosophic orthodoxy, it might be informative to look briefly at how the language of values increasingly informs all our judgments and see how a generation of innovators has made that language its social mission. Before considering the philosophic argument, let us hear first the voices of the last three decades, a time when the full significance of that language swept through the field of education. In the polyphony which brings together the apparently heterogeneous chorus of liberals, marxists, existentialists, phenomenologists, freudians, and deconstructionists, the immediate implications of the fundamental uprooting required to overturn the traditional teaching of 'ethics' and 'morals' display themselves in all their vigour and enthusiasm.

The result of the call for a new curriculum and new pedagogical techniques was a growth industry. How better to change consciousness than through values! In the United States, Louis Raths, Merrill Harmin, and Sidney Simon produced a program of 'values-clarification' as well as the text *Values and Teaching* in 1966 now enshrined in the agenda of the National Humanistic Education Centre and distributed by the Sagamore Institute. In England, John Wilson, N. Williams, and B. Sugarman in 1967 published *Introduction to Moral Education*, which was followed by Peter McPhail's work at the Schools Council Project and became the basis for the *Moral Education Project* kit. In the late 1960s Lawrence Kohlberg announced his findings on cognitive moral development in educational psychology journals. In the meantime numerous programs focusing on the 'components' of 'valid moral reasoning' have developed. Of these, Jack Fraenkel's 'analytic approach' and M. Meux's *Rational Value Decisions* and *Value Conflict Resolution* are the best known. Other programs, such as Don Oliver and Jack Shaver's *Teaching Public Issues in the High School*, focused on the 'value concepts' inherent in the idea of a democratic society, and these were converted to curriculum material by Frank Newmann as *The Public Issues Series*.

How widespread was the enthusiasm over these programs? A report in 1978 announced that the values-clarification movement operated within a network of over one hundred trainers and had reached over two hundred thousand teachers, counsellors, and other helping professionals. The Harvard University Centre for Moral Development and Moral Education has conducted seminars for educators and psychologists on the methods of evaluating cognitive moral development for the last twenty years. Widely used textbooks, such as the Holt *Social Studies Curriculum*, are based on Kohlberg's cognitive developmental theory. In Canada, the Ontario Institute for Studies in Education and the British Columbia Association for Values Education and Research promote training for teachers and distribute documentation labelled 'reflective approach' and 'value reasoning,' versions of formal operational reasoning. There is now a vast field and network of values education experts supported by international periodicals and yearly colloquia substantiating the argument that values are the one thing most needful in today's world.[22]

Permit me to extract from these materials the general tone of this revolution in education. The voices I briefly allude to here (before a closer analysis of some of them in later chapters) do not, of course, reflect the whole chorus of interest in values, nor are they necessarily the finest trained voices. By virtue of their bluntness and their visionary expectations, they do, however, in my view, illustrate the full import of the recurring refrain.

Clive Beck, a leading Canadian spokesman for progressive change, expresses the urgency with which the area of values education needed to be revitalized as follows: 'While our society has surged ahead in scientific and technological knowledge, the study of values remains largely as it might have been in the Stone Age. This vast domain of human knowledge and experience, of central importance to all of us, is left to chance, subjective impression, or dogmatic, unreflective assertion.'[23] Thus, 'progress in the realm of values would seem to be among the most important objectives of human endeavour in the present age.'[24] Teachers (Beck envisages) will be 'change-agents' on behalf of the progress that overcomes the confusions in the 'traditional curriculum.'

In his *Values Education*, Michael Silver explains the new role of teachers as 'change agents': 'The surge to introduce values education comes at a time when society is faced with questions arising from a breakdown of traditional values, cultural and racial conflict, and a deep distrust of the social and political institutions ... Because the social and personal problems are rooted in values confusion, the school should play a large role in helping children to identify and clarify their values, and to make moral choices.'[25] Silver's explanations are repeated over and over throughout the field. The immediate situation necessitates a revolution in education. The social system is in an unprecedented state of crisis. Rising statistics on delinquency, drug-abuse, pregnancy, and racial hatred combined with alarming concerns about the environment, poverty, and the threat of nuclear warfare make it necessary, like never before, to raise questions about the old curriculum. The power dynamics of the old curriculum, these experts say, are the single major cause of today's social disorder. And the social disorder is perpetuated by the rigid political forms inculcated in students in the classroom. Clive Beck voices a common refrain when he writes: 'I am convinced that the greatest single problem in education today is authoritarianism, a major aspect of which is the curtailment of people's freedom to think, do, and be.'[26] The use of fear and approval in the traditional curriculum, Beck suggests, had contributed to maintaining this authoritarian regime.

The general consensus is that the traditional curriculum advocates modes of learning which produce passivity and rule-following rather than creative and critical engagements between students, teachers, and the curriculum. As Paulo Freire terms it, the transmission of knowledge by rote is a 'banking model' of schooling, leading students to absorb uncritically the structure and contents of a predetermined society.[27] There is a 'hidden curriculum' operating, transmitting relations of hierarchical authority, reifying the educational process, inculcating obedience and docility, and perpetuating traditional class structures. 'Nothing,' as one contemporary writer challenges, 'can ever become morally right because someone says that it is so and ... obedience to an authority is, strictly speaking, irrelevant to the business of moral decision-making.'[28] There is, the new educators claim, a sterile conservatism present in the existing school technique of focusing on facts and rules, in the passive acquiescence to books, in memory drills, in the study of predetermined, finished knowledge and enduring ideas, and in traditional rituals and enactments of religious or historical events. All these, they say, simply reproduce present inequities. Teaching, the iconoclasts challenge, has become nothing more than the deployment of subtle forms of discipline ensuring the perpetuation of a structure of privilege in society at large. Education is now a mere form of social control, the school a custodial institution, and the curriculum a stale replay of the status quo.

Nowhere, the new educators write, is this more true than in traditional moral lessons, which Lawrence Kohlberg dismisses as using a 'bag of virtues' for indoctrination.[29] Traditional habituation to excellences and virtues, exercises of recollection, and emulation of historical figures is nothing more than 'values inculcation.' 'In this sense,' Kohlberg writes, 'character education is close to the unreflective valuing by teachers which constitutes the hidden curriculum of the school board.'[30] As R.M. Hare proclaimed in his call for a more self-conscious and systematic appropriation of values, 'in so far as moral principles are thought of as something inherited and external ... they are dead things.'[31]

Moreover, the new educators say, traditional centres of moral education can no longer be trusted with the complexity of moral existence. 'Our studies have shown that the field of values is so vast that the task of values education cannot possibly be left to one or two societal agencies, such as the home and the church.'[32] Indeed, the traditional centres would have to be transformed too and the classroom, serving as a laboratory for change, would be the starting-point. The school must be the source of social rejuvenation: 'working through society as a whole also appears an attractive possibility when one recognizes that without general changes in a society's value outlooks, it will be very difficult to achieve value development through that society's schools.'[33]

Evidently, then, the new education proposals have a wide-sweeping and revolutionary political agenda. As Henri Giroux, activist and reporter of the first rank in the movement, conveys it, 'any viable form of political action must begin with a notion of political education in which a new language, qualitatively different social relations, and a new set of values would have to operate with the purpose of creating a new environment, in which the non-aggressive, erotic, receptive faculties of man, in harmony with the consciousness of freedom, strive for the pacification of man and nature.'[34] The call for a heightened 'consciousness of freedom' was a revolutionary banner to reorganize the world. 'The meaning of liberation,' as Charles Reich pithily summarized the revolutionary aim, 'is that the individual is free to build his own philosophy and values, his own life-style, and his own culture from a new beginning.'[35] For such revolutionary *praxis* to be maximally effective it could not remain at the level of reforming institutions, social forms, or behaviour. The penetration had to bring about a change in the understanding of the very order of being – a new construct of reality, a new mode of existence, and new human relations.

It goes nearly without saying that the old pedagogy that used fairy tales and myths, historical adventure stories and sagas, biographies of leaders and legends, thereby appealing to a reality structured by the tensions of imminence and perfection, or finitude and transcendence, had no place in this vision. How could there be gods and monsters when the innovators, fearing that any definition would reproduce the old authoritarianism, refused to clarify what were the determinate characteristics of the 'human'?

Old modes of valuation would have to go, especially those like common sense or judgments of historical appropriateness. Henceforth, these were no more than 'constituted by taken-for-granted categories and practical activity divorced from the agents and conditions that produced them.'[36] Giroux cuts to the core of the spirit of the revaluation writing: 'Radical practice begins ... with a break from the positivist emphasis on the immediacy which daily deludes individuals with a nature-like invariance of their life relationships' and functions 'so as to perceive the past in a way that makes the present visible as a revolutionary moment.' Such uprooting must be 'informed by a spirit of relentless negativity, one designed to promote the critical independence of the subject as well as the restructuring and transformation of an oppressive social reality.' Human consciousness, in other words, must be moulded before it has been corrupted or, if that is not possible, radical pedagogy must prolong and deepen the already-present corruption as a prelude to a redemptive, reconstructed world.

The reconstruction of the world could proceed only if new forms of open communication were made available and the transfigurative power of speech was given an open rein. Thus, values education entailed a profusive explosion of speech. Students would have to talk and communicate, speaking the truth of their feelings, their perspectives, their anxieties. They would thereby be speaking a truth against power, against the status quo, against the censorship imposed by vested interests. This emancipatory speaking of truth, the innovators promised, would culminate in a new language and a new construct of reality. As Paulo Freire put it in *Pedagogy of the Oppressed*, 'to exist humanly is to *name* the world, to change it ... Once named, the world in its turn reappears to the namers as a problem and requires of them a new naming.'[37] The 'true words, with which men transform the world,' Freire adds, promise permanent release from the world as it is given, in its corrupt and corrupting concreteness.

Both the curriculum and the physical structures of the school itself would need to be changed. Closed classrooms, the position of the teacher, orderly desks, as well as examination procedures, course subjects, timetables, and promotion scales had to go. It was time for students to learn techniques of 'self-construction' and 'creative self-expression.' Students 'need to be placed in classroom social relationships that affirm their own histories and cultures while at the same time providing them with the critical discourse they need to develop a self-managed existence.' More self-confidence, assertiveness, and a greater critical bent were seen as the means to achieve such control.[38] The mandate was to develop processes which made sense to young people ('student-centred education' of 'basic life skills'), which were relevant to life as they knew it. 'Centres of interest' and interdisciplinary approaches would prevail over the divisions of the old curriculum. The new values, whose precise character could not be predetermined, were to be culled from authentic self-disclosures, based on empathetic assessments of 'feelings.' There could be no more ideal types, models of perfection, or ideas of finality or completion. Truths would be arrived at through pragmatic negotiation. Their value would be gauged by their capacity to contribute to effectual solutions.

Although the ends or goals of these dialogues could not be preordained, there was in the best of the programs an attempt to devise models of 'strategic reasoning' and 'decision-making.' These models, their inventors held, would be neutral in terms of substantive moral ends, thus avoiding an indoctrination of unachievable ideals. The premiss guiding such models was that 'in all areas of social action and interaction, a common pattern of reasoning can be used. This is possible because all decision-making and justification in these areas require the same sorts of factors: namely, those expressed in the model of strategic reasoning.'[39] Rather than teaching values, schools must 'teach about values' and about the 'valuing process,' 'to try to fit them,' as R.M. Hare suggested, 'to make for themselves, the choices with which they will inevitably be faced.'[40]

Not wholly surprisingly, the choices made in the reconstruction of values might bear resemblance to older 'values.' As Clive Beck writes, values that have their source in religion, tradition, and authority 'provide much of the essential raw material for the development of values.' Beck concedes that 'much of traditional morality can be salvaged,' but it will be chosen by new modes of valuation and deployed within a broader network of 'human life decisions.'[41] New syntheses and ideals could be forged using the new modes of valuation. With the teacher as a 'resource person' and the 'mutuality' of a small 'inner group,' students would engage their minds to discover 'ingenious political solutions to social problems.' Following Peter McPhail, Beck recognizes that the schools must be used as laboratories to simulate real-life situations 'without many of the insecurities and immediate pressures of real life, a context in which [the students] may engage in social experimentation leading to discovery of more satisfactory human relationships.'[42]

If they were to have that effect, for Beck at least, the old idea of the autonomy of morality would have to be jettisoned. There would be a new alignment of 'moral' values to other values (economic, political, and aesthetic). Keeping each distinct was, Beck argued, an 'unreflective adherence to maintaining a set of rather specific rules.'[43] By introducing such fluidity, one might see a new being emerging from the process, a 'total personality' whose relations to reality arose from 'transactional pragmatism.' Submissive participation would be a thing of the past.

The release from 'fixed ends' might remind us of John Dewey's injunction to tie moral beliefs to social serviceableness. It also reproduces his confidence concerning the greater ability to control moral beliefs when they are seen as units within a system of means: 'Why have men become so attached to fixed, external ends? Why is it not universally recognized that an end is a device of intelligence in guiding action, instrumental to freeing and harmonizing troubled and divided tendencies? ... Ends are, in fact, literally endless, forever coming into existence as new activities occasion new consequences. "Endless ends" is a way of saying that there are no ends – that is no fixed, self-enclosed finalities.'[44] A system of means, by this account, breaks down the authoritarianism of traditional transmission of morality by establishing relations which are, to use Clive Beck's terms, 'functional,' and which will actualize 'the possibilities of developing complex, horizontally interlocking institutions that effectively achieve their goals.'[45] The new education would mean more group decision-making, more team skills, and a better sense of broader societal interests.

Of course, expanding the concept of values did create problems. The haphazard and ambiguous range of what should be included under the term 'values' already signals the problem. In *The Sources of Value*, Stephen Pepper gives a definition of value 'in the broadest sense':

anything good or bad ... pleasures and pains; desires, wants, and purposes; satisfactions and frustrations; preferences; utility, means, conditions, and instruments; correctness and incorrectness; integration and disintegration; character, vitality, self-realization; health; survival, evolutionary fitness; adjustability; individual freedom, social solidarity; law, duty, conscience; virtues, ideals, norms; progress; righteousness and sin; beauty and ugliness; truth and error; reality and unreality.[46]

Values could be identified as preferences and tastes, but also as determinate needs and conditions of flourishing, or as allocations of interest or qualifications on desire. Further illustration of the problem is evident in the work of Kurt Baier, who could slide from 'the value of something ... is a certain sort of property of it' to 'value is the thing's capacity to confer a benefit on someone, to make a favourable difference to his life,' and finally end up with the statement that values are *tendencies* of people to devote their resources to the attainment of certain ends.'[47] The issue, as Pepper concluded, is 'how to bring order and clarity into this apparently heterogeneous mass of subject matter,' thus securing and rendering certain the processes of valuation.[48]

To prevent relapse into past ideas of truth, and to give some order to the fluidity which was being unleashed, there was a need for new representations of reality. These representations had to satisfy ambiguous, and perhaps incommensurate, objectives. There could be no absolutes, but there did have to be a rigorous method by which students would devise their own representations. The need for a single effective method, which might seem to run counter to the professed desire of plurality, was taken to be a temporary inconvenience in the service of more effective, self-conscious valuing. Indeed, the new methodism was, paradoxically, more definite that order could be introduced into human life. Instead of working from the probable and the feasible, and from the uncertainties of ambiguous contexts, methodic inquiry into values would bring procedures which provide a controllable and predictable realm of objects. It was expected that the aggregate of phenomena relevant to values assessment could be resolved to its clear and simple unit, and then the whole could be reconstructed so that the resultant compound – society – would have the unity and consistency of its elementary building blocks. Deploying such methodic procedures and thereby installing the work of the natural sciences within the moral sphere was expected to provide a 'settled, assumed subject matter.' Values would no longer be obscure or ambivalent but rather be effective and relevant.

The Deploying of Values

What cannot be separated from this keen enthusiasm 'to bring values under control' is the historical context in which the values education programs were devised – the postwar years. These decades were a period of historically unprecedented technological growth. The call for wholesale revamping of the school curriculum and for the introduction of the new values-education programs represented one example of the questioning embarked upon in North America as to what it should do with its new power and affluence. Aroused by the realization either that the traditional 'bag of virtues' was inappropriate in relation to the new productive forces, or that such development had neglected the 'human factor,' values education programmers saw their task arising from a growing tension between values and power. Many identified the contemporary form of power in which society's regime of truth manifest itself as technology. For many, Marshall McLuhan was right when he recognized that 'we are witnessing a clash of cataclysmic proportions between two great technologies' and when he cautioned that there would be a gross failure if society went ahead to 'a job demanded by the new environment with the tools of the old.'[49] In his *Gutenberg Galaxy*, McLuhan had suggested that 'two cultures or technologies can, like astronomical galaxies, pass through one another without collision; but not without change of configuration ... Even without collision, such coexistence of technologies and awareness brings trauma and tension to every living person.'[50]

Clive Beck strikes a chord one finds echoed throughout the literature. 'Modern technology,' he writes, 'while it has not achieved much so far in real terms, is the only means whereby man could ever have gained control over his own destiny.'[51] Thus, 'we must accept technique because only then will we be able effectively to develop techniques for keeping technique in its proper place in our thought and behaviour: largely as a means rather than as an end in itself.'[52]

What was properly understood by so many of these thinkers was that technology was not merely new machinery, new forms of organization, and new products. It was also a way of ordering, a way of seeing the world that was acquiring widespread approval especially in North America. The task for many of the new educators was to apply the model of technological growth to the realm of morality. Under the pressures of a new social environment, teachers and administrators would have to 'decide whether they want values to develop haphazardly in students without any conscious and specific involvement on [the teacher's] part, or whether they intend to help students explore and come to some conclusions about values ... explicitly.'[53] Closing the gap between individual well-being and the emerging technological forces required no more than 'upgrading' some values and 'downgrading' others, and activating 'the vast backlog of unexploited techniques found in research laboratories.'[54] It was possible to analyse values for certain regularities and patterns which would constitute a sufficient basis for 'a scientific teaching of values.' 'Values change' and 'values adjustment' could be researched to serve as a further basis for prediction. Aggregates could be statistically profiled, norms could be displayed, and proposals for change as well as the correction of deviations could be produced.

Again the spirit of John Dewey informs the argument and rationale for this co-penetration of values and technology. 'I have no desire,' he had written, 'to show that what we term "science" is arbitrarily limited by *outside* ethical considerations; and that consequently science cannot intrude itself into the ethical sphere; but precisely the contrary, viz., that just because science is a mode of controlling our active relations with the world of experienced things, ethical experience is supremely in need of such regulation.'[55] Once ethics has been satisfactorily reconstructed, such regulation could be pragmatically employed. For Dewey, operationalizing attitudes, preferences, expectations, and aptitudes allows the technician to coordinate valuation with the self-correcting process of adjustment of means and ends which characterizes a society that has accepted experimental and reconstructive science as its central principle. Indeed, until that is done, the many 'problems' of social organization would not be solved. As long as 'ends have values independent of appraisal of means involved and independent of their own further causal efficacy ... no sure progress was made.' Only when these problems were 'conceived in terms of analytic observation of existing conditions, disclosing a trouble statable in a problem, criteria of judging were progressively self-corrective through the very process of use in observation to locate the source of the trouble and to indicate the effective means of dealing with it. These means form the content of the specific end-in-view, not some abstract standard or ideal.'[56]

The new educators saw the values education initiatives as bringing about these new possibilities. So successful were these initiatives going to be that Lawrence Kohlberg could report that the state of values education is 'coming of age.' Clive Beck, conveying this same Deweyan expectation that the renewal of values would translate into social progress, suggested that 'progress in the realm of values would seem to be among the most important objectives of human endeavour in the present age.'[57] Methodic reorganization of the moral sphere was enthusiastically linked to a pragmatic operationalism committed to social reconstruction. 'Values' are the tools with which social experience could be reworked.

The enthusiasm to close the gap between valuing and technology, it has to be stated, was not universal. Others found the new technological and social transformations potentially dehumanizing and sought in

values education an antidote. 'The long-range implications of a cyber-
nated world for mental health,' they warned, 'are disturbing.' The field
of values, however, could be the operational site for a 'total shift of our
society' by way of a new 'mental hygiene.'[58] The key was in turning
from 'authoritarian' hierarchies to 'authentic' interpersonal relations.

This hope coincided with an important shift occurring in the mental-
health profession: the anti-psychiatry movement. This movement
reflected the efforts of leading anti-establishment figures like Thomas
Szasz, Erving Goffman, R.D. Laing, and David Cooper to 'humanize'
psychiatry. Repeating the denunciation of hierarchy and typal identification, but adding a critique of institutionalization and professional
expertise, these vocal figures advocated a society-wide 'human services
complex.' Once spread throughout society, they believed, diverse 'preventative' or 'pre-emptive' therapies could more effectively cure the ills
previously brought to the psychiatrist's office.

Erich Fromm expresses that connection with consummate candour:
'Neurosis itself is, in the last analysis, a symptom of moral failure ... a
neurotic symptom is the specific expression of moral conflict, and the
success of the therapeutic effort depends on the understanding and
solution of the person's moral problem.'[59] This link between morality
and psychic disturbance was to provide an opening for an entire complex of values-education interventions. The significance of that marriage
cannot be underestimated! Therapy and morality were to link up and
provide a new 'hygiene.' Behaviourist psychology would arm educators, facilitators, negotiators, and counsellors with new techniques of
self-empowerment, of confessional self-disclosure, and of crisis-resolu-
tion. Their mission was to create empowered individuals and authentic
human relations. Clive Beck commended Carl Roger's 'non-directive
therapy' enthusiastically. It is one in which 'the therapist constantly
encourages the individual to rely on his own judgments and feelings in
value matters,' and thus it 'can help a person gain confidence in his ability to make autonomous judgments.'[60]

The catchword was more 'open' or 'effective' communication. This
was taken to require more tolerance, greater inclination to conciliation,
and a greater sensitivity to others through empathy. The use of values
'therapy' to counteract the social problems of discrimination, delinquency, or rebellion was understood to be a more effective route than
explicit political actions since these problems, according to the reformers, actually had their root in behavioural disorders. The new role that
social work could play in this is expressed by Francis Turner:

It is only recently that we have become increasingly aware that the place of values in the therapeutic process is a more involved, subtle and influential factor than we had previously thought ... Social workers in clinical practice are finding in their caseloads individuals, groups and families whose stress in psychosocial functioning is directly related to value and value orientation conflicts, sometimes recognized and sometimes not. Thus we can no longer see the client's value system as a private domain. We are being asked to look at it, and get involved in it, and indeed to help alter it.[61]

The pressures associated with technological growth came to be identified as 'technostress.' The immediate manifestation of such stress was 'values stress.' Once named, these stresses could be organized, recorded, monitored, and intervened with. Thus emerges a whole vocabulary associated with 'stressors,' 'stress reactions,' 'technostress reaction patterns,' and 'stress personalities' (types A and B) which, systematized as a field of inquiry, served to justify the introduction of preventive, surveillance, and adaptive strategies ('stress audits'), thus providing an overall 'stress management' program.[62] Questions of 'moral deficiency' could be transmuted into problems of psychological maladjustment. Applied to the schools, the old role of schools as custodial institutions could now be relinquished in favour of using them as therapeutic centres.

Theodor Roszak's *Making of a Counter Culture* is a manifesto which distils much of this enthused expectation of social transfiguration. 'We must,' he wrote, go beyond 'the diminished range of experience to which urban-industrialism limits our awareness and its alienating dichotomies' and reach to the intersection of 'human psychology and natural ecology.' Roszak anticipates a focus on the 'specialness' of 'personhood,' and links between individuals and the life-affirming energies of the earth.[63] Associating the emerging networks of therapy and helping-professions with a new 'politics of the person,' he thought he could perceive a 'new historical script' being engraved in the environment. It was a script of 'confessional freedom and open self-expression,' of 'creative disintegration,' and of 'affirmative therapeutics.'[64] 'There is so much social pathology in urban-industrial society,' he writes, that a new global dispensation is called for, one 'imagining the Earth at large, including ourselves and our culture, as a single, evolving system of life, the great mothering organism of organisms.' The new pedagogy, he suggested, would be the prelude to a new age of psychospiritual renewal, a 'New Jerusalem.'[65]

Not all the proposals resonated with the expansive, and even chiliastic, note struck by Roszak, but other variations on the philosophical theme he was elaborating were popular. Thus, Heidegger's authentic *Gerede*, Buber's I–Thou relationship, and Goffman's performative techniques of the self, popularized by Rollo May and Carl Rogers, and given a social scientific tincture by Gordon Allport and Abraham Maslow, became familiar references in the literature, incorporated within either what some referred to as 'technological humanism' or what others saw as an antidote from 'outside' of technology. The idea was to limit technological power by activating subjects to speak of their 'values.' The school was only one, but in a sense the most important, site of a growing social complex designed to encourage talking about values. The facilitators spread throughout this complex needed to do little more than to identify values stress. Social rejuvenation depended on nothing more than the authentic confession of values confusion and willingness to begin everything anew. This regime of truth – this solicitation and production of speeches about values, about how we come to be 'in the true' – was taken as that which could be set against the dominant power structures of technological society.

The theme of Charles Reich's *The Greening of America* is also very characteristic of this hope and, again, its teaching resonated deeply among management consultants, facilitators, and educrats. Reich saw an antidote to technology occurring in the evolution of consciousness. Technology itself, he writes, has made possible the emergence of a 'Consciousness III' which promises a change in the system of values, a transformation of psychological behaviour, an alteration in the lives people lead. 'For the choice of a lifestyle,' Reich proposed, 'is an act of transcendence of the machine, an act of independence, a declaration of independence. We are entering a new age of man.'[66] To control technology 'it suffices to take hold of controls that no one else is holding.' Reich's view is characteristic for two reasons: first, it puts forward the notion that technology has brought humans to a new stage in which their true capacities are finally revealed. Technology and humanism co-penetrate: humans have become fully human only because of technology. Second, Reich states that now, where there is a danger that technology may overreach and suppress the new revelation, it is time for a new consciousness. Previous morality and ethics, because they took their bearings from a person's complex and synthetic nature, and thus were implicated in a pre-technological political and psychological configuration, could provide no guidance here. Consciousness has now come to its prime and it is sufficient to simply change consciousness in order to change reality.

Whether values were a corrective or an antidote to technological development, it was not doubted that the primary goal of the programs was to deconstruct, tear down, and dismantle everything that had preceded the current era. Root and branch, the break had to be decisive. The language of values celebrated a human subject who could demystify the cultural forms around him, and who could, through ideals as well as the force of imagination and will, create new realities. It was time, to recall Giroux, to unleash 'relentless negativity.'

It was also time, as a report to the Club of Rome challenged, to end 'reactive' responses to crisis and to encourage 'proactive' or 'anticipatory' skills to cope with global dangers. It was necessary to close the 'human gap ... the dichotomy between a growing complexity of our own making and a lagging development of our own capacities' by going beyond 'maintenance/shock learning' which is 'a product of elitism, technocracy, and authoritarianism' towards 'innovative learning.' Here was an opportunity for an orientation which 'prepares for possible contingencies and considers long-range future alternatives,' that is 'value-creating' rather than 'value-conserving,' that 'prepares people to use techniques such as forecasting, simulations, scenarios, and models,' that 'emphasizes the future tense,' and that works in the interests of 'global consensus.'[67] Within this 'general systems theory,' a circulating series of values would permit a 'comprehensive' examination of 'problems.' Values cannot be fixed to a tableau of predetermined order and coherence. And as Clive Beck writes:

In the realm of values, there will be constant change in the future because values are so dependent upon changes in knowledge and technology and related aspects of culture and society. Values also have a tendency to change in themselves, because of the need for variety, and because the bases of values, being somewhat arbitrary, can shift arbitrarily. The old notion that we are looking for *the* answer for all time – and the belief in each age that we have found it – must be replaced by an expectation that our value outlooks will require constant modification and a capacity to achieve such modification successfully.[68]

Such 'successful modification' entails a greater adaptability with respect to the many impermanencies of contemporary society. Concluding his argument that 'ultimate' moral criteria or values domains inhibit survival by exacerbating tension, ambiguity, and conflict, Beck writes: 'And part of my recommendation is that people abandon the "host of ultimates" approach to morality ... We must come to see the connections between our life goals, otherwise they will continue to be in conflict, and we will not know how to achieve any of them successfully. And as we become aware of the connections between our life goals, we will notice that there is more in common amongst the life goals of people around the world than we had previously thought.'[69] Such universality, predicated on the 'adoption of a scientific, rigorous pattern of inquiry, reduces variations that are due to error, superstition, and prejudice.'[70]

'Values': A First Approximation

In broad brush strokes, this is the spirit gripping the values education initiative. The many voices constitute, without doubt, a polyphony but nonetheless they are united in the message that personal, social, and political renewal will be the inevitable outcome of the new consciousness of values.

We need now to understand the philosophic centre of this revolutionary chorus, so as to elevate the meaning of its themes to the same degree of coherence as we acquired when discussing ethics and morality earlier in this chapter. One could say that these programs continue the predominant misgivings constituting modernity's rejection of traditional metaphysics. The language of 'values' we might see as continuing the turn away from a study of man in his relation to the eternal or divine, to an anthropology focusing on the intramundane personality, a subject whose acts of resoluteness could break the grip of man's indebtedness and subservience to what was given. Values, then, celebrate humankind's spontaneous freedom, its capacity to make and unmake, and its natural desire to alter the conditions under which life was given to us. Valuing is thus at the same time a revolutionary rethinking of the traditional question of limits, of directives of human conduct, of ideals of self- or social perfection, that is, the realm of 'ethics' or 'morals.'

Historically and etymologically this first approximation to the meaning of 'values' seems to be a correct one. 'Values' has its first usage in the late nineteenth century: in the neo-Kantian schools, in the economic theory of marginal utility, in John Dewey's pragmatism, in Max Weber's account of how phenomena are endowed with cognitive interests, in Nietzsche's perspectivism and account of the will-to-power. What we can observe in these thinkers or schools is the postulate that humans are called to a freedom fully conscious of itself. The language of 'values' evokes the expectation of a radical demystification: the liberation of subjective freedom from those contents and contexts of existence which until contemporary times have impeded the open growth of human perfectibility. With 'values' what is affirmed is the human subject in its desire for autonomy and in its capacity to 'nihilate' the brute, given conditions of existence by choosing constructs of reality in sovereign freedom. To affirm values is to have subjected to clarification the dark, dense, and arbitrary sources of personal and collective life, to have extricated oneself from primordial bonds of situational belonging, to have celebrated one's newly achieved self-consciousness and wilful subjectivity. The contents and contexts of primordial belongingness – the body, nature, the divine drama, culture – are not seen as opening us to meaningful structures, but rather as barriers to complete flourishing. As opposed to the participatory openness and receptivity of ethical or moral life to transcendence – either cosmological or political – values-positing demands a 'posture' and that posture is one of suspicion, resoluteness, and creativity. Evidently authority, obedience, and accommodation, built on foundational images of a reality whose proportionality and order are structured by completeness, finality, and perfection, and stimulated by reminiscence, paradigmatic types, and habituation, are moribund in this demand for the self's empowerment.

Jeter par terre, as Descartes epigrammatically summed up his revolt. But how far would the revolt against tradition go? Before we answer this question, let us step back, if only to proceed on a surer footing.

2

The World and Spirit as Possession

Although most of our lives is spent in the commonplace, quotidian rhythms of the everyday – acting by habit, interacting civilly, judging what appears, obeying authority, expressing anger, forgiving, fearing disease and death, resisting but accepting imperfection – and although the traditional understandings of ethics and morality have taken the everyday as the point of departure for a discussion of how to order human longing, a great denial characterizes the dominant discourse of our society, refusing to believe that the everyday is the source of important truths about ourselves. Indeed, the most significant philosophic voices of this century, Friedrich Nietzsche and Martin Heidegger, complete the Cartesian 'jeter par terre' and the Baconian 'begin the work anew' by suggesting that the common world we inhabit is indelibly marred with 'inauthentic everydayness.' Nietzsche comes to this conclusion after analysing the power dynamics operating in our everyday moral discourse. Heidegger conducts an investigation which leads to the dismissal of the everyday as 'idle chatter,' trivial 'curiosity,' and culpable 'ambiguity.' Their successors would be even more dismissive, recoiling at the 'slimy' or 'gelatinous' quality of the concrete forms, events, and experiences of the everyday human world. They would see these forms as threatening to 'engulf' or 'devour' the more 'authentic' (i.e. fluid and indeterminate) primordiality of human beings. The durable aspect of being which the everyday reinforces cannot, for these thinkers, be accepted as a significant or formative aspect of reality. There is a need to go behind the appearances of the world where a dynamic and primordial process preceding all forms and individuated phenomena pulsates. Plato and Aristotle's argument was that what most essentially *is* appears in the 'incompletable ascent from *proteron pros hemas* [what is first for us] to *proteron physei* [what is first by nature],'[1] and in this they affirmed their trust that the everyday holds within itself a structure which moves us towards the mystery of our being through images of finality and perfection. The common acts of possession characterizing the everyday invite us to deeper and more complex forms of reality. Nietzsche's and Heidegger's perspective demands a radical dispossession from the durative aspect of being and from the everyday in whose forms being lingers.

If we are to understand the full import of this repudiation of the everyday, it is necessary to dwell briefly on Nietzsche's and Heidegger's challenge. Why I raise the spectre of Nietzsche's and Heidegger's radical turn away from the durative aspects of being as they manifest themselves in the everyday is because I want to argue that this turn supplies the enabling context in which the values programs we are analysing were devised, implemented, and judged sensible. Only in Nietzsche's and Heidegger's thought is the full destiny of the language of values spelled out. I do not, of course, assume that the values educators have always directly confronted Nietzsche and Heidegger, or that they assented to all of the features of Nietzsche's and Heidegger's thought. Instead, I would speculate that they received the radical import of that thought, mediated piecemeal by lesser (though better known) thinkers like Jean-Paul Sartre and Albert Camus, and Gabriel Marcel and Emmanuel Mounier, psychologists like Gordon Allport and Erich Fromm, and social critics like Theodor Roszak and Alvin Toffler, and fused it to their own social ideals. We are brought back, however, to the thought of Nietzsche and Heidegger because there the full implications of adopting the view that what *is* is pure becoming are not shied away from.

Nietzsche's and Heidegger's 'anti-foundational' thinking, and their portrayal of humans as part of a dynamic process of Life, quintessentially fits our image of ourselves as vital, mobile, and expansive beings, constrained by neither history nor transcendent limits. Such a self-image and the philosophic thought which supports it have little patience for the possessive affinity to being that manifests itself in love of things, formation of character, or principles of truth. We need to understand what follows from this alluring image of vitality and we will only do so if we see the whole of Nietzsche's and Heidegger's teaching and follow out the idea that our age is playing out some of the darker and more sinister elements of their thought.

Nietzsche's thought is a sustained reflection on the human flight from finitude and transience. He rejects the human incapacity to live with the awareness of the temporality and mutability of all things as a disfigurement of consciousness. Nietzsche's analysis identifies the flight from finitude with the recurring human tendency to moralize life, that is to give permanence, structure, and prescriptive authority to some aspect of our being. By conducting a 'genealogy' of all past moralities, he hoped to lay bare the disfiguration of life that occurs when that life is judged from a moral point of view. He shows that all past moralities – of justice, love, or respect – could be seen as products of *ressentiment*, a deformed rebelliousness against vigour and superiority, and ultimately against human finitude itself. Their principles could now be seen for what they truly were: perspectival illusions or dramatic masks disguising the underlying impotence and spirit of revenge, arbitrarily reifying the transient dynamism of life. Our moral criteria, Nietzsche claims, are but 'values,' that is, psychological constructs, serving some arbitrary conception of utility, yet masquerading as predicates of being. Nietzsche's deconstruction of moral forms is an invitation to dispossession, to overcoming the need for stability. Overcoming possession is, at the same time, a conduit for our deliverance from a faulty tradition of humanism. A 'posthumanist' earth is one that has transcended the tensions and ambiguities of the all-too-human everyday.

Nietzsche's portrait of the landscape after this deconstruction is one in which no traditional compass points remain. His writings expose the core of the language of values and evoke the atmosphere of a destiny in which Man is no longer the central phenomenon, but is instead one insignificant component of an indifferent, dynamic process. From that perspective, the coordinates of the past can have no further relevance and projects to sustain them can be despoiled of their moralistic posturing.

Not only are our moral limits disintegrated, but the moral deconstruction becomes a vehicle for a radical repudiation of the entire tendency to stand in some relation of possession to being. In Nietzsche's thought the poles between which human thought and action in the past acquired their tonality – human/divine, immanence/transcendence, evil/good, desire/reason, truth/opinion – and which served to symbolize the human participation in reality simply disintegrate. Interpretations of 'truth,' or 'reality,' or 'morality' become mere signs of ascending or faltering life. The 'death of God,' which Nietzsche heralds, marks the end of all eternal justifications, all theodicies, and all grand systems explaining the motions of life. With all metaphysical foundations for our self-interpretation dissolved, our desires, practices, and thoughts can no longer be understood as actualizing natural potentiality, or contributing to a cumulative historical progress, or as the expression of a human freedom ruling the world by reason. Indeed, Nietzsche suggests that what we have called essences and forms, types and processes, are nothing more than ruses or strategies within the game of life itself. That game is pre-moral or amoral, unfolding without particular reference to human measure. It is a game furthest from the Pythagorean principle of all Western thought that the human is the measure of all things. The game of life is innocent and cruel, pure and compulsive, because, like a cat with a mouse, it plays with its objects, including the human, without regret, guilt, or promises. Human projects, born out of inflated self-importance, of a pretence to 'know' the world, or faith in the divine plan, or historical action or stylish aestheticism are nothing more than life's own self-experimentations, effervescently emerging from and withdrawing back into the generative abundance of life. Amidst this fluidic cycle of creation and disintegration, all ends, meanings, and boundaries become free-floating and mutable.

The terms with which Nietzsche attempted to account for this new destiny were 'will-to-power' and 'eternal recurrence.' They are as much counter to the traditional coordinates of distinct space and time by which we have ordered human experience, as they are indications of a fundamental revaluation of existence itself. Our location in a place and within a history is henceforth better understood as an episode within temporary configurations and fateful throws of the dice. Under these new configurational destinies, which are formations of power under continuous metamorphosis, Nietzsche predicted that the twentieth century would be an era of vast devastation, forgetfulness, and blending of previously distinct phenomena. It would be a wholly new age with novel forms of thought and action.

The 'future philosophy' and the 'new mode of valuation' are to be expressions of a fresh vitality and exuberance for life, beyond the 'mechanism' of Western metaphysic's attempt to legislate everything in its place in relation to a putative 'real world.' Nietzsche's vision is of a future in which we live dangerously and tragically by loving the fate of meaninglessness in the face of infinite transience, though Nietzsche knew that the many (the last men), released from order and authority, would respond with indifference or relief to the loss of meaning, comfortable in their self-absorbing consumption and diversions, whereas only a few (the nihilists) would rise above the spirit of revenge to be legislators and artists, a new cruel and noble aristocracy. Planetary rule was a possibility for these new 'supermen,' though no traditional (read 'metaphysical') conceptions of strength, power, knowledge, virtue, law, or moral imperative would supply the script of that 'life-enhancing' rule. To live dangerously means to live without justification. This political counterpart to Nietzsche's radical historicism is usually forgotten by those who celebrate today's 'new pluralism.' Nietzsche, however, did not share the naive optimism of liberals and socialists. Once the will-to-power is released from the stranglehold of moralism, the natural inequality of human beings reasserts itself.

Heidegger's thought reinforces this dispossessive mode of existence. In *Being and Time*, he sets up a chronicle of man's ways. Humans are the 'being' encumbered with the awareness of the transience of all beings and the sense of 'thrownness' or cosmic abandonment in this world. 'Care' and 'anxiety,' as primordial ontological states (not merely emotions or physiological conditions), inform our consciousness of temporality. *Dasein* (the term used to designate humans without a determinate nature or potentiality), though concerned about its own Being, is also together with other human beings and defines itself by projects in their midst. But these engagements take place against a backdrop that threatens to lead to *Dasein*'s 'fall' into 'inauthenticity,' a renunciation of *Dasein*'s way in a world of mutability and dispersion. Against *Dasein*'s capacity to disclose to itself, and project itself into, its own possibilities lies 'everyday' life and the 'they' which oppose the temporality of existence with certain, secure, dependable standards, roles, practices, and thoughts. Things and meanings acquire objective stability. *Dasein* falls into uncritical acceptance of this commonness and flees from the burden of finitude. Such flight constitutes 'inauthentic' existence, its inauthenticity arising not from lack of conformity to a primal state of human existence (the good soul, the virtuous person, the faithful servant, the dutiful citizen), but precisely from conformity to or 'absorption' in such definitions and the accompanying closure of its own possibilities.

Authentic existence is activated by 'authentic resolve' that is triggered when *Dasein* faces its own individual death and acknowledges this encounter alone as the impetus to project its own possibility. Under the recognition of death, *Dasein* realizes its burden is inalienable: the existential uniqueness of its own dilemma cannot be represented or become the common project of human striving. When death becomes *Dasein*'s own possibility, it sees the sham of the common programs to transcend death, based on linear time (immortality, salvation, a historical terminus), and realizes an 'ek-static' potential, an ecstatic temporality. Facing transience with 'resoluteness' means that the phenomena of the world will manifest themselves to *Dasein* as they are. *Dasein* will no longer fix on the 'look' of things, as if this stable aspect of beings constitutes their exhaustive reality, but will engage in the ongoing creative renewal of existence. Only then can *Dasein* be authentically with others too. Resoluteness, then, is understood not only as a practical (vs. theoretical) event but as the 'authentic' modality of 'care,' that is, acknowledging the finitude of all beings. What will bring *Dasein* to resoluteness? Heidegger writes of a 'call of conscience.' That call of conscience is not the Thomist *synderesis* providing substantive guidance for the moral life, but is rather a disclosure which awakens *Dasein* to and from its absorption in the density of the world. A purely formal, contentless call, conscience reveals *Dasein's* state of being lost in the 'they' and turns *Dasein* to its authentic Being. 'Hearing' the call implies no plan of action or program of development. There is even no state of preparedness, as if the call can be summoned; *Dasein* is called because care – awareness of the transience of being – is the very basis of *Dasein*.

The 'fundamental ontology,' within which this drama of *Dasein* and the 'they' occurs, reveals how a reason that is evading the nothingness of Being will fall into error. Primarily, the error occurs when transitional moments in the process of Being's emergences and withdrawals are hypostatized into permanent entities. Nonetheless, an entire tradition of thinking, Heidegger says, disposes us to repeat that error. He traces the source of this error, which he calls metaphysics, to Plato's allegory of the cave where philosophic (in)sight is shown by Socrates to take its bearings from the way each being is present or appears, as that which remains in place or is stable. Plato, Heidegger says, separated two aspects of being: the process by which things come to presence and withdraw and the temporary 'standing' they have in their appearance. Assuming, though, that what *is* is what appears, as a surface or a look whose apparent permanence seems to express the totality of a thing, is, Heidegger challenges, to abstract it from the emerging power through which it became present and from that same dynamism which will lead it to pass out of appearance.

Letting itself be apprehended by how it is seen means too that a thing is taken to have boundaries or limits. The 'truth' of phenomena becomes linked to the aptitude of a knower to measure and secure these boundaries. At this point, 'ideas' are the means by which the look of a thing is fixed; to make out the being of things is to have 'insight,' which means utilizing ideas that represent the look of a thing to give it a determinate

place as an element of knowledge, and this appropriative form of apprehension spirals all the way down, in man's attempt to know the source
of things, so that being itself is just another phenomenon securable by
ideas, relative to the sight of the knower. The distortion whereby the
being of things is reduced to how those things look to humans simultaneously makes things into lifeless objects and Man into wilful subject.

The way human ratiocination and speech are understood repeats this
disfiguration. Reason is understood as marking out the human knowledge of objects. Language is no longer the 'house of Being' but an instrument for making statements that indicate the correctness or rightness of
the apprehension of being by ideas. Both are no longer seen as conduits
through which the flow of Being passes, but as the instruments for laying the appearance of what appears open to sight. The correctness of
reason and speech, that is, their potential to attain to truth, is a function
of the right vision of the ideas. Certitude provides the attitudinal vector
confirming this correctness.

Not unlike Nietzsche, Heidegger sees a kind of moralizing imperative
at work in this legislation of stability to being. The deformation began
with Plato. His Socrates mediates the apprehension of things with a
sense of the Good. The Good is what confers visibility and intelligibility
on things; it is what makes it possible for a thing to appear. The Good
arrests dispersion, flux, aberrancy, as reason informed by the good
arrests passion and desire. Only in light of the Good are things noticed
and meaningful: they are fit for, appropriate to, suitable for, something.
But this means that things are because they are experienced in terms of
their fitness and appropriateness for humans. In making truth relative to
humanity, through the image of the Good, Plato released a logic that
would progressively exalt the subjectivity evident whenever the 'good'
is posited. 'Truth' or 'being' would, as the legacy of the Platonic thinking, be a mere function of a subjectivity that controls what *is* by the construct of value to which it is disposed. 'Values' comes from the same old
order of metaphysics, conferring the same sense of self-assurance and
self-certainty in the realm of human relations that had always been at
the core of the representation of reality. Values are simply the most self-
conscious expression of the project to make humans the 'subject' or sovereign centre of beings, 'so that as the tyrant of Being he may deign to
release the beingness of beings into an all too loudly bruited "objectivity."'[2] Exalting subjectivity, 'values' make the conditions in which the
things of the world are as so many objects to be manipulated.

For Heidegger, too, the human affinity to possess being is the problem. And for him too it is the inauthentic demand that being stand secu-rity for humanity, that being justify the 'tragedy' of our existence, which must be overcome. That will occur only when the fluidity and mobility of existence itself are permitted to define our lives and the inauthentic characterizations of humans as beings who possess something perma-nent are overcome. That overcoming will herald the end of our view of ourselves as tragic and as needing justification.

Nietzsche's and Heidegger's challenge goes to the very core of the her-itage and civilization we identify as 'Western.' From Homer to Hegel, the unrest and uncertainty experienced in human life has been tied to the per-ishability and temporality of existence. What characterizes the diverse thinkers over two and a half millennia of Western thought as a 'tradition' is their recurring need to address the question of this finitude as a ques-tion concerning human mortality. What this tradition has centred on is how the human anxiety regarding death, which opens to the larger con-cern over the perishability of all human things, is at the same time a hor-ror of oblivion or of boundlessness. Amidst perpetual change, the authors in this tradition have argued, there can be no meaning or order.

Not only in intellectual effort has the anxiety regarding human mor-tality been expressed. The record of human history is a testimony to that anxiety. In many examples of architecture, the public arts, political action, and procreation lies human anxiety concerning death. Recogni-tion of our own coming-into-being and the imminence of our passing-out-of-being motivate our projects to stabilize this flux and to find some meaning for it. Indeed, the very assumption that our brief sojourn is a coming-to-*be* and our departure a passing-out-of-*being* is built on the expectation that something permanent and complete structures what allows for meaning in our lives. Whether it is the Greek citizen for whom the durability of the *polis* outlasted his individual action and pro-vided a sepulchre for the immortalization of that achievement, or the ancient philosophers for whom the universal form through which eter-nity was intimated stabilized the flux of sense-perception and opinion, or the Romans for whom universal law could withstand all convention and contingency, or the Christian who found peace in an immortal soul, or the bourgeois whose 'continual prospering' permitted forgetfulness of transience with durables which constituted an 'estate,' or the modern search for identity and selfhood amidst the breakdown of traditional ties and obligations, what we witness is an attempt to rebuff death and to articulate meaning in the face of oblivion.

At both the individual and collective level, the search for an imperishable enclave is an attempt to bestow order on flux and contingency. Indeed, the very meaning of 'adequacy' itself – personal, moral, political, social, economic, militaristic, scientific, philosophic – has reflected the need to possess one part of life so as to experience it as 'real,' as incorruptible, and as a standard. Only by positing in things which are first and foremost to us (in what we 'possess'), and which we take as stable aspects of being itself, do our strivings, choices, reasonings, and thoughts have structure and direction. Action is by definition change: it unleashes the forces of transience and mutability. But the hope of possession prevents such action from being purposeless or frivolous.

In practice, we know all such efforts to be tragic. Only dogmatism would lead us to believe that the desire for self-possession, possession of the world, or possession of truth could be fulfilled. Indeed, so easily does this desire for possession derail that the same tradition which situates it at the centre of human activity has offered recurring indictments of it as corrupt and debased, sinful and prideful, and exploitive and psychotic. Self-possession, it is said, degenerates to audacity or smug self-complacency; possession of the world is fetishism or licence for rapacious acquisitiveness; and possession of the truth is the way to dogmatism and intolerance, or parochialism. The accumulated tradition of the West's moral and political techniques for establishing and enforcing order constitutes a grand arsenal of weapons for combating these disorders and legitimating genuine possession.

The issue which arises from Nietzsche's and Heidegger's challenge is whether a 'post-humanist' world and a dispossessed being can cope with the evident reality of those burdens of our existence such as scarcity, injustice suffered at the hands of the stronger, inescapable rivalry, and the acted-out fantasies of political agitators, not to say the personal traumas of despair, cynicism, boredom, and feelings of impotence and neglect, without the guideposts developed over the long history of our tradition. For Nietzsche and Heidegger those guideposts have emasculated our natural love of contingency and creative power. Sustained by the illusory hope that existence can be mastered, these life-denying values have finally produced a process by which they have caused themselves to be devalued, leading to drift, apathy, irresoluteness, craven guilt, and resentment. For them such moods are syndromes of the nihilism which saturates and saps our spirit. Only radical dispossession – the dismantlement of those possessive relations towards aspects of our being urged on us by the tradition of Western metaphysics – can save us from nihilism.

But there is another exposition of what nihilism is, and that exposition traces the collapse of human direction and purpose to the radical historicism put forward by Nietzsche and Heidegger. In this second account the source of our problems at both the political and the personal level is the devaluation of our traditional moral, political, and intellectual categories and the grounds which validated the purposes and ends we have traditionally pursued. And these problems cannot be resolved by resoluteness, or care, or empowerment, or structureless creativity.

Nietzsche and Heidegger pose the most radical challenge to this tradition, repudiating not only distorted possession but all possession, and thus the forms of the everyday, as inauthentic. Their call to dispossession is so radical because behind it lies the desire to overcome humanism itself and all its wearisome and paralysing antinomies and bring about a new world whose new inhabitants, authentic *Dasein* or the *Übermensch*, resonate authentically with the primordial process of pure temporality.

Two thinkers in the last decades have stood against the Nietzschean and Heideggerian celebration of dispossession: Hannah Arendt and Eric Voegelin. What is important about their thought is that they show it is possible to resist the nihilism (the declaration that there are no grounds for the purposes and ends by which we govern our lives) to which radical historicism leads us without merely restating the metaphysical doctrines of antiquity and modernity. Arendt offers us a powerful restatement of our political existence. Voegelin provides us with a rich assessment of our intellectual longings. I believe a composite can be formed from their thought which will permit us to judge the values education initiatives, recognizing what is beneficial in them and what is harmful. With their thought we do not retreat into a pocket of philosophic dogmatism, for both thinkers pass through the thought of Nietzsche and Heidegger to arrive at their own position; nor do we abandon either reason or freedom. At the political level, their thought has the virtue of holding together the aspirations of modern life – individuality, freedom, and the will to change towards a future – with more ancient concerns of commonality, meaning, and responsibility. Their thought seems to me particularly well suited to permit us to judge values education responsibly while avoiding both romanticism and presentism. In turning to the thought of Arendt and Voegelin, I want to depict a way of thinking which does not respond to the perception of the transience of all things with despair and by dispossession, but rather gets on with living by creating a world where we can live tragically but decently.

The World of Politics

The aim of Hannah Arendt's work is to remind us what it is about a distinctly *human* life that ensures such decency. All of her studies explicate the meaning of the unalterable conditions of human existence, and in providing such meaning she is seeking to re-establish limits to what we think we can do.

In her major works *The Human Condition* and *The Origins of Totalitarianism* Arendt develops two theses which are germane to our discussion. First, she portrays the implications of abandoning the common world of political engagement through the formation of mass society; second, she shows the connection between our prevailing form of knowledge and our vulnerability to political terror. What links these two theses is her overriding concern that the common sense and decency which ensure public order cannot withstand a condition where everything is rendered fluid and mobile.

In *The Human Condition*, Arendt argues that one of our major historical achievements was the creation of a public world in which essential facts of our human condition were ranked and given their due. Characteristic of this public world was the activity of politics in which the fact of human plurality and the capacity to act freely were acknowledged. The plurality and freedom of the political world were differentiated from the processes and necessities of the private world where the biological demands of nature were fulfilled. These natural demands, while essential for survival, are processes which cannot sustain the distinct human capacity for freedom and unique action in so far as they recur infinitely as necessary cycles of birth, growth, and decay. Thus, a clear demarcation separates this realm from the political world. The world is an artifice, and Arendt distinguishes it from the mere natural earth. The world is organized in such a way so as to allow action. Politics is about the action by which humans announce their freedom and introduce newness to the world. But politics is also about the power of collective enterprises and the delicate balance of preserving plurality and unique action amidst the 'web of human relations.' The question of how that balance is achieved is resolved by meanings.

Meanings come from two sources. One is the active participation of citizens who, like separate dinner guests around the same table, see and hear from a distinct vantage point and from different interests but participate in a common enterprise. What is known and found to be meaningful is negotiated in the interplay of different perspectives and public unity. Such meaning could not arise if everyone merely reiterated and reinforced a feeling-state or shared drive. The result would be simply a multiplication of one single experience, which however strongly felt, could not approximate the reality recognized in the exchange of many perspectives and interests which engender human meaning. The second source of meanings arises from the response to actions. Actions, once performed, constitute events, and events can be composed into stories which establish meaning. Story-making is very important, for in saving words and deeds from oblivion, it stabilizes the processes of contingency and errancy unleashed by action into forms which can become opportunities for renewing the world.

Action needs to be distinguished from work, which is the activity that creates a permanent world of artefacts characterized by durability and whose stability outlasts finite individual life and the novelty of action. Work, and the relations of possession it makes possible, are vital if there is to be sufficient continuity to form meaning. But work is an inappropriate model for the public sphere, since its logic is governed by means and ends. If politics is to respect genuine plurality and the capacity for expressing freedom in action, as well as the ongoing activity of negotiating meaning, then there can be no predetermined ends. Similarly, labour, that activity which reproduces the processes and relations of the private world, is an inappropriate model for politics. Labour's bonds of necessity, its futile cyclical and infinite repetition of nature's motions, do not allow the characteristically human capacity for action, or humanity's plurality, to emerge. Nor can labour produce meaning since its infinite cycles perpetually consume anything which could be enduring.

Arendt believes that the point of these distinctions was maximally clear to the ancient Greeks. Plato and Aristotle muddied the distinctions, though they preserved the idea of politics as the activity in which individuals excel and the importance of stability and permanence as manifest in possession for blocking the boundlessness of contingency.

Beginning in the sixteenth century, however, the distinctions disintegrated when the maintenance of life came to define the mandate of government. One reason that this occurred was as a consequence of the expropriations during the Reformation. The reason for having private property, as the Greeks had understood it, was to provide for oneself a permanent place and stake in the common world. The expropriations had the effect of destroying property without creating a new form of permanence. Millions of persons, deprived of their hereditary place in the world, were transformed into mere labour-power, and expropriators treated them as capital whose purpose was simply to generate more capital. Production could then be primarily understood as being carried out, not for the sake of fabricating a permanent world, but for the sake of consumption to continue the process of capital expansion. The values of a labouring world are productivity and abundance, values most closely allied to the processes of life itself. The worldly values of work – permanence, stability, and durability – vanish as humans are shifted from a stable home to a liquid movement.

The distinction between private and public became blurred as the relations and consciousness of the private sphere were extended into the public world. Such blending created a new realm: the social. The social was characterized by the collective organization of the natural biological processes in the form of the regulation of the cycles of production and consumption. Unlike the political world that had been characterized by a plurality of perspectives and interests, the social realm has a statistical uniformity arising from measurable and predictable regularities in human behaviour. Since a single aim comes to predominate, its rule does not require the conciliatory negotiation of different perspectives through public speech, but rather a government's undertaking to ensure that idiosyncratic particular wills are normalized and adapted to the general will. Politics becomes modelled on the activity of making, thus transforming genuine plurality from a condition of human existence to a problem to be solved. In the model of work the need for unique action is extinguished because the end has already been predetermined. Moreover, meaning becomes reduced to simple use. Such a state is run by functionaries, who are expected to behave efficiently, not act independently.

Society in time appeared inhospitable to the human heart. The turn away from society occurred during the period in which romanticism arose as a respectable form of intellectual resistance. It continues as a form of protest while social conformism continues to spread. Social others become merely similar organisms, reflecting back the same concerns and needs. The logic of labour – where all things are consumables within a liquid process – prevails in all things, replacing a human world with mass society, where nothing survives the instant under the anonymous cycles of social growth and decay. 'Socialized mankind' merely resonates in an efficient 'metabolism with nature.' Our doings become mere bundles of reactions to system norms. At this point humankind becomes a single mass. Not only is that mass now highly vulnerable in a manner we shall identify momentarily, but life loses those events whose singularity confers meaning on the process of life. This is as true of the time spent labouring and consuming, which must finally be experienced as boring, as it is of the free time spent pursuing hobbies, which are frivolous, or pursuing managed leisure periods, which become subject to the same laws of necessity as the labouring process. Persons will look desperately for an alternative.

The withdrawal from the social realm looks to the enclaves of intimacy and personal grievance for satisfaction. Such enclaves are refuges, of which the dearest and most pleasing are our inner, mental lives. Once so isolated, individuals have achieved the maximum 'worldlessness.' They may be global consumers, and participating in universal processes, but they are isolated and atomized. What Arendt means by referring to their 'worldlessness' is that the world, organized to acknowledge human plurality and to remember the distinctive contributions of individual actions, served a vital purpose. In the public give and take of politics, the plurality of perspectives guaranteed a common sense of reality. The certainties of the lonely heart cannot be assumed to correspond to the reality attested to and negotiated by a plurality of perspectives.

Moreover, for Arendt, this is an interior space which is easily manipulated. In the loneliness of the heart, nearly any phantom can arise. Isolation leaves individuals vulnerable to those sufficiently skilled in ideological propaganda. The general condition of worldlessness, Arendt notes, while apparently the necessary condition for supplying us with the many pleasing things of life, was 'also the necessary condition for the formation of selfless mass men, willing participants in ideological mass movements.' Ideology becomes the means for acting out the fantasies and grievances agitating the lonely heart. Ideological agitation is furthest from the activities and relations of the everyday world of embodied existence where things are possessed, events publicly witnessed and judged, and common sense consulted.

The experiment of 'politics' is one option through which humans could respond to the anxiety associated with consciousness of human finitude and with the fear of boundlessness. For Arendt it is a particularly benign and moderate option, truest to the various limits and possibilities conditioning human life and most likely to produce a decent world. The overturn of this experiment and all the relations it sanctioned by forces of expropriation dismantling the durable aspects of our being, and leading to worldlessness and dispossession, presented a different option. For Arendt this option holds some clear dangers which jeopardize the hope that humans will treat one another decently. These dangers were magnified, and became the horrific events of the twentieth century known as totalitarianism, only when they combined with another force. Simultaneous with the historical processes in which the public world was lost was an intellectual revolution contributing to and hastening the loss of the ancient Greek's clarity about things. This revolution was also a process of dispossession though of a different sort.

The second thesis of *The Human Condition* pertains to the advent of modern science and the spread of its methods into every human endeavour. Arendt begins with the metaphor of the 'Archimedean point,' which for her serves to explain important details about our modern age. Archimedes, she recalls, speculated on the location of the centre of gravity of a lever capable of moving the earth. By extrapolation one could imagine the mathematical question becoming the philosophic speculation concerning the perspective of those who could harness the forces of the world. Arendt suggests that this speculation was made into a concrete possibility by modern science. Modern science, as the thought of Bacon and Descartes attests, is characterized by distrust of worldly reality. It seeks in regenerated 'facts' or mathematical models a simplicity and coherence lacking in our ordinary perceptions and common-sense observations. It seeks a reference point which is universal and certain beyond the plurality of cultural and historical worlds and beyond the tentative, faltering efforts to find meaning. Nowhere, Arendt points out, has the attainment of such a reference point so clearly given us the power to imitate universal forces than in our extraordinary ability to release energy processes normally occurring in the sun, to initiate processes of cosmic evolution in a test-tube, to penetrate cosmic space to the extent of six billion light years, to build machines for the production and control of energies unknown to earthly nature, to attain speeds in atomic accelerators which approach the speed of light, to produce elements not found in nature, to disperse radioactive particles created by us through the use of cosmic radiation on the earth. In other words, we can handle nature from a point in the universe outside the earth. We can act on the earth as if we operate from the Archimedean point. And hence we deny that anything occurring on the earth is a mere earthly happening. All events are subject to universally valid laws. Both the geocentric and the heliocentric perspective betray a desire for a fixed centre, which modern science reveals to be an illusion. And thus, Arendt concludes, we see ourselves as universal beings.

Yet, at the same time as the expansion to universal being, Arendt points out, the Archimedean point was moved within man. This was already evident in Descartes's mathematical representation where all real relations are dissolved into logical relations between the mind's own products and in reference solely to the pattern of the human mind. The same internalization is applied across the fields of human endeavour. It occurs in the Protestant Reformation, which finds the proof of election in 'worldly asceticism'; in Benthamite utilitarianism, which establishes morality on the basis of the inner sensations of pleasure and pain; and in the philosophies of life where the primordial dynamic of life itself defines the principle of existence. In each case, the same mistrust of man has occurred: human senses cannot receive reality and human reason cannot receive truth. The worldliness of human experience is invalidated, and only the certainty of inner processes is authentic. In this way, private, internalized experience comes to be seen as more true than the worldly reality given in observed fact or common sense.

Modern science turns us away from humanism, that is, from seeing human concerns as paramount, for another reason. The modern paradigm of knowledge is characterized by the mutual action of knowing and production on one another. Galileo's telescope proved that the appearances of the world are essentially deceiving. Only the use of instruments can tear the veil of illusion away. Consequently, what we know arises not from receptivity to the order of being, but through experimentation in which reality is made to reveal its hidden truth. Modern reason is technical, regulative, and interventionist. Its progress relies on machines and laboratories. Hence our productive capacities are vaunted above our contemplative or receptive faculties. But if our productive capacities are able to penetrate and remake the conditions and limits under which existence appears to us, then it is not inconceivable that the regulative parameters defining our being can be overcome as well. Then, not only can we only know what we ourselves make, but what we are is the result of our making capacity as well. Modern science offers release from the inconveniences of our human condition.

Modern science ends up abetting some of the worst dangers of modern worldlessness in its form as 'socialized mankind.' Science proceeds as a form of making and that making is steered by a construct of reality conceived in the isolated processes of the mind. The scientist who uses his mathematically generated models to 'produce' technological results cannot be certain that in so doing he has made any statement about reality. Techniques appear to allow him to 'make' realities evident in vast technological growth and the accumulation and distribution of the good things of life. But technological success, while the modern test for the validity of a hypothesis, is not in itself a demonstration of truth, unless truth be reinterpreted to mean practical success. All that productive success means is that man can consistently apply the contents of his mind, regardless of the truth status of the propositions, to the practical world. Essentially incompatible rival theories can nonetheless generate identical practical results. As Arendt comments, though, 'there are no limits to the possibilities of nonsense and capricious notions that can be decked out as the last word in science.'[3]

Where truth is tested by doing, the activity of making is obviously supreme, not merely because of the dependence on technical instruments, but also because the experiment itself is a making and fabricating, the production of its own phenomena. We can only know what we make, and making therefore dominates the diverse realms of our intercourse. If we apply this mentality to our understanding of human action, we may believe that we can make and remake our own nature, unleashing processes which would not have occurred without this manipulation. Or we could make history, by conforming action to the means/end category. The dominant model of knowledge from the sciences supports such an effort, since science had acknowledged that we can only know things through the processes by which they became what they are. The scientist both reproduces processes and also initiates his own, concerned merely to elaborate how things came to be. Our 'nature' is our history, our coming-to-be.

With history also understood as a process, individuals and their actions could be understood as part of an objective and continuous movement. But like natural science, both the making of nature and history fall subject to the same dilemma: if the theoretical constructions guiding such making are human inventions, and any number of variations are possible, we can act successfully in nature and in history and the effects can verify the hypotheses and thus confirm them as the basis for consistent action. Any number of meanings can be found to emerge from these activities of making and the facts will obligingly fall into the many mutually exclusive patterns. But this expansion of power over nature and history as processes has the consequence that nothing can have meaning in itself but only as part of the process as a whole. Meaning is absorbed into historical trends or forces. When history has a pattern, we can be expected to conform to behaviour which substantiates the historical hypotheses. A whole mass society, Arendt warns, can be terrorized into acting in accordance with an ideology, and its elicited behaviour will be used to prove the 'truth' of the ideology. This can occur particularly where under the notion of 'socialized mankind' no public world relates and separates individuals. Instead, as elements within a universal process, and deprived of concrete particularity, what is left are 'atomized elements in a mass society whose completely heterogeneous uniformity is one of the primary conditions for totalitarianism.'[4]

The warning of 'nonsense and capricious notions' masquerading as 'the last word in science' takes us to the conclusion of Arendt's argument. What is at stake in the mass confusions of our lives today, we learn from Arendt, is the order of reality we negotiate among ourselves through observation, judgment, and common sense. Totalitarianism has supplied the jarring indication of the atrocious brutalities which accompany the eclipse of that order. Arendt's study of totalitarianism is disturbing and haunting for it reveals how similar our intellectual constructs are to the conditions under which Hitler's and Stalin's regimes arose. Totalitarianism, a quintessentially twentieth-century phenomenon, epitomizes the results which follow when the world comes apart and we lose the understanding of those distinctions which held it together.

Arendt's analysis focuses on how a 'mass' of human beings could be mobilized, agitated, and brutalized as specimens of experiments to make history and remake nature, conducted under the laboratory conditions of modern totalitarianism, and how this could proceed for many years without worldwide alarm and even with the apparent 'consent' of the victims. What had gone wrong?

The concentration camp is for Arendt the phenomenon which quintessentially conveys an answer to this question. Its capacity for total domination was built on the two dangers Arendt identified as having been posed by 'modern worldlessness': the loss of a commonly sensed reality and the reduction of humans to a bundle of reactions within a process.

Under these conditions, it was no surprise, she says, that the fictions and lies the internees and the German people as a whole were told could by their logical consistency alone insulate everyone from the brutal truth.

The camps served as scientific laboratories in which the totalitarian belief that everything is possible and hence permitted could be verified. The total domination was unlike any other political exercise of force and can only be understood as an ideological phenomenon because the mass murders were understood and carried out as rational programs of a doctrine that was completely logical. In those camps, fictitious realities were fabricated so as to make access to the reality given in common sense impossible. Individuals were held by the thrall of unified abstractions, by fictions insulating them from reality by logic and language. All actions were merely deductions from the accepted premises and followed logically. The rigorous consistency of logic does more than persuade. 'Totalitarian rulers,' Arendt notes,

> rely on the compulsion with which we can compel ourselves, for the limited mobilization of people which even they still need; this inner compulsion is the tyranny of logicality against which nothing stands but the great capacity of men to start something new. The tyranny of logicality begins with the mind's submission to logic as a never-ending process, on which man relies in order to engender his thoughts. By this submission, he surrenders his inner freedom as he surrenders his freedom of movement when he bows down to an outward tyranny.[5]

From 'our fear of contradicting ourselves,' we are caught in a logicality which entails 'You can't say A without saying B and C and so on, down to the end of the murderous alphabet.'[6] Thus victims and administrators alike behaved, following rules and believing they were obeying a necessity greater than their own judgment.

The laboratory of totalitarianism consisted of experiments in the remaking of human nature and history. Perpetual mobility and dislocation were used to produce a condition where no genuine plurality could exist and where individuals' capacities for memory, self-possession in shame, loyalty, and pride were simply destroyed. Choice and judgment were made meaningless by the arbitrary nature of the terror used, hence the extreme unpredictability of the actions of both guards and prisoners. But the use of terror also effectively eliminated that dependable self-interest which ordinarily underlies human deliberation and action. Individual psyches were disoriented, thereby transforming them into bundles of predictable response. Prisoners were remade in the image of the abstract theories of their oppressors, the success of which served to verify the hypotheses of the experiments.

Totalitarian concentration camps worked because of the absence of a world in whose stability judgment and experience could be anchored. Atomized and terrorized, viewed as abstractions and without concrete identity, men could become 'superfluous' because they had nothing but an indeterminate generality. 'The particular reality of the individual person,' Arendt noted, 'appears against the background of a spurious reality of the general and the universal, and shrinks into a negligible quantity or is submerged in the stream of dynamic movement of the universal itself.' Jews, Gypsies, or homosexuals simply lost their 'rights.' 'Rights,' Arendt notes, remain an abstract fiction when postulated for an '"abstract" human being who seemed to exist nowhere.' The solution to the degradation of Jews was not to say 'there is no such being as a Jew. There are only persons,' for then, as abstractions or indeterminate beings, they didn't exist, for their determinate characteristics had become superfluous and disposable. Even criminals find themselves in a better situation since their status was, at least, defined by a place in the world. 'It seems,' Arendt writes, 'that man who is nothing but a man has lost the very qualities which make it possible for other people to treat him as a fellow-man. This is one of the reasons why it is far more difficult to destroy the legal personality of a criminal, that is of a man who has taken upon himself the responsibility for an act whose consequences now determine his fate, than of a man who has been disallowed all common human responsibilities.'[7] The answer was not to eliminate the Jewishness of Jews but rather to protect it with a legal *persona*, under the equality of the law, and within a concrete community. 'Only the loss of a polity itself,' Arendt adds, 'expels him from humanity' and thus: 'Not the loss of specific rights, then, but the loss of a community willing and able to guarantee any rights whatsoever, has been the calamity which has befallen ever-increasing numbers of people. Man, it turns out, can lose all so-called Rights of Man without losing his essential quality as man, his human dignity.'[8] And as the events of the twentieth century have shown: 'The conception of human rights, based upon the assumed existence of a human being as such, broke down at the very moment when those who professed to believe in it were for the first time confronted with people who had indeed lost all other qualities and specific relationships – except that they were still human. The world found nothing sacred in the abstract nakedness of being human.'[9]

We can only fully understand the warning implied by Arendt's analysis of the camps if we note that the preconditions of their effectiveness – individuals reduced to 'mass' existence – have their equivalence in the social existence of individuals under the notion of 'socialized mankind.' The modern masses can be agitated and mobilized, as were their counterparts in the concentration camp, because, deprived of their concrete particularity and a public world, 'they do not believe in anything visible, in the reality of their own experience; they do not trust their eyes and ears but only their imaginations, which may be caught by anything that is at once universal and consistent in itself. What convinces masses are not facts, and not even invented facts, but only the consistency of the system of which they are presumably part.'[10] Under the condition of 'total domination,' what is attempted is 'to organize the infinite plurality and differentiation of human beings as if all of humanity were just one individual ... possible only if each and every person can be reduced to a never-changing identity of reactions, so that each of these bundles of reactions can be exchanged at random for any other.' When we are emboldened by our successes in making and remaking nature and history, and where the logical consistency of our ideas in conjunction with the practical success of their application is the sole criterion of truth, the greatest dangers of manipulation threaten us. The concentration camp is, by this account, only the extreme possibility already manifest in a 'socialized mankind.'

Arendt's analysis of totalitarianism focuses on the process by which men become 'desincarnated' and then by which they become a mere quantum within dynamic motion. In her book *Eichmann in Jerusalem*, she provides a case study of her argument. I wish to conclude this exegesis of Arendt with her portrayal of Eichmann because in a way he is the 'everyman' who so consummately is the consequence of some of the dangerous tendencies of our age we have been examining. Eichmann on trial appeared capable of recall and memory only in episodic and fragmented form, or through some curious act of simultaneous connection by which he would link incidents with feelings but never the events that occasioned them. Arendt notes that each of his emotions was viewed by him in isolation from any other, with no connection to other situations. It was as if each story ran along a different track in his memory. Or, he would conjoin hackneyed expressions like 'objective attitude' or 'economy' with an account of his administration of the extermination camps, speaking proudly of his detachment and efficiency, untouched by the callousness and moral obtuseness betrayed by his evident detachment from the horrifying consequences of his actions. It was obvious that among other things he simply lacked unity: his life did not constitute sequences continuously linked to give indication of a unified personality. Therefore, from one perspective, one would have to say that Eichmann was pathological. Yet, he 'behaved' effectively and used the necessary language rules to be understood by others. Little personal malice or evil revealed itself in his answers. He understood himself to be 'doing his job.' This self-insulation from the world, from the concreteness of fact, and from the meanings which arise in the exercise of common sense led Arendt to comment that the distinctiveness of wrongdoing under modern worldlessness is that it is an evil which is utterly 'banal.'[11]

The Questioning Psyche

Arendt's 'world,' its places and stories, and the common sense and appreciation for durable things by which it is preserved take us a long way in guaranteeing decency in human life. But we are still confined to an insufficient measure of what we are as human beings when we only take into account our public lives. Moreover, that which binds us as a community cannot survive without the parallel development of our own psyches. As Eric Voegelin reminds us, we are also thinking beings whose intellectual and spiritual experiences provide the substance which holds political citizens together. From Voegelin we acquire the other element of our argument that questions concerning the order and disorder of human existence in society are not restricted to questions of morality but are part of the larger issue of how we participate in the process of reality. If we are to understand the phenomena that are conveyed by the term 'values,' Voegelin teaches us, then they must become permeable towards the order of being.

Voegelin's work is a sustained inquiry into the ultimate units of analysis of human activity, namely primary experiences. Symbolized, these experiences give us a sense of order in our personal lives, in social existence, and in history. The force of those experiences comes to us in what Karl Jaspers has identified as 'boundary-situations,' where we are confronted with the stark reality of human existence and attempt to find meaning in these limits. Death is, for us, one of those boundary situations. The questions which arise when humans face their own finitude are distillations of the concerns we raise over the boundlessness and oblivion beyond the perimeter of human order. Neither our wilful protestations to the contrary nor dogmatic assertions of human omnipotence can forever escape the fact that this unlimited is inexhaustible and that it must remain an essential mystery to us as humans. But nor can it be denied that the infinite attracts and mesmerizes us, as a challenge and as a source of either our tranquillity or our terror. We seek either to know the infinite, or to overcome it; it causes us to recoil back into ourselves either in pious acknowledgment of our designated place in the ordered whole, or in an anxious sense of our own inadequacy in the face of a purposeless, random series of contingent occurrences. Either way, the infinite towards which we are attracted is a mystery, and the presence of such mystery, Voegelin writes, illuminates the nature of our existence as 'a disturbing in-between of ignorance and knowledge, of time and timelessness, of imperfection and perfection, of hope and fulfilment, and ultimately of life and death.'[12] The symbol 'death' causes us to recognize limits to our being and awakens us to a 'questioning unrest' at the heart of our existence. That questioning, the evidence of great thinkers both in the West and the East shows, 'seeks' in response to a seductive drawing and moving of the infinite. The 'questioning unrest' exemplifies the state of a philosophizing consciousness, one which realizes that once the event of awakening occurs it cannot slip back to an earlier state. It must now ask questions and place its entire mode of life under the demands of the 'questioning unrest.'

From this comprehensive perspective, 'death' and the fear of oblivion can no longer be restricted to being a catalyst for immortalizing political action. More important, 'death' becomes the symbol through which we enact the experiences of the questioning unrest towards the infinite.

By virtue of the testimony of those paradigmatic thinkers whose consciousness was wholly open to reality, the awareness produced by 'death' should not be the cause of anguish and despair. 'The concern of man about the meaning of his existence in the field of being does not [however],' Voegelin writes, 'remain pent up in the tortures of anxiety, but can vent itself in the creation of symbols purporting to render intelligible the relations and tensions between the distinguishable terms of the field.'[13] Through symbols, the tension of existence becomes an object of reflection and understanding. What is symbolized are movements of the psyche in its very natural and inevitable wonder evinced in movement both towards and away from the infinite. As symbols, they express the concrete manifold of experiences that belong to human existence: love, pathos, like-mindedness, spiritual persuasion, catharsis, trust, hope, longing, turning around, and turning towards.

These are experiences, articulated as symbols, expressing the nature of participation in the process of reality. It does not take philosophy to attune humans to these experiences. Myths, legends, fables, even rites, open consciousness, through the exemplary or paradigmatic beings they depict, to these experiences. The Greek philosophers 'differentiated' the experiences further than myth or fable allow and identified them not so much as actual events in the history of a people or distinct faculties of the human psyche but as moments in the psychic process of wondering, searching, questioning, and being drawn. The philosopher's symbols focus the psyche in its confused unrest to question the source of that unrest and lead to the further insight of that psyche's ignorance and desire for knowledge.

Myth is simply a more compact version of this movement. Historical recollection in the form of narratives is another. Philosophic symbolization merely means that participation has a greater degree of permeability to it. Heroic action in the myth translates to erotic tension to the ground of being in philosophy. Achilles is replaced by Socrates. Experiencing the cosmos full of gods, or thinking that gods have human or animal forms, is not merely 'false' or intended as a salutary, social lie. These are pre-philosophic articulations of the divine ground of the cosmos and of man. They are attempts to express the experience of the graduated ascent of reason metaphorically as the spatial distinctions of earth and heaven. The symbols are equivalent. Pedagogically, it is sound to initiate the young into a comprehensive participation in the process of reality through the medium of myth. Either through myth or through philosophic dialogue psyches are to be drawn to participate in the ground of being as a result of wondering. Wonder is not just idle curiosity; it opens one to a structure constituting the 'divinity' of the ground, that is to say a context which humans do not themselves create and which exceeds their interpretive efforts.

Voegelin restores to our vocabulary the term Plato and Aristotle use whereby the psyche explores the tension of existence. Reason is not just calculative, but 'noetic.' Noetic consciousness is an opening of the psyche towards the ground of being. Its experience of intelligibility is consubstantial with the order of the cosmos. The more regulative functions of reason – the control of desire, the consent to first principles – follow from that more important encounter. The activity of reason is what, in the final instance, establishes a structure and order for human life. Existential unrest, the desire to know, the feeling of being moved to question, the direction of questioning towards the ground, the recognition of the ground as stable – these are for Voegelin the experiential complex, the *pathos* in which the noetic process is actuated. If there is unity, proportionality, and order to human life, it is not simply a consequence of a right ordering of passion and reason, or a consequence of distinguishing right opinion from error. Instead, it is by virtue of an attunement in which 'the reality of divine-human participation ... becomes luminous.'[14] Why 'divine'? The word is not meant to invoke the many layers of dogma in institutionalized religion. 'Divine' is a symbol – not an external entity – that is put forward by consciousness when, in receptivity to the questioning unrest, it becomes aware that there is a structure to its questioning and reasons that such a structure cannot be the result of chance. Consciousness senses itself to be participating in a reality not of its own making and thus interprets that its 'primary experiences' of the world transcend towards the ground of being. Voegelin makes clear that such transcendence entails surmounting, not negating, the concrete experiences of a full human life: 'Participation in the divine,' Voegelin writes, 'remains bound to the perspective of man.'[15]

The experienced process of reality in the world, which includes political judgment, moral action, and intellectual questioning, points to a process within the divine ground of being. The 'divine' reality towards which consciousness transcends cannot be known as an object of knowledge, for consciousness is participatory. Thus, we must symbolize this process in which we wonder about the ultimate ground as 'reality,' or 'nature,' or 'divine.' These concepts do not have an independent, external existence. They are symbolic expressions of consciousness participating in an intelligible process flowing through human beings. They focus attention on the human psyche as a sensorium for the 'divine' source, or the 'other-than-human' source, of intelligible order. 'Truth' too is not a statement about the correct representation of reality. Instead, by it we mean the love drawn by the ground towards which the questioning consciousness transcends.

The participation of consciousness in reality means that all that one can speak of is the fundamental tension constituting the psyche. Its experience of unrest and the resultant desire to question are all that can be said of the structure of consciousness. There is no 'immanent man' and 'transcendent god' as if these are separable entities. Voegelin suggests that for the purpose of analysing human tension towards the ground of existence, one will speak of a human and a divine pole, as one will speak of a knower and a known to indicate the phases of cognition. But these poles really have no independent existence apart from the field of tension in which they are experienced as poles. A consciousness no longer fully participating in the process of reality is prone to fixate on one of the poles and to define that pole as a dogmatic proposition, or a doctrine, or a system of thought. The 'human' will be taken to be 'the rational animal,' or 'the labouring being,' or 'the maker of tools.' 'God' will be personified as the 'righteous judge,' the 'loving father,' or the 'redeemer.' But, Voegelin challenges, as mere 'concepts' these word definitions have lost their permeability for the reality of the primary experiences. No set of propositions concerning the human tension towards the ground can resolve the unrest of existence.

The tension means that our lives are an 'in-between' existence, where we are conscious of a spiritual quest which continually moves between the poles of ignorance and knowledge, mortality and immortality, organic, sentient life and divine perfection, death and life. Plato had identified this quest as the 'metaxy,' a process within reality in the effort to search for divine order. '... the in-between – the metaxy,' Voegelin explicates, 'is not an empty space between the poles of existence, but the "realm of the spiritual"; it is the reality of "man's converse with the gods," the mutual participation (*methexis, metalepsis*) of human in divine, and divine in human, reality.'[16] Humans, the unfinished and unfinishable beings, experience themselves as in-between. That experience constitutes their humanity. Recalling our in-between existence explains the ineradicability of certain features of our existence (such as those mentioned by Hesiod) and the importance of certain human virtues in responding to this condition (courage before death, fair cooperation with others, moderation). Even more significantly, it initiates our spiritual and intellectual questioning of the mystery of goodness, of existence itself, and of the order in which such mysteries are experienced by us.

The modalities of our distinctively everyday human existence – wonder, hope, anger, love, shame, promising, and questioning – all participate in this process of reality, manifesting its tensions and unrest, as well as the structure established by the existence of a transcendental, divine ground of being. The realm of human spirituality, then, rises in and through the immediate and concrete desires and passions, whose nascent order disposes the psyche to trust that its questionings have direction. Even in relatively low levels of existential tension – between desire and need, between sentient perception and right opinion – there reality shows itself. The experiences of the concrete everyday are events within which the psyche participates in transcendent being and allows itself to be structured by it.

Resistance to reality is, however, a continual temptation. Dissatisfaction with the given situation can lead, not to the reasonable assumption that man is inadequate vis-à-vis the goodness of the given order of being, but rather to the belief that the world is wrongly organized but capable of being reworked. Being is taken to be reducible to a cognitive construct.

In such reductions the 'primary experience' of existence is usually the target. Some will repeatedly assume that with enough techniques perfection can be made immanent and mastered. This presumption will appear either as salvational ideologies or as causal explanations of how consciousness can be reduced to controllable, organic processes. Voegelin warns that such control of reality only eclipses what is distinctive to human existence. Hypostatizing either pole of the tension (i.e. knowledge, perfection, immortality, or ignorance, imperfection, finitude) only results in extravagant expectations concerning human actions or a cynical unwillingness to pursue the life of reason.

Revolt against the ground of being reaches its peak, though in the phenomenon Voegelin refers to as 'gnosticism.' The 'gnostic,' driven by the expectation that a return to some original primordiality is possible, attempts flight from the intrinsic order of being. Speculatively or actively, the gnostic customarily tries to transcend the promptings, longings, and orderliness of the human psyche by appealing to the 'free powers' of the *pneuma*, or spirit. The self which is awakened, in its awareness of the deceptive complacency of the world, can no longer accept the traditional forms of accommodation to and survival amidst the tension of existence. With regard to the realm of the concrete, it must deny the limits of finiteness and creatureliness, of historical and social existence, imposed by its natural condition. Spiritually, it rejects the counsels of moderation and sees these as nothing more than arbitrary forms of domination by a world denying its true freedom. Alienated from these conditions and the world which has been built to mirror them, the gnostic self must do more than simply master the world; it must reconstruct itself into a closed system which shields itself from any further incursion of the unreconciled elements which threaten its new revelation about the true nature of the world.

Voegelin sees gnosticism as a disfiguration and suggests that it arises whenever political empires break down and where institutional and social disorder runs alongside intellectual and spiritual disorientation as well as moral insecurity. The ancient 'gnosticisms' responded to the historical and personal disorder by symbolically reformulating the meaning of existence. The concrete world was experienced as alien and inhospitable, a place into which man had accidentally strayed (or had been violently flung) and from which he had to flee to return to his true home. Seeing the world as evil darkness and *gnosis* as an illuminating light which promised an escape from the prison-house of this world and the everyday rhythms of the world, the gnostic had to reject what is taken as reality by the preponderant part of humankind. The *gnosis* was a new 'truth' wholly other than that knowledge which humans have by experiencing this world as an orderly whole. The gnostics were 'anti-cosmic' – nothing of this orderly whole visible to our senses and intelligible to our minds actually reveals truth to us.

While the ancient speculative gnostics sought a transcendental salvation (a god outside of the cosmos), the modern activist gnostic, still disenchanted with the order of this world, nonetheless anticipates an immanent release from the despotism of this world's order. In gnosticism of the immanentist variety, the reality of the cosmic tension between the eternal and the temporal is denied. Instead, the modern gnostic believes human tension to be the consequences of clashes in historical or social forces and further believes that there will be a historical resolution of those clashes, a development which will culminate in a new age of humankind. In this version of gnosticism, all that is needed is a prophetic intellectual who by evoking the shape and direction of history initiates the process by which humans can save themselves. But as Voegelin points out, the intellectual will be successful only if the psyches of the intellectual's followers are deformed, which is to say that humans have become wholly immanent beings for whom the promise of a major transfiguration of their existence is imminent. The 'magic' of this operation, Voegelin suggests, is worked by psychology. The intellectual persuades us that we are in a 'state of alienation.' The scheme of reality this 'magician' projects forms a system in which alienation is overcome. As a total and definitive system, the scheme permits nothing of first reality to intrude. Any thought that the tension of existence cannot be resolved in an immanent schema of reality is thereby abandoned.

Both ancient and modern gnosticism share the assumption that humans are homeless in the world as it has been given to them. Nature, society, and even the everyday events of personal life are alien and even actively hostile places. By virtue of their 'entanglement' with matter all these have become unwelcome dwellings for humanity. Salvation demands a revolutionary upheaval. First and foremost that upheaval involves recognizing that our current state is one of sleep: we must awake to an awareness of our alienation from this world. The promise is of a *gnosis* which simultaneously awakens humans from their condition of darkness and offers them the means of escaping from it. The whole tiresome business of human life – the recurring need to accommodate to material limits, the need to respond to perennial spiritual unrest – can be fled from by an act of consciousness or overt social action. Thus the order of being can be destroyed and the tension of existence which humans impatiently endure can be overcome.

Another way of stating what happens when the order of being is denied, or when the conditions of human life are re-created, is to say that the 'death of God' has occurred. What this means is that reality, or the 'created order,' is unmasked and revealed to be nothing more than the product of demonic forces or ignorance. The world cannot be trusted to bear the imprint of an intelligible ordering, and the human psyche's experience of meaning, harmony, or consubstantiality with the order of reality is dismissed as illusory. 'God,' or the existing order of being, has been murdered. Only then can the re-creation of being occur. Since it is germane to our inquiry, it is important to note that Voegelin sees Hegel as the archetype of modern gnostics and Nietzsche as the one who drew the inevitable consequences from Hegel's gnosticism. Hegel's *Phenomenology of Spirit* is the classic example of attempted mastery of the tension of existence, for he shows how 'divine' reason is, in fact, nothing more than the dialectical progress of *Geist* (or Spirit) in history, and how the state of alienation evident throughout human history will finally be superseded by a state of conciliation once history is over. Moreover, the modern gnostic as exemplified by Hegel ends up revealing that the order of being has become incarnate in himself and that, as creator of a New World, he can do away with the old 'God' by transfiguring his world.[17] Nietzsche simply drew out the obvious conclusion: the murderers of God ('humans' as the now embodied expression of *Geist*) must see their own death as a consequence of the death of God. Hegel, and for that matter all thinkers who posit a process of development wherein human unrest is once and for all ended, is not merely transmuting the substance of the order of being but also thereby ending whatever once may have been the distinctively human.

At the psychological level, this kind of transfiguration of reality occurs when a key component of reality is abandoned. For example, reason may be renounced because it is seen as too compromised with the world. The orgy of passion which remains is seen as the whole of reality. Or, a rigid asceticism is followed that sees all desire as alien and capable of being transcended in a pure, unalloyed act of reason. One sees the former in those romantic movements which followed Rousseau's idyllic portrayal of nature as 'sweet sentiment.' The latter is found wherever nature is seen as totally fallen and reason is believed to be radically free of it. Each one uses gnostic themes in its own way. In cancelling the tension between reason and the passions, the gnostic achieves that illusory state of such self-enhancement that he believes he can actualize his own salvation. Either the gnostic gives himself to an orgy of passion believing that the world can be consumed and thus cease to be a limit to human existence, or the gnostic presumes to have the *gnosis* which makes total escape from worldly constraints possible. In either case the soul's anxiety in the tension of existence is being denied, eclipsed by the temporary feeling of enhancement which follows the liberation from reality. Such a being believes itself to once and for all be free of the social, political, or intellectual forms of the previous age and free of the struggles of the psyche. It fantasizes a new world but it can do so only because it ignores an element of psychic reality. The 'second reality' will temporarily screen out the common experiences of reality, but this deception cannot last.

This deformed self, which Voegelin identifies as 'the *libido dominandi*,' is a will which ranges from acts of brute sheer political domination to the more subtle domination of reality by a transformation of the human search for truth. The *libido dominandi* refuses to accept its humanity. It abstracts one dimension of its existence from the overall process within which consciousness moves, pretending that politics, or economics, or morality, or technical expertise can be an autonomous realm of action. But, its schemes of second reality cannot work. Consciousness continues to function within the process of reality, for even with *ersatz* images (lust for wealth, power, purity, or wisdom) 'pneumopathological' disruptions in the existential order of the individual, or the social order of the community, will occur. 'In our time the loss of reality is not only registered by revolutionary violence, noisy propaganda, bloody executions, indifferent complacence, or dull apathy; it is also experienced and suffered as loss. The awareness of suffering a shadowy life, however, is the low point of turning around, the *periagoge*, from where the ascent from the cave to the light can begin.'[18]

The lesson to be learned from Voegelin's analysis is that reason is not simply a clever instrument for calculating how to maximize one's desires or how to acquire more technical control over things, but a faculty for illuminating the total context of personal existence. Given this scope, the exercise of reason cannot be contained by the social need to devise rules and regulations to prevent disruptions within the human community. There will always also be questions of the ultimate source of order and the place that human unrest has within that order, questions which are initiated when humans confront their own mortality. Behind political, moral, and social problems lies the deeper unrest produced by our relation to the ground of being. It is only if we are open to reality in this comprehensive sense that the anxieties of everyday existence, to which we are especially exposed in moral and political dilemmas, are met with a balanced state of mind rather than the state characterized by the Stoics as one of 'unreasoned fears' and 'fluttering uncertainty and overexcitement of passions.'[19] Openness to reality as the precondition of moral action also means that the moral reasoning activated whenever the appropriate relation between self-restraint and the passions is evaluated or when responsibility is assigned, or when the intention prior to choice is examined, must be located not as some criterion of 'meta-ethical adequacy' but as part of the experience of the process of reality. Morality is situated within the movements experienced by the psyche and it is directed by the divine presence within the *metaxy*.[20]

Voegelin's writings are a repeated warning concerning dogmatic resolutions to the tension towards the ground. At the same time, they are a report on the maximal amplitude of human experience in its various phases of wondering, searching, questioning, and being drawn as the authentic expression of the exploration of human unrest. Voegelin's account of what we are as humans acknowledges the process-character of life with its endless motions of desire, but it also recognizes a structure within which that unrest operates and which sets the tone for the human encounter with the process of reality. This tone, and the pull of the 'divine' pole, order the experiences activated by the search, providing humans with the proportionality, unity, and harmony which a balanced psyche uses in situations where a moral response is called for. As long as we remain 'humans,' there can be no cessation to the unrest, or even a permanent solution to the social and political, personal and historical, manifestations of that unrest.

Voegelin's analysis is a warning against extravagant expectations from politics and social action aiming to subdue the unrest and tensions of existence, as well as the spiritual *hubris* of pretending to dissolve the essential mysteries of our lives. There are limits on perfectibility. Enthusiasm for perfection diverted from the spiritual life and directed towards projects of radical transformation of human existence produces dangerous disruptions in personal and social life. The purpose of education is to cultivate a psyche receptive to order, one which participates through its experiences in a process transcending towards the ground of being. Such a psyche has a balanced view of the nature and extent of moral work, for it sees the ordering of the passions and the focus of reason within a wider process of reality.

Conditions and Balance

By drawing the concerns of Voegelin and Arendt together into a composite, we have restored the comprehensiveness within which, I think,
the question of values needs to be posed.

Neither Arendt nor Voegelin abstracts the phenomena understood by
'ethics' or 'morality' from political or intellectual life. To the contrary,
when they speak of 'judgment' or 'virtue,' 'disposition' or 'right,' they
are, at the same time, referring to a balanced reason and a psychic tonality arising from participation in the public sphere of speech and action,
as well as in the questioning process, within which the unique unrest of
our existence and the transcendental structure which draws us become
illuminated. The complex nature of human participation in the process
of reality, in which the psyche is pulled between rule and desire, and
constraint and freedom, and experiences the degree of self-perfection
which is granted it by nature, is the core from which radiates 'ethical' or
'moral' life.

In acknowledging this complexity, both thinkers make decisive the
importance of recognizing how the everyday opens us to the essential
structures of the process of reality. The everyday world of reputable
opinion, indignation at injustice, wonder at the presence of goodness,
anxiety concerning death, desire for individual recognition, cooperation
and competition, promise-making and forgiveness, awe before the
sacred, and shame and willingness to take risk forms the contours of the
process of reality in which we participate as human beings. For Arendt
and Voegelin they are also the origin and the terminus of political action
and intellectual questioning. They provide the substance within which
the ethical or moral phenomena arise and are given form. As well, both
writers warn that these phenomena will be gravely distorted and misin-
terpreted if, by ignoring the structures and possibilities of the everyday,
and taking instead as one's starting-point some apodictic first principles
or 'sentiment' of oneness within an unstructured primordiality, one
closes down the process of reality. Indeed, starting from either of these
errors, Arendt and Voegelin maintain, has been the determining factor
of the dreadful political atrocities of this century.

'Worldlessness,' for Arendt, and 'gnosticism,' for Voegelin, are
ways each has of speaking of the loss of the characteristically 'human' in
the face of the infinite or boundless. This dread of the boundless is not
new though it certainly runs against today's intellectual fashion, as we
saw in the celebration of permanent revolution in Giroux's 'relentless

negativity.' Such dread is conveyed in images of the ceaseless and futile desires, tasks, and punishments of Tantalus, Hercules, and Sisyphus, whose fate evokes the horror of the total oblivion of measurelessness, or of motion without cessation and purpose, or of permanence without novelty or hope. Indeed, one could nearly identify this dread as the first principle of Western philosophic thought. The absence of limit as per-petual transformation or undifferentiated identity entails, as Aristotle comments in his *Metaphysics*, an 'infinite regress,' and in the realm of human action that would make it impossible to speak of better or worse, superior or inferior.

So it is that Arendt characterizes 'worldlessness' as the infinity of an undifferentiated time and space.[21] Human beings, she states, and the common-sense decency and order they need to live well, cannot endure the unredemptiveness of an 'unbearable sequence of sheer happenings,' or that of a 'state of permanent instability.'[22] But nor can humans endure a condition where only certainty and finality prevail. Where time is the closed agenda of a historical script (dialectical materialism or progress), or space the site of 'total domination' by a schema of logic ('ideology'), there too is 'worldlessness,' the state in which the characteristically human cannot survive.

Where the characteristically 'human' does emerge is in the world. The 'world' for Arendt falls somewhere between motionless finality and boundless transience. The world manifests the rhythms and tensions of the intersection of order and generation. Thus it must stave off any slide towards either atomism ('heterogeneous uniformity') or monism ('the tyranny of logicality'), for in that slide is heralded the extinction of the human. The world is a *place* organized for the recollection of events by *stories*. It is a place given structure by the concrete and particular pres-ence of the individuals composing it. On the one hand, it is a space and time which have been invested with human proportion and measure. And, on the other, it is an organization sufficiently elastic and suffi-ciently tolerant of the ambiguities, inconveniences, and asymmetries of human existence to permit of new beginnings and new stories and to require the continuous exercise of practical judgment.[23] Without 'sto-ries' individual action would slip into oblivion. Conversely, without the spontaneous eruption of contingent individual action, there would be no need for 'stories,' no need to respond to the mysteries of birth and death, or of action and events. Moreover, if the world's distinctions and order did not express man's concrete existence and the primacy of his judgment, it could be no distinctly *human* world maintained by distinctly *human* stories. The 'world' is the juncture of limitless dispersion as one of its polar determinations and boundary or limitation as the other.

Voegelin depicts 'gnosticism' as a similar derailment towards the boundless. It is a psychic derailment produced in a dream of pure freedom from the world's 'entanglements' and the complexities of personal, social, and historical existence. But man, Voegelin counterposes, if he is to avoid 'pneumopathological disorder' and 'social disruptions,' cannot experience reality if oriented by an 'disembodied ego' anticipating union with 'ineffable greatness.' 'The leap over the bounds of the finite into the perfection of absolute knowledge,' he writes, 'is impossible.'[24] Alternatively, absorption in the merely finite is expressive of vegetative life. Participation that is fully open to the process of reality will know that its questioning unrest is grounded in embodied, historical existence and moved by attraction to a transcendental perfection. That participation cannot become luminous to itself if the process of noetic consciousness has become hardened, for example when formative experiences are transposed into 'dogma' (apodictic first principles, grand theories about the process of individual or collective history) or are reduced to the mere play of 'word definitions' in a signification scheme (the 'relativism' of 'non-binding subjective opinion'). When 'symbol' becomes detached from experiences in which it originated, and when it is employed within a closed system to deny the experiences of the questioning being, then 'gnosticism' has taken hold and the distinctively human form of consciousness cannot occur.

'Consciousness' (or *l'âme ouverte*), by contrast, responsively pursues its questioning unrest only in tension between the *apeiron* and the divine ground. 'Balanced consciousness' manifests its openness to reality only in a responsiveness that balances the pulls towards boundlessness and transcendent wholeness. Only then does it continue to question and only then will that questioning have a concrete basis and direction. Without the 'truth' of participation in a reality that is experienced as 'transcending,' there would be only 'non-binding subjective opinion.' Without the recognition of 'reality as process,' which thereby takes man's personal, social, and historical existence into the equation, there are only *ersatz* movements. These construct 'systems' by closing consciousness of the process of reality down to 'historical development,' 'the immanent self,' or 'the transcendental subject.' Constructs of reality which interpret the order of being as within human control, the givenness of which can be obliterated, signify a closure of existence. 'Consciousness' is a mode of participation in reality. Its characteristic activity is defined by movement between order and process.

Body and psyche, desire and transcendence, temporality and divine order – as the balance between these forces appears in the everyday, the tensions of the distinctively 'human' participation in reality show themselves and give evidence of man's 'synthetic' nature. What unites Arendt and Voegelin is their shared view that the 'elementary verities' of the commonplace and everyday provide the data for an understanding of the distinctions and structures which limit infinite boundlessness and thus preserve the distinctly human phenomena. The continuum of political, moral, and intellectual life must display an openness to the healthy tension between finality and motion, or between order and genesis. Arendt's account, which combines the stability of the world with the contingency of new events, is met by Voegelin's account of our double recognition of reality as process and reality as transcending. In neither thinker's work is one polar determination permitted to define the field so as to bring about the unreal experience that tension has ended. Balance is maintained in Arendt by counterposing places with stories and in Voegelin by squaring the human experience of 'truth' with consciousness of our existence as the in-between. Such balance serves the purpose of holding back a politically disordering encounter with the boundlessness of infinity as well as the destructive conclusiveness of final solutions.

Their positions, I want to conclude, reflect the everyday experience of human existence as a self-motion situated in a field of tension structured by forces tending on the one hand to limit, proportionality, and unity, and, on the other, towards transience, flux, and dispersion. This experience is evident in every human encounter, in acts of mercy as well as righteous anger, in judgments on actions as well as in thoughtful reflection. As we have already remarked, Plato had symbolized this tension as the intersection of forces apparently emanating from two polar determinations, the unmoved One and the boundless infinite, or *apeiron*. When the two forces are in balance, the tension and hence free self-movement of the psyche are preserved. Thought will display a rhythm that unites measure and dynamism, practicality and mystery. Practice will balance order with contingency and perfection with imperfection. But when one pole is abstracted and the field of experience is no longer structured by tension, the psyche no longer moves itself and thus loses its distinctive capacity for free thought. 'Worldlessness' and 'gnosticism' express the loss of balance. With them comes an assertiveness and impatience which would seek dominion over the ambiguities of our existence by schematic constructs of tensionless perfection. Such schemes either posit a consciousness without a somatic foundation or a somatic existence without an ordering consciousness. Abstracting consciousness from the bonds of the body, to illustrate, produces expectations of a Third Age of the spirit, of perfected reason, and of a new humanity.[25] Abstracting the body from consciousness leads to what Weber once described as 'specialists without spirit, voluptuaries without heart.' Both of these constructs of reality ultimately rest on the premiss that the evident and concrete experiences of living, as they manifest themselves in the everyday, are 'inauthentic.' For Arendt and Voegelin, the flaw in that argument is that it sees in the everyday only 'routine' and 'conformity.' It ignores the ongoing, and less visible, process of judgment and balanced reasoning by which the poles of existence are given their due and reconciled in forms and structures informing everyday existence. The search for authenticity in some primordial flow which is prior to the distinctions of the everyday is not only non-humanistic, it is anti-humanistic. It leads to neglect of or contempt for the political forms which hold together the fragile artifices by which human life and decency are guaranteed.

The result of the contemporary flight from the process of reality is, as both Arendt and Voegelin agree, that the embodied individual has been left exposed and vulnerable to the 'nonsense and capricious notions' and 'murderous schemes' of those who, sensing a vacuum, have been able to seize power.

For both Arendt and Voegelin, then, there is no self-delusion regarding the nature of human life, no expectation of 'universal enlightenment' or a 'new sensibility' bringing about a 'new humanity.' Opinions concerning the character and practice of justice for them cannot neglect the reality of power, of abused power, of cruelty and evil. But flight from the concreteness of the everyday lies at the heart of the messianic and chiliastic political and social projects of this century. Only recollection of the process of reality which ties the concreteness of our personal destinies to society, history, and those depths we must symbolize as 'mysteries' returns human judgment to that balance which serves as the bulwark for fantasy.

The composite drawn from Arendt's and Voegelin's work has provided us with a perspective in which the possibilities and limits of human experience can be discussed. They have given us contexts wherein the essential core of 'ethics' and 'morality' could be understood.

We will proceed in our discussion of values and technology more aware of the concreteness and complexity of political existence as well as the life of the spirit which experiences itself participating in a transcending reality. The principles of human order, which is all that is conveyed by ethical and moral life, can now be understood as rhythms in the movement between political and intellectual life. They are the forms of balance which give substance to human freedom and human questioning, thus inhibiting limitless and purposeless activism.

3

Values Education: Three Models

Despite a popular view that the schools have abdicated their responsibility to provide a place in the curriculum for morality and are fostering a general climate indifferent to moral phenomena, the classroom has been in the last thirty years, and nothing indicates that it will not continue to be, an active site of pedagogical practice and knowledge in numerous experimental efforts to put 'values' at the centre of concern.[1] In the next three chapters, from the great variety of such models, I extract the three dominant models and examine them, measuring their value against the composite sketch of the human condition of the previous chapter. I do not challenge these models as if they are theories which should be verified or falsified on the positivistic level. Nor is my exposition restricted to the explicit professions of their authors as to the meaning of what they are doing. As I have proposed already, the upheavals and crises within the history of political philosophy, and especially the important steps taken from Kant to Heidegger, provide the *enabling* context in which these models have meaning. My discussion therefore is of the philosophic positions from which each model arises, of the spirit or dynamic which drives each one, and of the implications for what I have depicted as the conditions of human order which follow on their implementation.

The three models which have predominance in this field are Louis Raths, Sidney Simon, and Howard Kirschenbaum's 'values clarification,' Lawrence Kohlberg's 'moral developmental approach,' and the program put forward by the Association of Values Education Research, 'values analysis.' From time to time, one or the other has been denounced by parent groups, school boards, or moral philosophers. Or, new empirical evidence shifts the field of positivity beyond the original intent. The result has been that the designers of the models have tended to re-conceptualize the models over time, incorporating the phenomena that were said to be missing, or synthesizing elements from other models.[2] A continuous process of readjustment characterizes the field and the identity of the models, making it difficult to typify the current state of each model with precision. Notwithstanding this flux, each separately (consistent with its own distinctive principle) continues to form one of the pillars of values education and each has its advocates among the teachers and administrators who have been exposed to these models for the past thirty years. Recent trends show a proclivity to avoid commitment to a single program and to adapt instead a vertical integration approach whereby each model is fashioned for maximum effectiveness into an appropriate learning experience, at a given stage in a student's growth, and then superseded by the next model.

However distinct each model may be, all three models share a majority of the features characterizing the movement as a whole. They are united in their stand against the 'traditional curriculum.' In all cases, procedure predominates over content, problem-solving over the understanding of facts and events, methods of gathering information over the acquisition of knowledge. All the models require the prior or the ongoing psychological work of forming a strong and positive sense of self, variably identified as 'self-concept,' 'self-project,' or 'self-image.' Once the self is empowered, 'skills' can be grafted to it: communication skills, organizational skills, conflict-management skills, decision-making skills, social skills, instrumental-reasoning skills. The result of such skill-training is not intended to be a movement towards understanding the 'truth' or unconditional 'compass points,' but an ability to perceive trends and relationships with sufficient openness so that conclusions can continually be retested against new information under a kind of operationalism that permits a 'floating' of what is known against new data. 'Facilitating' is less an actuation of the structures of the psyche's experience of the process of reality than an opportunity to encourage the student to concentrate his or her existence into the form of a resolute will able to repudiate 'reactive' behaviour and to create a lifestyle. The emphasis is on the possible rather than the actual, on newness rather than reconsecration, and on autonomy rather than tradition or transcendence.

Values education tends to be deployed in curriculum modules such as 'life in society' or 'social studies' or 'interpersonal skills.' The 'society' or environment which is the medium for such deployment is global 'society' or, when it is 'national,' it is found to be structured by universal functions which open to the wider environment. Values, or modes of valuation, in so far as they are functionally related to the environment, are instruments which can address specifiable, but changing, 'problems.' In these modules values connect individual creativity with system performance. Even where 'values' are seen to constitute an 'independent' sphere of individual self-regulation, and the mode of valuation is identified as *sui generis*, these are actuated within 'problems' which relate the self to the continuous processes of environmental integration – a health-care system, a public safety system, the workplace – endowing these with 'relevance.'

The relationship of the new pedagogy to the social sciences is one of either reproducing its methodological procedures or accepting its findings as definitive of empirical reality. All of these initiatives and the means of deployment depend heavily on the social sciences. The hypotheses and cognitive instruments of those sciences (the fact/value distinction, the naturalist fallacy, the self-evidence of logical structure) and their experimental activism (model-building, the resolutive-compositive method, heuristic circularity) are to have a direct presence in the classroom. In this dependence on the social sciences, the designers of the values education models are attracted to the experimental activism and operationalism of those sciences. The methods of the social sciences make it possible to achieve a wholly new direction for the future. Jerome Bruner could be speaking for all the models we are about to analyse when he writes, explaining the irrelevance of the past for today's values: 'But there is a more compelling reason to shift away from history toward the social or behavioural sciences. It has to do with the need for studying the possible rather than the achieved – a necessary step if we are able to adapt to change. It is the behavioural sciences and their generality with respect to variations in the human condition that must be central to our presentation of man, not the particularities of his history.'[3]

To recognize that all the values education models are united on these principles is to say no more than that they are all quintessentially modern projects, which are themselves a turning away from any last remnant of the political and intellectual structures of antiquity and a celebration of human freedom, the capacity to make and unmake, and the desire to alter the conditions under which life is given to us.

For reasons which should be obvious from my discussion of Arendt and Voegelin (and especially from my argument that their thoughts do not spring from nostalgia for antiquity but from a true encounter with the cardinal elements of modernity), many of these modern principles are highly desirable. There is no place in a genuinely liberal education for archaism or dogmatism. Metaphysical doctrinairism holds no favour in our modern age. Individual freedom and action, and the technical progress which makes possible that we use these to extend our good moral offices to others as well as bring the life of reason within grasp of more individuals, are unmitigated blessings of modernity.

But the question I am raising is whether, however concordant the values education modellers think themselves to be with enlightenment ideals, these models do not tap into some of the darker and more dangerous undercurrents of those ideals and, in so doing, promote a process by which those ideals overreach themselves and dismantle the grounds upon which they rest. For, what I wish to argue is similar to Grant's point to which we referred earlier, that the terms of language embody destinies and 'destinies have a way of working themselves out – that is of bringing forth from their principle everything which is implied in that principle.' I am proposing that the term 'values,' however the neo-Kantians, Austrian marginalists, or Weberians may have understood it, is a supreme candidate for Grant's general argument. However much the modellers may dislike any suggestion that the language of values embodies destabilizing principles and cannot prevent a self-destructive process of devaluation, I am saying that there is a seamless and ineluctable chain of inference unravelling the language of values and culminating in Nietzsche's 'the will loves even more to will nothingness than not to will.' I think the models I am about to examine bear out this contention.

Values Analysis: The Kantian Experiment

In its July 1983 prospectus, the Association for Values Education and Research (AVER), after echoing the common litany of complaints about the traditional curriculum and the previous sources of moral education, declared its confidence in modern moral philosophy's espousal of reasoning skills to solve values dilemmas. 'This program proceeds on the assumption that there is a rational approach to the solution of moral problems'[4]

Following the lead of John Wilson and operationalizing the concept of logical reasoning, AVER has developed procedures by which students can identify and resolve values problems.[5] In acquiring clarity concerning the principles of epistemological or ethical adequacy and then by setting out the terms of valid moral discourse – standards which any moral knower will see as the compelling criteria informing his or her cognitive processes – the student, following AVER's lead, will surmount values conflict.

'Value' judgments are understood as having numerous 'points of view' – moral, aesthetic, health and safety, economic, prudential, intellectual, environmental, and religious – each of which constitutes a distinct sphere of deliberation. Methodic procedure, the logic of which is drawn from a conceptual model, is applied to analyse the logical syntax of these judgments. Analysis of these 'speech-acts' will reveal a nascent logic, the measures of which can be used to overcome contradiction and inconsistency.[6] The form of rationality itself, as it is given in grammar, reveals the possibility of a universal morality. Following the dictates of reason alone brings one to what W.K. Frankena has articulated as the distinctly 'moral point of view': 'one is taking the moral point of view if one is not being egoistic, one is doing things on principle, one is willing to universalize one's principles, and in doing so one considers the good of everyone alike.'[7] The moral point of view is understood to override all others; the task of education will be to have its coherence and consistency manifest themselves throughout the student's life.

The moral point of view, however, does not arise spontaneously. Before it is actuated, preparatory work is required. The distinctively moral phenomena can only arise if valuing is a matter of personal choice and if the act of choice displays sufficient internal coherence. The range of relevant human phenomena must be delimited to what allows of clear and consistent articulation. The students must examine their desires and preferences, wants and needs, to make each an object of evaluation and assent. Tacit knowledge of principles is not sufficient for a distinctively moral point of view. Students must become 'autonomous,' which means they must become self-conscious, and they must be able to legislate consistency to their lives. Autonomy and consistency are the keys to non-egoistic and universalizable forms of moral principle. Only when these are in place will students legislate universally acceptable moral laws to themselves. One final feature must be added for the activation of the moral point of view to be successful: students must be brought to display altruism and empathy to others.

The philosophical pedigree of this model lies in Kant's account of moral autonomy, specifically the categorical imperative. In Kant's account too, the regulative laws of moral reasoning are necessarily separate from knowledge about the practical world. As he writes, they command imperatives rather than offer mere prudential advice. Moreover, the sphere of morals can be specified a priori: in so far as Kant sets out an 'ethics based on pure reason' (rather than on how individuals actually act), reason alone can fully articulate the obligations of morality. There are three features which distinguish Kant's account: the primacy of self-legislation, the elevation of a deontological over a teleological ethics, and the centrality of a procedural rationality issuing in universal maxims.

The first feature means that human agency must be enlisted under an imperative mode to legislate against its natural or social inclinations in favour of an ideal. Man is, in his highest possibility, a universal subject willing universal rules. The proper moral experience is one formed in the crucible of a conflict between desire and duty, resolved by a will able to impose order on the unpredictability and partiality of particular inclinations. The empowered will manifests its autonomy by effecting a subjugation of the experiences given immediately in day-to-day life.

The second feature removes moral law from an instrumental role in the achievement of pleasure, social utility, or happiness; maxims or rules of practice are not sufficient bases for morality. Morality must be *sui generis* (the 'formula of the ought' arises wholly from the concept of 'ought') and respect for it is to be unconditional. The moral motive of duty rather than the motive by inclination is to dominate, on the basis of its own internal and formal logic. There are, thus, no natural ends or historical purposes which morality is intended to serve. Morality concerns an a priori right rather than dianoetic (or, conversational) interactions that start from the matters of the world or opinions concerning the good. The ascent from what is first and foremost to ultimate reality Kant sees as a vain activity, merely 'dialectical.'

The last feature establishes a mode of reasoning which seeks for a minimal, universalizable basis for moral action. Rationality can claim no knowledge of substantive human ends or determinate structures composing the whole range of human experience. Instead, out of its own mechanism of logic and decision-making, reason can generate the a priori conditions of its moral activity. Where there is a truly 'moral' point of view, the law is acknowledged as absolutely and universally binding.

Kant understood these features to reflect the logic of simple sense and the workings of a good will. The 'commonest intelligence' and the 'commonest man,' he wrote, could be brought to see the moral law and the a priori right present whenever his or her moral reason is exercised. And he avowed that there was nothing so unconditionally good as a good will. The elaborate programs of education and habituation to the moral life were superfluous in the face of the common decency of the good will, a will which wills a universal law. No training of desire or passion will make duty be experienced as anything but a constraint; the imposition of law upon oneself is a pure act of a reasoned will.

Kant's concern was to demonstrate the possibility of knowledge of the universal subject who wills moral acts. To do this, Kant's account draws on a metaphysic which grounds the expectation of unconditioned conditions of possibility for moral reasoning. At the same time, though, what grounds Kant's account of morality is a theistic apparatus of 'postulates.' The free man, for Kant, respects the moral law because through it he acknowledges his participation in a supersensuous kingdom of ends, beyond the world of his sense experiences and palpable necessity, and realizes that he has a rational duty to believe in God and immortality as a guarantee of the substance of his moral freedom. This transcendental ego permits the three topics of the noumenal – God, freedom, and immortality (about which reason can have no knowledge) – to be projects of man's will. The primacy of morality and practical reason is an act of faith and a consequence of the synthetic productivity of imagination. Kant's account of human freedom is in the final instance intelligible only by virtue of this transcendental idealism.

For our assessment of the AVER method, two features of Kant's account must be clearly understood. First, Kant's radical separation of the phenomenal and the noumenal, which decisively informs his account of the autonomous will, has to be understood as reflecting a characteristically Protestant scepticism that nature reveals the order of reality (the law of God). That is, against the Thomist position of the medieval church, which accepted that the world provides signs of God's reason, and which formulated a natural-law doctrine based on observations of nature, the Protestant split of this world and the divine principle renders any knowledge of the *logos* of the whole impossible. It also deprives nature and the world of everyday practices, except in a wholly reconstructed form, of power to inform us concerning what it is good to do. The subsequent Calvinist and, in a more extreme form, Puritan interpretation of humanity's limited access to truth was to underscore the view that man most properly displays his piety by the methodic control of himself and his world, a project which cannot be guided by any dianoetic or noetic sense of finality. This interpretation also, of course, underscores the notion that the true life, the life of the spirit, is guided by rules drawn not from the ambiguous encounter of concrete human beings and their pragmatic doings, or from trusting participation in the process of reality at any point of its instantiation, but rather from an ideal point not of this world (the 'Archimedean' point of the transcendental ego). Yet this agnosticism concerning the incarnation of truth in the world also grounded Protestantism's strong sense of piety and, with it, the powerful restraint of human desire. The legacy of Kant that AVER adopts retains the Calvinist imperative of world mastery, while abandoning the Protestant imperative of restraint and tradition of piety.

Secondly, Kant's idea of morality runs parallel to liberalism, indeed supplying the formal defence of its major tenets: the division of the public from the private and the inviolability of the individual person. If liberalism can be defined by the primacy it places on the rule of law, and by the need it recognizes for an institutional guarantee of individual rights, as well as by its efforts to ensure a form of public legislative activity in which the public good is the result of a negotiative interaction over judgments, then Kant's account is its natural ally.[8] For by making the realm of human intercourse subject to right rather than good, ordered by procedural justice rather than a substantive assessment of the good, and linking moral action to the interior disposition of the autonomous individual, Kant's ethics dovetail with the sober core of liberal politics.

What AVER does not explicitly acknowledge is that the Kantian position also links up with liberalism's more equivocal legacies: radically delimiting the public sphere, privatizing (and eventually relativizing) substantive conceptions of goodness, identifying the source of authority exclusively in self-legislation, and the general perception that politics should confine itself solely to the bureaucratic administration of comfortable self-preservation. Kant also lays the basis for the elements of liberalism which put in place a dynamic that has potentially disrupting consequences: the notion of the 'person' which, while drawn from the Christian sense of the sacred inviolability of a unique life, identifies the pure activity of human motion as self-caused; a philosophy of historical progress, of a growing perfectibility of man and the gradual elimination of unsociable characteristics by reason and good will; and an end-point to the historical dialectic of universal cosmopolitanism and perpetual peace under universal enlightenment.

Finally, as if the instabilities must inevitably come home to roost, both Kant and liberalism, while grounding the principle of legitimacy on the cognitive will-acts of the sovereign individual, also set out strict limits to the exercise of that will; in both, too, though, there is an unresolved tension in the effort to hold the dynamics of the will back by ends legislated from within that same dynamism. To hold that dynamic back, both have put a significant premium on the respect for persons, with all of the undercurrents with which Christianity invested this existential modality with eternal significance. Only this spiritual dimension vouchsafes for liberalism's attempt to compose human order and Kant's efforts to prevent the will's derailment into limitless self-overcoming. Of course, like liberalism itself, Kant also shows that all of these factors must be thought together within a single paradigm.

The drama of power upon which this morality and politics of sovereign self-legislation rests can now be identified. Amidst the disorder of phenomenal life, rationality magisterially enacts authority by categoric, prohibitory power. It is an act which cannot help but be spectacular; invoking the categorical imperative, reason subdues by force. Every act of contingency, transgression, and deviation calls out for the restoration of reason's power. The law's imposition of order is meant to be witnessed in so far as dignity is central to its enactment – a visible sign of power, of responsibility, of participation in a community of rational beings. Grand and imposing, reason, nevertheless, cannot prevent aberration: there will, of course, be errors of judgment and derailments into unsanctioned imperatives. Sovereign legislation cannot eliminate human spontaneity and historical contingency, the sources of unpredictability. The sovereign act is impermanent and inefficient, for 'reason restlessly seeks the unconditionally necessary ... though it has no means by which to make it comprehensible' and thus is forever vulnerable to the escape of forbidden pleasures, desires, and taste.[9] Nonetheless, so little would Kant think it a task to subdue this unrest and ambivalence that he in fact recognizes it as the necessary tension by which the elevation of soul, spiritualizing the moral experience, is initiated. There is a limit to what man can unmake and a limit to the defiance against the given with which that unmaking is accompanied.

Kant still links morality with participation in a political world and with the experience of a transcendent reality. These two contexts supply the motivating factors and stabilizing balance necessary to moral activity. Although Kant sets in motion the processes which would eventually lead to their inanition as defining forms of human existence, he still offers a measured and defensible account of moral experience and a balanced conjunction of genesis and order. Morality is not a special form of reasoning, but a psychic tonality of righteousness and an understanding formed by the concrete particulars of human existence and the complex motions of the questioning psyche. With Kant, there are answers to why we should be moral and how we should encounter the fact of our own mortality, as there are limits to moral zeal, because morality is not one discrete segment of human existence but a psychic disposition which informs all the dimensions of reality – personal, social, historical, and transcendent.

Kant's epigones – the twentieth-century philosophers in the analytic tradition who are the immediate source of AVER's Kantian model – were less balanced. Moral philosophers in this school extracted the decision-procedure in which the formalized conditions of rational, moral agency are elaborated from Kant's account. Retaining the Kantian separation of nature and freedom, as well as the assumption that the structures of consciousness provide sufficient basis for understanding moral experience, they also accepted Kant's concept of truth as apodictic certainty. But the analytic philosophers' indebtedness to Kant stops there. They did not accept the notion of a transcendental subject, beyond the transience of historical existence, who postulates the reality of God, freedom, and immortality. Nor did they resolve the question of how a finite, historical being apprehends the enduring structures of his or her own being. Rejecting Kant's metaphysics would seem to require turning to his philosophy of history if the argument of 'basic logical structure' (read 'eternal') inherent in moral reasoning is to be upheld. The twentieth-century moral philosophers chose not to do so, adopting neither Kant's proto-Hegelian historical dialectic of the 'unsocial-social' nor his hypothesis of an end-state of perpetual peace and universal cosmopolitanism. Finally, the sole conditions of politics which the twentieth-century moral philosophers acknowledge are autonomy and tolerance. These are mere shells of the political action and civil respect of Kant's writings. The problem with the initiative of the moral philosophers is that they are attempting to ground moral norms and formal structure on the empty process of human finitude, while eclipsing the contents and contexts which in Kant supply some substantive direction to morality. The disruption of balance, as we shall see, has implications which are very questionable.

Setting this difficulty aside for the moment, let us look at the particulars of the AVER project. R.M. Hare (one of the most respected authorities for values-analysis education) sets out the proper procedures for determining the acceptability of assertions by delineating the logical characteristics of moral reasoning.[10] Morality, we learn, is a language with a specific form. A moral language – of 'rigorous and austere simplicity' – is prescriptive rather than descriptive, universal rather than parochial. Following Kant, moral action is such if it agrees with a universalizable maxim in accordance with which it ought to have been willed. But, unlike Kant, and following the lead of Stevenson's emotivism, the normative expressions do not arise from features of human existence which are metaphysically grounded. Rather, in Hare's case, they are conventional imperatives uttered by speakers.

The procedure of clarifying utterances is one of conjecture and refutation. The valuing subject aims, in testing his evaluation, to show that it is defective. Evaluative reasoning is understood to be logically distinct from a parochial rating of a value object. Moral judgments command us what to choose and do, and commit us to a rule that is to govern all similar cases. Moral maturity entails prescribing for all persons in relevantly similar circumstances. The essence of valuing, in short, is its universalizability and prescriptivity. Hare writes, 'I am convinced that if parents first, and then children, understood better the *formal* character of morality and of the moral concepts, there would be little need to bother, ultimately, about the content of our children's moral principles; for if the form is really and clearly understood, the content will look after itself.'[11]

One feature of Hare's account, however, fills out this formalism. Hare requires that students empathize with one another. Empathy more effectively sustains the effort at universality.[12] Here too the moral philosophers depart from tradition. While what is meant here is a very distant heir to *homonoia* (like-mindedness), which spoke to the spiritual unity of humans, or even to its Kantian liberal form 'respect,' which implied recognition of the concrete political community guaranteeing the rights of the individual, the tone of empathy is decisively different. 'Empathy' is an imaginative act of expansion into the world. It corresponds to, rather than moderates, the will's mastery of reality through universal legislation. As such, it is more like Descartes's notion of *générosité*, a passion which has the tonality of dynamic expansion, rather than of participation. We will return to this point in a moment.

P.W. Taylor is another of those authorities to whom AVER looks in operationalizing Kant.[13] Taylor claims that normative reasoning moves through four phases: verification, validation, vindication, and rational-choice. One commences by conducting empirical tests to qualify the phenomena being evaluated and to determine their conformity to the value rule chosen by the valuing subject. Subsequently, the value rule is validated by determining that the object being evaluated belongs to a class of things which are correctly judged by the rule, and that no other rule conflicts with the one being applied, or that the one being applied is to take precedence in the event of a conflict. The first condition is satisfied by determining that the rule can be deduced from a more general rule within the evaluator's value system or by showing that by fulfilling the rule, some other rule within the value system is fulfilled. The second condition is satisfied by showing how giving precedence to the rule follows logically from a further rule in the value system. Subsuming rules within more general rules continues to ensure logical coherence in the entire value system.

Absence of the principle of equivalence would give rise to dissonance. For example, the student is asked whether there should be a guaranteed annual income. The student may say 'no' because someone may receive income without working. The student is asked whether the case of inheritance does not invoke the same difficulty. Since the student may not hold two contradictory principles, he must disavow inheritance or accept a guaranteed annual income, or find another valuing principle that permits the differential.

Where further justification is needed, vindication involves adopting the value system and determining whether that system has instrumental value in light of the life one considers desirable. Finally, it is necessary to show that the way of life was rationally chosen, that is, that the choice was 'free,' 'impartial,' and 'enlightened.' Unconscious motives, compulsions, and external constraints have to be excluded. Likewise, emotional prejudices, the desire to protect privileges, and biases resulting from authoritative influence, illiberal education, or narrow experiences have to be neutralized.

The moral philosophers' demonstration of a 'moral language' relies on a pragmatic operationalizing of Kant whereby the synthetic a priori are understood only as ideal constructions. On this account, nothing better can be expected. No substantive rational defence of the goodness of such constructions is given or can be given. The moral philosopher can only assume that there is a 'meta-ethical logic of reasoning, the result of philosophy having done to words what mathematics did to numbers.'[14] As in Kant's 'metaphysics of morals,' the exercise of such rule-governed reasoning is intended to surmount 'heteronomy,' or in other words the ambiguities and ambivalences, arbitrariness and idiosyncrasy, of particular judgments of everyday life. Surmounting the everyday, however, now proceeds without a 'metaphysics.' Validity, replacing truth, rests on the consensus of rational minds participating in the form of reason immanent in human existence. The apriorism is, at one and the same time, more speculative and more restrictive than Kant's. The twentieth-century philosophers' disruption of the balance in Kant's thought raises the question of why individuals should be moral and also how far their moral zeal should extend, for whereas in Kant, moral experience at the same time answers to human anxiety about finitude and speaks to the ends of political action, now no existential contents condition the formulation of moral imperatives.

The eschewal of Kant's metaphysics is a deeply troubling matter. The absence of ground constitutes a crippling, destabilizing factor in the model. Having disavowed the assumption of fixed designs and purposes based on a hierarchy of natural ends, while raising to paramount status humanity's linguistic capacity to critically clarify and define the determinations rendering humans into objectifiable phenomena, means that history, consciousness of time, and temporality preside over the conditions constituting knowledge. Further denying that time as history proceeds towards finality means that the model simultaneously seeks knowledge of the definite formal structure of human existence while acknowledging the indefinite conditions of possibility of that structure. Human historicity is being expected to stand in to permit a transcendental deduction of the form of human existence but the insurmountable irreconcilability of being and time denies the possibility of such 'standing in.' Resolutely asserting *the* forms of reasoning does not make them any more coherent. This is why Nietzsche called the Kantians 'the great delayers.'

To return to the specifics of the values-analysis model, the AVER model follows Frankena, Hare, and Taylor in identifying moral experience as epistemological and logical clarification. The assumption is that such clarification will generate logically compelling directions for human conduct. The exercises proposed in the model are intended to solicit reciprocity, universalizability, prescriptivity, and finality, which are taken to be universal features of our cognitive faculties. Sound moral assessment requires applying a set of procedures to social phenomena and, just as scientific method can be taught without determining the outcomes of investigation, so there is a method specific to moral discourse which will permit students to conduct their own investigations of moral phenomena.

The AVER model provides a classroom application of Frankena, Hare, and Taylor. The student is required to examine the world through the form of the practical syllogism. The practical syllogism is to display the distinctive form of values reasoning, and to do so the fact/value dichotomy is employed. The form of the syllogism consists of a major premiss which is a value standard, a minor premiss which gives the relevant fact, and a conclusion which applies the principle to the fact. Values reasoning is an attempt to account for both the factual considerations and the value principles which appear in a syllogism. A valid values argument entails a conjunction of relevant facts (those associated with our economic well-being, our health, our aesthetic satisfaction, etc.) and 'moral reasoning.'

The student is to understand that the determination of facts requires discerning those statements that are empirically verifiable or, to be more precise, those which are measurable by scientific means. Information will need to be 'tested.' Values statements must be further distilled to the moral point of view. Descriptive and emotive claims are not in themselves morally relevant. Factual information is necessary to assist values decisions but cannot determine them. The designers of the model are keen to avoid the 'naturalist fallacy.' Values arguments are instead to be scrutinized for their logical consistency. They will have to be examined to permit 'getting clear about the meanings of the words in the statement.'

What mediates metaphysically neutral facts and values statements? The vital link between factual claims and value judgments is the 'value standard,' which is the coupler in the deductive argument used to generate values conclusions. To validate valuational claims and to determine their acceptability the student must have recourse to the rules implicit in universal rational discourse. Since all value reasoning has the same structure – the practical syllogism – it is simply a question of acknowledging the binding requirements of rational discourse as it proceeds through the practical syllogism. What can be determined, however, is only the validity of an argument, not the truth of the premiss.

The value premiss can be evaluated by the application of four logical tests, the products of which suffice to establish the bases of moral competency: the Role Exchange Test, the Universal Consequences Test, the New Cases Test, and the Subsumption Test. The overall point of these tests is to eliminate preferment or partiality except in relevant situations, and to activate the processes which produce universal agreement. All moral positions, once so clarified, can be shown to exhibit the same 'basic logical structure.'

The Role Exchange Test appeals to the student to exchange places with a person maximally disadvantaged or adversely affected by a value principle. Such exchange 'is necessary to consider how such a person would feel and whether he had any rights in the situation.' The Universal Consequences Test requires the willingness to accept a state of affairs where everyone acted according to the same principle. On the basis of respect for persons, and in the absence of justifications for differential treatments, each is to be treated equally. The New Cases Test asks if all the judgments arising from the principle in question are acceptable and permits legitimate exceptions to be built into a new principle. The Subsumption Test requires logically deducing the value principle from acceptable higher-order principles; in the absence of such deduction, new reasons for holding the value principle must be found or a reconsideration of that principle should ensue. The instruction for the Subsumption Test sets out that it is necessary to elaborate the reasons for holding a value principle on the basis of the facts about the class of things judged by the value principle. Participating in the essential form of reason assumes endorsement of universalizability, prescriptivity, reciprocity, and finality. 'Responsible judgment' is the product of following the cognitive interests of pure reason itself.

The student activities associated with the formation of 'responsible judgment' involve factual claim/value judgment exercises, points-of-view exercises, practical syllogism exercises, the production of a Reasons Assembly Chart, dilemma discussions, role-playing exercises, attitude surveys, and principle-testing exercises. Defining the relevant issues, distinguishing the field of positive fact, determining the reliability of authorities by collecting empirical evidence to justify factual claims, imaginatively sharing the feelings, hopes, and ideas of others, and practising the recognition of 'relevance' establish a consciousness which has grasped the principle by which all the facets of its existence can be integrated into the 'moral point of view.'

There are many objections which could be raised in assessing this model. The obvious critique is that this eviscerated Kantianism is even less likely than Kant's own project to provide more than a highly general and even uninformative backdrop to moral judgment. It is not necessary to repeat here the common argument that reciprocity, universality, and prescriptivity hardly are sufficient for characterizing distinctly moral experiences, or for guaranteeing moral conduct. Without massive import of more substantive images of good and noble conduct, one might sceptically conclude that the tests of valid reasoning at best render the actions to satisfy the objects of desire singularly consistent.

Equally one might raise another common objection that not only is there an annoying circularity in the argument linking rationality, universality, and prescriptivity where each is permitted to validate the other, but one might seriously question the image of uniform and homogeneous reality lingering behind that circularity. It does not require as ancient an authority as Aristotle to make the argument, as innumerable physicists and biologists are asserting against the paradigm of unified field theory, that being is essentially heterogeneous, or multidimensional, and that the harmony of the whole depends on maintaining that heterogeneity.

But my objections to the AVER model are different and follow from the discussions of the preceding chapter. It is doubtful, in my mind, whether the AVER model displays the kind of balance essential to human order that we have been discussing, given that the form of moral reasoning which it sets out has so little regard for those political and intellectual contexts within which the moral phenomena are given stability and substance.

The moral reasoning the AVER model proposes is in two ways clearly antithetical to the conditions required for a political world. First, the model is fitting for a society of isolated individuals whose moral certitude is underwritten exclusively by self-certainty and supported by facts which can be mathematically represented. No palpable things and events seen and heard in common and no process of intersubjective negotiation in a public space ground these projects of logical coherence. Meaning (or 'validity') is derived from the sheer sequence of deduction. The 'empiricism' which is to be factored into the values evaluation is itself grounded in subjective self-certainty, for it is based neither on public negotiation nor on experience, but on scientific explanation. The only factor which is added on to this apodictic certainty is an operational necessity to regulate values by considering their general acceptability in an ideal society of rational persons structured by these principles. No concrete world, constituted by the web of human interaction, provides a limit to these logical exercises. Empathy serves merely to confirm the premium put on logicality. A regulative ideal of a yet-to-be possibility informs moral valuation. To recall Arendt, this orientation cannot avoid dovetailing with the mentality of *homo faber*, who instrumentalizes the world and makes it over by appealing to imagined ideals. *Homo faber*, as Arendt points out, is unable to distinguish use and meaning, and thus no meaning emerges besides that which he makes. Thus while AVER's values analysis purports to be a deontological model (right has priority over good), and thus in opposition to the teleological model of utilitarianism, it must eventually, for having operationalized morality into a social project, derail into instrumentalism.

Secondly, the AVER model, however formally, in true Kantian fashion, it supports the highest principles of political liberalism (respect for the rights of persons, acknowledgment of the plurality of individuals, obligation based on rational consent), makes little effort to maintain the conditions of the political world we examined earlier.[15] Nor does it promote the renewing action which prevents those meanings we negotiate in the world from degenerating into dogmatism and archaism. There is nothing which acknowledges the centrality in life of the radical contingency of novelty actuated by every human action. In contracting the 'human' to the capacity for a formal willing of universal structures, the freedom to initiate redemptive new beginnings is not factored into the equation. The AVER model does nothing to encourage the belongingness within the concrete particulars and forms of historical communities which would provide a permanent and stable bulwark to the contingent processes unleashed by action. It does not encourage care for the permanence of the world through the possession of durable things. The turn from concrete to formal, internalized mental operations disregards the practical world in which everyday human existence is stabilized and given meaning. The AVER model underwrites free-floating universality, structured by logicality alone, providing little foundation for the concrete, community-guaranteed recognition of rights, and as little occasion for the public discussion of meaning.

Nor does the AVER model actuate the structured openness of the questioning psyche, a psyche which is receptive to the 'pregnant possibilities' of the world. With 'obedience' or 'consent to otherness' reduced to 'blind submission,' there can be no openness to a process of reality not of human making and no retrieval of the primary experiences which order moral reasoning beyond itself. This rejection of psychic receptivity is already evident in the positivistic reduction of those Platonic existential modalities of participation in reality referred to earlier. The tonality informing AVER's moral life is a dynamic expansiveness of the will into the world, rather than the *periagoge* (the turn towards transcendence) which, in the older and, in my mind, more balanced account, more effectively moderated irascible desires. The 'universality' of the *logos*, to which Plato appeals, speaking of the 'comity of humankind,' concerns transcendence of the soul beyond the here and now. In contracting universality to generality (as in Rousseau's or Kant's 'general will') what has been lost is the psyche's openness to the full amplitude of human experience. The elimination of the transcendent pole which structures human motion means, too, that the entire range of human existence (the organic, sentient, dianoetic, and noetic dimensions) is believed to be capable of human mastery. This risk that the world comes to be seen only as something to be controlled is particularly acute because the AVER model, like most contemporary formalistic rationalisms, denies that unrest in existence is permanent and refuses to see it as the source of our most essential human virtues. In the AVER account the essential unrest of existence is observed only in the moral struggles of desire and duty, and thus, since that unrest is not seen to emanate from the structure of existence itself, and manifest itself as fully in the political, intellectual, and spiritual dimensions of our existence, it is believed to be wholly controllable by a single legislative act of the will. This means that in the AVER model the moral phenomena – right, justice, empathy, universality, prescriptivity – become mere 'concepts' or regulative ideals. They have lost their permeability to the comprehensive reality encountered in primary human experiences.

In isolating morality *sui generis* from the political, intellectual, and spiritual dimensions of human existence, the AVER model cannot ensure balance. It is a proper thing to encourage reason over feelings, coherence over inconsistency, respect for others over selfishness. But, what in their account encourages a moderation of morality? What supplies the existential incentive to exercise moral judgment? As it stands, I fail to see how the AVER model can prevent moral irascibility and moral zealotry. In its failure to encourage plurality and its equal immodesty regarding the human possibility of intellectual ascent to first principles, AVER's contraction of morality to *the* universal form of reasoning cannot prevent in my view a derailment which, to use the language we have been using thus far, constitutes a move towards one pole, eclipsing the pull of the other. The derailment to which I am referring is marked by an excessive desire to reorder the world by a contraction of its rhythms, and it is achieved primarily by supporting a view of society as isolated individuals confirming their moral obligations on the ground of self-certainty alone, confirming this self-certainty solely through empathy, which is nothing more than self-certainty extended to a multiplicity of other like-minded individuals. We have referred in the previous chapter to the vulnerable state this creates.

Moreover, I would argue that this reasoning is not moral understanding and thus cannot give rise to balanced moral judgment. Understanding is formed by an appreciation of how the motions and forms of everyday life are structured by meanings and ends supplied by the contexts of human existence, and of how the distinctions that structure the world and the modality of human questioning form judgment. Reducing values to a formal and abstract model of reasoning cannot produce that understanding or judgment because the reasoning does not include a recognition of or encourage debate over what humans believe is worthy.

Should it matter that these concerns are not met by the AVER model? If, as I have been arguing, values are more than simply products of a compartmentalizable modality of reasoning, to be brought out under the special circumstances of valuing, and if values are more correctly the measures of a balanced disposition engaged in a comprehensive participation in reality, then it does matter that the model cannot meet these concerns. Without the perspective that situates values within all the dimensions of human reality, there is nothing that supplies motivation or persistence to the purpose values are meant to bring about. If values cannot answer to our anxiety about our finitude, to our fear of boundlessness, to our desire for possession of simple goodness in life, and thus endow our actions with deeper significance, then those values are empty and easily disposable.

But there is a graver difficulty which no formalistic ethic that believes morality is *sui generis* can overcome. Grounding values on will, and expecting the will to cease its own self-overcomings and see its perfection in willing the universal form of itself, in the absence of other experiential parameters, is, I would argue, to have an unfounded optimism that the will can deliver moral limit. In excising the political, intellectual, and spiritual contexts of moral action, what is to prevent the overreaching dynamic that propels the will's self-overcoming towards a restless will-to-will? Even if universalizability, reciprocity, and prescriptivity did confer a distinctly 'moral' aspect on reasoning (which is widely debated in moral philosophy, with the advantage going to those who say that it is not; they are at most a precondition), why should these constitute a *finality* to willing? An unconditional end towards which the will is willing is excluded by the very motions that inform the will. Will, to recall Augustine (who points forward in a straight line to Nietzsche's account of the phenomenon), is self-caused and self-moving. What it legislates to itself is to continue willing. The finality set up by 'universalizability' and 'prescriptivity' is a legacy of, and abstraction from, the more comprehensive classical Greek and Christian teaching concerning human participation in reality. When one leaves behind the transcendental realm one is also abandoning the source of those imperatives by which humans were bidden to be moral beings. The logic upon which

AVER's moral reasoning is grounded (the will willing the form of itself, universality, as a limit to itself) seeks to hold together the enduring autonomy of the individual with the will's process of self-overcoming. It may hold back the degeneration of the self into pure process temporarily but mere resoluteness cannot hold *the* form of reasoning stable because the principle sustaining the subject is commensurate with the logic which denies the stability of its being. To see in the will's postulates a guarantee of limit is a deception because its motions constitute a declaration of the essentially conditional character of all limits. Reasoning gives us the form of our justice, but that same reasoning as pure will must deny that justice is either sacred awe in the face of eternity, or the recognition of natural limit, or respect for the meanings collectively narrated in concrete conditions in which a response to historical contingency is negotiated. Its tonality is one of struggle and perpetual self-overcoming. For the will to adopt finality is for it to cease to be.

There is in the model of moral reasoning being proposed by AVER a foreshadowing of a dangerous dynamic towards nihilism. This potential outcome is already prepared for in AVER's turn away from what is 'first and foremost,' that is, in its positivistic reduction of the forms of human existence to mere 'everydayness.' The methodological apriorism of linguistic philosophy from which the AVER model springs operates in the same rarefied atmosphere as Heidegger's 'fundamental ontology.'[16] The consequence of that is not only the disregard for politics and those institutions which guarantee the political world but also the structure of intellectual questioning itself which prevents reason from derailing into dogmatism or radical scepticism. The AVER model's dualism of desire and autonomy, subjective and objective, and nature and freedom dismisses out of hand the view held by sensible educators from Greek times to the present that there is a teleological structure in everyday forms and that the purpose of education is to form and sublimate desires so as to produce good citizens and thinking beings.

The question of what stabilizes AVER's model of moral reasoning takes us back to an earlier point, namely the role of the social sciences. AVER's reliance on the fact/value distinction, and the positivistic social sciences authorized by that distinction, adds a twist to (or makes explicit what is only nascent in Kant) the question we raised earlier regarding the ground of the formal structures of moral reasoning. Conventional utterances, an image of the life persons find desirable, and the mutable facts of human existence, we recall, are being asked to stand in for Kant's transcendental deduction. AVER's apriorism, lacking the guarantor of a noumenal realm, and thus the intellectual act which transforms finite apparati of cognition into the transcendental conditions for cognition, has to permit the phenomenal realm to 'presence' its formative determinations long enough to acquire the effect of transcendentality. This requirement gives to those social sciences which collect and analyse data of the phenomenal realm a vital importance. Their progress plays out the instability which occurs when the trans-historical order of the infinite is rejected and transience cannot be surmounted. Theirs is the unique problem that their subject is the paradoxical being who *is* the forms of humanity's finitude and yet also the historical consciousness which realizes that those forms are arbitrary categories imposed on the temporality of a being who has no essence. 'Ideal constructions' only temporarily obscure the problem that the dynamic of historical categories of knowledge (conventional utterances) destabilizes the representations of beings, structures, needs, and desires. The scope of the social sciences' observations, but also, as we noted in our discussion of Arendt, their active intervention into human phenomena, is determined by the hopeless expectation that the positive facts of human finitude are representable. The various modalities of humanity's being in time are divided among the paradigms of the social sciences. Each proposed model immediately has its critics who reveal that the conditions of possibility of the transcendental demonstration are arbitrary, that is they are merely rationalizations of historical contingencies. In rejecting its 'crude' empiricism, these critics propose another, more 'scientific' model and establish what they believe is a more certain empirical field that will reveal human possibility. A perpetual oscillation between positivism and critical reason ensues. This recurring dialectic has meant that the social sciences, upon which AVER's moral reasoning so decisively relies, are given over to considerable vacillation. Each model and discipline attempts to secure the 'human' from a different perspective in an attempt to account for the possibility of representation itself, but none can gain total assent to its positivist reduction of experience to its phenomenal forms. And the forms, increasingly, do not look like the forms of everyday existence. Modern social science knowledge is inherently unstable. It is forever elaborating forms which, in principle, it refuses to accept. Ours then is a 'will-to-knowledge' which appears to have a direction, but in fact, as our more honest researchers admit, its end and conditions are hypothetical and unverifiable. Creative and organized efforts to form new disciplines and to concentrate intellectual output cannot render the social sciences any more intelligible.

Nietzsche, as we already mentioned, identified the Kantians as the 'great delayers.' Nowhere is Nietzsche's charge more appropriate, in my view, than when it is applied to the neo-Kantians to whom we have been referring. Nietzsche's epigones have been ruthless in unravelling the vestigial moralism of the neo-Kantian moral projects, logically extending the consequence of discarding a transcendental structure down its inevitable path of deconstruction. When Nietzsche calls for the inanition of the moral remnants of the past in his pithy summary of the history of philosophy, writing 'The real world – an idea no longer of any use, not even a duty any longer – an idea grown useless, superfluous, and *consequently a refuted idea*; let us abolish it; broad daylight, breakfast, return of cheerfulness and *bons sens*; Plato blushes for shame, all free spirits run riot,' his French deconstructionist followers (Gilles Deleuze, Michel Foucault, Jacques Donzelot, Jacques Derrida, Henri Bataille) were not impulsively advocating nihilism but were following through the inexorable consequences of the 'death of God.'[17] For our purposes, Foucault is an important ally in truly pulling up and examining the roots of the AVER project, for in his works he took Nietzsche's method of 'genealogy' and pillar by pillar dismantled the empty expectations behind our will to knowledge and the equally empty moralism of the sciences of the modern age. The will to knowledge of the human sciences, Foucault writes, given its paradoxical mandate, must secure the subjects and objects of inquiry. Social scientists may believe that they are inquiring into what are autonomous objects, but the conditions of the experiment are ones in which the interventions in the laboratory are themselves the condition of possibility for those objects (a point made by Arendt as well). Both the contents and the form of modern knowledge are made possible and are maintained precisely by the objectifying and subjectifying techniques employed by the social scientists. They offer up 'models' and devise 'methods' which make it possible to constitute aggregates of phenomena as so many 'objects' for a field of knowledge. Their 'knowledge' is possible only through those various projects of distribution and aggregation they themselves form and, to complete the circularity, the propositional truths which emerge from their surveys serve as the basis for more interventions. Advancing empirically and historically, they nonetheless assume transcendentality, but this assumption, as we noted before, is inevitably subject to refutation, requiring new rounds of experimental control.

A complex intertwining of the will to knowledge and power ensues, permitting the human sciences to compose and recompose their own objects and subjects, trying unsuccessfully to rescue the 'pure form' of the transcendental condition of knowledge. The experimental activism of modern knowledge is inseparable from an entire complex of power permitting endless subjugations and disciplinary controls. That experimental activism and the diverse forms of control it must employ are not coincidental to the possibility of knowledge – they are its very condition. Foucault's main point is that the diverse technologies of managing humans are not accidental by-products of the modern social sciences. To the contrary, they are the objectifying and subjectifying techniques which maintain the space in which the human sciences conduct their investigations. The social sciences tactically collude with strategies of power, organizing and disciplining human beings.

As we have already pointed out, Kant's transcendental synthetic apriorism had the noumenal realm as its guarantor. AVER's apriorism does not. In the absence of a noumenal realm, the phenomenal realm which the social sciences monitor has to suffice, and it must 'presence' its formative determinations long enough to gain the effect of transcendentality. One cannot help but speculate, especially as one looks at the applied modules which AVER supplies with its model of moral reasoning, that the force and substance of AVER's apriorism is not simply the compelling logic of an internally self-consistent and coherent deduction but the equally compelling dream that the world itself can come to display the regularity and unity of *the* form of moral reasoning.

The apriorism which lies at the heart of the demonstration of the conditions of possibility of the human will willing a form of moral reason to itself, combined with the repudiation of any essential metaphysical structure which would support that apriorism, leads one to the conclusion that the persuasiveness of AVER's demonstration lies less in the realm of theory than in the realm of praxis. A projected future society, which is in the process of being progressively fashioned by human will in conformity to the pure image it can posit of itself, supplies the postulates of moral reasoning and provides the justification for the 'moral point of view.' The actuality of that society is not merely an ideal. AVER's model presents an actual program of social action which can be operationalized by a concerted exercise of power. At the core of the AVER model is a project to reconstruct the world, to make it over so that nothing besides the willed universal form of reason remains to guide human activity. The possibility that this program can produce an actual new society stands in as the synthetic a priori.

The social vision which confirms the ideality of *the* form of moral will, which substantiates it beyond mere declaration, is implicit in all the modules AVER supplies with its packages. These modules are all directed to the resolution of social problems – war, population, the aged, illiteracy, poverty, and hunger – and the moral reasoning that will be used to solve these problems is one which is indistinguishable from the praxis required to order the world into a wholly new society with a wholly new humanity.

The modules present an image of society focused on matters of food distribution and socio-economic development, concerned with mortality rates, inequalities in resources, and inequities in the distribution of services. Economic productivity, social security, expanding job opportunities for minorities, universal education, and national health and nutrition programs are the themes within which the moral equation is to be formulated. This is not surprising. A society committed to peace and safety, economic success, and individual self-enhancement, and all the disciplinary forms of organization needed to keep such a society efficient, would seem to be the natural ally, and condition of possibility, of the form of moral legislation that confines itself to universality and reciprocity.

To illustrate, let us examine a few particular modules.[18] In the 'Population Unit,' the issues to be discussed include religious and moral objections to birth control and abortion, the right of governments to manipulate birth rates and immigration, the sources of scarcity, the means of resource distribution, and the extent of the right to a decent standard of living. The form of moral reasoning is expected to exhibit itself in working out issues associated with statements like 'food is an example of the inequity of resource distribution in the world' in so far as 'it seems that an adequate supply of food is a necessary condition for human growth and dignity,' by finding solutions to mortality differentials for various groups, by taking on a 'personal responsibility for population growth,' or by working 'to relieve population pressures in other parts of the world.'

Central to the module is the assumption that the phenomenon 'population problem' and the factors organized around it giving it positivity, such as 'human growth,' 'resources,' 'decent standards,' 'rights of government,' and 'responsibility,' are universal, or that the only logic with which the question of population can be consistently discussed must establish itself universally if there is to be any cessation to human 'problems.' But what AVER is saying here is that any alternative moral position will be counted as such only if it will relate its metaphysical principle to phenomena its adherents may not even acknowledge (and, even, articulate itself as a metaphysical principle). If this alternative position fails to do so, it risks being dismissed as failing the eligibility criteria required of a moral point of view. Let us be blunt in saying what is occurring here. One aggregation of social interests is being absolutized as a universal form. But that form, recalling our point about the crucial role the social sciences have in putting forth the objects of knowledge, is simply a function of the prior existence of a specific historical configuration with a reading of its future potential. What we have is the study of the 'population' given positivity by the criteria which the exercise was meant to prove. It should go without saying that the point of view being demanded emerges from a specifically liberal and technologically progressive society and that this society's interests are serving as the criterion of relevance for valorizing certain phenomena as 'moral.' At its very roots the moral point of view must exclude other moral understandings as unintelligible.

For example, the question of voluntary limits to family size in other countries is to be discussed by considering the 'points of view' for which reasons are given in opposition to such limitation. This demand can have only one result. Since the universalizing and homogenizing tendency of the four tests displaces metaphysical positions whose principle is that reality manifests itself heterogeneously (such as in Hinduism), and since the 'moral view' overrides all others, a case for defending reproduction on any ground besides its effect on population growth is deemed inadmissible. For example, the quite defensible arguments that reproduction is fulfilling the principle of generative spiritual order as stated in the divine command 'go forth and multiply,' that being able to parent or bear children is a condition of full humanity, and that the birth of a son is needed to ensure subsequent passage in the next cycle of reincarnation cannot lay claim to being 'moral' points of view. It is not surprising, then, to read the concluding exercise wherein students, acting on the very form of moral reason itself, are asked to 'develop a program to reduce the fertility rate of several of the poorer nations.'

Similarly, 'patterns of food consumption,' nutritional levels, the mental and physical health of children, and 'resource use' are assumed to be empirically verifiable phenomena and, moreover, are assumed to exhaust the field of positivity within which the principles of justice are intended to do their work. In a typical case of solutions looking for a problem, students are invited to consider the global situation in terms of 'continued population growth for resource use' and the fact of 'pollution and environmental degradation.' The various 'brainstorming' techniques, simulations, and role-playing activities associated with solving the problem of birth rates categorically dismiss the fact that there are some intelligible and *moral* reasons for resistance to seeing birth rates as a 'problem.' One question the students are to ask themselves is 'Will people decide to have fewer children if the needs children satisfy are filled in other ways?' – a question that can be asked, because ultimately the module posits that the only reason individuals have children is to 'fill needs.' It should hardly have to be stated, but this is a functionalism which from the ground up precludes most of the answers which would have meaning within any other metaphysic. The students will consider methods of delaying marriages in countries 'with loose standards about premarital sex' or 'limited use of birth control devices' and work on syllogisms composed of such value premises as 'People ought to have only as many children as they can afford to support' or factual claims such as 'Enabling people to be economically secure leads to lower birth rates.' The students are to consider statistics on infant mortality rates and birth rates. It is expected that this 'researching' will render them better able to reason about the legitimacy of political action. Any resistance to the terms of the debate can be dismissed as 'points of view' which moral reason will actually come to see as invalid reasoning and as impediments to solving the human problem.

The unrest and tension of human existence to which we have been referring since chapter 2 are understood here as nothing more than the social factors behind poverty, hunger, and illiteracy and asymmetry in the relations between persons within society and between societies. These constitute technical problems which can be solved by redistribution of wealth, 'family planning,' and an increase in technological competence.

Students are asked to reason about the global population problem within a 'broader development strategy,' within 'a more comprehensive socio-economic policy':

As we have seen when we discussed family planning, as one's standard of living improves, large families are not as important to one's economic security. An adequate diet and better health care reduce the rate of infant mortality, and decrease susceptibility to disease. Healthier, smaller families have increased educational opportunities and new employment options. A better educated and more affluent population has more access and is much more receptive to family planning programs.[19]

Students are taught about the 'poverty cycle': poverty, they learn, breeds malnutrition and disease, which reinforces poverty; lack of medical care reinforces malnutrition and disease, reinforcing poverty. Only more data and more means of technical control – understanding of which is organized by the students in charts that reveal the linkages of multiple problems ('You can add as many boxes and arrows as you need') – will provide the basis for a valid moral resolution of the crises of the modern world. There will be a need, AVER says, quoting from a UNESCO document, for 'new ways of thinking about man's needs and values': 'The vastly increased sizes of population in every form of settlement ... may require forms and methods of economic and social organization unlike those successfully used in the past ... Some goals of humanity may have to be reformulated. Revolutions in thought, feeling, and attitude of one kind or another may become necessary – and, in fact, such radical changes appear bound to occur.'[20]

The same vision pointing to a well-managed and regulated society is manifest in the unit 'War,' the central feature of which is to show that taking the 'moral point of view' leads to a recognition that 'the psychological pressures of war result in a breakdown of rationality.' War 'is by definition an act of violence and hostility' and as such activates 'moral hazards': 'pain, death, loss of property, and loss of trust and hope.' Indeed, it 'involves the systematic breaking of moral views' and 'puts a stop to the benefits of peace, when people can go about the business of living in reasonable confidence that the rules hold.'

In this module, students participate in 'moral dilemmas,' which include 'speaking out against the war,' arguing for pacifism, 'showing compassion to a person from the enemy side.' While students will learn that there might be wars conducted under 'the claim of right,' it is evident that the application of the four tests composing the 'moral point of view' shows war to be morally unjustifiable. In the construction of the 'Reasons Assembly Chart,' 'conscription restricts freedom,' 'food rationing interferes with the operation of a free market economy,' and 'conscientious objectors are not doing their duty to fight for their country' are put forward as factual claims, while 'people have a duty to defend their country' and 'a nation is justified in waging war only when attacked' are offered as value claims. In one activity, students are presented with the distinctly apocalyptic statement that 'mankind is at the crossroads of life or death' and the activity proceeds by showing that it is not idealistic, but in fact implicit to the very form of reason, to actuate the 'concept of brotherhood.' The universal form of moral reasoning is recognized as being operative when students use crisis-management techniques, the Prisoner's Dilemma model of rational reasoning, and simulation activities meant to underscore the need to work for peace. The world, as yet deprived of the full effect that moral reasoning and technological reconfiguration can work, is one of 'shameful inequality' and a 'balance of terror.'

We do not need to go any further, merely replicating the same evidence over and over as it appears in AVER's modules. Suffice it to say that the social world of the AVER modules is one where endless interventions guided by the social sciences are employed to supervise and pacify the sources of crime, poverty, inconvenience, and disorder. Control of the forces of social existence is to be accompanied by a moral reasoning which sees its true form in universality, reciprocity, and finality. In other words, reality can be made to display a new uniformity, and consciousness will find satisfaction in the justice made actual.

Foucault's study of the social sciences and the practices of disciplinary management raises the question 'what is the necessity of this image of society?' Is it in every way evident to reason that the human world should be organized as a continuous process of efficient production and consumption? Is the animus behind the stand against war, the fight against poverty, the war against crime, and the battle against drugs the sole and even best way to ask the question as to how we ought to live? How is it that moral reasoning finds its own only in a social world given over to technological intervention, comfortable self-preservation, and the expectation of perpetual peace? What are the conditions that make such a society a possibility and that make the form of the moral will sustaining it a self-evident 'logical structure'?

Foucault has a very interesting essay entitled 'Governmentality' in which he answers the question of how an age can come to be so certain of the form of moral reasoning it upholds.[21] I think historical evidence clearly bears out his argument. In order for there to be a 'population,' 'population problems,' and a 'reasoning' appropriate to analysing and solving these, he argues, there must be an organized social body whose regularities fall within a field of visibility, can be counted upon, can be formalized as knowledge, and can become the basis for regulative intervention. But the emergence of such a social body is a historical datum. Neither the Greeks, nor the Romans, nor the medieval world, nor the early moderns had 'populations.' 'Population' is a quite specific organization of power and knowledge. Foucault calls it 'an economy of bodies within a specific set of political power.' It was only when an aggregate of individuals could be analysed by a new science of statistical demography which 'discovered' and then measured human intercourse in terms of the probabilities of large numbers, under the categories of wealth and prosperity, health, longevity, and response-behaviour, that humankind could be said to constitute a 'population.' But these regularities could acquire positivity only when wholly new and vast spheres of human life came under observation, surveillance, and control: sexuality, mortality, health and hygiene, wealth, fiscal theory, beggary and vagrancy, fertility, birth rates, and urban safety. What become valorized, for the first time, as objects of knowledge and of political control were phenomena which all relate back to the biological processes of individuals – the climate, irrigation, and fertility of the environment; the social impact of famines, epidemics, and death; sexual promiscuity and aberration. Once their regularities were made visible and were enumerated they could be distilled to form the 'social interest.' Foucault's analysis complements well the portrait supplied by Arendt in her discussion of the emergence of the social world. And, if Foucault's analysis is correct (as I believe it is), one must come to the dismal conclusion that the social homogeneity encouraged and depended on by the AVER model of reasoning is bound to strengthen the isolationist features we already identified, by producing the reaction Arendt observed, namely that of romanticist withdrawal from the political world.

Foucault, however, turns our attention elsewhere. For him, in social management lies a conception of the political state not merely as watchman or as sovereign ruling from above. Instead, Foucault argues, rule proceeds by linking scientific, juridical, industrial, and familial enterprises, a complex whose relations of power are maintained by an active monitoring for regularities which support the social interest by producing 'normal' statistical profiles. Social ideals of health and safety, productivity, and yield permeate all the spheres of social life by a process in which power and knowledge are constantly reinforced by one another.

Under this image of 'regularity,' such phenomena as contingency, uniqueness, and action have to be seen as social problems, as dangers affecting the social interest. They can be recorded as 'deviances' and can with the help of the social sciences in turn be corrected and pacified. It is evident, Foucault reminds us, that there are such regularities or 'normalcies' only because there is simultaneously a manner of controlling and managing them. Abnormal cases need to be identified, surveyed, documented, and monitored. Thus, criteria of the 'standard case' develop through the policing function of the political apparatus, as it appears in the judiciary, the schools, industry, corporations, and the medical profession. A continuous process of control mechanisms establishes itself in the social world. Essential heterogeneity or what Arendt called 'plurality,' as well as mystery and ambiguity, needs to be organized and marginalized as a spectacle of unreason and disorder. Values education situates itself firmly on this constituted field where deviance and inconsistency can be labelled and neutralized.

As cynical a view as this may appear to be, Foucault is not a romantic nostalgically longing for primordial liberty. Rather, the conclusion of his analysis follows quite inevitably from the premises from which the social sciences proceed. For our discussion, what we can say is that while we are being asked to take the achievement of *the* form of moral reasoning to be a purely epistemological breakthrough (sudden clarity brought to a world whose darkness stems from its tolerance of ambivalence and ambiguity, risk and mystery), the postulate of the form of moral reasoning is clearly substantiated only by a new organization of social forces. The condition of possibility for *the* form of moral reasoning is no transcendental synthetic a priori, but the process of world transformation by which universality and homogeneity are actualized. Efficiency, safety, high productivity, and the administrative neutralization of the sources of injustice can occur only with new forms of control, intervention, and constraint and with the declaration of a 'social interest.' The emergence of a new economy of power substantiates the postulate of moral reasoning.

Here, finally, we arrive at the instability at the root of the AVER model which causes it to have to overreach itself into a different model. While AVER's postulate of *the* form of moral reasoning is entirely hypothetical, its processes unleash a dynamic whose work will secure the proof of the validity of the hypothesis. But this dynamic leads to contradictions at the base of the model, between a 'Kantian' image of individual sovereign acts of self-legislation and a 'Hegelian' image of the systematic organization of life forces. On the one hand, the AVER model operates with a mechanical image of power whose principle is that of the autonomous, concrete subject legislating rule and right but, on the other hand, the a priori of the values imperative substantiates itself by the possibility of the formation of a society whose motions are regulated by a generative vitality which sees the individual only as an instantiation of developing structures and which sees unrest as capable of administrative neutralization only within the system as a whole. The postulate of *the* form of moral reasoning anticipates the results of a model and a social configuration which takes the expectation of universality and homogeneity beyond the realm of the hypothetical into the historical possibility of a systematic management of life.

The AVER model demands the stability of the ego, but the moral vision it wishes that ego to embrace depends on a power dynamic which must finally outstrip the idea of the autonomous individual will, bringing about a process which will be intolerant of exclusive and prescriptive spaces, and which cannot prevent a self-overcoming towards forces that affirm the generative vitality, rather than the mechanical constraints, of the will's will-to-will. The AVER model overreaches itself, then, into a technique of values management which is developmental and whose processes, in the systematic organization of life in its entirety, are continuous.

4

Values Development:
The Hegelian Experiment

Lawrence Kohlberg echoes the familiar refrain that 'character education for a set of virtues' is based on an unjustifiable 'hidden process based on authority.' But Kohlberg's opposition is not limited to principled objections to authority. According to Kohlberg, more simply, that process did not work. Drawing on the Hartshore-May study of habit and character formation, and its finding that the consistency and persistence of moral characteristics were not guaranteed by traditional educational approaches, Kohlberg holds that the classical habituation to virtue is empirically demonstrated to be conducive to only short-term, situation-specific, and reversible moral conduct. Kohlberg therefore looks elsewhere. He claims that in the structure of the democratic process lies the key to a non-authoritative, effectual moral system. Indeed, democratic negotiation is the only just source for moral judgments. There can be no order of justice and no moral necessity, he argues, which is not derived from interactive consultations among equal persons.[1] We can analyse the structures of cognition and observe their development in our relations with other social actors and there we will find our moral obligations.

Kohlberg calls his approach 'progressive interactionism.' He suggests that it is an 'ideology' avoiding indoctrination but also relativism. Its sole purpose is to foster a cognitive skill which develops ineluctably as a result of the student's 'natural interaction with a developing society or environment.' The outcome of a spiral of such interactions and successive points of equilibrium is the 'moral point of view' – agreement on the definitive characteristics of morality as pure form without necessary agreement on the contents or substantive principles of morality. The moral point of view is meant 'in the sense of *prescriptivity* ... speak[ing] with a universalizable intent.'[2] Kohlberg's method stimulates the student to organize experience of the world in a 'logical fashion.' The mature moral student is one who has experienced 'a dramatic shift from concrete to formal operations by which old conceptions of the world are restructured in terms of a new philosophy.'[3] From such a vantage point, the student will realize that all previous conceptions of moral and personal order are only prolegomena, or pre-moral states, which have been superseded by the self-consciousness of the pure logical structure of reasoning. The compromises and practical conciliations of everyday human intercourse are replaced by a drama in which the fragments of human existence come to be ordered into a logical system.

Like values analysis, then, the form of rationality itself will provide the ground and mode of valuation. 'Logic,' Kohlberg writes, 'is a case of a normative model,' adequate to the task of a rational reconstruction of morality.[4] A moral point of view entails the maximal assimilation and integration of the sources of cognitive conflict, and logic is the technique by which this ideal equilibrium of mental processes is achieved.

For Kohlberg, the regulative ideal structuring moral skill is the idea of 'justice as equilibrium.' The first task is a delimitation of the relevant field of phenomena. What counts as a moral judgment is a judgment constituted by the formal characteristics of impersonality, ideality, universalizability, and pre-emptiveness. The delimitation is justified for two reasons: first, because 'it is not clear that the whole realm of personal, political, and religious values is a realm which is nonrelative, ie. in which there are universals and a direction of development,' and second, because 'it is not clear that the public school has a right or mandate to develop values in general.'[5]

But educators can with certainty and justification stimulate the processes that produce a moral point of view. A judgment is properly characterized as moral when (unlike aesthetic, technological, or prudential judgments) the judgment is made in such a way that students are prepared to say that everyone should make judgments that way, that the judgments are good in terms of some impersonal ideal standard shared by others, and that students themselves, as well as others, should act in accordance with what the judgment mandates, whether the students wish to or not. 'Regardless of who it was' implies universality; 'in spite of fear or reward' implies impersonality and the ideality of obligation. These are logical tests which are sufficient to determine whether principles are moral, without a further need to consider their specific content (the action judged), or whether that content agrees with the student's own personal judgments or standards. The *morality* of the 'moral point of view' is its conformity to the invariant forms of conceptualizing rules, rather than the historically and culturally specific contents given to those rules. Kohlberg, too, accepts Hare's characterization of the distinctive formal features of morality as 'prescriptivity' and 'universality.'

Like the AVER model Kohlberg denies that the conditions of possibility of moral reasoning are the synthetic a priori of a transcendental ego. Instead, he states, they emerge as the result of a universal invariant development of moral growth reflected in evolving structures of moral reasoning:

[T]he existence of six qualitatively different systems of moral apprehension and judgment arising in invariant order is clear evidence that moral principles are not the intuitions of an inborn conscience or faculty of reason of the sort conceived by Butler or Kant. And if stages of moral judgment develop through conflict and reorganization, this is incompatible with the notion that moral judgment is a direct apprehension of natural or nonnatural facts. Our interactional theory claims that moral judgments and norms are to be ultimately understood as universal constructions of human actors which regulate their social interaction, rather than as passive reflections of either external facts (including psychological states of other humans), or of internal emotions.[6]

This 'historicization' of moral consciousness, at the ontogenetic level, means that values education is a form of self-development understood in terms of a progressive, irreversible actuation of the formal criteria of reasoning. Judgment is not given once and for all time but rather forms through a comprehensive series of developing desires, passions, cognitive skills, and thought. Specifically, development is defined as increased capacity for differentiation and integration, thus satisfying the imperative of 'structural adequacy.'

To substantiate his own empirical studies of the evolution of the capacity to conceptualize rules, Kohlberg links Kant's formalist moral theory to Piaget's structuralist psychological theory.[7] Kohlberg draws from Piaget's account of cognitive mastery as development through invariant sequences, a development which transforms both the structure of reasoning and 'aspects of personality.' Piaget had explained that the logical operations of adaptation and assimilation were central to the cognitive domain. Two tempos coordinate such operations: *horizontal decalage*, which refers to generalizing across experience and activities, and *acceleration*, which refers to movement through stages. Maturation entails moving from the concrete to the formal by an increasing mastery of disequilibrium, a transition *from* logical inference as a set of concrete operations *to* logical inference as a set of formal operations, or 'operations upon operations.' The measure of adequacy of such adaptation is successful integration of experience and fortified ego strength. The development is understood as invariant. Such invariance follows a law of necessity because knowledge as structure is transformative and, as Piaget proposes, self-regulating systems continually transform themselves to achieve equilibrium. The interactive assimilation and accommodation to the environment is the endogenous or automatic function of an organized system. Two conclusions follow from this microcosm/macrocosm integration. First, the assumption that equilibrium in the system is 'normal' makes it possible to identify recurring disequilibrium as pathological mental states. Second, the microcosm/macrocosm integration means that social disorganization or disintegration can be identified as a manifestation of cognitive dissonance.

Kohlberg adapts Piaget's model to structures of 'interpersonal' interaction and suggests that they have the same 'logical necessity.' There is, he claims, *a* structure of distinct moral reasoning defined by 'justice operations' and 'moral conflict resolution.' Moral reasoning contains a structural logic which can be not only philosophically analysed but also empirically tested. 'Moral principles' are 'cognitive structural forms of role-taking, centrally organized around justice as equality and reciprocity.'[8] The appeal of these universal moral principles is so great, Kohlberg declares, that his studies show that students advancing through his stages will positively affirm these moral principles rather than focus on the 'badness' of certain practices. Moral maturity is primarily a cognitive and not an affective development. Structures of epistemological consistency and moral development work together under the logic of reciprocity to form respect for self-legislated, universalizable rules and respect for persons who are worthy of respect by virtue of their rational autonomy.

A logic lies at the centre of morality which validates equality, equity, and universal reversibility, or reciprocity.[9] The student is successful in fully activating those operations when connecting a moral value with the logical rules of reason itself rather than with rewards, approvals, or social utility, and assessing action wholly with the intention of maintaining epistemological clarity. This internal self-regulation, Kohlberg claims, 'helps us avoid the problem of finding some "objective" standard for making an aretaic judgment of the moral worthiness of an action or actor. Instead, it allows us to rely on the subject's own response to define what is right and helps us to understand increased consistency between moral judgment and moral action as a phenomenon related to moral stage growth.'[10]

The shift to greater cognitive differentiation, integration, and adaptation is, at one and the same time, a 'rational reconstruction of ontogenesis' and an actuation of moral reasoning from within the universal philosophical norms, namely the formation of the moral operations of reciprocity, role-reversal, and universality. The outcome is 'a better equilibrium of the structure in question' able to 'handle more moral problems, conflicts, or points of view in a more stable or self-consistent way. Because conventional morality is not fully universal and prescriptive, it leads to continual self-contradictions, to definitions of rights which are different for Republicans and Democrats, for Americans and Vietnamese, for fathers and sons. In contrast, principled morality is directed to resolving these conflicts in a stable self-consistent fashion.'[11]

Pedagogically, moral education is a process of moving from egoism to universalism, from situation-specific rules to universalizable and reversible judgments of principle. This is achieved, not by a direct teaching of rational morality, but by an indirect stimulation of its development. Moral reasoning, Kohlberg explains, 'depends upon theories as rational reconstructions of the tacit meanings of experiences by human subjects.'[12] The activation of moral reasoning occurs through cognitive conflict.

For example, the student is brought to confront a conflict between heteronomous concerns for obedience to authority and autonomous concerns for rights and welfare. The key story Kohlberg uses is a story about a man named Heinz who must debate whether or not to steal a drug he cannot afford to buy to save the life of his wife. To the question 'Should Heinz steal the drug?' students offer opinions which by successive questioning confront them with the rival claims of life and property, and the whole resolution will depend on activating formal properties of rational thought.

The responses of different students, or a student at different times, can be viewed as representing the different stages of reasoning. The stages form an order of increasingly differentiated and integrated structures, with higher stages integrating and transcending the forms of the lower stages. A set of transformational laws govern the operation and its development. Such laws will structure the full range of human responses since each level is a total configurational organization of reasoning operations. There are three levels – preconventional, conventional, and post-conventional – each of which has two stages.

At the first level of reasoning, the preconventional level, the student responds to cultural rules and ascriptions of good and bad, and right and wrong, interpreting these either in terms of the physical consequences of action, i.e. punishment, award, exchange of favours, or in terms of the power held by those in authority. In stage 1, the student responds obediently for fear of punishment. What makes this the lowest level of moral reasoning is the absence of reflection, or respect for an underlying moral order, or a consideration of the human meaning of the consequences of action. It is therefore an 'undifferentiated and egocentric perspective.'

At stage 2 the student makes an instrumental-hedonist calculation to satisfy needs. On the one hand, such reasoning introduces proto-moral criteria such as fairness, reciprocity, and equal sharing but, on the other hand, since these are interpreted solely in a physical or concrete way, they are not yet moral. Since human relations are viewed only in terms of the market-place, stage 2 reasoning introduces the relativity of value and a naive egalitarianism. These are necessary conditions (sense of loyalty, gratitude, or particular principles of justice) but not sufficient conditions for self-conscious moral reflection and thus are unstable enough to degenerate back into selfish calculation.

At this second conventional level of reasoning, moral issues are differentiated from the immediate calculation of consequences. The student realizes that form rises above content. A sense of universality and ideality has evolved, though it has not grown beyond a rudimentary form of recognition of higher goals.

At stage 3 reasoning, conformity to images of behaviour approved by a majority of others emerges. While not yet formal moral reasoning, and not yet a principled sociality, stage 3 introduces life as interpersonal concordance with the image of morality and thus the motive of recognition. At the same time, considerations of intention emerge, making symmetry between internal motive and external action a factor of moral ability. Intentionality reconfirms the principle of equality that defines the exchange of recognition, for it seeks to prevent non-reciprocal or hierarchical relations.

At the fourth stage of reasoning, the student abandons images of normal behaviour and orients himself towards authority, rules, and the maintenance of the social order, acknowledging their intrinsic value.

The student now encounters an objective order which he or she can will to be his or her own, and the logical principles of reversibility coordinate this support of the general will. But there is still not an adequate differentiation of 'rights' and 'shoulds' and thus stage 4 does not generate the distinctive form of moral reasoning, which would distinguish it from prudential considerations. At stage 4 reasoning, the moral subject still only sees himself as part of a local social system.

At level 3 reasoning, 'post-conventional,' 'autonomous,' or 'principled' reasoning emerges, overcoming all the ambiguities and recurring tensions of the previous two levels by abstracting and idealizing the fragments of relativity, universality, equality, reciprocity, and transparency inherent in the two earlier levels. The transition here is the crucial one: from logical inference as a set of concrete operations to logical inference as a set of formal operations or 'operations upon operations':

'Operations upon operations' imply that the adolescent can classify classification, that he can combine combinations, that he can relate relationships. It implies that he can think about thought and create thought systems or 'hypothetico-deductive' theories. This involves the logical construction of all possibilities – that is, the awareness of the observed as only a subset of what may be logically possible. In related fashion, it implies the hypothetico-deductive attitude, the notion that a belief or proposition is not an immediate truth but a hypothesis whose truth value consists in the truth of the concrete propositions derivable from it.[13]

The process of moral reasoning entails the logical deduction of possibilities from the construction of ideal worlds. In maturing, the student acquires formal mental operations which lead to a new view of the external and the physical world. 'The external and the physical are only one set of many possibilities of a subjective experience. The external is no longer the real, "the objective," and the internal the "unreal."'[14] What Kohlberg is saying is that, under the dynamic capacity of the mind, the world once requiring the traditional principles and dispositions we discussed in chapter 1 as ethics and morals can come to be seen as means, while the means of those projects – reciprocity, prescriptivity, reversibility – must come to be understood as the true ends. Concomitant with this transformation comes what Kohlberg praises as a healthy scepticism, 'the clouding and questioning of the validity of society's truths and its rightness.' Having wholly abstracted the mind from the concrete and given permits a pure form of logical operations to emerge, and allows for the fabrication of social possibilities dictated by the form of logic alone: 'The shift in adolescence from concrete to formal operations, the ability now to see the given as only a subset of the possible and to spin out the alternatives, constitutes the necessary precondition for the transition from conventional to principled moral reasoning.'[15]

At the 'post-conventional' level, moral values and principles are defined as having validity and application apart from the authority of the groups or persons holding these principles and apart from the individual's narrow interest in identifying with these groups. The emerging order is one where rights are mutually recognized, where the subject as a person (not as a member of a race, gender, nation, class, family, religion, or social group) is recognized, and where everybody is in principle satisfied. Human beings, once at odds because of different purposes, interests, desires, and perspectives, are now reunited and all fundamental differences are overcome. This homogeneity satisfies the logical requirements of the process of development and it overcomes both natural and social unrest.

In stage 5 reasoning, a social contract of individual rights and social standards is forged. Here the full relativity or arbitrariness of the origin of all values is accepted, but a device for recognizing procedural rules for reaching consensus is also accepted. The result is the formation of a legal point of view, with an accompanying emphasis on the possibility of changing law to accord with rational calculations of social utility. The rigidity of law and order is thereby tempered. Free agreement and contract are recognized to be the binding elements of obligation, thus establishing deontological reasoning as the essence of justice. But stage 5 can provide no guidance for when it is morally right or obligatory to violate the law.

Finally, at stage 6 reasoning, the logic of procedurality is fully abstracted from the residual utilitarian concerns of the social contract, and universal principles of justice based on reciprocal, equal human rights, and on the respect for the dignity of human beings as individual persons, are fully affirmed. Now earlier forms of reciprocity, such as mechanical equivalence or the exchange of gratification, can be denounced as inconsistent and unfair. Stage 6 resolves the inadequacy of stage 5 by 'recognizing the primacy of justice over all other moral considerations.' These are principles any member of a society would choose for that society even if he did not know what his position was to be in the society and even if he might be the least advantaged in that society. Principles chosen in this stage, Kohlberg claims (and in this he borrows from Rawls), entail the affirmation of maximum liberty compatible with everyone else's and the admission of only those inequalities in goods or respect which are to the benefit of all, including the least advantaged. Concern with the least advantaged might not seem to be inherent in the principle of stage 6 reasoning. Kohlberg does, however, see this concern as a logical extension: 'We take it as the characteristic logical fallacy of conventional morality that it fails to reduce the welfare and 'claims' of the group as a collective abstraction to the welfare and claims of its members as individuals ... From our point of view there is a logical fallacy parallel to elevating the group above its members: the fallacy of treating a principle as elevated above the individuals in the situation to which it applies.'[16] Stage 6's 'principled form of thinking' completes the emerging idealization of reversibility.

Reversibility is that property of a justice structure of moral operations which enables the structure to construct solutions to dilemmas in such a way that these solutions can be considered acceptable or just from the points of view of all relevant parties. At the highest level of moral reasoning, reversibility implies a conception of justice as 'moral musical chairs,' a conception which requires each person to systematically take the position of everyone else in the situation until a fairly balanced solution emerges.[17]

In the Heinz case this entails the conclusion that claims to life take precedence over claims to property, while in another story, 'Joe and His Father,' the adequate solution for Kohlberg is the recognition of a moral hierarchy in which promise-keeping, whose maintenance is logically necessary if there is to be the possibility of speech-acts at all, takes priority over the claims of authority in father–child relationships. The rule of 'reversibility' renders the alternative untenable. Because to prefer property over life is to allow particularistic principles to stand over fully universalizable and maximally consensual judgments of rightness and obligation, 'morally relevant criteria' favouring property over life and filial piety can lay no claim to 'universal rules of justice.' The moral conclusions are necessary and inevitable for all rational persons.

No further change is now needed. No other natural or historical givens need to be determinately negated. Autonomy, mutual respect, and reversibility, the objectives of the process, are now fully actualized as moral wisdom.

The achievement of stage 6 cannot be dismissed as being purely formal and contentless. To the contrary, one value has risen to paramount status: the primacy of life. At stage 1, life was valued only in terms of the power or possessions of the person involved. At stage 2, life was valued for its usefulness in satisfying the needs of the individual. At stage 3, life was valued in terms of the individual's relation with others and their valuation of him. At stage 4, life was viewed in terms of social or religious law. But at stages 5 and 6, life itself is seen as inherently valuable.

For Kohlberg, the dialectic of moral reasoning is not merely an intellectual exercise confined to the classroom. It is also playing itself out on the historical terrain of active social life, where the negating acts of controlling nature and social opposition, as well as isolating and neutralizing atavistic dispositions standing in the way of the total system's evolution, are occurring. This interactive process between ego and society arises because as an 'integral' system, each part will respond to every other. '[I]ncreased sociopolitical complexity,' Kohlberg writes, 'poses new problems for members of a society which give an impetus to the growth of a new stage to cope with these problems.'[18] The 'cognitive moral ego' requires transactions whereby it sees its own activity mirrored back to itself and thus is confirmed to itself wherever it acts. Its activity of seeking equilibrium requires that the ego project an imaginary realm of 'ideal role takers,' alike in their expectations from one another, and work at actualizing reciprocity, equality, and equity, which can be confirmed by tests of psychological maturation. Role-playing is central to this interaction, for it allows reproducing the parallel or complementary evolving structures of the social world. 'One side of such role taking is represented by acts of reciprocity or complementarity, the other side by acts and attitudes of sameness, sharing, and imitation ... These tendencies, intimately associated with the development of language and symbolism, form the basis of all social institutions which represent various patternings of shared or complementary expectations.'[19] The culturally universal invariant sequences imply, Kohlberg claims, some universal structural dimensions or invariants of the social world. 'Universal physical concepts relate to a universal physical structure in somewhat analogous fashion,' he writes, as 'the social stages imply universal structural dimensions of social experience; this is based on the fact that social and moral action involves the existence of a self in a world composed of other selves playing complementary roles organized into institutional systems. In order to play a social role in the family, school, or society, the child must implicitly take the role of others toward himself and toward others in the group.'[20]

Thus the formation of the moral self coincides with, and interacts with, the evolving structures of the social world. Such mutual adjustment is driven by a 'functional or pragmatic epistemology, which equates knowledge with neither inner experience nor outer sense-reality, but with an equilibrated or resolved relationship between an inquiring human actor and a problematic situation.'[21]

Given the interactive development of ego and the evolving social system, it is no surprise that Kohlberg admits that his model requires specific stands on various political issues. The recognition of the primacy of life and the social satisfaction of even the least advantaged means, for example, that such inhumane events as 'the clashes in which Americans and Vietnamese kill one another in the name of justice' are signs of the lowest level of moral reasoning, just as 'no postconventional reasoning could lead one to endorse the Aztec practice of human sacrifice.'

As emphatically Kohlberg writes that since there can be no predetermined limits to the challenges which an evolving life brings, 'the very meanings of abortion and divorce change historically,' and consideration of abortion and euthanasia issues changes 'with each new biological or technological advance in knowledge, changes that 'cannot be overlooked by principled reasoning.'[22] And capital punishment is inadmissible for 'murderers are to be treated as anyone in their position who also took the roles of others would wish to be treated (as an end rather than as a means).'[23]

In light of these commitments, Kohlberg has been charged by his critics with having merely absolutized a Western model of rationality and liberal thought. Moral reasoning, Kohlberg has retorted, is emphatically not a mere matter of 'the Western liberal content of reasoning.'[24] A 'principled form of thinking,' he discloses, was corroborated by testing in India, Turkey, Taiwan, Zambia, and other non-Western societies, where stage 5 responses to his program were recorded. Functional correlations underlying mere epiphenomenal cultural differences reveal that the structures of development are neutral. All societies, he claims, have the same basic institutions: family, economy, social stratification, law, and government. 'In spite of cultural diversity in content, these institutions have universal transcultural functional meanings.' The functional correlates display the same proto-moral processes which can issue in principled moral reasoning: 'all morally relevant rules and institutions are conceived of as interpreted through processes of role-taking directed by concerns about both welfare and justice.' and: 'All institutions and societies are alike in the sheer fact of being societies, that is, in being systems of defined complementary roles. The primary meaning of the word 'social' is the distinctively human structuring of action and thought by role-taking, by the tendency to react to others as like the self and to react to the self's behaviour from the other's point of view.'[25] As Kohlberg says, 'the ideal principles of any social structure are basically alike, if only because there simply are not that many principles that are articulate, comprehensive, and integrated enough to be satisfying to the human intellect.'

His critics, Kohlberg responds, confuse 'the cultural origins' of a theory with its 'validity.' Responding to E.L. Simpson's claim that his approach merely expressed the bias of a specifiable social environment and the norms of the subgroups within that environment, Kohlberg wrote:

[W]e believe that the way to avoid bias in the development of a theory is to subject its development and validation to the scientific method and critical appraisal. The intent of Kohlberg's theory is that it be used, verified, or revised by people other than himself; by people of different social origins, cultures, and classes. The scientific method as we understand it is a product of modern Western history. However, we claim that it represents the most adequate cross-culturally understood method available for avoiding the type of bias that Simpson is concerned about and that it constitutes the best available method for assessing the truth value of claims to objective knowledge.[26]

While not denying the Western source of his account, Kohlberg argues that the criteria of moral valuation correspond to the terms of philosophical (i.e. universal) adequacy. His theory, Kohlberg writes, is not merely empirical-analytic. It is a 'reconstructive' scientific theory which reads into empirical data the universal mode of reasoning which is the product of impartial philosophical scrutiny.

Moreover, he claims, the model can sufficiently accommodate apparent alternatives. Responding to Carol Gilligan's suggestion that his version of human development is based on the study of men's lives and reflects the importance of individuation in their development, Kohlberg proposed that her perception of moral development focusing on care and understanding and on special relationships could be fully integrated into his system, and was in fact presupposed by the moral logic of philosophic reasoning and the empathy by which it is psychologically maintained.[27]

Kohlberg's answer has not satisfied the sceptics. Kohlberg's answers to his critics are, in truth, generally so unpersuasive that one cannot help but return again and again to the question of what precisely grounds the invariant process of transformation. Let us again step by step examine the argument of what grounds his theory.

First, Kohlberg denies the dependence of his account on the assumption that the cosmos is an ordered whole. 'We make no direct claims about the ultimate aims of men, about the good life, or about other problems which a teleological theory must handle. These are problems beyond the scope of the sphere of morality or moral principles, which we define as principles of choice for resolving conflicts of obligation.'[28] This disavowal is intended to underscore his argument that moral education is 'not a process of transmission of fixed moral truth but rather a stimulation of the child's restructuring of his experience.'[29] Second, the stages he describes are not enduring structures which human beings merely accommodate themselves to: 'moral judgments and norms are to be understood ultimately as universal constructions of human actors which regulate their social interaction rather than as passive reflections of either external states of other humans or of internal emotions.' Thus the 'views of most of humanity' that judgments of right and wrong correspond to a right and wrong external to the 'judger,' Kohlberg says, are indicative of only the most rudimentary state of reasoning. Third, Kohlberg does not wish to explain his stages, and especially the structure of stage 6, as 'emergent totalities,' implicit in the emergence of the constituent parts of the mature ego. Thus, while 'historicizing' the truth claims of AVER's Kantianism, by seeing progressive stages of human reason as moments within the historical coming-to-be of a wholly adequate moral reason, he denies that there are predetermined a priori forms. Moral stages are not, for example, the result of an unfolding of biological or neurobiological structures. Kohlberg is particularly insistent that he does not want to be seen as committing the naturalist fallacy, that is, deriving an 'ought' from a metaphysically and prescriptively neutral 'is.'

So what is the link between the scientific claims arising from the psychological theory of ontogenesis and the ethical theory of the rational reconstruction of moral judgment? In his earliest efforts to explain this Achilles heel of his model, Kohlberg suggested that the two paths of progress are fused together: 'The scientific theory as to why people factually do move up from stage to stage is broadly the same as a moral theory as to why people should prefer a higher stage to a lower.'[30] When he was criticized by Jürgen Habermas for this suggestion, Kohlberg adopted a 'complementarity thesis,' acknowledging that the normative adequacy of the ethical theory could not be empirically demonstrated. A psychological theory of ontogenesis that is objective, he admitted, must be distinguished from a normative-ethical, rational reconstruction of judgments, but the two may complement one another. 'Science, then,' he wrote, 'can test whether a philosopher's conception of morality phenomenologically fits the psychological facts. [Nonetheless] ... science cannot go on to justify that conception of morality as what morally ought to be.'[31]

Despite this concession, the truth of normative speculation can, at least, be subjected to empirical testing. Explaining Kohlberg's 'complementarity thesis,' Habermas claims: 'the success of an empirical theory which can only be true or false can function as a check for the normative validity of a hypothetical reconstruction of moral intuitions.'[32] Although the empirical evidence of ontogenetic development does not 'prove' the normative reconstruction of moral judgment, it presupposes that reconstruction, because it is informed by it, and the rational conception of justice can be shown empirically either to 'work' or to 'not work.' The normative claim that a higher stage of development is 'better' is incorporated into the psychological account of sequential stage movement and the latter contributes to the coherence of the normative theory by explaining ontogenesis by such mechanisms as cognitive conflict. Falsification of the empirical hypotheses of the psychological theory, moreover, would 'cast doubt on the validity of our normative theory of justice.' The standard of adequacy organizing the empirical investigations is 'assessed by the extent to which that standard provides order to empirical data and by the intelligibility of the order it defines.'[33] The complementarity of empirical evidence and normative reasoning 'allows us to have our psychometric cake and hermeneutically interpret it too.'[34]

Steering closer to Habermas's theory of the evolution of communicative action, Kohlberg now claims that the stages are the products of the student's interaction with others. The process is one of moving up the scale and playing out the inevitable rational logic of interactive communication.

In other words, what lies at the core of the theory of moral ego development is the expectation that the gap between mind and society can be progressively closed, that the ideals arising from the logical structure of reason can be taken as 'social concepts' to coordinate life, thus making life display the same characteristics as the developed mind (more differentiated, more integrated, and more universal) and that once life is wholly systematized, and all its logical linkages made to work effectively, then the intellectual is also in a position to genuinely substantiate the hypothetical deductive model.[35] The development of moral wisdom is inseparable from the interactive, progressive, and irreversible process wherein ideals are redefined and re-employed to bring about the total coordination of the moral spirit and its social world. In order for this process to unfold, those conceptions of moral and personal order of earlier ages, derived from the concreteness of the everyday, must be abandoned, for they are the single greatest obstacle to the fluidity of the ideal proportions and relations unifying the system.

The language we have used to restate Kohlberg's thesis is not our own. We are taken by Kohlberg necessarily back to Hegel. For all of Kohlberg's stated disavowal of teleology and ontology, his schema of the operative causalities which govern sequential stage development, and his notion of moral knowledge as functional adaptation within a system of ego balance and social concepts, are utterly dependent on a metaphysics of time. It is not possible to identify an exchange of equilibrated and disequilibrated structures or processes of assimilation and adaptation as the dynamics of stage development without such a metaphysics. For Kohlberg to determine that these are the paramount criteria of development requires a predetermined assumption that the dynamic is not only continuous but that it also has an identifiable origin and a knowable terminus. Without such a tacit assumption nothing would be legitimate about his explanation of the operative dynamic, and nothing would stabilize the motions from embarking in wholly different directions. Continuity, origins, and ends come as a complete package. But this is simply to say that to analyse process under the concept of development is to see time as historical succession. It is necessary, if we are to understand fully the meaning of Kohlberg's model, to spell out the full implications of analysing process within a metaphysic of time, that is, of apprehending time as history.

Hegel's *Phenomenology of Spirit* supplies the most comprehensive account of the meaning of that metaphysic. There, Hegel provides an exposition of the process of thinking the moments of temporality, whereby such moments are recognized as fragments of the *logos* dispersed in time, available to be recollected as phases of historical development. I am arguing that Kohlberg's phenomenology of the moral spirit runs parallel to, and even reproduces, the logic of Hegel's system, that its coherence is confirmed by purchasing in full to Hegel's exposition. In both, the tensions of existence, the contingencies of human action, the formative events of everyday life, and the presence of mystery are transformed into transitional moments within a dialectical consciousness whose processes are unfolding towards a system of absolute knowledge. But it is not for the sake of mere resemblance alone that I am drawing the reader's attention to Hegel's parallel exposition. Rather, behind the soft, liberal language of Kohlberg's method lies a darker and more aggressive Hegelian teaching whose sombre hue Hegel's most incisive twentieth-century interpreter, Alexandre Kojève, has depicted in his commentary on *The Phenomenology of Spirit*.[36]

Hegel's exposition is a theodicy which draws all of human time together into a history. He hopes to justify both the apparent futility of historical action and the apparent inconclusiveness of past philosophic controversy by revealing all previous human enterprise to be but transitional moments in a dynamic of creative self-expression experimenting through time and culminating in the modern achievement of subjective freedom and universal reason. This theodicy, unlike the theodicies of theologians, is intended to produce the consciousness that the temporal world is capable of containing truth wholly within itself. Hegel's exposition is a reconstruction of everyday reality which sees its imperfections and tensions as temporary inconveniences to be surmounted historically by a transfiguration where all discord in reality is put to an end. The agent of this theodicy is Spirit, an impulse of world-creation and a process of consciousness which, while initially bearing a resemblance to the God of the old theologians, turns out to be the divine principle in the spirit of man-yet-to-be. And unlike the old God, Hegel's Spirit is not complete and perfect before all time, but rather the history of the world is conceived as the record of Spirit-in-the-making. Spirit needs to become conscious of itself as a world-self before it is complete and perfect.

Hegel's *Phenomenology* is a story of Spirit's passage not only through history but also through the evolution of consciousness. The vehicle of Spirit's slowly growing consciousness of itself is the consciousness of man weaving together what had hitherto been the source of tension, discord, and imperfection into a pattern revealing the coincidence of Spirit's self-consciousness and human freedom. Spirit's characteristic act is to express itself – to assume various concrete, objective forms. Combining the impulse to self-consciousness with creative self-expression, Spirit manifests itself as substance, so that it might become conscious of what is other than itself and then recall that this other is but itself. Spirit's self-externalizations are in space as the world of nature and in time as the succession of culture-worlds in history. Nature is externalized Spirit unconscious of itself as Spirit. As inert and mute, it must be negated by human will-acts. The creativity of humans in these acts is the continuation of the original self-expression of Spirit by which nature and human existence came into being. Human actions whereby mere given-being is negated are really Spirit in the act of becoming conscious of itself as Spirit. Spirit will pass from primal unconsciousness in the form of nature to ultimate self-consciousness in the works and ideas of historical humans. As creators of culture-worlds, humans are Spirit in its creative, self-externalizing phase. In their capacity as knowers, they are Spirit in its move towards self-consciousness. The successive human actions correspond to the cognitive activity which recognizes these actions as fragments of reason and order, to be recollected as phases of historical development. In the process of coming to this historical aware- ness, historical consciousness (humans) overcomes its finitude and ele- vates itself to the level of absolute self-conscious Spirit – Spirit complete, perfect, and omniscient.

This desire to know is not the same as the traditional God's loving observation of his created order or the classical Greek philosopher's experience of wonder. Knowing is Spirit's reintegration of itself from the state where, divided against itself, it is conscious subject (humans) con- fronting itself as external object (nature, history). In the subject/object relation, which is the relation permitting Spirit's self-estrangement and self-recovery, Spirit experiences otherness as alien and hostile, because from its consciousness of itself as absolute being, it now has to acknowl- edge a limit to that absoluteness. The experience of non-absoluteness is a mortal challenge to itself. Otherness must be divested of its objectivity to neutralize the sense of bondage humans experience when a limit threatens their idea of themselves as free and creative.

To know is a desire to dominate and see through the apparent objec- tivity of the world which confronts us so as to apprehend it as subjective in character. The activity of knowing entails defiantly divesting the objective world of those features which appear different to us and trac- ing these differences back to our own cognitive interests. Human cogni- tive activity is Spirit's repossession of itself in consciousness.

Hegel depicts this cognitive experience as a great battle. The reappro- priation in which the world is re-internalized in thought exhibits the will-to-conquer. For the object to be mediated by understanding, every facet of the world and experience must be grasped, clarified, and absorbed into the logical schema of historical development, thereby losing its autonomous, independent status. Hegel makes clear that the dialectic is a process of self-aggrandizement to infinity and that, since the process is both cognitive and political, expansionism cannot stop short of the totality of absolute knowledge and the empire achieved by world-conquest.

The final breakthrough to infinity occurs at the moment of the history of the world when all the creative potential of Spirit has been exhausted, when all the objective world-forms Spirit is capable of assuming have been posited, and when consciousness has cognitively conquered all the historical dimensions of the *Logos*. Then Spirit experiences itself as the totality of being, and absolute knowledge arises in the minds of humans in the form of philosophical science. The whole world is now known by the world-self as itself; it is fully self-conscious Spirit in the minds of humans. And it is free, for the successive acts of overcoming objectivity culminate in a state where self-consciousness experiences no opposition, limit, or resistance. The moment of self-awareness represents the culmination of Spirit's odyssey in nature and history. This is the end of history because the totality of possibilities has been achieved: in art, religion, and philosophy; in politics, war, and statecraft. The end is perfect, for all have achieved their full humanity and no further pursuit of perfection is necessary. The sole remaining intellectual activity lies in extending the system of logic down to the minutest capillaries of social and personal life. All that remains as social activity are the administrative chores of tidying up those atavistic pockets where deviance remains.

For Hegel, the odyssey of consciousness as Spirit is played out as significantly in the political world. History, for Hegel, is the process whereby freedom and rationality are actualized. Hegel's exposition reveals that Spirit's repossession of itself by divesting the other of its objectivity leads humans to realize that all previous philosophic and political accounts, historical explanations, and economic or social relations, while presented as truth in the past, are in fact 'ideologies.' Under the pretence that these accounts were truth, the enduring condition of humans up to Hegel is one of false consciousness. The dialectic of history does not 'simply' destroy those historical fragments, but it eviscerates their substance, reducing and transfiguring them into pure form. Looking at the historical inventory of actions and discourses, Hegel identified structures whose traces could be idealized into the dynamic of historical development. Hegel saw such traces in the practices of the Greek city-state, then in the political actions of Alexander, in Christian and Roman society, and finally in the achievement of the French Revolution and the creation of the modern state. Each stage reveals a new, but incomplete, aspect of freedom.

What makes Hegel's 'empirical' historical audit possible is a recollective reconstruction that starts from a total definitive reality, in this case the modern state (complete and perfect), by which historical fragments can be woven together. The total definitive reality of the modern state is the full reconciliation of subjective and objective freedom, or the resolution of the particular and the universal, so that a state where the quintessentially human desire to be recognized in one's eminent dignity is realized. What the modern state has permitted is the right of the subject's particularity to be satisfied. Subjectivity will have a place in a universal and collective life. The regime is one of mutual recognition of subjective rights. The ethos of Greek life, the mores of Roman society, the graces of Christianity, the moral code of Protestantism, and the virtues of the modern bourgeois are not responses to permanent structures of existence, or a natural hierarchy of ends, but are transitional moments of the historical dialectic. Greek and Roman, Catholic and Protestant, fulfil purposes which exceed their own professed ends.

For Hegel the increasingly self-conscious politics of modernity does away with traditional philosophy and religion, while their 'spirit' (their pure form) is fulfilled. The rational state can now be constructed by joining subjective freedom and universality. The possibility of a universal and homogeneous world order is real because the traditional political and moral forms have been fully deconstructed in their appearance as heterogeneous aspects of being and idealized as the operative dynamic of world history. The end of history occurs when freedom is revealed as the essence of man and when the objective organization of government (such as that provided by the Napoleonic empire) is mandate to recognize individuals in their particularity. At this point, each and every person, in a mutual acknowledgment of everyone's right to be recognized in his dignity, is fulfilled. History is over, all historical human possibilities have been achieved. All philosophical and historical work has been completed, and wisdom is actualized in the full comprehension of history's order as well as the full definitive reality of the universal and homogeneous state.

Hegel knew precisely what he was up to in this audacious exposition and he did not shirk from drawing out the immodest and impious implications of his account. If he stood at the privileged point in time which permitted the only authoritative recollection of the fragments of the *Logos* into a history, and which made it possible to recognize that history had consummated itself, it was also an achievement which he took to complete and perfect the eschatological promises of Christianity and to elevate to divine status the exegete of this theodicy. Indeed, the new god was an improvement on the old God, for the act of cosmogonic recollection identified as the process towards self-consciousness had overcome the imperfections, tensions, and inconsistencies of the first creation. Hegel also revealed that the completion of creation in the universal and homogeneous state had brought about a condition where all human possibilities were now actualized. Historical action and philosophical discourse were henceforth unnecessary, short of the rote-transmission of the logical schema.

So that there is no mistaking what Hegel (and by implication Kohlberg) is overturning once and for all, let us recall again the conditions we identified in chapter 2 required to be met if we are to educate a balanced political, moral, and intellectual being. Hegel opposes ancient reverence and receptivity to otherness as the hallmarks of an erotic soul. He rejects the conditioning power of the everyday forms of love, courage, loyalty, friendship, possession, and work, whose recognition would further necessitate attention to the formation and training of practical judgment. Authority, obedience, and accommodation can no longer have any relevance as those foundational modes through which the unity and harmony of reality are observed. Hegel's logical schematism denies that knowledge is an uncompletable ascent. It simply makes the human desire for transcendence and meaning a manageable world-immanent project where wholeness and truth are actualized in a society where everyone is fully satisfied. Such an achievement permanently neutralizes the unrest and tension of human existence by eliminating the gap between the world and our idea of it. Such an elimination, as we already noted in examining Voegelin's argument, is the first step of the gnostic's eclipse of reality.

Kohlberg's development model reproduces this Hegelian alchemy. The dross of everyday existence has been transmuted into a system construed as a succession of phases of moral consciousness proceeding in dialectical development from primary consciousness of self-interest to the final stage of universal recognition of the primacy of life and full self-consciousness of the procedural norms of right. The last stage of moral consciousness signifies the golden perfection of Absolute Knowledge, where 'right' is fully known and has become science in the medium of the concept. Stage 6 is the Hegelian end of history, the regime of mutual recognition, and the actualization of wisdom in the universal and homogeneous society. From its vantage point all previous moral understandings – obedience and happiness, law and order, utility and contract – and all their accompanying ambiguities and tensions, not to say the complex pedagogy associated with training practical judgment and the noetic ascent towards the divine pole of existence, are overcome once and for all in a methodic actuation of *the* form of moral reasoning. Kohlberg's process of moral development is simply the microcosmic replay of Hegel's historical drama, where phylogenetic process is duplicated in ontogenetic development.

The ideal-speech act of stage 6 is the completed and perfect speech. Whereas earlier speech merely symbolized the tension between thought and phenomenon, or ratified the historical work of negating given-being to produce culture, the ideal-speech act reconciles humans with nature, self with other, and time with eternity. Stage 6 realizes a perfect moral order. With it the uncompletable struggles for justice present in the 'premoral' state are given a conclusive solution. All are in a position to enjoy their full humanity and the pursuit of perfection is fulfilled. The traditional notion of ethics or morality as a daily and unending struggle amidst the pressure of passions, the changing images of the desirable life, the tensions of the intellectual and spiritual quest, and political circumstances which constantly change – all moments of man's permanent individual imperfections – is swept away by the achievement of a system of the development of moral reason which actualizes perfect morality.

In Kohlberg's model, Hegel's audacious daring in which the immanentization of the Christian, eschatological drama of the Fall, the arduous way of the Cross, and the ultimate redemption of Eden regained in the universal and homogeneous state whose principles are articulated in the science of the concept, has become unproblematic, even commonplace. Liberal platitudes are unabashedly grafted onto a design of immanent, systematic perfection.[37] Stage 6 is the terminus of the moral spirit's successive cycles of self-division, self-alienation, and reintegration, the completion of the necessary alienation from an original unity and the negating work needed to regain that unity.

The political meaning of Kohlberg's Hegelianism is equally clear. His technique is both a moral theory and a program for restructuring social life which advances a global project of forging all persons together under the concept of historically achieved rationality. 'We claim,' he writes, 'that there is a universalistically valid form of rational moral thought process which all persons could articulate, assuming social and cultural conditions suitable to cognitive moral stage development. We claim that the ontogenesis toward this form of rational moral thinking occurs in all cultures, in the same step-wise invariant stage sequence.'[38] Can there be any doubt that nothing less than a world empire, which to many cannot help but appear as a global tyranny, is the precondition for a truly moral consciousness?[39]

What is the social world portrayed by Kohlberg? What are the social conditions within which Kohlberg's moral development theory both works as a regulative ideal and is refined? Let us recall briefly where 'values analysis' left us. In the AVER model the condition of possibility of the 'transcendental' deduction of the legislative actions of the moral will was a population concerned with the generalizable needs of peace, safety, and prosperity. These needs are seen as best met by formalizing human association in line with the principles of procedural reasoning, thus supplying the population with a representation of itself in its most general and indisputable form – that is, linked by a single social interest. We observed in the previous chapter that while individuals and the organized form of the collectivity are identified as autonomous centres of power, legislating order on the confusion of everyday existence, a bureaucratic government, administering and reinforcing the social interest, enables such autonomy. The AVER model establishes the connection between moral values and the monitoring of population growth and decline of patterns of wealth and prosperity, sexuality, health and hygiene, and safety of urban and domestic spaces. Moral values underwrite the social need to watch, count, tabulate, and design frequency standards. But there is no imperative within the AVER model itself to systematize these processes, nor are the rhythms themselves the conditions of moral debate. The moral order remains centred on the sovereign act of self-legislation and on the prescriptive implications of an autonomous act of reason for producing sound behaviour. Moral training involves constraint and supervision for the purpose of enlightenment and emancipation. The invocation of reason, limit, and order is formidable and imposing, carrying the robustness characteristic of a healthy liberal democracy.

In Kohlberg's account of the moral phenomena, the fusion of morality with the dynamism of life alters what is understood as morally relevant from the mechanical sequences of sovereignty and self-legislation to the organic cycles of bio-norms and adaptation. Moral self-control, as it is self-consciously understood by stage 6, is no longer a subduing or impeding of desire, or focused on the individual in relation to other free individuals, but is instead a structural resonance within the dynamic rhythms of life itself, whose invariant regularities set the direction for individual and social adaptation and enhancement. By looking to the rhythms of life to determine the nature of morality, Kohlberg's method necessarily expands the net of relevant moral phenomena far beyond the domain of the AVER model.

To situate morality within the scope of life and to expect it to replicate life's dynamism is to realize that all the impulses of life are interdependent, co-conditioning and relevant to moral capacity. This assumption means that a dynamic coordination must occur both at the individual level (psychomotor impulses, the affective realm, communicative capacities, reasoning skill) and at the social level (efficient production and consumption, physical and mental health, safety). The rhythms of life as they appear in social norms are suddenly no longer irrelevant phenomena, for they provide insight into the measurement of the life processes in terms of frequency in statistical regularities of aggregates of human behaviour.

Systematization involves the integration and reconstellation of infinite numbers of relations and forces into a set of fluid and unified linkages like life's own automatism. Foucault has a first-rate term for this new dynamism – bio-power. It is a technology of power centred on life. Rather than restraining and impeding the processes of life, bio-power, as an art of rule, is 'bent on generating forces, making them grow, and ordering them.' The coordination of these forces gives a single purposiveness to the totality of human doings. Kohlberg's technique allows the psyche to be seen as merely a functional component of social organization according to bio-power, enhancing its characteristic capacities by conforming to the general process of structural dynamics.

Of course, not all life is developing sufficiently rapidly or regularly to conform to the prescriptive implications of these norms. But moral education can be the conduit for bio-power's imperatives. Moral education will then no longer attend only to manifest expressions of conduct or the ritual performance of self-legislation. It must, in the spirit of the growing web of linkages and interdependences, and in conformity to the ineluctable rhythms of bio-power, attend to all the sources of disequilibrium, maladaptation, or abnormality. Unlike the moral constraints and limits of the sovereign enactment of reason (characterizing the AVER model), conforming to the dynamic of life involves continuous regulatory and corrective mechanisms and the distribution of all of life's moments around the formation of norms. Fusing moral capacity with life's natural dynamism means corralling the myriad life processes into a system where surveillance and optimalization are so integral to moral valuation as to have become transparent as incursions on privacy and as neutralizations of singular and spontaneous action.

Thus Kohlberg's method requires a proliferation of methods of observation, techniques of registration, and procedures of investigation and research especially as the population moves towards the end of the spiral of equilibrated balances in the universal and homogeneous society. Such surveillance and incitement to conform to the norm operate both by aggregating behaviours and by isolating individual dysfunction. The actuation of the spiral of equilibrated balances becomes interpenetrated with the disciplinary techniques which make normalizing assessments viable, differentiate bodies according to types of observable behaviour, and calibrate these bodies according to optimal patterns of preserving and enhancing life. No sovereign authority (either society or conscience) needs to be consulted to conform to the dynamics of life. The power of moral proscription is no longer perceived as a limit but rather as a general social function of maintaining equilibrium and stability, linked to the health, welfare, and productivity of the body and the population. Under a condition of such efficient power, no conflict between individual desire and the law needs to arise.

Under this general imperative of system expansion, Kohlberg's method must necessarily open up beyond the classroom into the broader social concerns of the general population. Indeed, as we have noted, he has made this a condition of the 'proof' of the theory of moral development. Once tensions in social life can come to be seen as expressions of latent moral stress, and moral disequilibrium can be seen as remediable and situated in a continuum of normalcy to deviancy, new domains of intervention are opened and legitimated. Such intervention rides on the expectation that the deviant conditions or causal factors under which morally disequilibrated individuals develop can be detected. The moral education method used in the school produces knowledge of frequencies and distributions of individual deviance and devices for possible normalization. Moral development points beyond itself to a whole ensemble of diagnoses from different agencies, so that the object of education becomes shared among psychiatrists, social workers, demographers, and social-policy analysts. The discovery of moral abnormality demands a surveillance to which the entire society needs to be subjected.

The areas of housing, sexuality, nutrition, health, and economic prosperity must of necessity fall within the gambit of moral education's investigative order. Precedents and subsequent life-histories become relevant areas of control. The details of family life – its neglectfulness, laziness, dissoluteness – cannot escape the gaze of the system coordinating efficiency in the entire process of life. The educator who is a facilitator rather than a figure of authority is only the most direct representative to the student of a multidimensional field, surveyed by an all-inclusive scan. As 'bio-power,' the forces which are reordering and systematizing are invisible because the continuum of regulative apparati does not appear as constraining or impeding. But, the pan-optic monitoring obviously situates each element within the system and in the process confirms and verifies the empirical generalizations which serve as the social scientific categories of normalcy and deviance by which the ensemble of interventions is steered. The categories operate as the principles of a more efficient and expansive economy of power, ensuring regularity, refinement, and universality.

Rather than the inconsistency and irregularity of a juridical enforcement of sovereign legislation, this synoptic regime circulates in a dispersed network, committed to enhancing 'life' by recomposing intention and conduct at the level of desire. It entails a gentle, rhythmic application of power. Being 'synoptic' and 'dispersed' it becomes less random and more accurate through a continuous, administrative regulation of the life-process, adjusting individuals to the norm. Spectacle and ritual are replaced by an incremental, but continuous, transmission of power, producing homogeneous effects. The principle of this power does not lie within the control of any particular person, institution, or rule, but is instead operative in the impersonal distribution of bodies and disciplinary mechanisms. Power radiates from an uninterrupted play of calculated gazes conveying the norms of life by the positive adaptation of individuals.

In this net of control, there is no chance that aberration, whimsy, contingency, and unpredictability will not be neutralized and caught by the synoptic gaze of the mental and social health network of agencies promoting social welfare and public safety. There is a permanent, exhaustive surveillance which, as Foucault suggests, makes all things visible and becomes itself invisible. Life and its tempos are, in this way, brought into the realm of explicit control. Kohlberg's method paves the way for fusing the questions of morality with the questions of health, and for focusing the diagnostic and therapeutic interventions away from the curing of unhealth to the production of health. Unlike AVER's method of stigmatizing through the juridical category of judgment, Kohlberg's development approach establishes an encircling, preventative pedagogy of supervised normalcy. We observe here a transition from moral judgment as juridical appraisal to a psychological continuum allowing sustained surveillance and adjustment. There is no genuine politics here of the sort we discussed in chapter 2 but only a surrogate more properly called social administration.

We must be quite clear what extolling life in its regular patterns of resistance and integration means. To recall Arendt's analysis, we can see here a reduction of the manifold of human actions and worldly events to the rhythms of the life-process. Yet Kohlberg sees himself as doing otherwise. He presents the emergence of moral principles as the very model of the democratic process: 'The concepts of role-taking and justice, then, provide concrete meaning to the assumption that moral principles are neither external rules taken inward nor natural ego-tendencies of a biological organism, but rather the interactional emergents of social interaction.'[40] But he does not understand that this 'social' interaction is precisely that of *social*, not political beings, and that the behaviour of social beings, that is, labouring and consuming, is directly linked to the tendencies of a biological organism.

Kohlberg's moral values are quintessentially those of 'socialized mankind.' At the individual level, moral values are those which simply adjust and coordinate the distinctive person to the rhythms of the whole. At the social level, these are the values where the norms of the system's regularity establish conformity and unquestioning acceptance of the system's dynamic expansion. Spontaneous and unique acts are simply 'noise' in the feedback loop or 'dysfunctional' deviations of a normal distribution profile. Moral self-consciousness has been rendered into the values by which life functions well, which is to say that conditions of existence, to paraphrase Nietzsche, have become predicates of moral being. There is then neither action nor meaning negotiated by a genuine plurality. There can be no stories because there are no exemplary deeds or singular events. Moving through the spiral of equilibrated balances, all experience is increasingly systematized, and all everyday forms and relations are progressively rendered 'transparent,' as the process moves towards its completion in the expression of self-consciousness as identity with the pure form of the motion of life. Kohlberg may extol the achievement of moral consciousness as the result of 'speech-acts' but the achievement of stage 6 replaces speech by what

Heidegger called *Gerede*, or chatter. One must also realize that Kohlberg retains the subjective test of self-certainty (which we observed in the AVER model) as the individual's method of discerning truth. While students interact, their benchmark for discussing appropriate movement towards moral wisdom is 'equilibrium,' a self-regulating, self-validating automatic and irreversible self-examination. Kohlberg's valuing selves are every bit as isolated from the public world (which we discussed in chapter 2) as are AVER's students.[41]

The meaning of Kohlberg's model does not end with the spurious politics of supervised normalcy. We must also observe what scope his model leaves for the life of the intellect. As we have noted, the force substantiating the concept of 'moral adequacy,' and justifying the pedagogical interventions, is 'life.' But who determines what life is? What experience of definitive reality grounds the image and whose experience is it?

To answer these questions, we must return briefly to Hegel. Hegel's account establishes himself as the privileged being in whom Absolute Knowledge became self-consciousness. The language with which he conveys this is borrowed from neo-Platonic and Renaissance mysticism. The metaphors the mystics employed to envisage the unity for which they strove were those of an oceanic effusion of absorption and enchantment, a polymorphous wholeness, and an undifferentiated identity. In a world without negativity, where what *is* is identical with the mind's idea of it, where, in short, desire is fully satisfied, all difference – particularity/universality, time/eternity, passive/active, emotion/reason – is gathered into absolute unity and transubstantiated into a mystical modality of existence, revealing the world as a living totality constituted by an inexhaustible life process repeating itself rhythmically. Hegel's own mystical evocation of the end of history has to be seen as the regulative ideal which substantiates the interactive dynamic in history and the intellect. Only from the standpoint of such a mystical vision, which reconciles all the contradictions of historical existence, is it possible to see the multiplicity of human ends and purposes as fragments of a history whose equilibrated balances spiral towards an absolute end.

Having already observed the kinship between Hegel and Kohlberg, it is not surprising that Kohlberg has 'discovered' a seventh stage, beyond the social regime of mutual recognition and the affirmation of universal rights. He discovered that many religions affirm a higher religious stage based on *agape*, 'or universal responsible love, forgiveness, and compassion "beyond justice."'[42] This higher moral stage is one that 'arises out of a religious or metaphysical notion of the ideal unity of people with each other and with God or Nature.'[43]

In two essays entitled 'Moral Development and the Theory of Tragedy' and 'Moral Development, Religious Thinking, and the Question of a Seventh Stage' Kohlberg affirms that this highest stage might be the decisive feature which renders his account of morality intelligible, for in its absence, he acknowledges, there seems to be no answer to the question 'why be moral?' It may be astonishing but Kohlberg now admits that the universal ethical principles of stage 6 do not answer to the sceptic who denies the claims of reason.

I am not saying that Kohlberg's discovery is eccentric or unimportant. It should be evident that I am in considerable agreement with the comprehensiveness of Kohlberg's model, with his understanding of the development of judgment through a series of equilibrated balances, and with his ideal of reciprocity, as the harmony of difference within unity (freedom within a unified and complete life), just as a Platonist might find much that is agreeable in Hegel. Quite reasonably, and in correction of the AVER model, Kohlberg now indicates that the very possibility of values entails the further questions 'Why live?' and 'How face death?' 'so that the ultimate moral maturity requires a mature solution to the question of the meaning of life.' This, he continues, is not a moral question but an ontological or religious one, and 'not a question resolvable on purely logical or rational grounds as moral questions are.' This highest stage, Kohlberg offers, entails a mystical union with the whole, or individuation brought into the perspective of the infinite.

But it is at this precise point that Kohlberg's system derails, degenerating into the gnosticism we examined in chapter 2. It is a derailment which rebounds back onto his spurious politics, for it is only when an intellectual hopes for immanent wholeness and perfection that politics and the inconveniences of the everyday become impediments. Stage 7, Kohlberg insists, does not require a theistic 'union with God': 'Its essence is the sense of being a part of the whole of life and the adoption of a cosmic, as opposed to a universal, humanistic Stage 6 perspective.'[44]

Kohlberg comes to such enchantment through a characteristically gnostic lament, that of world despair. He writes: 'the world order, then, is one that has established humanity's sense of justice and then left it in conflict with the forces of nature and society.'[45] In broader terms, this conflict is born 'in [the] despair [that] we are the self seen from the distance of the cosmic or infinite.' The possibility of overcoming this conflict, and thus resolving the duality and contradictions of human finitude, not to say the whole intelligibility of his moral system, depends on the possibility of a stage 7 experience.

Kohlberg, to be sure, stops short of the traditional gnostic myth of an unpolarized consciousness which regains its original wholeness, overcoming wholly the division of subject and object, or knowledge and being. Yet, everything in his model points to a desire for the unification of opposites, the transcendence of all dualisms, and the resultant perfection consisting of a unity-totality to be achieved in a new type of humanity.

What prevents Kohlberg's model from being a traditional, speculative gnostic lament is the strong residue of characteristically North American Puritanism informing his thought. The meaninglessness which Kohlberg says comes from the despair we experience when contemplating our distance from the infinite can be addressed only when we face the contradictions between 'humanity's sense of justice' and 'the forces of nature and society' with a new determination.[46] Kohlberg writes:

The resolution of the despair which we have called Stage 7 represents a continuation of the process of taking a cosmic perspective whose first phase is despair. It represents, in a sense, a shift from figure to ground. In despair we are the self seen from the distance of the cosmic or infinite. In the state of mind we have metaphorically termed Stage 7 we identify ourselves with the cosmic or infinite perspective itself; we value life from its standpoint. At such a time, what is ordinarily background becomes foreground and the self is no longer figure to the ground. We sense the unity of the whole and ourselves as part of that unity. This experience of unity, often mistakenly treated as a mere rush of mystic feelings, is at 'Stage 7' associated with a structure of ontological and moral conviction.[47]

In other words, Kohlberg's solution to world despair lies not in absorption into a transcendent and infinite One, as the ancient gnostics would have it, but in the formation of resoluteness and conviction in the service of moral reconstruction. If the infinite cannot be known, nor the meaning and justification of our suffering divined, and if we cannot interpret existence, we can at least be self-righteous and determined in our efforts to change the world. The 'wisdom learned through suffering' in tragedy 'is not the wisdom of a generally higher stage of morality but a new attitude toward justice.'[48] From this 'cosmic perspective,' the post-conventional principles of justice of stage 6 are understood as natural laws, 'principles of justice which are in harmony with broader laws regulating the evolution of human nature and the cosmic order.'

Kohlberg initially explains the meaning of such conviction with the example of Marcus Aurelius, whose moral austerity and appreciation of universal principles of justice are akin to stage 7 thought. However, stage 7's cosmic unity is in fact one 'in which the cosmic vision has a larger influx of union, love, joy, and grace as well as moral force.'[49] The example of Andrea Simpson's *agape*, he claims, is more appropriate. Her early pacifism and activism were indications that in early adulthood she had attained post-conventional morality, and her later exposure to an Indian Vedanta teacher centred her 'on the sense of oneness with "God, cosmic flow, or reality."'[50] This she combined with Western religiosity – to be precise, her Quaker Christianity – 'which identifies inward spiritual union with God with active love for, and service to, fellow human beings': 'She exemplifies the striving for a cosmic or infinite perspective to answer the problems and questions raised but left unsolved by principled (stage 5 or 6) morality itself, the problem of undeserved injustice and suffering.'[51] 'Agape,' Kohlberg claims, 'minimizes the differential merit, deserts, or social utility of people, as does justice as reversibility that centres on equality and consideration of the perspective of the least advantaged.'[52] Uniting the natural-law pantheism of Spinoza, and the evolutionary process philosophy of Whitehead, Bergson, and Teilhard de Chardin, one has, Kohlberg affirms, 'the comprehensive statements of the ethical and religious philosophy exemplified by Andrea Simpson.' The mystical experiences thus achieved permit the disclosure, Kohlberg suggests, of the oneness of being and the overcoming of the subject/object duality.[53]

How are we to understand the full meaning of Kohlberg's model in light of this discovery? It is time to be blunt. I want to argue that Kohlberg's theory of moral development is a totally arbitrary and parochial reading of privileged moments in time, from the perspective of active, modern gnosticism (whose roots lie in Calvin and whose methods are perfected in Hegel). This gnosticism is read through contemporary linguistic philosophy into the concept of 'moral adequacy.'

Let us return again to Kohlberg's 'proof.' As we have seen, first Kohlberg attempts to find a correlation, but then complementarity, between the empirical evidence and the philosophic model. The problem is how few reach the upper stages of the process. In the model, preadolescents move through the preconventional level, adolescents usually achieve the conventional level, and adults move towards the post-conventional level of reasoning. Yet, less than 20 per cent of the adult population Kohlberg has audited reasons at the post-conventional level. Indeed, stage 4, the law-and-order orientation, is always the most common stage, and it is even possible for adults to reason at the lower stages of moral development. Kohlberg admits that none of the longitudinal subjects examined in the United States, Israel, or Turkey have attained stage 6, acknowledging 'that the case materials from which we constructed our theoretical definition of the sixth stage came from the writings of a small elite sample; elite in the sense of its formal philosophic training and in the sense of its ability for and commitment to moral leadership.'[54] Moreover, Kohlberg also admits that stage 4 and 5 reasoning was not found in small-scale villages but only in urban areas. Explaining this, he writes: 'Given the urban findings, however, it seems fair to conclude that the fact that Stage 4 or 5 reasoning is not found in small-scale villages is not because these stages simply express Western values. Rather, it seems more likely that such stages have not been observed in these villages because of their relatively simple degree of social-structural complexity and because their populations have little or no formal education.'[55]

The data do not seem to support Kohlberg's hope that the reality and rationality of stage 6 are empirically grounded. The lack of evidence appears to jeopardize the whole account of the process of development. The lack of empirical corroboration, however, is not decisive since Kohlberg does not claim to ground his moral theory on psychological findings. So stage 6 is retained, 'because we conceive our theory as an attempt to rationally reconstruct the ontogenesis of justice reasoning, an enterprise which requires a terminal stage to define the nature and endpoint of the kind of development we are studying. In other words, a terminal stage, with the principle of justice as its organizing principle, helps us to define the area of human activity under study.'[56]

But Kohlberg immediately steps back from the assertion that stage 6 is 'analogous to norms of scientific rationality in the discussion of the philosophy of science.'[57] First he admits that stage 6 of moral development may only be recognizable by the practitioners who have themselves reached it: 'only the philosophical formalist who views morality as an autonomous domain with its own criteria of adequacy or rationality ... is likely to evaluate more arguments by formal moral criteria and hence to clearly recognize stage-six reasoning as more adequate than the reasoning at lower stages.'[58]

But then Kohlberg admits that 'it is not necessary to endorse the philosophical adequacy of our normative claims in order to begin the psychological study of moral development as we have done,' and in a startling admission writes that 'personal endorsement of the philosophical adequacy claims of higher stages is a matter of choice, and one's personal stand may simply be that using the moral stage framework is a fruitful tool for scientific research.'[59] His moral prescriptions, he acknowledges, may not be based on a more satisfactory meta-ethical position, or a more rational formal normative ethic, or one that is more scientifically true. This admission echoes the general incoherence displayed in all of today's values education models for it denies on the one hand the ultimately rational status of the end, while demanding the reasonableness of the means through which it is achieved on the other. Finally, in a characteristically contemporary resolution of such incoherence, Kohlberg ends lamely in pragmatism: 'the validity of my assumption of such a standard of adequacy in describing the moral development of individuals,' he writes, 'can only be assessed by the extent to which it provides order to empirical data and by the intelligibility of the order it defines.' In an even more revealing passage, Kohlberg writes: 'It should be noted that at a philosophical level these assumptions remain controversial, but their use has led to the discovery of empirical findings which seem to justify their continued use.'[60] Just like the social sciences we referred to earlier, and confirming Arendt's point about the circularity of proof in modern science, Kohlberg finds a way out of the impasse of his model by turning to an operationalism whose generated effects will be allowed to verify the hypotheses.

We have, then, as the sole basis of what justifies the entire complex of interventions and enticements, constraints and discipline, two facts: a small number of professional philosophers who have seen *the* form of moral adequacy, and an effective operationalism whose results confirm the correctness of their speculations.

There is really only one conclusion at which one can arrive in thinking about these shifting 'proofs.' In light of the 'discovery' of stage 7, I believe we are observing here an exemplary gnostic invention, born out of intense discontent with the simple goodness of existence and sustained by the symbolism of a shallow mysticism onto which has been grafted a messianic resoluteness. Let us observe the stages through which this deformed consciousness moves. The concept of 'moral adequacy' and the means by which it is implemented are informed, in the final instance, by the desire for 'oneness with "God," cosmic flow, or reality.' Humans desire, for Kohlberg, a mystical leap out of the differentiated world and an absorption into the One. But that desire cannot be satisfied, for life is 'an ultimate tragedy,' or, as Kohlberg laments, ours is 'the meaninglessness of the finite from the perspective of the infinite.' Thus desire is infinitely thwarted: 'in despair we are the self seen from the distance of the cosmic or infinite.' But unlike the romanticist who escapes into a golden era, Kohlberg does not let this despair form into enchanted self-absorption. Since the 'tragedy' for Kohlberg is not simply a general despair at the human inability to experience cosmic unity, but has a quite specific source ('the world order, then, is one that has established humanity's sense of justice and then left it in conflict with the forces of nature and society'), there is a specific direction which human despair can take to satisfy itself wholly. Kohlberg permits frustrated despair to be converted into righteousness, which is to say that the despair that cannot find the transcendent infinite can be turned to morality. To repeat some earlier quotations, but now in the context of understanding what Kohlberg is doing, let us examine his explanation. The 'wisdom learned through suffering,' Kohlberg writes, 'is not the wisdom of a generally higher stage of morality, but a new attitude toward justice.' The experience of unity, 'that is often mistakenly treated as a mere rush of mystic feelings, is, at stage seven, associated with a structure of ontological and moral conviction.'

But morality, as Kohlberg depicts it, is a progressive inanition of the everyday forms of human existence and the formation of an ideal schema of relations and proportions as the one and true order of existence. Morality is indistinguishable from world transfiguration. The despair which has become righteousness and conviction finds in morality the vehicle for obtaining the simulacrum of 'unity of the whole' in the consolidation of a global, homogeneous society united under the sign of logic.

As we have observed, the regulative ideals of this society are the internal rhythms of bio-power. While bio-power needs no full-time policy directors, its essential dynamic has to have been initiated. Replacing the old God of creation was the work of an exclusive society of moral philosophers who, as speculative gnostics unable to live in the world of differentiation and mediation, fantasize reunion with the One, and whose personal 'deformations' lead them to write a script of their own self-divinization, and set the agenda for the sometimes unwitting agents, and sometimes activist gnostics, who play out their part in the bio-power complex. The true tragedy here, in my mind, is that, all the while, these field operatives think they are fulfilling their moral obligations and doing their best for humanity. The fruit of the life of reason becomes the intoxicating drink of world revolution.

In chapter 7 we will return briefly to the enchantment of the gnostics and relate it to modern technology. Before we leave Kohlberg's fantasy, one final point should be made. Kohlberg writes that stage 7 is one which shifts consciousness from figure to ground, where the finite is 'individuated in the perspective of the infinite' in a new 'cosmic perspective.' But as a consequence of the process whereby the everyday forms of the finite have been discarded, where everything enduring, stable, and capable of being possessed has evaporated on the route to this 'experience of unity,' the 'cosmic perspective' cannot, despite Kohlberg's fervent declaration, hold the 'structure of ontological and moral conviction' secure. It must, precisely because of its indeterminate nothingness, its relentless negativity, finally overreach itself, in a dispersion in which the last remaining stable parameter, life itself – as it was fantasized by the gnostic – disseminates, and produces a state where finite and infinite merely resonate as modulations of one another in a kind of episodic enchantment. *Incipit Nietzsche.*

5

Values Clarification:
The Nietzschean Experiment

The schools must not be allowed to continue the immorality of morality. An entirely different set of values must be nourished.

Sidney Simon, 'Nourishing Sexuality in the Schools'

In this strategy, the leader is probing deeply into individuals who have private thoughts. It is hoped that they will want to share their thinking.

S. Simon, L. Howe, and H. Kirschenbaum, *Values Clarification: Handbook of Practical Strategies for Teachers and Students*

The values clarification technique is associated with Louis Raths, Sidney Simon, Merrill Harmin, and Howard Kirschenbaum.[1] In both Canada and the United States programs like the Human Development Program kit, the Magic Circle, the Dell Home Series, and others employ the values clarification techniques. It is the method probably best known of the values education programs, both for its notoriety and for its uncanny ability to reproduce itself and appear in countless social situations – ice-breakers, initiation rites, management seminars, catechetic training, social work therapy, and university residence counselling to name a few.

Like the other models values clarification (VC) takes as its point of departure the values confusion of contemporary social life. 'We believe that people today cry for help with values ... with so much change and instability in the air, with so many people struggling to find a centre and meaning for their lives, we believe the methods provided by values clarification can make a significant contribution both to personal and social fulfilment.'[2] Moreover, VC adopts a similar Deweyan pragmatism rejecting traditional methods of habituation and moral training. These, the values clarification advocates argue,

have not and cannot lead to values in the sense that we are concerned with them, values that represent the free and thoughtful choice of intelligent humans interacting with complex and changing environments. In fact, those methods do not seem to have resulted in deep commitments of any sort. The values that are supposedly being promoted by those methods in our society – honour, courage, devotion, self-control, craftsmanship, thrift, love, and so on – seem less than ever to be the values that guide the behaviour of citizens. On the pragmatic test of effectiveness alone, the approaches listed above must receive a low grade. They just do not seem to work very well.[3]

Endorsing the *Encyclopaedia Britannica*'s account of John Dewey's pragmatism, Raths, Harmin, and Simon write: 'Similarly there are for Dewey no self-evident or universally valid rules of conduct: moral rules are hypotheses which have been found to work in many cases and hence offer helpful suggestions; they offer nothing more.'[4] It is appropriate, they add, to 'see values as being constantly related to the experiences that shape them and test them ... they are the results of hammering out a style of life ... after a certain amount of hammering ... certain things are treated as right, desirable, or worthy. These become our values.'[5]

Finally, VC repeats the opposition to the traditional content of learning. To date, the experience of the classroom has been of 'a punitive atmosphere,' a 'sterile curriculum,' and 'anger.' In contrast, values clarification aims to foster 'nourishing school environments' as models of new social relations.[6] As opposed to the 'heavy moralizing, inculcating and indoctrination' which, 'in [their] extreme form, led to the horrors of the Nazi regime,' values clarification avoids the transmission of a code in favour of 'honest sharing.'[7]

VC's solution is more radical, however, than that of the other two models. Where the AVER approach and Kohlberg's model, whatever their internal instabilities and flaws, align themselves with an enduring and persuasive philosophic source (Kant and Hegel), VC embarks on the most radical revaluation of all values. That radicalism arises out of the lethal combination of Rousseauan romanticism (nature is good, civil society is corrupting; the highest good is the sweet sentiment of existence) and Nietzschean empowerment ('the will loves even more to will nothingness than not to will'). This linkage is evident in the eclectic pastiche of Deweyan pragmatism and Maslovian/Frommean self-actualization and authenticity.

VC follows Dewey in a commitment 'to a belief in a plurality of changing, moving, individualized goods and ends, and to a belief that principles, criteria, laws, are intellectual instruments for analyzing individual or unique situations.'[8] Central to such commitment is demurring from stable distinctions and permanent ends.

We all tend to relapse into this non-moral condition whenever we want any one thing intensely. In general, the identification of one end which is prominent in conscious desire and effort with the end, is part of the technique of avoiding a reasonable survey of consequences. The survey is avoided because of a subconscious recognition that it would reveal desire in its true worth and thus preclude this action to satisfy it – or at all events give us an uneasy conscience in striving to realize it.[9]

VC's approach and specific techniques are based on the assumption that 'by definition and by social right ... values are personal things.'[10] A value is 'a preference for something cherished or desired; it is linked to one's satisfaction of his needs, his realization of goals, and the maintenance and enhancement of his self-concept.'[11]

VC's identification of values with personal choice and the fulfilment of one's 'self-concept' suggests VC's proximity to the 'emotivism' expounded by A.J. Ayer and C.L. Stevenson. According to these moral philosophers, what can be said about morality is limited to the recognition that like all language statements moral speech-acts are not descriptive statements of fact, but express only emotional attitudes. When individuals express their values they are at best only seeking to persuade others of the same feeling of approval or disapproval. There is nothing enduring or unconditional about the measures of such approval and disapproval, and thus essentially contested difference is inevitable. The range of contestation can only be reduced by ensuring that the contestants are clear about the difference between statements of fact and expressions of value.

The emotivist opinion is clearly evident in VC's affirmation of the dynamic creativity underlying values. In the techniques they propose, the primacy is on the process itself and that process is not intended to produce enduring virtues but rather to be valuable in itself.[12] A world that 'changes as rapidly as ours,' the VC authors write, cannot assume permanence or possession. Shifting aspirations, purposes, attitudes, feelings, activities, interests, beliefs, and worries in a world which is similarly undergoing perpetual change requires in turn that individuals remain adaptable and mobile. 'Planning,' Simons in his characteristically gnomic fashion writes, 'is a fear of living.' A perpetual revaluation of values is expected. 'Heavy moralizing, inculcating, and indoctrination' rely on a metaphysic for which contemporary society has no place. H.V. Perkins, whose writings closely connect to VC, comments:

We believe that each person has to wrest personal values from the available array ... values that actually penetrate living in intelligent and consistent ways are not likely to be produced in any other way. Thus it is the process of making such decisions that concerns us. 'Instead of giving young people the impression that their task is to stand a dreary watch over the ancient values,' says John Gardner (1964), 'we should be telling them the grim but bracing truth that it is their task to recreate those values continuously in their own time.'[13]

VC's handbooks supply the techniques, simulation games, and role-playing and awareness exercises through which students can identify and clarify their values.[14] The facilitator's role is one of stimulating awareness of values by requesting quick responses and authentic self-disclosures through which the true self is revealed. To begin, the facilitator focuses the student on his or her own feelings of unrest, discontent, and anxiety. The bruised self and the fractured world are to be seen as in need of cure: 'both individuals and societies are suffering from many ailments, not the least of which are *value problems*.'[15] The facilitator is not permitted to persuade the student of his or her competence in managing 'values stress,' but rather he can demonstrate the power that the self can have over reality. The empowered self equips itself for such control with a 'self-concept.'[16]

The process of fabricating a self-concept involves a rapid-fire succession of identity questions and a visceral reaction to 'issues.'

Are you more a No Trespassing Sign or a Public Fishing Sign, a file cabinet or a liquor chest, a fly-swatter or fly-paper, here or there, breakfast or dinner, yellow or blue? Would you like to be cremated when you die? Do you think we ought to legalize pot? Would you mind having classes without textbooks? Would you like to keep a compost heap? Would you like to have spoken with homosexuals about their lifestyles? Reveal who in your family brings you the greatest sadness, and why. List all the people you've been in love with. How did you first learn to kiss? Recall the last ten times you have cried. What was each about?

Share the most intense religious experience of your life. The subject I would be most reluctant to discuss here is ... How many of you think that parents should teach their children to masturbate? Could you tell someone they have bad breath? Is going steady important to achieve social success?

Initially students are to give 'yes' or 'no' answers, simply affirming by gesture, or verbalizing the intensity of their feelings about the varied topics. In the same expressive manner, students will complete sentences like 'Secretly I wish ...,' 'My parents are usually ...,' 'I'm trying to overcome my fear ...,' 'I am most proud that ...,' 'If I won a lottery I would do the following to make the world a better place in which to live ...,' 'I feel most deeply about ...,' 'If I had to write my own obituary, I would include ...' Discussion, informative questioning, and factually linked argument are not encouraged at this stage because these overly cognitive skills may render 'experiencing a self-concept' inauthentic. Students are to engage in 'value-voting,' and 'feeling-whipping' around the classroom is encouraged. Following the arousal of feelings and the formation of a self-concept, students participate in brainstorming, free-wheeling discussion, and fantasizing. What would you do if you had a million dollars? what would you do on the moon? and what would you rather be doing than being in school? Students are to conceive of limitless permutations of situations, thereby enhancing their own creativity. How will people look a million years from now? What is life on other planets like? Imagine new kinds of inventions.

Simon's games require honest commitment to 'openness.' Perfect candour and self-display are the basis for a positive sense of self and effective interpersonal relations. Lacking such openness indicates a return to the expectations, rules, and demands of others, to 'shoulds' which are meaningless if they have not been affirmed through personal preference.' "Shoulds" come from external sources, "wants" come much more from our inner selves, our own beliefs. They come from the real me.'[17] The atmosphere of these sessions, Simon says, is to be open and non-judgmental. Suppressing feeling is an inauthentic mask, just as negatively assessing another person's values is a mere defence mechanism. From time to time, candour will require pre-verbal communication and the legitimate suppression of verbalized evaluation and judgment. 'Non-verbal communication,' students learn, is more authentic. It breaks down 'inauthentic' role-playing. To assist in breaking down inauthentic behaviour, the classroom is to be positive, supportive, and non-judgmental, and students will give one another 'warm fuzzies,' pat one another, and hug. These public validations of 'relating' are meant to break down individual isolation and false pride, modesty, and inhibitions.

The 'facilitator' does not express preferences or offer direction. 'Authenticity' demands that he or she acknowledge his or her own values confusion. At best, the values held by the facilitator are to serve as the equivalent of 'smart-shopper's tips.'

Making values a matter of choice and feeling does not, according to VC's designers, entail the radical relativism implied of the emotivist position. 'Some people have charged us with being ethical relativists. By that they seem to mean that we accept one value as being as good as another. That is far from our position. We believe in clarifying values, helping people better integrate their beliefs, feelings, activities, purposes, and so on, through awareness and reflection.'[18] The valuing process is, for them, methodic and structured. The valuing process is a technique in which preferences are subjected to 'clarification.' A clarified value is one which has passed through seven methodological criteria:

a) choosing freely b) choosing from among alternatives c) choosing after thoughtful consideration of the consequences of each alternative d) prizing or cherishing ('values flow from choices that we are glad to make') e) affirming ('we are willing to publicly affirm our values') f) acting upon choices ('Life must be affected for a thing to be of value,' 'nothing can be a value that does not ... give direction to actual living') and g) repeating (if it's a value it has to persist, and we repeatedly act in accord with it).[19]

'Unless something satisfies all seven of the criteria ... we do not call it a value.'[20] Where the seven criteria are not met, such as where there are only goals or purposes, aspirations, attitudes, interests, feelings, beliefs, convictions, activities, worries, problems, and obstacles, these are 'value indicators', but not yet values.[21] As stimuli, however, values indicators nonetheless need to be elicited so as to be compiled on value-information sheets. Their status is raised only when the entire valuing process is completed.

And while in the first edition of *Values and Teaching: Working with Values in the Classroom* the centrality of 'thinking' was diminished (there is 'a greater quality of uncertainty about the thinking process'), in the revised edition, VC's designers acknowledge that 'values and thinking are inextricably linked' and affirm the need 'to train [students] in the process of valuing and thinking.'[22] Indicating how this 'thinking' relates to expressing preference, they write: 'we conceive of thinking as processes associated with inquiry and decision making. Whenever decisions are made, value judgments are involved.'[23]

However 'soft' VC's values remain, the final test of the value of values is whether they work. 'Whether values clarification makes a difference ... is, we think, a question to be tested empirically and personally by those who are interested in it. It is less important to us to wonder if the theory can be made true for all people and all times than to wonder if it can serve particular people in these times ... we say: try the theory and see if it works for you.'[24] Values are appropriate when their implementation has results: 'whatever values a person obtains should work as effectively as possible to relate that person to his or her inner and outer worlds in a satisfying and intelligent way.'[25] Under this mandate of pragmatic operationalism, VC sees its value in alleviating 'certain behaviour problems' which to date have caused youth to 'act impetuously, erratically, and sometimes destructively.'[26] The values procedures of VC will, the designers believe, defuse those feelings of 'resentment and hostility and alienation' which 'stem from their lack of personal power or hope for the future.'[27] Students under the traditional curriculum have 'a lower level of life than need be.'[28] The 'truth' of VC's methods lies in their effectiveness to release 'personal and social productivity' and the extent to which its 'thought provocation' activates 'the use of personal power' and 'independence.'

And studies 'using sophisticated designs and large populations' have shown values clarification to 'work.'[29] Students exposed to values clarification, the VC designers argue in pointing to tests, correlate with low drug abuse, reduction in juvenile delinquency, and lessening of racial conflict.[30] The tests show improvements in initiative, self-esteem, self-concept, self-direction, attitudes towards learning, personal and social adjustment, intra-class relations, appreciation of deviant behaviour, and setting of values priorities. Repeated testing reveals, the authors argue, that values clarification techniques reduce 'the frequency and acuity of such negative behaviours as apathy, flightiness, uncertainty, inconsistency, drifting, overconforming, overdissenting and role-playing.'[31] Thus, the VC authors argue, there is no basis for the widespread charge that the program is 'relativistic' and 'controversial.'[32]

Nonetheless, the common charge against VC is that it is relativistic and that it reduces morality to mere states of feeling. Are there not absolute prohibitions of certain acts, ask the critics, and must those prohibitions not be stated and applied through the exercise of reason? Is it sufficient for responsible conduct to merely hold a moral value *resolutely*, and is mere consistency sufficient as a criterion of coherence in a moral position? Are empathy and mutuality sufficient between persons to ensure that each is given his or her due, that is, treated justly? Is it appropriate for moral educators to probe the 'authentic me' which in the past has been the exclusive domain of religious ministers or psychiatrists, and de-emphasize acts and consequences?

These are important questions, and the issues associated with them have fortunately been systematically addressed by many commentators. My concerns lie elsewhere, though my conclusions dovetail with the views of many of these critics. In values clarification, I am arguing, the inevitable destiny of the term 'values' unfolds. I have referred earlier to Grant's argument that philosophic terms embody destinies and 'destinies have a way of working themselves out – that is of bringing forth from their principle everything which is implied in that principle.' When values clarification refers to moral experience and conduct as values, it sums up and completes the philosophic and social uprooting of six centuries of rendering the moral phenomena wholly transparent, highly formalistic, unworldly, and appropriate only to a construct of reality where humans, in a freedom become fully conscious to itself, have demystified all the images of order and finality previously defining humanity and now relinquish their 'all-too-human' being by affirming their belongingness to a more primordial force.

Values clarification is a remote heir to Heidegger's analysis of the temporality of human existence, to the theology of 'mutuality' of Buber, and to Sartre's existentialism of freedom (as well as work of his followers such as Erich Fromm and Abraham Maslow in the field of psychology). One could say that VC operationalizes the radical overturn of metaphysics which all three thinkers undertook philosophically, attempting an equally radical transvaluation of everyday existence. But VC shies away from the inexorable logical deconstruction intended by the philosophers and instead eclectically blends with this relentless negativity a pragmatic liberalism celebrating the creative self, a sentimentalized romanticism of authenticity, and an assertive ethic of decisionism. The fanciful fusion of incommensurable theoretical elements means that VC's philosophic core is tenuous at best. The riotous blending is, indeed, the source of the essential instability in the VC model and the origin of the radical undertow which makes VC the most revolutionary of the values education programs. What I observe and wish to restore to visibility in VC is the lurking phantom of Nietzsche, whose aggressive politics and morality of empowerment distil with ruthless candour what follows when the 'real world' and the 'apparent world' are deconstructed and relentless negativity unleashed. VC's optimistic presentism, its unambiguous praise of unbounded freedom, and its innocent appraisal of the potent emotions it unleashes shield this darker figure from appearing. I am arguing not only that it is Nietzsche's thought that gives 'coherence' to VC, but that the effect of VC is very much the perspectival, playful, but also lethal, episodic ornamentalism which Nietzsche intended to bring about.

We must recall that the traditional curriculum, and the vestiges remaining in AVER's and Kohlberg's values programs, attempted to educate students and attune them to the process of reality. The traditional curriculum was constructed on the principle that the structures of that process could be crafted into topics and practices which would serve as icons for the movements of consciousness in its development towards intellectual and spiritual maturity.

In values clarification, by contrast, no idea of what a human is, no account of the ends of human society, no sense of authority, no permanent principles of rationality, nor any conception of a structured life grounds the proliferation of values. Much more radically than AVER or Kohlberg, VC dissociates itself fully from any program of character formation. There are no programs of habituation, no exercises of reminiscence to collect self-identity into the durations of past, present, and future, and no efforts to produce a total personality. No permanent or centring principle orders or limits the effervescent willing of the valuing subject. Neither recollection nor commemoration leads the psyche to paradigmatic experiences or exemplary historical events. No sense of the sacred or the divine, the heroic or the public, gives the new mode of valuation and its values substance or continuity.

That VC extols freedom and uniqueness is not, obviously, the basis of my apprehension. After all, these are aspects of our human existence which, following Arendt, we have praised as essential to political life. By clearing the ground of so many of the dogmas, systems, schematic constructs, and sententious moralizing of the past, VC opens up opportunities and re-establishes the importance of the redemptive quality of novelty.

Politically, values clarification urges that activity which leads to singular action and unprecedented events. It thereby frees individuals from constructs of existence based on spurious doctrines of natural necessity or historical development. Intellectually, VC razes the accepted opinions of the dominant schools of psychology and philosophy to the ground, by undercutting the dogmas and schematic formalizations which have blocked genuine openness to the primary and elementary questions of existence. The freedom of a young student's consciousness from the logical necessity of systems, or the web of social determinations, makes the search for meaning once again a direct encounter with the experiences of movement within the process of reality.

But the momentum of VC goes far beyond the idea of liberal education we discussed in chapter 2 and have used as a measure throughout this book. To accept the language of 'creativity,' 'uniqueness,' 'authenticity,' and 'openness' uncritically would be to overlook the more revolutionary and destabilizing aspects of values clarification. Of the medley of objectives values clarification aims at, it is the conjunction of authenticity and empowerment, which, in my mind, unleashes those potent and lethal tendencies to which I referred earlier. Authenticity and empowerment, while in some ways antipodal, work together to repudiate completely the forms of the 'everyday' by aiming at a much more nebulous and volatile retrieval of a primordial genesis prior to all order. VC follows Sartre in affirming its commitment to a *true* humanism. But, in dispensing with the structures in which the 'human' is situated, VC ultimately renounces genuine humanism, favouring a type of existence given over to randomness and contingency. The techniques by which the self is empowered and ratifies its values, as well as those by which interpersonal relations the self has with others are forged, are united in their disavowal of those everyday forms which once wove together motion and finality, contingency and order.

Let us begin with the self of values clarification. The self is nothing more than an open possibility directed into an indefinite and infinite future. As an expression of pure self-overcoming, its existence is a perpetual deferral of determinate characteristics maintaining the adaptability and movement which Simons, Raths, Harmin, and Kirschenbaum praise. The self is 'proactive,' as the vernacular identifies this mobility, as long as it is a will-to-will, activating values operationally under changing circumstances. It must avoid being 'reactive,' a state the self would exhibit if it settled for forms of existence which reflect accommodation to or obedience to the given, unified, or complete.

The criterion for the self's appropriate activity is not based on what has traditionally constituted the determinate being of what essentially *is*. To be is not to be what one is in the tension towards the divine pole of existence, or in relation to the actualities of concrete being, or through the ways of life and practices of historical cultures, or in relation to the palpable 'things' which are occasion for historical recollection and appreciation of worth. Each of these, being determinate boundaries to the rhythms of human existence, established that permanence or stability which was an intellectual, spiritual, emotional, or material possession. That possession was a nucleus around which and upon which genuine acts of freedom, choice, thought, and action could become processes of perfectibility. To 'be' authentically, however, for VC is to adopt an attitude of superfluity or disposability towards these possessions.

One must conclude that the fluidity and dissemination which values clarification fosters are meant to bring about a radical dispossession from permanence and from that recollection which we identified as the means by which a retrieval of the *arche* of intelligible speech is possible. Indeed, to refer to the psychologist Erich Fromm, whose thought so quintessentially underwrites the central features of VC, 'possession' and 'recollection' are modalities of 'necrophily':

... the necrophilous person loves all that does not grow, all that is mechanical. The necrophilous person is driven by the desire to transform the organic into the inorganic, to approach life mechanically, as if all living persons were things ... *Memory, rather than experience, having rather than being, is what counts.* The necrophilous person can relate to an object – a flower, or a person – only if he possesses it; hence a threat to his possession is a threat to himself; if he loses possession he loses contact with the world ... He loves control, and in the act of controlling he kills life.[33]

For Fromm, to have is to orient oneself by stable forms which are erroneously taken to symbolize permanent structures within reality, or to orient oneself by a false sense of continuities and purposes, or even to orient oneself mistakenly by a tangible arrangement of things. In all these cases, Fromm indicates, one is arresting the effervescent genesis of life itself. To 'be' a self is to divest 'being' of its possessive character. Genuine being cannot include having.

Sartre, whose influence similarly radiates in VC and who is more candid as to the full implications which follow from denying that images of order and finality are grounded in structures of being, is even more emphatic as to the inauthenticity of durability. At the very core of our existence, Sartre writes, 'is a useless passion.' We seek durability which would make us what we are not (an 'in-itself'), but being as we are, we must destroy the stable elements with which we surround ourselves.

While humans are the unique source of value and thus the measure of the nothingness of the world, we cannot continue to be the being aiming towards an open and indefinite future (a 'for-itself') if either our values or our identity have permanence or ontological stability. The 'in-itself' can never be a value or serve as a condition of existence for the 'for-itself.' The essence of the self is temporal and conditional. As much as the 'for-itself' seeks to render itself permanent and to maintain its stability, it renders itself inauthentic to its true possibility. The self is a spring-board situation. Self-identity needs to be repeatedly deconstructed since if the 'for-itself' is authentic to its 'being' it must be a dispossessed self. The 'for-itself' truly *is* precisely in the destruction of the 'in-itself.'[34]

To refuse 'essences' and 'continuities,' 'primal meanings' and 'structures of intentionality,' is to say that the self must give itself over to perpetual cycles of self-overcoming. The self can be only temporarily sufficiently stable to affirm some value, but it must refuse, on pain of bad faith, that appointment which would see itself as that same stable being in the future. True authenticity affirms a kind of nothingness, as Sartre describes it, entailing an endlessly refracting effect of evacuation from situations by a self perpetually engaged in the extrication of itself from its own bad habit of desiring stability and wholeness. Free of precondition and determinacy, the 'for-itself' is a process of 'empty spontaneity,' a freedom willing to risk all possibility, and a joyful will to episodic novelty.

This self which I argue lies at the core of VC experiences life as an eternal cycle of objects made available to it but also immediately to be disposed. The apprenticeship which leads to such vitality and the accompanying sense of the superfluity of all things aims at a radical dispossession – from the order of being, from historical artefacts and recollected memory, even from the characteristics identifying selves as singular. The self is simply an empty possibility. Thinking back to Arendt's idea of singular action and individual uniqueness, and the determinate circumstances in which they acquire their form, one can hardly say that these selves are either genuinely free or individual persons since neither the world nor a structured process of reality directs and substantiates their motions.

In opposition to existentialism's and values clarification's optimism that such a self is truly free in any human (read 'moral') sense, and any expectation that such a self is immune from the brutalities which can be inflicted on individuals by others, I would argue that this self, reduced to sheer emptiness, has been irresponsibly left utterly defenceless and exposed to the ruthless and exploitive play of power. This wholly exteriorized self, as simply a temporary presence in one situation and then at the next moment dispersed into an infinite variety of options, is 'empowered' but this means nothing more than that the self has become a vacuum to be filled with perpetually changing profiles of whatever is declared to be the 'state of the art.' Beyond shame and remorse, discontent and hope, and deprived of the experience of integrity based on persistence over time, the self is indeed 'empowered' and its circumstances are 'demystified,' but it is unable to resist or challenge any image presented to it. If we recall Arendt's warning about the vulnerability of isolated beings who, deprived of a stable identity and a durable personality within a concrete community, have become superfluous and disposable, this celebration of dispossession should give us pause. The selves of VC are individuals reduced to mass existence. They are locked within their own amorphous and receding subjectivity, isolated from others and yet primally connected through a web of affectivity. No genuine plurality or opportunity for composing the actions of such selves into meaningful stories can be found in such a web. In the absence of detachment and critical distance from this primordial web, these selves are going to be greatly susceptible to the 'nonsense and capricious notions' by which masses are mobilized and terrorized, unable to distinguish propagandistic fiction from reality.

The 'authentic' encounter is no haven from this danger. While derivative of Buber's understanding of non-objectifying, non-hierarchical, and mutually satisfying human relations, Buber's I–Thou relation took place as a truly transcending event within the process of reality. The mystery of the other and assent to its otherness which Buber calls 'rehallowing' is not enchantment with expressive feeling-states, but genuine experience of a transcendent reality in which the whole of existence is affirmed as a gift. VC's encounter, in which the 'real me' and 'empathy' are the source of animation, takes the most elementary primal impulses and, disallowing any image of order or perfection to structure the pure expressivity of the event, transmutes these into an epiphany.[35] The immanence and mutual absorption of the encountering selves, where each approves and empathizes with the other, is nothing more than a spurious mystification, an obsession with the most primitive, trifling states of being. The 'real me' is an affectation of enchantment with mere sentience.[36] VC's 'empathy' radiates neither from a being with a determinate personality nor from an actual situation.[37] Neither spiritual substance nor concrete political interest (literally, between beings) is formed. The encounter is therefore neither friendship nor civic respect. It is not a negotiation of collective meanings or an opportunity for the formation of judgment.[38] Unlike AVER's 'reciprocity,' which was a harmony of difference within unity, 'empathy' is a mere affective resonance. Its immediacy permits of no distance. Where 'planning is a fear of living' there can be no purposes or balanced points of view actuated in the encounter. The 'encounter' finally refers to a resonance of occasional beings, thrown together by chance. Just as the individual has become a wholly exteriorized self, simply a temporary presence in a situation, so the engagement with others is vaporized and depleted of its substance.

Now let us turn to the self's values. Surveying VC's 'values' – honesty, self-disclosure, commitment, resoluteness, self-scrutiny, self-abandonment, empathy, authenticity, consistency, reciprocity – one cannot help but be struck by the eclecticism. What is the *arche*, or foundational principle, which unites or ranks these values? The anarchism in VC's values is not surprising, however, for it follows from the very process VC identifies as its distinctive perspective on moral education. Clarifying values means summoning forth ways of life, practices, and understandings and exposing the contents and contexts of life to be arbitrary arrests of the effervescent motions of existence. Once 'clarified' as objects whose origins, motivations, and sources have been fully exposed, values become mere 'data,' available and disposable at will. They are not the enabling conditions that animate us, but instruments which empower us. As instruments values can become endlessly processed and reprocessed since they are no longer symbolic expression of participation in reality. They can be denied their enduring representational or referential role since there are now an infinite variety of constructs of meaning. As abstracted signs of former ways of life, skills, and understandings, they can be stored, deployed, and recirculated and they lend themselves to limitless creative rearrangement.

Let us look again at the 'values' which empower VC's self: honesty, self-disclosure, commitment, resoluteness, self-scrutiny, self-abandonment, empathy, authenticity, consistency, reciprocity. The array is only vaguely reminiscent of the traditional cardinal virtues. Where is the ordering principle which could account for this eclectic and discontinuous pastiche? How incommensurable its components are can only be understood if we place the pastiche up against the principles structuring Plato's 'philosophic soul,' Aristotle's 'magnanimous man,' St Paul's or St Augustine's 'spiritual person,' St Thomas's 'saint,' Machiavelli's acquiring and glorying prince, Hobbes's and Locke's calculator of advantage, Calvin's or Luther's 'pious believer,' Rousseau's compassionate, perfectible child of nature, or Kant's 'mature citizen.' VC's values are all, and thus none, of these. Having abandoned nature, God, history, and reason, VC's values can only be an *an-archic* pastiche.

Is this a fair statement? Reading the values clarification handbooks, one does experience that one is observing another form of the great romantic themes of frustration, alienation, anger, rebellion, projection of an idealized wholeness, and self-recreation. But then, with the addition of resoluteness, a deeper disruption occurs which vitiates this simple search for referents and thematic coherences in romanticism. Nor is VC true to the late-nineteenth- and early-twentieth-century analyses of the psychopathologies of the self described within the polarities of alienation/unity, authenticity/inauthenticity, false consciousness/self-consciousness. Instead, the stream of values is a random collection of deracinated ideals utterly separated from the great themes associated with the ideas of a sacred cosmos and spiritualized souls, a sacred cosmos and obedient stewardship, an orderly nature and intellectual consent, or a moral community and civic respect. VC's amalgam betrays utter pragmatism: whatever works is true. But it is not even, strictly speaking, 'pragmatism' if pragmatism is understood as deciding action by its use to the individual or for the social interest, for in VC there is no concrete context for valuing. There is no interpretive work within which one might conduct an analysis of VC's valuing process or values to produce a true vision or a coherent image of human reality.

But is this celebration of human creativity and freedom not simply the end-point of the great modern humanist project of liberating the self from all determinations? I would argue that it is not. While VC's use of language is mischievous, I do not think that we should see its techniques of the self as merely a new opening for the full richness of subjectivity in feeling, emotion, and affect, or another aestheticism of expression and taste based on the effort to dramatize an internal feeling outward. VC's value-clarifying self is not expanding into an embrace with all existence. To the contrary, its movement is an interiorization of experience to the point of an implosion of all meaning and itself. An implosion is not a retrieval of interiority. Values just play on the surface here, for the depth or ground has been vacated. Morality has become extreme ornamentation. The traditional values are all there and yet, in that, none of them are there.

These are 'values,' in short, which have lost their reference point, the human perspective. Infinitely permeable, substitutable, wholly exteriorized, random 'styles' of an empty self, they can only be seen as tools of experimentation. They are simulacra (copies for which there is no original) of former principles of ethics and morals. No structure with stable boundaries or a determinate tension provides values with valency. Where ethical ways of life and practices, or moral acts and norms, may have been grounded on a sense of what a human being is fitted for and situated within the regulative poles of such oppositions as divine/human, good/evil, virtue/vice, transcendent/imminent, soul/body, or reason/desire, which supplied them with meaning, values merely circulate randomly. Neither metaphysical boundaries nor historical ideas of space and time define values. How can we give others their due, or allot what is appropriate to each aspect of existence, if these parameters no longer have determining power? VC's values have no possessive affinity to being at any level – in oneself, in things, in truth. Instead, they shift and transfigure, manifesting themselves as no more than temporary intensities or affects. VC's array of values is a great encyclopaedic compendium of past morals or ethics but now this array is simply an aggregate of disconnected signs. Nothing endows them with coherence. These values are the furthest reach from the already unstable notion of value as it was used in the neo-Kantian schools, in the economic theory of marginal utility, in John Dewey's 'instrumentalism,' and in Max Weber's social science methodology. These new values function to achieve the effect of truth in a dehistoricized and desocialized space, but they can be understood only as simulacra. They are now mere imitations of dead styles. 'Neo-edition' can exist alongside 'classic-edition' because neither substantive structure nor historical time any longer holds. When this eclectic fusing of values is combined with the des-incarnation of man, the 'values' of values clarification even overreach the conception of 'values' as a creative expression of 'personal style' – there is no longer even a self who can apply a signature to the array of values.

The same anarchic and post-humanist eclecticism is evident in what VC sees as the 'skills' with which the self creates values. Again, in examining the handbooks one is struck by the random listings of processes, and the eclectic fusing of disparate techniques, practices, and capacities of consciousness. While the 'values' which the self embraces need not be so very different from 'traditional' excellences and virtues, what has changed is the mode of valuing. Skills are not practices, or talents, or aptitudes, for all these bring about something more complete or more unified. The objective of skills is not to retrieve an *arche* or to re-collect the transience and moments of existence into durations of past, present, and future. Skills simply do not restore or actuate order. No account of the human potential which can be actualized, no sense of historical progress, endows skills with purpose. As a consequence, skills cannot be situated in a structured, sequential time-frame. The point of skills is not to bring something into being but to consume and empower. 'Skills' are revolving means, which for having been divorced from ends, are merely exercises of power. Their exercise is not an 'employment' but a 'deployment,' an episodic effusion of power. As much time is spent 'deskilling' as in using skills, for the point of skills is empowerment, not production.

'Brainstorming,' the quintessential skill encouraged by VC, is a perfect expression of this episodic overflow of power. As VC puts it, brainstorming can deploy any known method or technique from any field, regardless of its designated area of applicability. Any strange and exotic option can emerge from these sessions for there are no bounds, no purposes, and no ends in this exercise. Brainstorming is a free-for-all allowing all the strata of existence (organic, vegetative, sentient, and rational) to appear simultaneously and to mix into any scenario imaginable. With 'brainstorming' individuals do not speak, they chatter. What emerges from chatter might be the gift of tongues or it might be Orwellian doublespeak, but no student will know the difference.

The chatter of values clarification, however lacking in coherence, is intended by the designers not so much as a statement on the order of reality, but as the vehicle for the spontaneous release of primal freedom. Despite VC's optimism that layers of repression are being lifted by the process of clarification, the promise of emancipation has met with extensive scepticism by critics. Is the destruction of the forms and sensibilities of everyday human intercourse not an exhibition of raw revolutionary power, its relentless negativity and resoluteness the very antithesis of genuine freedom? ask the critics. Does the dissolving of inhibitions and defence mechanisms not leave the student vulnerable to the potential bullying tactics of the facilitator? Is it not a political paradox that students on behalf of a politics of authenticity are being forced to be free?[39]

I, too, question with suspicion the claim that a benign and spontaneous freedom is being released through values clarification. Values clarification proceeds on two highly naive assumptions. It assumes that after stripping away the political and social roles from individuals, and the everyday forms of human relationships, there will remain a substratum of emotions and feelings which are non-destructive and attuned to reality. It also assumes that the facilitator will have no motive besides that of care. Such optimism flies in the face of the evidence. An audit of what important thinkers have argued, and of the cataclysmic events they were often observing, reveals a singular human capacity for exhibiting powerfully disruptive passions – the desire for glory, the lust for domination, the longing for total satisfaction, the will's tendency to slip into weakness and despair. The thinkers and events of the past supply compelling evidence of the vital need to tame and sublimate these passions through a sound education and laws, thus forestalling their lethal impact.[40] As we saw earlier, Hannah Arendt was highly alert to the vulnerability of those who, amidst a general deprivation of concrete communities and stable political personae, were in a position to be victimized by the more powerful. And we should also recall both her and Voegelin's observation that in a general climate of perpetual mobility and dislocation, however deep the primordial 'authenticity' may be, individuals are highly susceptible to 'fictions' and 'second-realities,' through which the powerful rationalize their barbarous acts. Values clarification commits itself to a simple optimism regarding human behaviour, doing little for the protection of the weak and the restraint or education of the strong.

This problem is particularly acute, in my mind, in the facilitator/student relation, a relation modelled on the analyst/patient relationship. What is poignant about values clarification's intellectual indebtedness to Rousseau's 'natural education' is that in the treatise in which this education is presented, Rousseau leaves the reader with the uncanny realization of not only how manipulative the tutor is in achieving a 'natural education' but also of how much the relation of tutor to student flatters the desire for power of the tutor.[41] Emile, the wholly 'natural being,' is delivered from utter dependence on the tutor's sovereignty to the absolute power of his beloved, Sophie. Both the tutor and Sophie hold total control over Emile's fervent desire for unity and wholeness in so far as they hold the reins of the potent passions to which he has been reduced as a 'natural being.' His virtue is indistinguishable from their management of his being.

So, too, values clarification facilitators appear to be the prime movers causing the 'authentic self' to 'be' and thus managing the student's 'true being.' While the VC designers see the 'natural' fluidity and mobility they arouse as politically superior to the constraints of the traditional curriculum, they can provide no evidence that 'authenticity' is any less an artifice than what they claim the forms of the past to be. Moreover, it cannot be overlooked that they have produced an environment in which the student, deprived of all resistance, 'is' only at the behest of the facilitator's power to name one or another behaviour as 'inauthentic,' and in which the facilitators, unlike in all other teacher/student relationships, are the least accountable for their actions.

I would argue that VC offers the opportunity not only for regulatory control, but also for a dangerous emergence of the potent passions associated with boundless power, because of the centrality of 'authenticity' as its objective. Earlier we referred to the sheer emptiness of the self and its values, and to the fragile and vulnerable state the individual has been reduced to as a consequence. 'Authenticity' significantly contributes to this vulnerability because, by definition, it has no presence. 'Authenticity' is a resonance with some primordial being informing our existence. Leaving aside whether there is such a substratum (wholly unlike Aristotle's more sensible *dunamis* or even Rousseau's 'sweet sentiment of existence,' though akin to Nietzsche's will-to-power and Heidegger's Being) it seems to me that VC's efforts to *operationalize* authenticity, while linking it to empowerment, are where the opening for political abuse occurs. 'Authenticity' is not a presence, or a state, hidden beneath falsifying social roles, needing only some interpretive work so as to be retrieved. To the contrary, authenticity is a process of disentanglement and withdrawal. To be 'authentic' is precisely to defer the 'real self,' for authenticity works on the assumption that the dichotomy 'real' versus 'illusory' is itself a form of inauthenticity (in the language of VC it is 'judgmental'). Yet, in trying to operationalize authenticity and fuse it to empowerment, authenticity is made to stand in as the 'real.' This means, as I see it, that the 'authentic' can at best be staged, or better 'simulated,' for how can nothingness be retrieved? Simulation of authenticity is, in operation, necessarily a spiral of proliferations of simulated 'reals' as the only way of exhibiting authenticity. The simulation of authenticity is moved by an overwrought anticipation of the 'real.' This 'hyper-authentic' mode of being is, I argue, a desperate simulation of feelings intended to recapture a real which always escapes it.

Such uncertainty and repeated frustration make the values-clarifying self an obvious, and I would argue inevitable, target of the facilitators' capacities to exhibit and enhance their power. It is naive to think that the facilitators' motives would be deeper, though the truth of their actions is often covered over by a moralizing discourse of therapy and care.[42] In the absence of the 'real,' the facilitator is offered a boundless opportunity to exercise power in an unaccountable manner, disrupting and gaining control over dimensions of an individual's life previously held

inviolate by shame, honour, pride, humility, good taste, tactful indifference, and particularly sound judgment. These moderating dispositions
and virtues still held sway, albeit weakly, in AVER's portrait of conflicts
and rules and in Kohlberg's system of functions and norms, supplying a
limit to power. In VC, the absence of limit, and the riotous celebration of
what the deconstructionists identify as *différence,* in the context of operationalizing 'authenticity,' justify, I believe, the argument not only that
has VC supplied an occasion for the limitless exercise of power, but, stating this more strongly, that there is a seamless web linking the 'authentic
self' and the powerful interventions of the facilitator.

Under values clarification, I would argue, the classroom has become a
laboratory in which wilful desire is diversified and proliferated. This
control of desire occurs in two ways. There is a perceptual field in which
desire is excited and mobilized. Watching and gazing, the facilitator
monitors for any signs of apathy, flightiness, uncertainty, drifting
behaviour, and dissension. The surveillance gives positive form to a
myriad of passing moods and actions, making them measurable intensities, visible problems, and effects which can be controlled.

The classroom is also a controlled environment for what is permitted
to be enunciated. Certain things are allowed to be said and must be said,
while others must be suppressed. The flow of speech is guided, quietly,
by an authorized vocabulary and a policing of statements. Those feelings which contribute to unbending behaviour, single-mindedness, or
even trust in convention cannot be esteemed or expressed.

These forms of visibility and enunciability do not, to repeat, reflect
permanent purposes or structured potentialities. But, for being highly
fluid, they are no less the object of power and temptation, under the
guise of therapeutic self-help. Facilitating supplies a continuous regulatory and corrective mechanism. Here we have an expression, I believe,
of that modern paradox in which freedom and control increasingly reinforce one another.[43] But in the case of VC, the ambiguity surrounding
the nature of freedom under the elusive label 'authenticity,' and the glee-
ful embrace of empowerment as the vehicle for authenticity, draw our
attention less to VC's praise of freedom than to VC's use of control.

The facilitator invokes and listens to an endless stream of self-disclosures, running the gamut of feelings, moods, attitudes, thoughts, worries, anxieties, aspirations, and guilt. His task is to identify and name
these amorphous sentiments as 'values indicators,' organizing them
around the student's 'self-image,' and consolidating the values field by
encouraging self-ratings on 'self-analysis reaction worksheets.' The

facilitator has the complex role of composing the 'real me' by means of incitement and confession, while maintaining files and dossiers of student biographies and the circumstances of variously exhibited behaviour, and, at the same time, maintaining a high degree of mobility, in which the range of emotions and moods fluidly modulate within a total, living experience.

We referred to the facilitator's power to sustain a continuous regulatory and corrective mechanism. It has to be immediately added that such policing does not rest on the traditional model of power, in which authority is exercised to restrain power. Akin to Kohlberg's ability to stimulate desire and internalize authority so that the normal functions of the life process are valued, VC too has found a positive manner of gaining the student's wholesale commitment to the net of control in which it enmeshes him, so that the student sees his control, not as an exercise of force, but as a pleasure-inducing diversion. Power, in this case, gives desire new avenues of excitation, subterfuge, transgression, intensification, and, above all, pleasure. With the encouragement to profusely pursue the 'real me,' wilful desire is incited to indulge in an infinity of new permutations and scenarios. The self is not a docile, or repressed, product of the facilitator's power, but rather an active, creative pursuer of empowerment. For example, VC encourages body motions and body language. The overt actions are permitted to be deciphered in terms of latent potentialities. Inside and outside acquire a meaningful vitality and the transgressions this new vitality permits give the valuing self a feeling of expansiveness and power. Its self-disclosures have opened wholly new temptations, forms of complicity, and experiences of enchantment. Risk and violation have become pleasurable feelings and are linked to the satisfying rewards of 'self-esteem' and a 'positive self-image.'

But what is this positive enhancement of human experience? Is it free of ideological manipulation? To the contrary. Exclusively, the confessions and temptations, the seductions and the prurience, are in the service of the radical disentanglement of the individual from the world and the formation of a disposition of permanent revolution against the world. Fears and desires, moods and pleasures, which confirm in any way the trust that the world exhibits unity and proportionality, or harmony and balance, and therefore that meaning is in some way pregiven, are forced to appear as spectacles of unreason. They are formed into images so as to arouse, shock, annoy, and cause revulsion. Being thus formed, they have been flattened of their genuine depth and have been offered up as so many mere signs to be consumed by the eyes and ears. Everyday human speech, common sense, and the virtues and judgment formed through habit are disposed of as idle talk, busyness and routine, and compulsive behaviour. Against the traditional view that these forms opened us to the pregnant potentials of meaning and truth in the world, in VC they have become merely vacuous scenarios, void of any permanence or coherence. Values chatter has named them and allowed them to be revealed as arbitrary and reactive. Of all the values education models, VC is the most disruptive, its 'relentless negativity' limited by no bounds when it comes to the forms of everyday life. Those forms are dismissed as so many 'inauthentic' states of being. But VC knows how ineluctably students are naturally drawn into trusting in permanence, desiring enduringness, developing balance in judgment. These reactive modes must be continually controlled and ridiculed as reactive. Thus VC's vigorous regulatory mechanisms, which serve to keep the student in perpetual mobility, have to erase the possessive affinities of remembrance, dialectical speech, genuine love, intellectual intuition, consent to otherness, and the promptings of conscience. VC's mission is defined precisely by the need to disentangle students from these natural expressions of human longing or observance of limit. Only by a continuous management and control of the student, in which empowerment is optimalized, can the student be 'authentic.' The sensations may be ineffable, the gestures enchanted, and the interactions affective, but they are no less contrived by the facilitator. The facilitator gazes and records. The facilitator is decisive in provoking and seducing. VC's designers know too how extensive the net of control has to be: the facilitator's information sheets on which data of 'general patterns of behaviour' are recorded must be regularly updated by the observations of 'the school nurse, the student personnel services staff, [and] parents' for the 'students' permanent record folders.'[44] The discourses on feelings and values do not develop outside of or against power. The data and knowledge, the moralizing discourse of therapy and care, required to form the student's authenticity are not an alternative to power. They appear, instead, in the domain and as the means of its exercise. Power and force are not experienced punitively, since the classroom atmosphere is one of titillating release. Authenticity and empowerment reinforce one another to unite pleasure and control.

And finally we should add that the combination of these modalities of authenticity and empowerment lead to a unique contemporary outcome. In the effort to be authentic, the self is drawn into the deepest recesses of its own being. But the student's construct of reality is not restricted to his internal states of feeling. He also participates, through empowerment, in the vast contemporary array offered for his consumption. Empowered, the self is in an assertive mode of relentless negativity, but also creativity, ranging abroad amidst a global collection of available scenarios (sexuality, internationalism, environmentalism, peace, racism, sexism, machines, television, censorship, propaganda, abortion, bureaucracy, corruption, violence).[45] Values clarification produces the strange and wholly novel condition where the primordial affectivity of the imploded self confronts directly the powerful dynamics of the global environment without any mediation by the concrete historical forms of the human condition (the family, political community, or nation-state). The turn inwards in search of primal substratum comes simultaneously with a resonance in a wholly new global existence, where all events, experiences, and opinions modulate with one another. As a consequence of values clarification, the student is at one and the same time a self-absorbed monad (the dangerous condition Arendt identified as loneliness) and a bundle of reactions tied to the single membrane of the global environment.

6

The Technological Environment

It is now, at last, time to introduce the second term of my analysis. I would like to situate the discussion of the preceding three chapters – specifically my detection of those destabilizing factors which in a series form an ineluctable chain of self-overcomings culminating in the frivolous nihilism and dispossession of values clarification – against the backdrop of technology. It is not self-evident that an analysis of values education should intersect with a discussion of technology. Beyond the obvious points that certain technological advances have raised unprecedented moral dilemmas, and that successful technological development depends on skills and attitudes which appear to require new 'values,' the necessity of linking these phenomena together might appear puzzling.

Contributing to the disinclination to connect the two is the view expressed by many of today's technicians and managers that technology is nothing more than an aggregate of isolated technical apparati and that humans alone determine the use of the available techniques by purposes independently identified as important.[1] The contemporary era, according to this view, is not to be distinguished from any previous age, for it is assumed that the power to steer the world by an idea of what is good for us still lies wholly within human hands.

Contrary to this view, I want to examine technology as a phenomenon which is more than a system of mechanical apparati, and argue that it is instead a postulate concerning reality which underwrites the vast range of enterprises and justifications we characterize as modern existence. Moreover, I will argue that technology is that postulate to which we are giving our unconditional endorsement, anticipating in its successes the final meaning of our capacity to act and definitive answers to the full range of human questions. Thus, with every technological innovation we believe we are observing the full opportunity our power to act offers, and when we ask such questions as what is good? what is order? what is just? what is love? what is death? and what is freedom? technology appears to be in the process of answering all of these. Where we may have once looked elsewhere – in religion, in art, in philosophy – and while a few continue to do so in private enclaves, the construct of existence which has gained ascendancy in the modern world has either promoted a deconstruction of the forms by which these activities offered up the symbols once understood as truth, or brought about a reconstruction of those activities themselves so that they reinforce the technological imperative. And finally, I want to argue that the growing interdependence of technologies has begun to follow its own internal laws of systematization and development, and that when this phenomenon is combined with an accompanying lack of confidence that realms of human activity outside of the technological system can provide us with knowledge of the purposes and ends we ought to pursue, it is 'as if' technology has become autonomous. At that point, technology will have seriously endangered the fundamental human need to act and to ask questions.

Yet, questions concerning technology obviously do come to light in everyday experience for those who are not technicians and managers. Such questions arise in the gap between expectation and result. We all know that technology has given us, in terms of implements and productive means, powers of making and unmaking that translate into the vast alleviation of pain and suffering, the expansion and 'democratization' of a wide range of leisure pursuits, the projection of ourselves into wholly new environments like space and subatomic-particle fields, and the extension of a myriad of opportunities for more choice, involvement in decision-making, and expression of subjective freedom. But, as if to frustrate our satisfaction, technology has also given us new forms of pain and suffering, widespread boredom and social atomism, fallout zones of nuclear waste, and a severe trivialization of many human opportunities. In the space which opens between the presumption and the despair accompanying existence under the vast technological growth we have experienced, come questions awakened by the novelty of our condition. What should be made? What should be left unmade? How far do we push the frontiers of human re-engineering? How do we judge the new forms of human control? To what extent and under what circumstances do conceptions of individual responsibility still hold?

Traditionally, our moral discourses, within the contexts of our political communities and intellectual or spiritual journeys of exploration, have supplied us with answers to these questions. Can we expect the same of 'values'?

Speaking against this expectation is the novelty of our present condition. We must not ignore that our era exhibits an unprecedented convergence and interdependence of technologies as well as a growing co-dependence of political or moral understanding and technological progress. This systematization has not occurred simply overnight, but in a protracted historical struggle where accounts of knowledge, understandings of human nature, and ideas of cosmic order, supporting a scientific viewpoint external to the immanent logic of technology's momentum, have been progressively delegitimized as coherent forms of thought. This struggle, moreover, is marked by the progressive success of a singular modern desire – for the unconditioned, or for a pure experience of undetermined wholeness. Modern science in the form of technology, it can be argued, was the conjecture which allowed modern humans to experiment with the fulfilment of this desire. And with technology's growing ability to satisfy that desire, allowing that desire to expand and eclipse all others, technology acquired the formidable and paradoxical responsibility of justifying our existence in the very process of extinguishing those conditions which needed justification.

What complicates our efforts to speak of these things is the situation where our tremendous capacities to make and unmake – to make synthetic materials and radioactive waste, to unmake genetic abnormalities and species of life – bring forth forces and crises exceeding human measure, yet which also appear to be transfiguring the regulative parameters of the 'human' and the human perception of reality. Because of this impact on traditional understandings of what a human is we are having singular difficulties in comprehending technology. How can we explain a phenomenon which shapes and conditions the very categories, if not indeed our humanity itself, through which we attempt to explain it to ourselves? As George Grant once warned, 'we are apprehending our destiny by forms of thought which are themselves the very core of that destiny.'[2]

In this chapter, in setting out what distinguishes technology from technique, what form of psychic tonality accompanies technology, and how technology's development proceeds through specifiable stages, I want to demonstrate why Grant's words so succinctly go to the heart of the question of values. My aim is to depict how closely our construct of ourselves as a self who asserts values mirrors the core of technology, and thus how, in the very pocket from which we might speak of limits to technology or of resistance to its growing anti-humanism, we draw ourselves deeper into the fateful inner emptiness of technology. And, in identifying a commonalty linking technology and our values, namely the wilful desire to eclipse and escape the world of human limit and measure, nowhere more evident than in the new age of digitalized sound, computer networking, biogenetic splicing, data-environment patterning, 'virtual realities' simulation, and artificial intelligence, I want to demonstrate how technology increasingly falls under the conditions Arendt and Voegelin respectively identified as 'worldlessness' and 'gnosticism.'

Yet, at the same time, my view is that only the deepest, unfounded pessimism could lead one to the view that any phenomenon or process of the human artifice ever wholly defines human reality. The grip under which technology may hold us is, I believe, formidable. But I agree wholly with Hannah Arendt when she notes that it always 'lies within the power of human thought and action to interrupt and arrest such processes.'[3] I also agree with Eric Voegelin that, however powerful a 'second-reality' construct of truth is in denying the validity of the symbols through which our intellectual and spiritual longings are expressed, such eclipse cannot forever extinguish the human need to ask questions. I adopt their faith in human potential in so far as it is always given to human beings to act and to think. Finally, I believe that as human beings we have moral duties such as charity and, thus, I am in full agreement with Grant's comment about those intellectuals who complain of the frivolity and boredom of the technological age and who would have us somehow dismantle the achievements of the last five centuries so as to seek some other pure form of wholeness. These intellectuals overlook how technology (especially the economic and social reform under its auspices) has provided us with the opportunity of extending our moral offices to others (especially those in the non-West) as never before. 'Let none of us who live in the well-cushioned west,' Grant cautions, 'speak with an aesthetic tiredness about our "worldliness".'[4]

The Novelty of Technology

Since the sixteenth century technology has come to take a central place in our lives. This is not to deny that there were mechanical apparati and complex tools before that century. But technology is something novel, suggested by the neologism *technology* itself, a word which explicitly links *techne* with *logos*. One way of understanding this novelty is to recall Aristotle's distinction between two forms of knowledge – *techne* and *episteme* – and to reiterate the point of his distinction between *techne* and *praxis*, for these distinctions, and the metaphysic which supported them, in great part governed the direction and extent of intellectual enterprise for the eighteen centuries of our history before the emergence of technology. Aristotle understood these divisions to correspond to distinct and irreducible 'faculties' of the human psyche and, thus, to essential structures within reality itself.

Techne, he observed, is the skill employed to produce a thing. *Techne* is one type of *poesis*, or bringing forth, which is mediated by human agency. With *techne*, and the tools and procedures through which technical activity proceeds, humans aim at achieving what they cannot do unassisted. *Techne* enlarges the human repertoire. The techniques and instruments of a craft extend the human sense apparatus, or enhance capacity, or make amends for deficiencies in the nature of things.

Two points follow from how Aristotle understood *techne* as a *poesis*. First, *techne* is a situated knowledge. It is appropriate to refer to it as 'craftsmanship' because it is a know-how which is intrinsically connected to a practice. The practice composes the relation between the craftsman's skill and the things upon which he works into a constitutive relation. This is why a pure ideal of a perfectly functioning scheme of mathematic relations and proportions is anathema to the realm of *techne*. The genuine craftsman must accommodate to the variability of things since he operates in a domain where he is bringing about what need not be and what could be otherwise. The craftsman participates in bringing forth, rather than reconstructing available objects. The work of *techne* is an actualization of a potentiality seen to dwell in the matter which is being worked. It is a form of communion, rather than one of negation. The craftsman displays an openness to an inner principle which he brings forth as the shape and design of a thing.

It would be excessive to say, however, that the artisan has a raptured immediacy with the material out of which a thing is crafted. *Techne* is not enchanted magic. Technical activity has structure and is guided by rational intent. There is inner structure to material because what the craftsman sees are designs and purposes arising, not so much from the material or process of work itself, but rather from the shape or look the thing is to have. Crafting is governing, grafting *eidos* on matter. The surgeon removes what is malignant, the shipbuilder corrects and enhances the wood he forms. *Techne* is not poetry, for unlike the poet's enchanted inspiration, *techne* is guided by rule and principle. Means are directed towards ends, and ideas of purpose establish the regulative parameters of the making activity.

Second, *techne* is always a mediation between humans and nature, governed by perceptions of reality which are the context for how things appear and have a look or shape, establish how the craftsman acts with the things of his trade, and endow practices with coherence. These perceptions are not a direct result of the technique itself. They arise out of a context – culture, religion, the customary – and define the effective use of the technique. The looks and shapes that the craftsman actualizes arise from purposes which relate him to the world. Crafting is governing or steering, but the rules of technical practice arise from the practices which best illustrate human ways and human purpose.

Two distinctions follow from the principle that *techne* is a governing of the effective means to a specified end and a bringing forth of what need not be. *Techne* is distinguished from *praxis* which, as we have already seen, is the public engagement of human beings, acting and speaking with others so as to actualize the human potential and the virtues afforded by political participation. In so far as *techne* is a *poesis*, its dynamics are foreign to genuine action, although it does supply what Aristotle calls 'equipment,' the material making it possible to act.

Techne has also to be distinguished from *episteme*, the theoretical science. *Techne* is not the complete and best form of questioning and knowing. Only in theoretical science do humans pursue, not what might only be, but what always is. Since *techne* deals with what might be otherwise, there is no complete *Logos* in *techne*, a term properly reserved for the medium and object of intellectual inquiry, as the achievement of a mind attempting to apprehend the rational ground of what is itself. The search for the *Logos* is for things which are eternal and unchanging and whose possession justifies the human sense that the world displays proportionality, unity, and coherence. In short, for Aristotle, making, doing, and knowing are all distinct. Each has its own modality and, to reiterate, each reflects an irreducibly distinct dimension of human activity.

The intellectual revolutions of the early modern era severely eroded the intelligibility of Aristotle's distinctions. Where Aristotle kept *techne* and *logos* apart, thus ensuring that *techne* was judged from outside its own domain, modern science (the form of reason which would dominate and foreclose the option of rival accounts) did not accept the metaphysics which made these distinctions intelligible and made it impossible to rationally establish parameters, external to its own expansion, which could guide its growth. There are numerous ways of explaining how this came about. Alexander Koyré does so by depicting the modern scientific turn from closed world to infinite universe, which had the effect of dissolving the boundaries by which worldly phenomena had been kept distinct from one another. Hans Blumenberg points to the growing consciousness which legitimated pragmatic human self-assertion, and the accumulation of knowledge beyond the point of its contribution to human happiness or desire for salvation, as the hallmark of the epochal threshold during which Aristotle's science was overthrown. Edwin Burtt traces the shift to Newton's and then Bacon's rejection of Aristotle's depiction of a fourfold causation in nature. Their refusal to retain Aristotle's observation of formal and final causes inherent in nature (and thus design and purpose in the universe) meant that what *is* was no more than matter-in-motion. For Newton and Bacon design and purpose were not given, but were expressions of human self-assertion.[5] On either account, modern theory rejected Aristotle's division of the realms of human activity and the distinction between the finite and the infinite, or the temporal and the eternal, upon which that division rested.

This intellectual turn radically altered the meaning of truth, an alteration to which we alluded in chapter 2 when we noted Arendt's point that the modern paradigm of knowledge is characterized by the mutual action of knowing and production on one another. With the rejection of the idea that reality informs us of our substantive purposes, truth could no longer be a symbol of participation in things presumed to be unchanging and everlasting, or a consent to otherness. Questioning would no longer take its bearings from the evidence of forms of completeness and perfection, or of the structure of transcending reality, within man's personal, social, and historical existence. Human institutions and everyday practices could not be assumed to be carriers of essential facts concerning reality since they were only conventional and temporary constructs reflecting varying historical needs. The modes of human experience articulated by the ancients had to be rejected because, if the environment is structured by necessity and chance (matter in motion), as modern science seemed to show, rather than by purpose and substance, as Greek metaphysics and Christian theology maintained, then those modes were only historically contingent. This shift further entails that the understanding acquired by common sense and by the experience of intelligibility in speech, or indeed by any of the elementary forms traditionally taken as conduits to knowledge of the whole, is deprived of any serious status. The 'looks' of the world provide no insight into what most essentially *is*. The everyday has to be stripped away or reworked if genuine knowledge of reality is to be available. The expectations that the concrete conditions of our existence provide opportunity for wonder at mystery or sacred limit, or that nature's impulses contain some guidance as to the character of the human good, or that cultural and historical ways of life reveal an essential relation that humans experience within the process of reality are all increasingly superseded, seen as belonging to a prehistory of humankind's progress to technological enlightenment. Equally, the contingencies, spontaneities, and risks of everyday life are henceforth to be recognized not as the occasions of mystery, madness, or evil, and thus, inversely, affirming the primacy of the sacred, the rational, and the good, but rather as events to be subdued, pacified, and managed. Existence consists of 'problems': modern science is seen as the 'art of the soluble.'[6] Technology promises a cessation of all ambiguity and unrest, its rationalized control systems replacing the need for older modes of human experience. To become, as Descartes hopes, 'masters and possessors of nature' requires, to use Bacon's language, the 'vexing and torturing of nature,' a 'putting nature to the rack' by instruments, both cognitive and technical, which dissolve the sclerosis of wrong opinions regarding the sacredness of nature, the mysteries of existence, human purpose, and the paramount importance of the political context of our lives emanating from the ancient and medieval intellectual tradition. Instead, the new project is to conduct experiments whose product heralds a wholly new age and humanity. The principle of *verum factum* replaces receptivity to the order of being. The 'real' becomes equated with that which is more controllable and certain. Bacon and Descartes, in an effort to restore the economy of algebraic demonstration, legitimize the effort to lay waste to the everyday.[7] To 'know,' and thus to actualize man's true purpose of freedom, entails subjugating nature, and the false reality of elementary observation. The only sure route to knowledge is the radical suppression of experiences and perceptions through a method which avoids precipitant acceptance of what is given in the primary experience of personal, social, and historical forms of existence.

Whether the distrust of the concrete forms of existence was a recrudescence of gnosticism, a remainder of anti-worldliness insufficiently extinguished by Christianity, or an emerging confidence in the human ability to control, the result was that the very act of knowing became regulative and interventionist. And thus the language of science undergoes a fundamental change. Science summons 'objects' rather than receives 'otherness.' The positing of objects before subjects relies on the technical arts that are able to disturb the randomness of phenomena and order them under the constraints of the 'experiment.' The resolutive-compositive method demands reducing compounds to their discrete elements, and then reassembling them with a view to permanently overcoming their imperfection. Here theory has become 'hypothesis' and 'conjecture,' a working model whereby reality can be extracted and probed to give forth its truth. The facts of the world, as they appear in elementary experience, are now only provisional. Truth is nothing but the controlled aspect of being. There is to our will-to-knowledge, moreover, an escalating dependence on control. As we disrupt what is first and foremost, a suspicion lingers that the conditions under which knowledge is being acquired themselves contaminate what is coming to be known. Science must recurringly subject its own constructs, its laboratory environment, and its instruments to interrogation. With each successive intervention, knowing comes to rely more heavily on making. The *logos* depends on *techne* and *techne* constitutes the essence of *logos*, or as George Grant says with customary economy, knowing and making have wholly co-penetrated.

At the core of the knowing activity, and in the intrascientific statement of human purpose, emerges the imperative of reconstructing ambivalence and disorder. Now, the craftsman of the past also had a tendency to instrumentalize the world, to break things down, both mechanical and natural, and rebuild them or find ways of simulating their movements. But in his actions there was little of the will-to-mastery that optimalizes each of the elements, so that in reconstruction the thing displays not only the teleological purpose already inherent in it, but a new ideal of a perfectly logical schema of relations and proportions. Traditional *techne* restrains the will to reconstruct because it is regulated by the constraints and imperfections of the natural or historical contexts in which it is employed. What distinguishes *technology* is the will to reconstruct the personal, social, and historical contexts in which the making activity occurs.

Understanding technology as reality-reconstruction is inherent in the self-consciousness accompanying modern science. The quandary of modern science, as it grasps the full significance of its dependence on technology, is that perhaps the scientist only has come to know the 'reality' he has altered or to which he has given temporary permanence with his own machines. The Heisenberg challenge – that what we know under modern science is confined to the constructs and position of the observer – leaves us with the uncomfortable realization that science, rather than uncovering reality, in fact makes reality. One cannot deny that the construct of reality we employ gives rise to innumerable practical uses, in other words, that it can be made to work. But if knowledge rests primarily on the success of its application, and the widespread effectiveness simply reveals how readily we can apply the contents of our own minds, we are left with Bacon's observation that, in fact, knowledge is but power.[8] The regularities and laws modern science discovers, the algebraic proportions and relations it takes to belong to existence, are indissolubly linked to the constraints under which the 'experiment' places reality. Scientists direct their inquiries to what are purportedly their 'objects' but by interventions that are, in fact, the condition of possibility for those objects.

Descartes's method, whose imperative of world-denial and world-reconstruction is a vital step leading to the distinctive character of technology, is important for another feature. His is a method that demands universality and homogeneity not only because Descartes and his successors understood the method to be applicable transculturally and to all fields of study, or only because they counted on its consistency to guarantee unanimity and thus the elimination of diversity and particularity, but because it assumes a reality that is essentially unidimensional, clear and simple, its parts equally commensurable with one another, and to which the changing rhythms of human ways do not effectively contribute anything substantial.

A construct of reality which adopts universality as the predominant factor, and which finds proof of universality through that reconstructive activity by which technology is so successful, legitimates a process of world mastery which is not complete until the world is a single, efficient system. This is how technology has come to mean the 'systematic' deployment of instruments, procedures, and skills under 'organized' rules to achieve the effect of optimal 'efficiency.' 'System' suggests a process of growing interdependence of controlled environments whereby single components are 'rationalized,' thereby rendered equivalent and substitutable. Industrial, social, cultural, and psychological phenomena are ordered into subsystems and installed within an interdependent web. Separate and distinctive techniques tend to integrate and function within continuous processes. The emergence of multinational production cooperatives and information networks points to a correlation of manifold technologies so that they function according to overall processes of development internal to the system itself. All systems function by the process of 'dynamic disequilibrium': as long as they continue to be challenged by countervailing tendencies and by margins of indetermination they are vital, for the system's strength is measured by its capacity to grow in power by isolating and neutralizing dysfunction and assimilating intruding forces. Once that challenging forth ends, they become inefficient.[9] Thus, such systems are expansionary; to avoid profound internal dissonance, a system, coming up against other systems, will enhance itself by competition and then incorporate these or demand their realignment in conformity with its own logic. 'Organization' refers to the progressive deployment of a single logic of abstraction, optimization, and idealized reconstruction at every level to maximize the management of information. The conjunction of systematization and organization universalizes all internal processes to a single logic and then expands the system to incorporate other ensembles. Once systematization and organization proceed together, and maintain the dynamic self-modification of recurring innovation, technology progressively displays a single *efficiency*. 'Efficiency' is the process whereby the plurality of ends and means is reduced to one system of means – the most efficient.

The novelty of technology does not stop there. Technology makes it possible not only to push the parameters of reality ever further away but to remake reality and then to cause its own manipulative intervention to, in effect, disappear. Technology's infinite plasticity and power of creation are only perfected when its interferences with reality become invisible, leaving its programmers and users with the impression that there is no gap between reality and their idea of it. From the point of view of its own internal regulative principles, technology's greatest achievement is transparency. Reality and 'virtual-reality' then are one and the same. This is where the simulation and optimization of reality characterizing technology join together with the uniquely modern desire for the wholly unconditioned, only now being progressively actualized in the contemporary era. Throughout modernity, the longing to break from the restraints of reality has driven our understanding of freedom. The final stage of that desire is the reduction of reality to language alone, specifically, as the post-structuralist would have it, the dispersal of reality into *différance*, a free play of signifiers in which there is no remnant of the grammar and logic which to the present day has been taken to represent the inherent structure of reality. Technology offers the opportunity to directly experience the free happening of decentred poststructuralism, with its infinitude of possible worlds, processing anything that has ever happened or ever could happen in a self-moving feast of production and consumption. Information 'superhighways' provide the vehicle to realize the dream of non-reifying practices and desubjectivized environments. No analytically and politically stable conception of limit remains. As the technological system is refined, transparency is revealed as the *telos* of efficiency and as the means of realizing this desire for the unconditioned. The technology to which we increasingly tie our most fervent hopes promises us permanent release from the 'sloppiness' of existence. We can have both the absolute power to re-create the order of existence by simulating it and freedom from the disappointment that accompanies the loss of immediacy with reality characterizing the production of substitutes. A transparent technology gives us perfect control – absolute power without consciousness of having mediated reality. Technology has made it possible to separate potentiality from actuality and attribute to potentiality the possibility of perfection, as if the actuality was no longer a limiting and regulating factor. The ideal of total rationalized control is realized in transparency: a recaptured immediacy which, like the first act of divine creation, needed only the Word and divine thought to make the world. At the core of technology is the desire, then, to make the world over and over so as to experience absolute power over reality.[10]

From particle-laser weaponry, time-resolved holography, genetic imprinting, superconductor technology, and chemical-based microprocessing, to cyber-punk, Disney World, and virtual-reality, we are participating in a momentum which is producing the desubjectivized environment dreamed of by those in whom the longing for the unconditioned reaches its consummate expression, namely the 'post-moderns.' Technology and contemporary self-interpretation cooperate in eliminating the human subject, whose longings and needs sustained modernity for three centuries with ideas of autonomy, individual responsibility, and personal merit. Technology coincides with these powerfully disruptive contemporary philosophic movements by dispersing the modern subject while refusing standing to any substantial aspect of humanity. Disrupting not only the sober modern idea of the individual, and the political institutions and practices which guaranteed common sense, decency, and protection for individuals, the post-modern push aims at breaking all the constraints of the old grammar and reasoning which gave stability and unity to the modern person. Our recent advances in technology eschew the 'human,' seeing individuals as encumbrances to the goal of transparency at least until such point as the complications arising from their worldly concreteness is utterly extinguished. This inanition of our incarnate being occurs when humans are seen as nothing more than translucent pure will, as mere registers of the technological environment, summoned forth within 'scenarios' or 'perspectives,' and subjected thereby to the multiple regulatory mechanisms of the system. When we see ourselves finally only as accidental episodes within the free play of the technological system – and this we do when we contract the reality of our existence to a minimal self whose sole impulse is affectivity – 'man' is fully enmeshed in the system. When technology has become utterly transparent, humans themselves have been absorbed into technology.

This systematization and rationalization of all the dimensions of reality, where even the characteristically human experiences are either assimilated in, or simply denied public significance by, the dominant discourse accompanying technology, leads Jacques Ellul to define technology as 'the totality of methods rationally arrived at and having absolute efficiency (for a given stage of development) in every field of human activity.'[11] Langdon Winner, agreeing with Ellul, writes that modern society displays a nearly total assimilation in the logic of technology, a 'reverse adaptation' where there is a total 'adjustment of human ends to match the character of the available means,' so that none of the traditional purposes remain intact.[12]

Ellul's seminal analysis of technological society was written thirty years ago. Twenty years later he wrote a second study arguing that the era in which the phenomenon 'technology' could be seen as merely a qualification of what we have traditionally understood as 'society' had ended. The present age, he now argues, is a 'technological system,' a condition in which the processes which had eroded the autonomy of social interest and social need are perfected and 'society' disappears. Ellul's point is that human resistance to technology has been nearly entirely co-opted.

Ellul's analysis focused on technology's two major characteristics: rationality and artificiality. The former refers to the process by which all phenomena are reduced to their logical dimension alone: 'every intervention of technique is, in effect, a reduction of facts, forces, phenomena, means and instruments to the schema of logic.'[13] The latter aspect refers to the destruction, subordination, even elimination of the natural world, where technology 'does not allow this world to restore itself or even to enter into a symbiotic relation with it.' Once technology establishes its laws of development the human environment comes to include fewer and fewer natural things. The combination of rationality and artificiality, in turn, generates technology's automatism, self-augmentation, monism, universalism, and autonomy.

The progressive rationalization of the world, and the production of an artificial, technical milieu, Ellul challenges, lead to a situation where technology has become automatic, for the 'prime aspect' of automatism is that technology itself 'selects among the means to be employed. The human being is no longer in any sense the agent of choice.' Technologies are applied because of choices 'induced by previous technologies,' as if 'the technological phenomenon contained some force of progression that makes it move independently.'[14] Such progression 'self-augments' because 'every technological apparatus, when discovered or about to be discovered, is (or will be) necessarily useful. At no time does man forgo using a technological apparatus.'[15] If a new technology increases productivity, yield, or control, it will inevitably be deployed, even where there are costs in other sectors. In fact, such costs make it possible for the technological system to augment itself with new reparative or risk-management technologies, thus preserving and enhancing its overall power. The increasing mutual interdependence of all components within the technological system implies their mutual action on one another. With a shift in one, all others must coordinate their movements, thus exhibiting technology's dynamic of spontaneous adjustment, or what Ellul terms 'accelerated progression,' by perpetual renewal. Such renewal will automatically aim, he suggests, to achieve 'the one best way' – the reduction of all ends to one, namely efficiency. This 'monism,' Ellul argues, is inevitable. The technological system is inevitably universalizing because the operational efficiency of any one unit depends on a symmetry with its entire environment. As equipment, operational technologies, and organizational subsystems are linked up to make each maximally effective, the environment automatically expands and becomes all-inclusive.

The most fervent hope of that early modern liberal tradition which embraced this universalizing tendency of modern industry was for the emergence of a comity of humankind, a community of cooperative beings living under a regime that, having freed it from the drudgery of work and the onerousness of old repressive political hierarchies, has thereby satisfied the human desire for freedom and knowledge. But, Ellul argues, what more than anything distinguishes the resulting 'system' is its 'absence of finality': the continuous exchanges and recurring renewals which belong to its dynamic of spontaneous self-adjustment and self-augmentation mean that all human purposes and ends, those once taken to be of intrinsic worth and inherent value, are deprived of their autonomy and absorbed into a process of 'revolving functionalities' which exhibits its own causality.[16] Freedom is reduced to choosing the objects the technological system exudes, and the accumulation of knowledge has been freed of the limits imposed on it by humanism, the anthropolitical principle that knowledge must serve human need. It is only then, Ellul observes, that technology seems to be 'autonomous.' It has been freed from the measures of concrete existence. It is a process exhibiting an entirely self-moving and relentless resolve of purposiveness without purpose. Ellul argues that the technological system which has emerged in no way merely affirms the power of humans to free themselves from what conditions them. To the contrary, the technological system 'performs unintentionally':

it produces a new kind of objectification which has nothing to do with Hegel's: it is no longer an objectification of the subject, and does not enter a subject-object dialectic. Now, anything that is incorporated, or seized, is treated as an object by the active system, which cannot develop or perform without acting upon a set of elements that have previously been rendered neutral and passive. Nothing can have an intrinsic sense; it is given meaning only by technological application. Nothing can lay claim to action; it is acted upon by technological process. Nothing can regard itself as autonomous; it is the technological system that is autonomous.[17]

Ellul's thesis has been denounced as fantastic and fatalistic. Such denunciation, however, follows, I would argue, from a distorted reading of Ellul's work. Ellul is not demonizing technology as if it were a Frankenstein or Golem, which in having become a force of its own making has broken free and acquired its own external existence and now legislates human ways. Nor is Ellul denying that the human capacity for spontaneity and transcendence remains. Ellul does not say that the 'reality' of the technological system now exhausts the full range of human possibility, that it has closed off all other forms of participation in the process of reality. He realizes that were he to be saying these things, he could be accused of displaying the symptoms of the very totalizing phenomenon he is analysing.[18]

Ellul is simply pointing to the implications which follow from the dominant paradigms and constructs of contemporary life. If what we

know is within a paradigm that cannot dissociate reason from techni-
cized production and that insists on destroying predicative reasoning
and 'centred' logic in every realm of human doing, and if, as a consequence, we find ourselves surrounded by a system of 'revolving functionalities' where nothing has intrinsic worth, finality, or is a vehicle for
our transcendence, and which simultaneously reduces the 'human' to
simply pure will, then it is 'as if' technology is 'autonomous' and
humans mere instruments, or perhaps error deviations, within the process. Ellul is saying that mathematical operationalism and technological
activism have the potential to be profoundly 'anti-humanistic.' Proceeding from the perspective of a universal 'Archimedean point' and thus
oblivious to what is 'first and foremost' for concrete human beings, technology finally reduces man to just one element within an indifferent
process whose dynamic bears less and less relation to the human sense
of proportion. Individual responsibility and judgment, common sense,
the desires once expressed through politics and our intellectual longings, all of which together constituted a matrix in which moral decency
arises, are so effectively diverted from their natural object as to be extinguished in force.

From Will to Will-to-power

Technology is not only an epistemological construct. It is at the same
time a specific tonality of the human psyche within the process of reality.
Unlike us, the Israelites, Greeks, and Christians had a relation to Being
in which they witnessed, receptively, in reverence and wonder, and
with a sense of mystery, open, as Heidegger remarks, to the 'pregnant
structures' of possibility at the source of all beings. Modern human
beings express their perception of reality under the sign of the will. This
is as evident in the modes of making and controlling by which we affirm
our freedom as it is present in the declarations of rationality by which
we announce our self-consciousness. To use Heidegger's terms, humans
no longer resonate with the possibilities of Being by 'bringing forth' its
rhythms but rather exhibit themselves in 'challenging forth' beings. That
exhibition has a tone of defiance which runs in opposition to reverence,
obedience, and commemoration. The experience of absolute power no
longer humbles but emboldens us.

Before we examine how seeing ourselves as willing beings reinforces
the technological imperative, and in the interest of giving a balanced
assessment of the consequences of seeing human activity under the sign

of the will, we must immediately remember that this tonality has its origins in an account of our humanity which attempted to hold together obedience and volition, and which saw humanity's proper purpose achieved when the will's resistance and defiance were educated to form assent to reality. The Stoic and Christian account of the will, to which we have already referred, historically sets up a vital and positive image of our humanity, many elements of which we continue to find attractive. For both Stoic and Christian the will was the source of our active power, that volitional component of our being which defined our singularity and freedom as much as our capacity to command and legislate. The will is the hallmark of a being who truly exercises choice. Without the understanding of ourselves as will, there could be no genuine human uniqueness or the distinctive self-enhancement we understand as moral autonomy.

But the will for both the Stoic and the Christian was less an answer to the questions 'what is the human good?' and 'what is human order?' than the context in which these questions are posed. When the slave Epictetus realized that he could will a subjectively certain world where he had no master but himself, he signalled the ease with which volition alone could transpose the concrete circumstances of the world into internal impressions. Such formidable power impressed not only the Stoic but also the Christian for in it lay not only the opportunity for moral fortitude but also the danger of a will so overly pleased by its negating action that it is inclined to dominate not only over others but even to deny reality itself. In the will's power to will the world anew lay not only the reasonable desire for renewal of the world's depleted forms but the passion for destruction, the 'relentless negativity' Giroux and others find so attractive.

Christianity's view of the destructiveness of the will is particularly important for, having made the isolated Stoic philosopher's thought-experiment the general condition of humankind, it cast its impression more deeply into Western consciousness.[19] St Augustine's *Confessions* are paradigmatic in this case, testifying with tremulous emotion to the ambiguities in the natural motions of the unique will. These motions reflect the struggles of a fallen nature which is driven to confront a loving, though demanding, God. The Christian understanding of the will is more pessimistic concerning successfully linking volition and obedience. Under Christianity, humanity came to see itself as in a ceaseless struggle to know God. That struggle was ambiguous, interwoven with the strongest counter-impulses towards pride, domination, and private fantasy. Command and obedience, intractability and relinquishment – these, rather than wondrous receptivity to truth, characterize the Christian's experience of reality. The Christian still seeks a transcendent truth, but now the subjective defiance and the labours of the human will are integral components of that search.

On the one hand, the recognition of such struggles means the important discovery by Christianity of the spiritual singularity of persons, to which our idea of the individual is still indebted. On the other hand, Christian participation in the divine/human encounter becomes considerably more complex than its Greek predecessor: the will is forever on the brink of sliding towards solipsism and unorthodoxy. Why is this so?

St Paul, as we have already noted, discovers his will not in its dynamic legislating mode but as impotence: 'for to will is present with me; but how to perform that which is good I find not.'[20] That impotence, however, is broken by the eruption of the acting will. Human freedom appears as an exhibition of a force tied to no necessity.

That wilful exhibition of freedom was, as Augustine knew, ambiguous. Commanded by reason, or more commonly freed by grace, will assents to the order of reality, even endowing that assent with moral approval. The virtues of faith, hope, and charity are symbols of will's receptivity to being. That they are chosen freely reveals the spiritual intention behind them. Left to its own motions, however, the will, which loves its own power, isolates itself from reality and from the comity of mankind that exists through mankind's common spiritual participation in reality. The will thus forgets its dependence on the existing order. Ultimately, it may seek to dominate reality, accepting for its direction no cause or purpose, outside those emanating from its own motions. It may attempt to dominate created being; it will believe itself to be self-sufficient, to have the power of divine creativity.

How does this derailment occur? The dynamic which ends in such derailment lies within the will itself. The will, as Augustine makes clear in his *On Free Choice of the Will*, is self-causing: 'For either the will is its own cause or it is not a will.' Of all human faculties it is the only one that is self-creating, that owes its cause to nothing either internal or external to the human being. As it rests on no grounds outside of itself, the will is guided by nothing that draws it. The answer is simple: the will simply wills to will. 'For the will,' Augustine writes, 'commands that there be a will, it commands not something else but itself.'[21] The will accepts no constraint from the past. It does not bind itself to commitments in the present, or to the future. The will is a will-to-will and as such disavows anything which impedes it. Its power denies limits whether those are conditions of actual existence or are forms of completeness to its own activity. The will is the vehicle of the human desire for the unconditioned.

From the point of view of the individual, the experience of power and control of freedom from determination and limit is one of great exhilaration. This excess of life, however, also carries forward the extravagance of destruction. As Nietzsche would remark, the will 'would rather will nothingness than not will.' This destruction exhibits itself most acutely in what endures. The will's motions against the complete and perfect, its *telos* of more power to itself, and its modality as a future-oriented force underwrite an image of human excellence in opposition to accounts of the human which focus on the thinking remembrance of things eternal or past, and which see the human task to be that of forming a loving union with the structure of what is. For Augustine the turbulence and solipsism integral to the will are finally self-destructive even though the will does not come to this conclusion on its own. Its motions are finally arrested only by the intervention of an experience wholly external to it: love. Only love brooks the conflict and equivocation within the will. Love does not arise spontaneously in man's heart. As Augustine makes clear, were it not for the unmerited and unanticipated advent of grace, the *libido dominandi* would not be restored to the order of being.

So potent a faculty was the will that Christianity designed a formidable education to curb its destructive capacities. If the will's love of the unconditioned was not educated to the reality of otherness, a lesson reinforced by guilt and fear of eternal damnation, and if the will was not brought to will virtue, human assertion could become a passion for destruction. Christianity combated this danger by rigorously suppressing and sublimating the desires, bringing the will to exercise its power of command on behalf of moral freedom. Without linking volition and obedience, the Christian realized there could be none of those forms characterizing our humanity – respect for the dignity of the person, observance of the sacredness of existence, charity towards and forgiveness of human weakness, the cultivation of humility and patience – nor the moral robustness needed to walk the fragile line between despair and presumption.

The Christian era precedes by many centuries that age which would devote the preponderant part of its intellectual and material resources to technological mastery. Yet, Christianity sets in place the powerful dynamic which culminates in technological consciousness. This is so for two reasons. First, in Christianity the idea of nature, as an orderly whole displaying rhythms which reason might understand, is radically demoted. The doctrines of Creation, the Fall, and the Incarnation express the subordination of human and non-human nature to divine power. Nature is now contingent on God's will, and its rhythms (such as they are when subject to miraculous intervention) do not display an order which reveals to humans the working of divine reason. In the absence of direction available from nature as to how humans should see their true purposes, God becomes humankind's supreme focus since only his grace can redeem fallen nature. And in this relation, too, the demotion of nature is reinforced, for humans cannot consult their natural longings or natural reason in hopes of discovering signs of divine favour, for God's will and love is inscrutable. Moreover, the gift of grace cannot be earned, for God is not subject to the most evident and sensible principle of justice, namely that of reciprocity. With charity replacing justice as the paramount act of love, human and divine reason part company, losing that distinctive mediation central to Plato and Aristotle – the natural order. Even with the brief re-emergence of respect for nature in the Thomist idea of created order, and the re-establishment of a teaching of virtues based on the education of natural longing, the supreme virtues are theological rather than natural ones, owing their formation to divine grace and not natural longing. Nature has very little standing for Christianity and even if Christians are to see themselves as stewards in God's creation, their stewardship is an indenture to God rather than to nature.

Second, if humans are made in God's image and if God's character is best revealed in his creative and triumphant powers, as Genesis informs believers, and if God's offer to humans to join him in creating order by naming all living things reflects his genuine desire to permit humans to exercise their powers, then it is appropriate for humans to see themselves as willing and legislating beings. When humans are given co-creative responsibilities to be exercised in the fashion of God's creation *ex nihilo*, their power to command and rework is given free licence. Even obedience to divine power, in which human freedom is intended to culminate, exhibits at its core an assertive volitional element, for the will is engaged not merely in turning the spirit around (as in the Greek *periagoge*) but in renunciating the flesh and imposing unconditional imperatives upon its own activity. This dynamic of conflict and rule occurs precisely because the will in its unreformed mode is not receptive to limits on its relentless negativity. Awareness of the baleful consequences for social order and human salvation of this truculence is what underlies the extensive cultivation of moral forms in Christian education.

When the forms upon which this education are based were deconstructed, as they were in early modernity and continue to be in our times, we enter the period when we see ourselves as pure will and autonomous. The will's love of the unconditioned is now released with impunity. The release of the will from restraint and sublimation coincided with the unprecedented growth of man's making capacities. The will's free activity supports the technological model where knowing and making co-penetrate. The will has been released from traditional fealty to the order of existence. Its natural tendency of self-overcoming is now reflected in its subduing and mastering all that conditions it. The empowerment of humans as pure will is based on an image of humanity extricated from all determinate characteristics – either those arising from their natural attributes or those acquired from historical conditions. When a being's worth is based on the will's capacity to defy nature, and thus all conditions and purposes outside it, and this coincides with an image of the world's phenomena which has reduced them to mathematical proportions, the technological imperative has been fully internalized.

But the full power of the will to command and legislate to reality, 'laying waste' to all that is, as Heidegger would say, is exhibited only when the individual acts of technical control and mastery are coordinated and integrated and are seen as events in a sequential process called 'history.' Once the historical drama is seen as a succession of human will-acts wholly under the authorship of human control, and as a means of systematizing the technical achievements of the human will, a process has begun in which the cumulative effect of such organization is for growth and expansion to become wholly self-justifying. The idea of 'History' is the consequence of focusing on man's power to act and to control the future. The willing will now overreaches its own local activities and contributes to an overall effect. Its self-causing motion exceeds the constraint of individual intention: to will is to activate forces which eventually dissolve the singularity of the willing being into general processes. Moreover, the will's love of the unconditioned can now achieve unprecedented satisfaction because the coordination of technical forces permits an exhaustive control over all of existence. 'History' still confines these forces to a script – the process called 'progress.' When history replaces nature or providential plan as the enabling context of human doing and thinking, then the restless will-to-will is given a schedule and itinerary: the progressive march of history towards the achievement of immanent perfection. Successive will-acts now have a purpose and a timetable, and achievement is measured by the extent to which every facet of existence can be brought within the growing interdependent system.[22] The register of man's will-acts has a *telos* and a structure of development.

Hegel, as Voegelin argues, transforms that enterprise into a philosophic system.[23] Both liberalism and socialism, the two great ideologies of the modern era, acquired coherence in their indebtedness to the Hegelian system, and in both ideologies the ability to coordinate and systematize humankind's technical achievements is paramount. Humanity's highest purpose is tied to the progressive, coordinated mastery and control of all facets of existence for the sake of efficiency. Rationality is redefined to mean precisely establishing a single, integrative logic of universality and homogeneity in the political, social, and technical spheres. Integral to such systematization is the mastery and rationalization of both human and non-human nature. The particular now only has relevance within the general process which is unfolding towards maximum interdependence of all parts. The will's assertive negations are steered by a science which anticipates a future of pure efficiency. Faith in this historical script, like faith in the providential plan, stabilizes the self-overcoming of a human's will, humanizing and civilizing the potent passions of mastery emancipated when the transcendent order of being was spurned.

Such faith, every bit as much as Christian faith and Greek trust in eternal truths, as the major spokesmen of historical progress knew, does not arise spontaneously. No better example of the argument for the centrality of an education which tempers the aggressive dimension of human autonomy and love of the unconditioned and ensures the overall beneficent effects of system integration can be offered than that found in Hegel's educational writings. Hegel understood the corrosive impact of a will which asserts itself against natural, hereditary, and customary limitations. He knew that the political regime of mutual respect achieved in the march of history could only be maintained with an education which resituated the isolated individual of modernity within more integrative subsystems. Such an education, if it was to prevent the fragmentation of humanity into solitary producers and consumers and if it was to cultivate intellectual independence in a society prone to the tyranny of public opinion, had to free students from present social and vocational urgencies and form their inner personality, 'the essential inwardness which is the matter of self-control and self-possession.' The achievement to which history had brought humanity, by the dialectic of negation, would be lost if modern society could not now hold in check the relentless negativity by which freedom and rationality had been won and which exhibited themselves so remarkably in the imperatives of capitalism and modern technology.[24]

But why should the relentless negativity of the will not explode the bounds of the historical script? Is the assumption of a historical script not merely an artifice arbitrarily construed to deflate the vitality of life, its capacity for perpetual self-destruction and self-creation? Indeed, to go further, is not even the instantiation of the power of the will in the subject not merely a temporary episode of a deeper, pre-human primordial genesis? Then, is not the lesson of history, and the various variations of historical development, precisely the continual and unending self-overcoming of the will beyond itself, and should this process not be completed by renouncing the last constraints, those of the will as agent of history, as subject, and as value?[25] *Incipit Nietzsche.*

The full sense of the will-to-will's passion for limitless destruction beyond simple ennui with worldly forms, and thus its ability to break free from those projects of renewal and redemption to which Christianity and early modernity had harnessed it, is wholly understood first by Nietzsche. In Nietzsche's thought we see the true meaning of the 'relentless negativity' which Giroux and others find so exhilarating. Nietzsche takes the love for the unconditioned to its logical conclusion, arguing that the myth of the human will is merely a fiction played out by a subterranean force he called 'will-to-power.' It is Nietzsche who teaches us that our century alone will come to understand the fate which lies in seeing ourselves as pure will, for our age would finally grasp its being within the dynamic activity of the 'will-to-power.'

It is the nature of 'will,' Nietzsche explains, to express itself as command and obedience. Will is power and thus by nature expansionary: 'Power,' he writes, 'exists only in so far as its power increases and in so far as the will commands this increase.'[26] Nietzsche draws out the inexorable consequences which follow from permitting the will to rise to paramount status. Once the will is released from submission to divine power, nature's limits, or the past, as it inevitably must be, then the residual fiction that the will resides in human nature and is the instrument by which humankind preserves and enhances itself also evaporates, revealing that acts of the will are not the foundational source of human measure and legislation but temporary stations for further exercises of power. The will's continuous self-overreaching finally consumes the substantive bases from which that activity originated. The result is the will's subsumption in a vitality of which it is not the author. The will by its own activity is brought to sense its own actuation by the egoless effervescent genesis of primordial life itself.

Nietzsche describes the 'will-to-power' as unrelenting negativity. Fixed ends, stable meanings, and limiting boundaries are processed and transfigured, dispersed in a continual process of displacement, transference, and creation. Power begets more power, within cyclical motions of creation and disintegration. Space is no longer that uniform, continuous, and visual location which humans invest with meaning to create 'places,' for the will-to-power is like a field of electric circuitry where events are only discontinuous constellations of ever-transforming instances. The perpetual metamorphosis of such a field makes arbitrary those all-too-human categorizations of simple/complex, normal/abnormal, pure/tainted, intact/fragmented, standard/irregular because there is no longer any substantive form, or instantiation or individuated being, legitimating the distinctions.

The total release of the will-to-power also necessitates a major transfiguration in ideas of time. Nietzsche proposes to identify the new consciousness of time as 'eternal recurrence.' Time is no longer history, as it was conceived since Herodotus and Thucydides. Nothing of Newton's absolute, continuous flowing time remains, nor is the new conception of 'time' distinct from 'space.' To the contrary, there is what would be like an implosion of linear time and continuous space into a field of active tension. Time is deprived of its universal and homogeneous character, its continuity, and its irreversibility. Its coordinates are revealed to be relative to the reference system in which they are experienced. Position and succession no longer serve as orienting points. The thought of the eternal recurrence is an attempt to think outside of change reducible to sequentially ordered, graduated, spatialized arrangements and outside of the idea that time is irreversible. Such time is also no longer subject to the causality which posits one instance immediately before another. Eternal recurrence signifies an instantaneous present always being renewed. Nietzsche called this escape from the tyranny of time 'the innocence of becoming.' The eternal instant of the 'present' cannot be tinged with regret, vain hope, or condemnation because time's 'it was' is no longer. What is relinquished is the once and for all. Time is dispossessed of beginning, purpose, or goal. Time need not elapse nor need there be intervals between events. Moments manifest themselves now simply as active or reactive intensities. Within this affectivity, instances now become multiple phenomena, inhabiting an infinitude of realities, arbitrary effects of the forces which episodically constitute them.

Nietzsche's transvaluation of reality by a widespread fragmentation of all our traditional reference points is articulated in arch metaphor. Once human perspective is taken away, language becomes a bewildering array of floating signs. But Nietzsche understood the new perceptions of reality to which he wished to enjoin us under the terms 'will-to-power' and 'eternal recurrence' to be thought-experiments, valuable less for their truth about the physical world than for their ability to elicit maximal creative willing. Once our perspective shifts as if self and non-self no longer confront one another across the distance of space, once the orders of here and now, this and that, no longer stabilize our will to will, and there is simply a perpetual metamorphosis of expansion and contraction of the will-to-power, a new lease on existence will have begun.

Many of Nietzsche's enthusiastic epigones, while approving the dissolution of all barriers to our desire for the unconditioned, also acknowledge the meaninglessness of the new world to which Nietzsche pointed us: 'every unique and singular centre disappears and with that disappearance, all hierarchical judgment and comprehension becomes impossible ... Now all transcendent centres pass into total immanence, and "centre" as such ceases to be either singular or distinct. Therefore, real distinction becomes impossible; no longer is it possible to apprehend boundaries between things, to know a "this" which is "other" than a "that."'[27] And thus: 'When all things are firmly bound together, no lines or limits are possible, and all things spontaneously or immediately flow into each other. Now everything is a centre, is *the* centre, because the centre is everywhere. God as the centre that is everywhere? Yes, but only when God is dead, only when the negation of his sovereignty and transcendence invests every point and moment with the totality of Being.'[28]

Whether or not this is a type of existence understandable in any human way, the important thing about Nietzsche's analysis is that he shows this all to be inherent in the idea of humans as 'will.' Our destiny is to suffer the consequences which follow when everything is brought out which had been entailed once humans began to understand themselves as mastering and overcoming all determinateness and approved those acts of striving to fulfil absolutely the desire for the unconditioned. The destiny of that choice has, according to Nietzsche, produced a relentless overreaching in which humans themselves are now wholly delivered over to the will towards more will. Our spontaneous acting from a detached point of origin, which defined our earliest exhibitions of our capacity to will, has become the simultaneity of all existence in a resonating field. Humans, who understood since the birth of modernity the process of ordering or 'enframing' things so they would be useful and at hand as 'standing-reserve,' now are themselves used and at hand, ordered and reordered by the will-to-power. Humankind is irrevocably caught within the networks and relations, strange fusions and pointless images.

Nietzsche exhibits a morbid fascination with the detritus of civilization achievements left over once this deconstruction has firmly transfigured the traditional understanding of reality. Truth, law, right, justice, inner experience, and community – all of which had once symbolized human participation in the movement of being – are now, after the 'death of God' and 'death of Man,' as well as the 'murder' of all the master scripts explaining human existence, merely transitional episodes within the infinite displacement and metamorphosis of life's contingent forces. Nietzsche foresaw that without the humanist centre which had ordered existence in the past, all the traditional forms of politics and culture would be swept into a vast gyre of devastation, forgetfulness, riotous play, and eclecticism, played out in the technological domain. As well, our age, he realized, would be permeated by 'the smell ... of the divine decomposition,' that is, the putrid aroma of reactivated fragments desperately plundered from the decayed gods.[29] Humankind's disappearance into the effervescence of the will-to-power might, he thought, lead to greatness and new forms of creativity, but it was as likely that it would lead to cynicism and boredom and end with the whole earth inhabited by despicable 'last men.'

Now even Nietzsche still recognized the need of genuine education to prevent this. In the *Use and Abuse of History* and *Schopenhauer as Educator* he recognizes how dangerous the boredom and futility accompanying the human will can be. He despairs of the loss of distinction between higher and lower and of the atrophy of culture in its wake. But, at the same time, Nietzsche's enthusiasm for relentless negativity and the unrestrained love of the unconditioned retains the upper hand in his writings. Nietzsche leaves us with the uncertain legacy where as modern beings we are distraught over the flat drabness of modern existence and yet can establish no limits or parameters to contain the lethal corrosiveness at its core. And thus Nietzsche leaves our age with no reason to refuse, and many reasons for embracing, the radical self-overcoming which wills the dynamic willing of technology, a relentless purposiveness without overriding purpose.

Phases of Technological Intervention:
From Mechanical to Organic to Electric

No historical process is structured by invariant stages or moves towards completion. Philosophies of history are the sorts of metaphysical dogmas with which thorough philosophical analysis in the twentieth century has happily dispensed. But the reality of our power to organize and systematize, thereby promoting a single construct of reality through the explicit creation of forms of laws, institutions, and education, and through encouraging certain types of knowledge while prohibiting others, cannot be denied either.

All societies have regimes of truth – public discourses explicitly legitimated by elites and tacitly reinforced by our conformity to society's dominant images. Since the sixteenth century, as I have argued, technology has come to dominate as the discourse by which we have legitimated our enterprises. But the terms of that discourse have changed over time and within different spheres of human existence, conforming to shifts in the modalities of coordination and integration as technological apparati grew increasingly interdependent and were systematized. The laws of development of such growth can be tracked empirically as new forms of organization succeeded in enhancing efficiency. I do not intend to review this empirical evidence, but I would like to propose that a historical examination of technological expansion over the last four centuries reveals that certain symbols expressing human self-understanding of its movement in the process of reality can be mapped, bringing to light distinct phases of technological consciousness. Since history is transience, without end or purpose, we can understand the succession of these historical phases only heuristically and in metaphors. What I intend to summarize now is a succession of metaphors of order – the mechanical, the organic, and the electric – which appear to have played a significant part in structuring the public discourse at distinct periods of technological development.

As a guide to the distinctive features of each phase, we can turn with the promise of considerable enlightenment to the thesis of Marshall McLuhan, who analyses how technology at different times reorders sense-ratios and patterns of perception. His schematization of technology works on the assumption that once we have 'outered some part of our being in material technology, our entire sense ratio is altered' and 'in beholding this new thing, we are compelled to become it.' Once such extension occurs, 'it tends to allow all other functions to be altered to accommodate that form.' McLuhan's studies, predicated on the centrality of the categories of time and space to human consciousness and to the articulation of human experience, do not exhaust what needs to be said about the way technology steers our way of existence, but they do suffice as a first approximation.

In his schema, the first phase was the period of print culture. Print entails the isolation of the visual sense from the totality of experience – a print culture of alphabet and typography reduces experience to the patterns of sight-experience. McLuhan suggests that this reduction contributes to ideas also being derived from the Newtonian-Cartesian paradigm – temporal sequence and spatial allotment. Print links distribution in space with sequence in time. Space comes to be seen as enclosed, homogenous, and continuous, while time is linear, successively durational, and irreversible. Causality comes to be seen as having only one form, namely the efficient, and it is seen to operate wherever durations of time are linked in a single place and in successive order. Experience is segmented and interpreted sequentially. Phenomena are understood as having a discrete identity and to resist one another. This is a way of seeing the world which accords with the resolutive-compositive method of 'break down, simplify, and rebuild.' Out of it flow the human experiences of sequentiality and continuity.

Print culture encourages a view of the world which sees its forces as mechanical and its phenomena as mutually exclusive components. Each compartment or departmental boundary is seen as having a separate order of constitutionality, a regime understood as having a singular function and purpose. The sense coordinates of print culture hallow the idea that we are sovereign beings who may challenge forth the 'objects' of the world, as if they could be consigned a space on a taxonomic grid, and make them available or dispose of them so as to comply with our vision of progress.

McLuhan suggests it is no accident that this first phase of technological control was an age of industrial initiative and of production in the commodity form. The wilful inscription of power on formless nature, the 'empirical' studies constituting controlled environments, and the 'research plans' which produced controlled patterns, all operate on the same assumption that space is enclosed and events occur in time. Each empowers individuals to order the world and to overcome conditions which in the past had been left as intractable mysteries, tragedies, and contradictions. This first phase of technology is an age of objectification and standardization where the plurality of existence is reduced to the logical operation of a machine and where a growing number of resources are organized in the relation of means to ends, analogous to the relation between machines and functions, where a simple process is repeated many times over. Vast improvements in medicine, food production, public safety, and economic production are made as a consequence of the simple, uniform scientific models which now govern.

McLuhan proposes that distinctive political, moral, and social practices followed from a consciousness structured by the categories of enclosed space and sequential time. The political question becomes confined to the problems of sovereignty and individual freedom. How is power distilled into authority? What vector of force causes the effect of constraint? How can human relations be seen within the series objectification, alienation, resistance, and reconciliation? The traditional causalities and sequences constituting the activity of autonomous states, the contract relations between self-interested agents, the coordination of centres and peripheries of control, or the composition of political personas are recognized to be stable and secure. Political actors identify their space from others, insisting that all spaces should conform to the patterns of their own and devising strategies to move political spaces from one time sequence to another. The stable coordinates of the mechanical phase – uniformity and repeatability, homogenization and fragmentation, distance and separation – constituting a 'point of view' underlie the formal equality and recognition of a plurality of legal persons under the law.

The same ideas of specifiable boundaries, localizable phenomena, and mechanical interaction of spaces and durations legitimate certain ways of seeing moral questions. The relevant human phenomena are seen within a system of provinces. The chief ordinance of morality is one of limit, and injustice means breaking the bounds. Eros and hubris transgress order and violate the limits of *moira*, and morality necessitates a punitive response. The problematic moral relations are all about boundaries, either between individuals and collectivities, each of which inhabits a distinct space and proceeds on a discrete time-line, or between separate faculties like desire, the passions, and reason. An autonomous will can legislate moral order by identifying a stable form located at some 'origin' or 'end-point' in time. 'Moral judgment' means an independent and autonomous capacity of thought (a point of view or perspective).

In education and social life, too, the categories of the first phase of technological consciousness exert their influence. Students are to acquire a memory which is built on the idea that there are material objects stored and moved in space and time. Acts of recollection involve retrievals from one space to another. Social exchanges assume a stable world where words refer to things, ideas represent reality, and signs have referents. Work is production structured by specialization and division of labour. In all these cases, ideas of extended bodies, resistance, force, and homogeneous repeatability govern.

McLuhan's focus on categories of consciousness for describing the first phase of technology takes us far in understanding the reorganization of existence which began in the sixteenth century. But his account needs to be supplemented with an analysis of the power mobilizing these processes. We have already referred to Foucault's concept of 'juridical power,' a power he relates to the primacy of the principle of sovereignty and the commodity form. This political 'Newtonianism,' which I suggested was present in the AVER program, assumes that there are fixed centres from which force is imposed to achieve some predetermined outcome. Foucault's analysis of this form of power echoes McLuhan's observation that a single prototype is identified and then repeated across the social spectrum: 'The role of political power,' he writes, 'is perpetually to reinscribe this relation through a form of unspoken warfare; to reinscribe it in social institutions, in economic inequalities, in language, in the bodies themselves of each and every one of us.'[30] Power is something to be distilled into a single will whose sovereignty – as autonomous subjects who control desire, or as rulers who repress and subjugate their subjects – is a relationship of forces bearing down on individuals. Strict notions of causality, limit, and zero-sum gain govern the use of power. There is a fixed quantum of power within which political relations are formed. Power is an opaque force imposed, resisted, stolen, and retrieved. Its efficiency is limited by the range within which it is allowed to be exercised, namely a world where all relations are defined by conflict and rule.

The emergence of the second phase of technological expansion (which many industries and nations continue to be undergoing) makes it possible to overcome the inefficiency generated by technological apparati whose effects were too often isolated and restricted by traditional notions of unconditional limits on human existence. The second phase entails a growing systematization of all human phenomena into aggregates of processes, a reorganization best expressed with a language drawn from organic biology. Technological apparati now are deployed within total systems, as growing numbers of tools, machines, forms of organization, and knowledge form a stream of 'revolving functionalities' and are installed as subsystems within an interrelated and interdependent web. As subsystems they will 'transact,' integrating with one another and maximizing efficiency.

This 'organic' phase is described in Ellul's analysis of the inevitable systematization of technology. The emergence of supply networks, multinational production cooperatives, and knowledge-linkages points to a correlation of manifold technologies so that they function according to overall processes of development arising from the modulation of interdependent subsystems. Technological change will come to appear as 'automatic,' and the indicators of success and improvement will seem to have been generated from within the system. Ellul describes this systematic coordination into a fluid system of means as one where 'all parts of the social body [are] so conjoined and interconnected as to make that organism all-encompassing and uniform.'[31] Mechanism, the hallmark of the first phase of technology, will appear insufficient to explain the emerging vitalism of system interdependence.[32]

The locus of attention is no longer the extraction, stockpiling, and transfer of material objects extended and located in space, but the continuous processes in which the system's components interact and integrate. McLuhan sees this phase of technological growth as progressively overturning the Newtonianism and the Cartesianism of the previous phase: absolute space and time, irreducible discrete units, linear causality, material substance, and homogeneity appear as primitive analytic tools. What emerges is a new paradigm of interaction and energy, nonlocal connections and simultaneity. Instead of the strict, efficient causality and taxonomy of spaces ('a place for everything and everything in its place') of the first phase, there are now configurational or unified fields where everything is correlational.

At this point in his description, McLuhan becomes highly metaphorical. However, his language mimics the tone and expectations of standard textbooks in system design and engineering. Gone are the ideas of independent phenomena, linear sequences, localizable entities, discrete instances, and detached points of view, in favour of a new image of total fields of simultaneous relations, simultaneity, indeterminacy, and 'interstructural resonance.'[33] The world, in the minds of the new technicians, is becoming a total configurational tension at once differentiated and decentralized. The 'unique,' 'singular,' 'embodied,' 'possessed,' and 'instantiated' are dissolved into relations. Under this phase of techno-logical control, each element fulfils variable functions, objects have no fixed substance, space and time interact, and change is continuous. Space is no longer seen as containing things, but rather as an effect of the tension among opposing forces. Matter is viewed less as something dis-crete and inviolable than as the effect of a 'force field.' Motion is under-stood not in terms of discrete objects moving in an inert void, but as modulation within the wavelike variations in the curvature of space. Events are not so much contingent novelties as situations in probability patterns.[34] Here 'difference' is no longer experienced as distance, but as relational differentiation. 'Our specialist and fragmented civilization of centre-margin structure,' McLuhan writes, 'is suddenly experiencing an instantaneous reassembling of all its mechanized bits into an organic whole,' differentiated and heterogeneous and yet totally and simulta-neously 'involved.'[35]

McLuhan understands this shift in orientation to have significant political, social, and economic consequences. To take maximum advan-tage of the opportunities offered by the new order, the idea of 'compart-mentalizing human potential by single cultures' has to be relinquished in favour of an 'organic wholeness,' 'a unified mode of perception,' a 're-tribalization' into a 'simultaneous field in all human affairs so that the human family now exists under conditions of a "global village."' The age of imperial politics, of sovereign legislation enforced from the centre onto the periphery, is also outmoded. Global systems are self-organizing and their dynamic principles require no central planning authority.

McLuhan sees a different human potential being tapped by the sec-ond phase of technology. Leaving behind a world ordered by detached, non-involved control of distinct spaces means the potential for social arrangements that are no longer exclusive but integrative, no longer divisive but cooperative. Arranging social life and moral order using ideas of function and norm promises forms of discipline that are no longer punitive but that arise from a continuum of mutually adjusting processes. Social existence comes to be seen less as a field of isolated agents confronting one another from within static structures than as an interconnected web of relations and responsibilities dynamically bal-anced. Work is less a succession of discrete tasks, organized to maximize the performativity of each isolated component, than a continuous process of feedback circuits in which instruments, skills, and forms of production are dynamic functioning components in an integrated, growing organism. The free-market model of competitive exploitation focused on national sovereignty stands arraigned as counter-productive within the complexity of multinational interdependence. Educationally, knowledge is no longer directed to a detached mental apparatus but to the interactional processes of the reunified mind/body.[36] Compartmentalization as a whole is overcome in a new 'multisensual' and 'multidimensional' world of 'total configurational effects.' The new consciousness is no longer unique but manifests itself as 'intense sensitivity to the interrelation and interprocess of the whole.'

Under the mandate of 'interstructural resonance' a very different modality of power appears. We have already referred to it in examining Foucault's idea of bio-power. His argument is that an economy of efficiency dictates a shift in the flow of power. Now, sovereignty and the commodity form no longer structure economic, social, political, and scientific discourses, while power loses its 'representational' role. It becomes an anonymous, uncertified and disembodied dynamic circulating within dispersed networks of apparati. Bio-power is more efficient because, diffused into the tiniest capillaries of human life – sexuality, nutrition, sentiment, et cetera – micro-investments of effective power have been made in desire and pleasure.

Instead of requiring spectacular displays of force, whose success is not guaranteed, bio-power 'runs through and produces things' – 'it induces pleasure, it forms knowledge, it produces discourse.' It is a power far more subtle and nuanced, more efficient and continuous, for it is always already there where there is pleasure and speech, knowledge and truth. Once power can insinuate itself in the investments of desire in ordinary relations – inciting, proliferating, and instrumentalizing healthy bodies, productive bodies, normal attitudes, pleasurable feelings – and thus is no longer the macro-force dominating high-profile events (coups, acts of oppression, battles of liberation), it has overcome the wasteful expenditure and unpredictability of the old economy of power. It operates with optimal efficiency.

Bio-power is, nonetheless, a regulative force. It drives technologies which discipline by normalizing: 'taking charge of life needs continuous regulatory and correcting mechanisms ... it does not have to draw the line that separates the enemies of the sovereign from his obedient subjects; it effects distributions around the norm.'[37] But a diffused power is not perceived as power but is understood as a general social function of maintaining equilibrium, stability, and dynamic balance. Bio-power is invisible and not easily resisted. Its great achievement is that it permits a constant supervision of all the system's processes by creating an interest in maintaining the strength of the system. The continuum of regulatory agents – social workers, the medical profession, psychologists, social demographers, and aid societies – all play their part in the one interest we all share, life. 'A normalizing society,' Foucault notes, 'is the historical outcome of a technology of power centred on life.' When the 'natural body,' or holistic person, becomes the paramount concern an entire field of total visibility, an all-inclusive scan, can be installed. A vast arsenal of 'biopolitical' population-management technologies replace traditional politics. Society has become a continuum of an uninterrupted play of calculated gazes.

Can there be political or legal recourse from this web of power? Whom could one hold responsible for unjust exercises of power? Power emanating from subjects who can be held accountable for their actions has been replaced by anonymous transmitters, exchangeable relays, and polyvalent gazes. 'Now, the study of this micro-physics presupposes that the power exercised on the body is conceived not as a property, but as a strategy, that its effects of nomination are attributed not to "appropriation," but to dispositions, manoeuvres, tactics, techniques, functionings; that one should decipher in it a network of relations, constantly in tension, in activity, rather than a privilege that one might possess.'[38] Power had taken on an immaterial and dispossessed form, no longer encumbered by the obdurate world of concrete particulars. The scope and effective penetration of its control are now unlimited, with a constant articulation of power with knowledge and knowledge with power. This does not mean that the illusion of resistance and moral independence does not occur. 'There are also times when force contends against itself, and not only in the intoxication of an abundance, which allows it to divide itself, but at the moment when it weakens. Force reacts against its growing lassitude and gains strength; it imposes limits, inflicts torments and mortifications; it masks these actions as a higher morality, and, in exchange, regains its strength.'[39] Despite the all-pervasive control, or perhaps because of it, there is no end to the academic pretence that the new configuration is 'progressive' and its effects are the outcome of a moral refinement and maturation of the human spirit.

The second phase of technology optimalizes efficiency and brings us one step further towards fulfilling wholly our desire for the unconditioned. By establishing a continuous process of interrelated and interdependent components, a self-referential feedback loop whose means are the ends and whose ends are the means, the single biggest problem of the first phase of technology is nearly overcome. The first phase remained inconveniently dysfunctional because of the one component which remained arbitrary, unpredictable, dissatisfied, unreliable, complex, and wilful – humankind. Now, in the 'organic' phase, all these inconveniences can be identified as risks and can be managed. The 'organic' phase of technology is about risk-management and absorbing humans into the ecology of the life-system. As Norbert Wiener rightly recognized, 'we have modified our environment so radically that we must now modify ourselves in order to exist in the new environment.'[40]

The need to absorb humans as quanta (though still privileged quanta) in the life-system was not as important in the mechanical phase. Now, with more unity in the technological system, it is more vulnerable to colossal breakdown, for the interruption in one subsystem spills onto all of its interdependent relations. Moreover, since the variables effecting outcomes are no longer local but can, by virtue of the instantaneous interconnectedness of the whole system, arise to effect the process from anywhere, even the most contained fields are vulnerable to disruption. Hence, the development of risk-management technologies becomes the most important by-product of technological development in this phase. Risk-management does not mean stepping down the momentum of technological development, but rather altering and transforming the conditions under which the damage occurred. Risk-management becomes preventative or pre-emptive when it can sufficiently recondition a phenomenon so that it no longer produces a stress when it interfaces with another element under contingent circumstances. The most effective preventative measure is eliminating the functional exclusivity of any one component in the system. Optimal efficiency of the whole requires closing the margin of danger, contingency, ambiguity, and unrest by having concrete, historical persons see themselves as nothing more than universal form. With the systematization of the second phase of technology, the plurality of concrete persons is transformed into species-beings who are merely carriers of the universal form of 'Humanity.'

Despite this dispossession of a human being's everyday reality, a remnant of humanism still remains. 'Humanity' still exists as a regulative limit – as species-being, as labouring and consuming being, as embodiment of the equilibrated norm. Under the second phase, individuals are not merely passive 'victims' of technological processes, but active carriers of the life code sustaining the human species and giving it peace and prosperity. But, why should the system's dynamic of contending forces move towards equilibrium and balance? Why should the vitality of the whole inevitably ensure functional adaptation? Why should the expenditure of forces exhibit itself as a benign maintenance of the whole? Why should it not be that 'all events in the organic world are a subduing, a becoming master'?[41] Why should the 'invariant' process of efficiency not break away from the regulative limits of the system's organizational forms and begin to exhibit 'entropy,' an increasing disorder?

The third phase of technology erupts as the enormous technological capacities brought about through system coordination break the harness of standard frequency curves, profiles based on the norm, and central planning. Once again the principles of efficiency have had to be reassessed, expansionary forces redeployed, and a new lexicon formulated. Yet, the least can be said about the third phase, for its formative patterns and regulative rhythms are barely evident. All that can be alluded to are highlights of certain trends, though speculation will permit some reflection on how humankind's relentless desire for the unconditioned seeks new satisfaction. Moreover, since the preponderant part of the world is still undergoing the revolutions of the first phase in attempting to industrialize and since the systematizing of the second phase of technology is still the explicit and self-conscious agenda in the most technically advanced states, our situation is one where a third phase is only a nascent hint, an eccentric, prophetic dream.

The third phase optimalizes a formative rhythm of the second phase – the transfiguration of reality in such a way that the sloppy ambiguities of everyday existence no longer impede pure efficiency. What the third phase adds is the achievement of transparency in which technical mediation appears to vanish, leaving consumers of its novel products with the sense that the real gap between word and thing, desire and satisfaction, intent and deed, lack and perfection, has vanished.

On the surface, the third phase appears to fragment the homogeneity and uniformity of the earlier stages. Instead of global integration strategies, there are multiple local centres which allow mass production and consumption to be expressed in infinite variety. Instead of concentration of ownership or integration of industrial policy, there is diffusion in the management of information. The centrality of a logic of production gives way to an infinite variety of market probes of consumption patterns. Not so much the producer, but the variable tastes of the consumer determine the range and focus of technological innovation. The tools of the new processes are signs and images, and the focus of research and development is the transmission of information. The third phase, then, is the phase of communication networks where the electric metaphor predominates. As Marshall McLuhan points out in *Understanding Media* (p. 307), 'With electricity as energizer and synchronizer, all aspects of production, consumption, and organization become incidental to communications. The very idea of communication as interplay is inherent in the electrical, which combines both energy and information in its intensive manifold.'

Instead of the mechanical metaphors of the machine phase, but like the organic metaphors of the systems phase, the regulative language is one of liquidity and flows. But the concepts of Euclidean space conceived as enclosure and exclusion and those of Newtonian time, understood as succession and direction, which are still residually manifest in the totality of the organic system, are now relinquished in favour of a dynamic field of dispersion and simultaneity. There is growth, but no finality. This is why Ellul claims that the new information order involves a 'polyvalent and nonlinear growth': where industrial production and early systems-organization entailed a 'closed, repetitive world, with linear evolution,' the contemporary situation is 'inevitably open, nonrepetitive, with a polyvalent evolution.'[42] Life in the third phase is a perpetual metaphoric creation of simultaneous pasts and futures, producing a new creativity and vitality, an infinitizing feeling of identification with the entire course of past and future possibilities, past and future events.

The environment of the third phase is consequently complex and puzzling. It links phenomena that are believed to be antinomies from any known human perspective: globalism and monadism, disembodiment and viscerality, primitivism and redivinization, detritus and vitality, consumption and the end of production, liberation and the effacement of man.

The extension of electronics wholly shifts our focus from the evident and sensible distinctions still at home in a materials-based technological society. McLuhan envisages a 'global village' that has overcome the order of centres and margins: 'Electric speeds create centres everywhere. Margins cease to exist on this planet.' The proliferation of information networks means 'intense sensitivity to the interrelation and interprocess of the whole.'[43] 'During the mechanical ages,' McLuhan notes, 'we had extended our bodies in space. Today, after more than a century of electric technology, we have extended our central nervous system itself in a global embrace.'[44]

But, at the same time, the new 'comity' is not a form of sociality. No central perspective collects the globe into a unified universal. As McLuhan notes, the marginal areas are no longer homogenized through the extension of power over them, because the electronic age has dismantled the coordinates of lineal and irreversible progress: 'Our speed-up today is not a slow expansion outward from centre to margins but an instant implosion and an interfusion of space and functions.' Implosion means a 'bursting inwards,' to an Archimedean point of universality, to a simultaneous and infinitizing resonance with the whole globe, to a 'mysterious coincidence.' To activate 'the cosmic membrane that has been snapped round the globe by the electric dilation of our various senses' there must be a withdrawal from the mechanical world's static spaces and sequences mediated by the inter-est between one being and another.[45] The disappearance of the 'social' brings about isolation, but this is the prelude to a state in which the web of electric signals produces a universality 'stimulated by mutual proximity.'

McLuhan sees this new state in a positive light. It marks the beginning of a whole new age of dispossessed and therefore creative and peaceful existence: 'a global embrace abolish[es] both space and time as far as our planet is concerned. Rapidly, we approach the final phase of the extensions of man – the technological simulation of consciousness, when the creative process of knowing will be collectively and corporately extended to the whole of human society, much as we have already extended our senses and our nerves by the various media.'[46] Thus, as he comments in *The Gutenberg Galaxy*, 'we can now live, not just amphibiously in divided and distinguished worlds, but pluralistically in many worlds and cultures simultaneously.'[47] Yet, the 'psychic permeability' causing the globe to resonate with one rhythm is, at the same time, enjoining us to participate in a 'resonance' which returns us to primordial affectivity.

The electric age, McLuhan notes, is 'quickly recreating in us the mental processes of the most primitive men,' rupturing the static and pictorial mode of perception and the arbitrary, privileging closures of the mechanical and the organic world. Electric technology points to an extension of the consciousness which bypasses the human need for verbalization. Language, McLuhan suggests, has been our 'Tower of Babel,' imposing arbitrary distinctions and static meanings. By overcoming language, the electric phase of technology will bring about a 'general cosmic consciousness,' a 'condition of speechlessness that could confer a perpetuity of collective harmony and peace.'[48] Humankind's 're-divination,' one could say in linking McLuhan's and Nietzsche's dreams, combines the pre-human with the yet-to-be superman.

McLuhan's enthusiasm for the full transfigurative effect of electric technology should not blind us to the fact that his is a classic gnostic dream which attempts with striking metaphors to evoke a *parousia* in which the ambiguities and ambivalences of everyday reality are radically transcended. The dream is also a second-order reality, eclipsing essential features of human reality. To return us to the world and first-order reality elaborated by Arendt and Voegelin, we can turn to the insights of a social thinker of the first rank who sees clearly where McLuhan's retribalized existence is taking us.

In his disturbing account of the processed world of mass communications, Jean Baudrillard accepts all of McLuhan's prophetic description, but suggests that the outcome of this vitality is, in fact, 'waste' and 'detritus.' Baudrillard suggests that the information age is noted less for creating conditions for new meanings and opportunities for renewal than for circulating abstract and 'hypersymbolic' diffusions of images and information.[49] Baudrillard argues that the contemporary age is playing out corrosive aspects of the post-modernist's 'philosophy of difference,' contributing to a new superficiality of empty ornamentation and stylization. The chief technological indicator is the shift in focus throughout the corporate industry from research and development in production to consumption. Whereas the commodity exchange, he argues, was the predominant economic form of the mechanical, industrial order, as well as of the organic, general systems order, now consumption of signs and images prevails. Rather than concentrating resources on maximum production, the focus is on 'skilling' and 'deskilling' individuals towards varying consumption habits. Rather than organizing technical resources for the sake of higher yield, the priority is managing information and marketing images. Aggregating information in scenarios and profiles takes precedence over profit and extraction of surplus value. The law of market value is no longer the decisive, necessitating strategies based on linear rationality, since information processing employs a 'polyvalent rationality' which need not be bounded by the everyday range of human experience. Indeed, research expresses precisely the strange reversal of the third technological phase: it produces novel procedures and solutions for which there is as yet no problem or use.

The substitution of consumption for production, Baudrillard believes, is at the same time a profound anti-metaphysical revolution. Production, he writes, is always a summoning forth, in which what *is* is rendered visible, caused to be collected, indexed, and assigned limits. The an-archy of consumption, in contrast, is an unending refraction of signs and thus is without coherence. Consumption is a *seduction* rather than a production, a withdrawal rather than a presentation. 'Seduction,' Baudrillard writes, 'withdraws something from the visible order and so runs counter to production.'[50] The seductive image of the information age is, for Baudrillard, an abandonment of order and of the humanist perspective. No stable value arrests the commutability of the sign, for the infinite metamorphosis of signification means that there can be no 'real.' In an age where consumption and seduction increasingly monopolize the resources of technological research and development, order is fragmented, decentred, and disseminated. Human life can no longer be understood under the sign of conflict and rules, or of functions and norms, but is traversed by a reversible play of simulacra and scenarios.

The infinite array of signs, Baudrillard argues, is a polyvalent and unstable series which devastates traditional political and rational meanings. The new an-archy of images is unintelligible within any known political horizon or rational understanding. Our technological environment is thus a 'hyperreality' – a non-place or non-history of semiological transference and feedback. 'Hyperreal' refers to the withdrawal of the 'real,' and its return as highly stylized, formalized, hyperbolic forms and styles, refurbished and copied even though the original may never have existed or where the original, lived context is completely refabricated. Past cultures, ways of life, and experiences become eclectic signs which have lost their referents in the service of mass consumption and innovative marketing. Their use and deployment in the media as circulating signs permit of no recollection or reminiscence to a primal point endowing them with meaning.[51]

The consumption age, Baudrillard documents, is an *absence d'oeuvre* – work of the sort we referred to in chapter 2 cannot retrieve the original to establish human meaning. But without meaning, Baudrillard notes,

the medium also falls into that indefinite state characteristic of all our great systems of judgement and value. A single *model*, whose efficacy is *immediacy*, simultaneously generates the message, the medium, and the 'real.' In short, *the medium is the message* signifies not only the end of the message, but also the end of the medium. There are no longer media in the literal sense of the term ... – that is to say, a power mediating between one reality and another, between one state of the real and another – neither in content nor in form. Strictly speaking, this is what implosion signifies: the absorption of one pole into another, the short-circuit between poles of every differential system of meaning, the effacement of terms and of direct oppositions, and thus that of the medium and the real. Hence the impossibility of any mediation, of any dialectical intervention between the two from one to the other, circularity of all media effects. Hence the impossibility of a sense (meaning), in the literal sense of a unilateral vector which leads from one pole to another.[52]

It is a situation where everything appears only as data within technological cycles of availability and disposability. The facts of existence are circulated around as great masses of detritus and excess, dead images which can be endlessly consumed and recycled. In the great celebration of playful *différance*, all is different, but different in the same an-archic way and for the same alogical reason. The disorder of simulation finally means sameness and uniformity. Are cynicism and boredom far behind?

Baudrillard's second major concern about the emerging technological environment is the character of the new global embrace. This 'whole,' he argues, is more accurately described as a 'mass,' for, unlike the 'social,' this transparent aggregate of human beings lacks those forms which would give it an interest. The 'contact' between isolated beings, Baudrillard comments, is no more than 'a ventilation of individuals as terminals of information.' 'The social,' he writes, 'only exists in a perspective space, it dies in the space of simulation.'[53] Baudrillard's description of a mass 'swirling with currents and flows' should remind us of the similar point made by Hannah Arendt, who warned about the 'heterogeneous uniformity' of the 'mass' whose togetherness is nothing more than an abstract and formless vitality of simulated interests.[54]

Under these conditions, the traditional idea of humans acquiring knowledge to improve their faculties or to perfect their abilities becomes outdated. Knowledge can no longer be an interiorized possession conferring stability on our being. Instead, we should, Lyotard writes in his work *The Postmodern Condition*, 'expect a thorough exteriorization of knowledge with respect to the "knower" at whatever point he or she may occupy in the knowledge process. The old principle that the acquisition of knowledge is indissociable from the training (*Bildung*) of minds, or even of individuals, is becoming obsolete and will become ever more so.'[55] The traditional curriculum, as we noted, placed a singular premium on memory, both as the historical remembrance of events which could be composed into stories and as the stimulus for an anamnetic recovery of being. Where there are no substantive selves, but only simulations of styles and values, a memory whose modality was retrieval will inevitably be seen as dispensable. Only an 'affective memory' can authentically contribute to that feeling of an eternal present to which the information age invites us.[56] The withdrawal of reality, and its re-creation in infinite variations of different information simulations and scenarios, overcomes the condition in which, with an older experience of human memory, humans had to respond to their own mortality by stories (the remembrance of immortal actions) and to encounter the essential mysteries of their existence (the anamnetic retrieval of the structure of being).

The third phase of technology brings the gnostic desire for the unconditioned to fulfilment. The goal of simulated immediacy where reality-reconstruction has become transparent is within reach. Reality remains only as a simulacrum of itself. The electric age has taken us to where, in Jacques Ellul's words, in humankind's enthralment with technology 'the world and man's idea of it have merged.'

But to be more precise, we should say that the play of information bits, processors, and communication networks goes on without the 'human,' for 'Man' as the being who acts and asks questions, and from whose perspective the world of politics and the experience of the transcendent were articulated, is no longer.

'Today,' to recall McLuhan, 'our science and method strive not towards a point of view but to discover how not to have a point of view, the method not of closure and perspective but of the open "field" and the suspended judgment. Such is now the only viable method under electric conditions of simultaneous information movement and total human interdependence.'[57] Transcending meaning-endowed places and action-centred histories, and the stable structures and forms of human experience, leads to sensing 'life as a series of emotional intensities involving a logic different from that of the rational world and capturable only in dissociated images or stream of consciousness musings.' What *is* is primordial, humanless genesis, experienced only as visceral affectivity within 'electric dispersion.'[58] Man – participating consciousness, questioning being, acting political being, subject, individual, or autonomous will and thinking ego – is nothing more than an incandescence of intensity.

Even McLuhan, the inveterate champion of the new dynamism, hesitates at this point, perceiving implications which are unsettling: 'Terror,' he wrote, 'is the normal state of any oral society, for in it everything affects everything all the time.' The neo-primitivism of the technological environment has the tonality of constant panic. Co-opted within a universal membrane, and empowered by global efficiency, nothing discrete, exclusive, and unconditional remains. 'General cosmic consciousness,' McLuhan recognizes, is at one and the same time isolation and universal resonance. Looked at in political terms the new global network is one which links a kind of retribalized existence with instantaneous reactivity to the whole globe. Each reinforces the other. That situation is one where the imploded self confronts directly and without mediation the powerful dynamics of the global environment. Monad and global force resonate with one another without any dialectical intervention, without any of the everyday forms of the political world. No distinctive modalities of mediation arise in this pure affectivity.

With the spectre of this dream before us, we are well advised to remember Arendt's point (a point she shares with Hegel) that the destruction of mediating institutions such as public space, as well as the common sense which develops in political engagement with others, leads to a state where masses of lonely and vulnerable people can be easily agitated and mobilized to commit murderous acts. 'Total domination,' to repeat Arendt's chilling warning, 'which strives to organize the infinite plurality and differentiation of human beings as if all of humanity were just one individual, is possible only if each and every person can be reduced to a never-changing identity of reactions, so that each of these bundles of reactions can be exchanged at random for any other.'

Whether this is our fate we cannot know. But we can remember with Arendt that it always 'lies within the power of human thought and action to interrupt and arrest such processes,' just as we can agree with Eric Voegelin that, however powerful a 'second-reality' construct is in denying the validity of the symbols through which our intellectual and spiritual longings are expressed, such eclipse cannot forever extinguish the human need to ask questions.[59] But such hopes are dashed if we remain in this uncanny place where our 'values' reverence nothing, represent nothing, and signify nothing.

7

From Dispossession to Possession

Values and Technology: A Modulating Couplet

Values education swept in with the promise of revitalizing flagging moral spirits, overcoming conformity, and enriching the place of humans in a world increasingly dominated by technological planning. In contrast to the objectifying imperatives of technology, values education was going to renew human subjectivity and to provide measures with which to steer our way around the new powers which were making it possible to manage, control, and optimalize all facets of life.

My argument is that the dominant models achieve none of these aims and that at the deepest level the metaphysic underlying them colludes with and reinforces key aspects of technological mastery. Values analysis, values development, and values clarification are producing a generation of students in whose fervent longings values educators have directly installed the technological imperative. And in so doing, values education has abdicated the responsibility of education to prepare a human being for the world and for the work of intellectual and spiritual questioning, both of which, under a more traditional moral education, would furnish unconditional limits to technology and the opportunity for genuine personal fulfilment.

What we have in each of these models are fragments broken off from a comprehensive whole, which for never having been made explicit in the traditional curriculum now founder at the hands of eclectic innovators and social activists. The result is a series of unstable values programs which cannot contain the dynamic each places at its centre and which fails to preserve an enclave or resistance point against technology.

This instability is evident even in the model of reasoning which places the autonomy of moral ideals and the freedom of the individual at its centre – AVER's values analysis. To be precise, of all the models we examined, the AVER model comes closest to preserving the distinctly political boundaries and experiences we examined in chapter 2. Seeing that the AVER model is derived from the thought of the thinker who supplied the moral and intellectual ballast to liberal democracy, Immanuel Kant, it is not surprising to find in the AVER model paramount recognition given to the juridical person – an image of humanity identifying individuals as bearers of legal rights guaranteed in a political community. The ideal of moral autonomy also supports the important notions of the dignity of the person, of civic respect, and of a political state as a regime of mutual recognition. The legal fiction upon which the common sense and human decency of this regime rest is a sensible and sober artifice. Its greatest virtue is that it restrains the dynamic power of human desire.

Yet, despite this noble heritage, AVER's self does not have the stability demanded by the legal fiction of an autonomous person. Unlike Kant's moral agent, AVER's self has no metaphysical substance, and unlike Hegel's concrete person, AVER's self is not an embodied historical being. The self has no concern for a permanent world whose stability would substantiate its claims to rights, and it is not invited to contract with a concrete community guaranteeing the enforcement of the required political forms. The empathetic skills and tolerance which AVER assumes will produce substance in the self cannot do so because the self the techniques form expresses itself as dynamic expansiveness, rather than receptivity.

AVER's self is intended to be the juridical, autonomous person of modern liberalism. But the dynamic at its centre – the pure process of perpetual self-overcoming – is a highly unstable basis for preserving the inviolability of genuine human autonomy. And the same dynamic reinforces a technological consciousness. The contraction of human existence to an autonomous will supports the notion that order must be legislated on the disorderly, phenomenal world.[1] The empowerment of the individual as pure will is based on an image of humans as extricated from all determinate characteristics – those emanating from either his natural gifts (intelligence, talent, temperament, sensibility) or his historical culture (religion, class, locality) – which might have been the grounds of action. As pure will, AVER's self must project itself into an infinite and indefinite future. Expressing itself in self-overcoming, this pure will must divest its being of any possessive relation to itself and things. Neither virtues, habits, talents, durable things, stable meanings, nor the permanent structure of the human attraction towards the transcendent may provide stability in life. A pure will expresses itself as a freedom from condition, as a subduing and mastering of all that is permanent and enduring. As subject, the only posture is one of defiance towards the merely 'heteronomous,' for in commanding it, this self expresses its moral freedom and worthiness. Nothing stable qualifies these motions – the willing self posits its own conditions and purpose, rather than receiving them. This is why the AVER model cannot provide limits to technology, for there can be nothing outside of the form of willing itself that defines the will, an assumption which both the AVER model and technology share.

At the same time, the fact/value distinction to which AVER ascribes and which constitutes the calculus by which things in the world are evaluated sets the world up as composed of mathematical objects. Worldly density, whose rhythms reflect the ambiguities and tensions of existence, is reduced to the simple schema of algebraic relations and proportions. As object, the world has become available for mastery and control, especially since, from the perspective of an autonomous subject, the world's rhythms of genesis and order are now merely heteronomous – that is, to be subjugated. The Cartesian dualism of mind and nature, as well as its use of apodictic certainty as the criterion of truth, which AVER adopts, is the quintessential mathematical model reinforcing the notion that what is must be mastered.

AVER's valuing subject represents the world on a classificatory grid (autonomous/heteronomous, facts/values, and moral/aesthetic/economic/prudential points of view). This assumes that compounds of human experience can be broken down, their elements clearly and simply identified, and that the reconstructed whole will be an object of certainty and consistency. The correctness of its actions, like the circular justification of knowing and making, is guaranteed solely by its own internal logic. The subject will accept consistency as the imperative of its actions, but this is because the homogeneity it produces accords with its own logic of recognizing only what it has itself made and can control. The subject will also accept the imperative of reciprocity, but not because it acknowledges the existence of others as 'other' (genuine plurality is inimical to the will's project of self-overcoming). Rather it will do so because the universality it produces allows the will to see only itself, confirming its power to re-create the world in its own image.

AVER's self, in other words, may appear to stand apart from the powerfully embracing touch of technology, but at its core lies a deep complicity with the conditions which drive technological mastery. This conclusion is reinforced if we accept the argument made in chapter 3 that the vision of a technologically reconstructed future society is what, in the final instance, substantiates the form of the moral will. The AVER model demands technological mastery because the new world must stand in as its synthetic a priori.

No better brake on technology is offered in Kohlberg's project. To be true, there is a sound insight contained in Kohlberg's model which acknowledges that human beings develop and that a life of reason manifests itself in the unity formed among diverse aspects of being. Moreover, it seems sensible to me to see moral understanding evolving through a spiral of balances in which motion and order are equilibrated successively, forming gradually enhanced capacities for judgment. Undoubtedly, if the full significance of these insights were developed (as it could be if it were brought closer to the thought of Arendt and Voegelin), Kohlberg would have supplied a powerful resistance to technological consciousness. But, the force of Kohlberg's idea of moral development is derivative of a comprehensive program of development theorized by Hegel. The consciousness which drives development to its resolution at the 'end of history' in this narrative, and which is present in any subsystem (such as Kohlberg's), is the pure expression of technology's dynamic. Spirit's self-externalizations and reappropriations entail the same procedure as the technological act which orders up reality as object to a subject, thereby enhancing human wilfulness and subjecting the unruliness of the world to control. The Hegelian system not only justifies technological mastery but is a form of it, for mastery is the operative dynamic of self-consciousness. Here too humans are masters who will the world into order and whose limits are self-willed.

Now, this contraction of human existence to the being who challenges forth the other as object, and who subjects the world to standardization and uniformity, was already present in AVER's Kantianism. But in the phase of technological consciousness that model underwrites, humans remain autonomous agents and singular beings who legislate and subdue a recalcitrant reality. In this phase humans are external to the technological apparati – values are the means to actuate our distinct human ends.

The Hegelian dynamic, and Kohlberg's version of it, suggest a new phase in technological consciousness. The organic metaphor of unity which now prevails requires a continuous process of mutual adjustment and integration of the system. What emerges under this phase are linkages and interdependences which fuse the diverse human phenomena into one system. Kohlberg's model puts a premium on that dynamic which establishes the rhythms of the life system as such, and not simply their individual instantiation, as the regulative measure of all human experience. Kohlberg's account of the development of moral reasoning establishes growth and coordination, under which the diverse human phenomena acquire the constancy and organization of life's laws of structuration, as the primary imperative. Human experiences come to be seen in light of an ineluctable necessity which homogenizes them as functional equivalents. The everyday clutter of human passions and commitments, desires and ambitions, is reduced and simplified, instrumentalized and coordinated, by being made a function of a cognitive need for equilibrium. What has been relinquished is precisely what defined the means/end calculus: a conception of something irreducible and unconditional outside the process.

Under the second phase of technology, we recall, phenomena are coordinated and integrated into an efficient continuum, their interdependence finally allowing the system to operate by its own laws of development. Ellul had identified this phase as one of self-augmentation and self-systematization. Kohlberg's account of moral understanding as a spiral of functional adaptations, and his wholly internal criterion of moral adequacy steering this spiral, reproduce the logic of this technological phase. Moving through the spiral of equilibrated balances, a student's experience is increasingly systematized, and all everyday forms and relations are first designated 'dysfunctional' and then rendered 'transparent' as the process moves forward. Kohlberg's development model relies heavily on a philosophy of life that extrapolates from the processes of biological systems to the conduct, actions, and thoughts of individuals. By so doing Kohlberg aligns human experience and meaning in perfect synchronization with the technological environment which has become the contemporary form of that life. The distinctly human phenomena are transformed into purely formal, transparent components of a life-system, as mere moments within the system's process of continuous self-modification and self-optimalization.

To understand how thoroughly individuals become enmeshed in the technological system by the time they reach stage 6, let us see what has occurred to the means/ends relationship. The moral adequacy or effectiveness of the moral subject is gauged at stage 6 by his or her total identification of values with the means used to develop them. The most effective values are not those which are unconditional or which reflect enduring and permanent facets of a human being, and which would then stand outside the valuing process, but rather those which are in closest approximation to the valuing process itself. Optimal effectiveness is achieved when the valued ends are actually the means of valuing themselves. We see here not merely the primacy of means over ends, but the collapse of the ends into means. Ellul argued that technological efficiency is maximally achieved when a system of means replaces external ends. By stage 6, Kohlberg's means and ends have become revolving functionalities. Dynamically interacting with one another, they have become sufficiently rarefied that human life has been brought to exhibit a kind of pure efficiency.

The organization of moral phenomena within a developmental model produces a morality which is like a perfect homeostatic system in which the ego makes decisions on the basis of an 'input' – a quantum of relevant data received – which, in turn, produces an 'output,' which is an effect upon the environment in which the system exists. What makes the system homeostatic is the existence of a feedback loop by which outputs resulting from one decision become inputs for the next cycle of decision-making. Difference serves as negative feedback, in the technical cybernetic sense, because as an output it tends to bring about a contrary effect in the next cycle, thereby restoring balance. The spiral of equilibrated balances progressively controls the inputs so that there is increasingly less negative feedback and a consequent acceleration towards perfect equilibrium or the perfect transparency of the ideal moral speech-act of stage 6.

Kohlberg's cybernetic system is not, of course, a closed system. Its mechanisms are not fixed or given, for it undergoes structural change in response to environmental conditions. However, since the environment itself constantly changes under the impact of the mind that organizes it, the emerging, total cybernetic system is effectively a closed system, with equilibrium and stability acting as the principle functionally integrating all difference. It is an inherently expansive process which incorporates more and more of the environment into its own logic. Using dynamic balance and synergy as regulators of performance, the system is increasingly successful in enlisting the smallest capillaries of individual and social life into the rational systematization of existence.

If my argument to this point is accepted, one would have to say that

Kohlberg's moral system not only parallels the path technological development is taking, and not only mimics its logic, but is in fact fully integrated into it as one of its key subsystems. The values of universality and reciprocity, ideality and dynamic balance, become nothing more than an expression of the perfect symmetry between values and technology. 'Morality' produces behaviour and a self-consciousness which contribute in a singular manner to the effective functioning of the technological system. Once again, conditions of existence have become 'predicates' of moral being.

All this may appear to be contradicted by Kohlberg's discovery of stage 7. At that stage Kohlberg appears to restore a mystical quality, a 'cosmic vision,' to moral life and thereby supply an alternative to the technological system in its expanding process of objectifying and managing all facets of existence. That Kohlberg's 'cosmic vision,' or mysticism, is not an alternative to technological mastery is demonstrated with considerable poignancy in Mircea Eliade's study of alchemy. In his book *The Forge and the Crucible*, Eliade considers the fourteenth-century alchemists, whose aim was not only to transfigure matter but to achieve in the process a mystical oneness with being by reproducing the experience of divine creation. Eliade sees the alchemists as prototypes of the modern technologist. Placing themselves in the place of cosmic time, the alchemists attempted to accelerate natural time to bring to completion what nature seemed to achieve irregularly. By dissolving the naturally given matter to a primal, inchoate, and larval state, their engineering was meant to make possible the re-creation of perfect matter.

In their presumption, the alchemists believed themselves to be standing at a point before the coming-to-be of worldly differentiation, contradiction, and tension and to fully experience the oneness and wholeness of divine unity. The dream of satisfaction expected from this moment was the powerful force driving the desire to produce perfect matter. Alchemy was not simply pre-scientific – its aims and expectations became legitimate in subsequent modern science.

The ancient alchemist knew that he was meddling in dangerous places. Since the modification of matter and the regeneration of time through the re-enactment of creation were divine prerogatives, the alchemist realized that he needed to protect himself from divine wrath with ritual.

Using the social-science laboratory and the classroom as the modern crucible, the modern alchemist too seeks to transubstantiate matter by regenerating time. There is, of course, a difference. First, modern alchemy requires no sacramental purificatory ritual because the technical act is not seen as spiritual pollution. At worst, experiments which fail and produce new problems can be corrected by further technical acts. Second, the modern crucible is controlled not by a *techne*, but by technology, which, as we have noted, is more than willing to dispense with those measures steering technical control drawn from the perspective of humans (beauty, immortality, or truth – the ends sought by the ancient alchemists). The modern alchemist, using modern science and technology, can fulfil Nietzsche's words, 'Love yourself through grace, then you are no longer in need of your God, and you can act the whole drama of fall and redemption to its end in yourself.'[2] What the example of alchemy shows is not only the hidden affinity between mysticism and technology, but also just to what extent the mystical desire for oneness may actually drive the projects to reconstruct the world and the self.

Finally, least of all can we hope for limits to technology arising from values clarification. This is a disappointing conclusion to draw because unquestionably there is enormous potential for the renewal of the world in the vitality values clarification taps. VC effectively clears the ground of dogma and doctrine and offers the opportunity to genuinely act on new opportunities, retrieving understandings of the past, opening individuals to experiences excluded from public discourse (the rich tapestry of non-Western ways of being, the subtle nuances of women's understanding, the cosmological visions of our aboriginal peoples), and restoring the conditions necessary for genuine freedom in action and thought. The potential VC releases appears particularly heartening as we seek answers to contemporary anomie and dislocation, loss of depth and narrowing of meaning.

But this potential is squandered, and the new heterogeneity VC celebrates seems less an answer than a symptom of the ailing contemporary society it diagnoses. VC's fragmentation does not cultivate the opportunity for return from dogma and arbitrariness to primary and elementary possibilities. To the contrary, in disrupting the principle of identity, and letting everything be different, it makes everything different in the same way and for the same reasons. Ways of being, understandings, visions, and practices become under VC so many lifeless images unable to contribute to the human search for meaning. No measure has been left with which the individual could discriminate among the plethora of images. Moreover, values clarification might start out as the final celebration of modern subjectivity, but it is a project which cannot contain its own momentum and finally extinguishes the self it has elevated and empowered by destroying its interiority. With its humanity wholly exteriorized, and its being 'decentred,' will it be able to resist any of the images with which it is traversed? The 'human' has become sheer availability with semiology as the tool that would perpetually re-create an individual's existence. As the mere carrier of data, as simply the 'state of the art' of various scenario-positing technologies, the self has lost that human perspective which would give meaning and establish the regulative limits of experience. All the concrete forms of its existence having been deconstructed, VC's self is a vulnerable, isolated being with no reference beyond self-certainty to verify whether its self-definitions and creations correspond to the structure of reality.

The abandonment of reality is not an accidental by-product of values clarification. The problem lies with VC's central value – authenticity. Authenticity is the value which is to reflect a person's resonance with primordial genesis. It is not merely a presence hidden behind falsifying forms, demanding simply some interpretive work so as to be retrieved. To the contrary, authenticity is a withdrawal, a disentanglement, and thus cannot permit of instantiation. The project to be 'authentic' must entail a repeated deferral of the 'real' self, for there is no primal substratum which it can seize and use against the inauthentic.

VC's demand that authenticity be operationalized is the attempt to make authenticity stand in as real. But since there is nothing that can be retrieved, the authentic can at best be staged or simulated. Simulation of authenticity requires the proliferation of simulations – simulations of simulations. The simulation of authenticity is driven by an overwrought desire for the real. This hyperactivity is a desperate simulation of feelings and moods to recapture the real which always escapes it. VC finally cancels out the difference between authenticity and inauthenticity for the positing of values requires a simulation of the real it cannot have. Indeed, authenticity is verified by its simulation – it is shown never to have existed. VC does not merely challenge the real, it suggests that the real is nothing more than a simulation. With the fusion of the real and the illusory in simulation, reality proliferates wildly and every scenario becomes real. In the process the self and the authentic disappear in the play of signs. In the sixties VC could be used to proliferate progressive values. In the seventies and eighties, VC was used to proliferate 'back to basic' values. On either account VC's values are simulations and they can be more potent than their originals. More real than their originals, these are 'hyperreal' values, each one different but authentic.

Another strange manoeuvre plagues values clarification and its hope for genuine human freedom. By conjoining the values of authenticity and empowerment, as we have already noted, values clarification implodes the self and simultaneously disperses that self over the whole earth. The move is characteristic of the third phase of technology. The implosion is not an act of retrieval of a rich interior core, such as that intended by the Christian imperative of renewing one's person, nor is the transcendence of the individual beyond place and history an invitation to participate in the universal comity of humankind. Instead, values clarification implodes the self towards a primal affectivity, while simultaneously extending that self outwards in an immediate embrace with all the globe. Values clarification produces a deracinated monadism which is brought to resonate with an abstract globalism. Operationalizing authenticity and empowerment merely brings the isolated self into a field of frantic energy where it is nothing but the empty synthesis of an infinite commutability of information signs. What we finally arrive at, having left Kohlberg's life-system, in a great celebration of indiscriminate *différance*, is what Ellul describes as 'a sort of schematizing of life by technology.' Given the enormous capacities of modern information and media technologies, and the absolute absence of any remaining trace of ordering symbols to direct those capacities to make and unmake, is it sensible to optimistically affirm that all clarified values will be benign? The ascendancy of the values of 'mobility,' 'superfluity,' and 'disposability' nearly guarantees that VC's self will be insulated from reality, incapable of receiving even the most elementary forms of possession which give human existence meaning. Once values clarification and technology work wholly in tandem, the contemporary age has produced an enormously efficient enterprise for wholly desincarnating reality. We are left in a situation, to paraphrase Neil Postman, of simply 'amusing ourselves to death.'

Moreover, belying the promise of freedom, the effect of VC's dispersion of all order is to merely substitute new forms of control and expose individuals to a new vulnerability. The autonomous and emancipated individual is nothing more than endlessly refracted effects of power, no less subject to an apparatus of total, continuous, and efficient surveillance and management. Such a self's complete openness to infinite and indefinite possibilities is not so much freedom as an emptiness which is an invitation to any number of experimental possibilities.

VC's primordial freedom, however evocatively its designers use metaphors to suggest new opportunities for human renewal, is in fact a new form of manipulation and control. Psychologizing values has meant turning from understanding 'moral' phenomena fundamentally as analogous to judicial categories, to articulating them as psychological constructs. This has meant that individuals can be enmeshed within an entire complex, a continuum of helping- and care-profession agencies whose concern it is to monitor and enhance their 'quality of life.' At the same time, as objects of knowledge, their desires and longings have been made available to be reconstructed and optimized. The therapy VC offers for 'values stress' is not the basis for a renewal of the forms which give human existence direction and substance (and which are in need of the new opportunities which genuine novelty offers), but rather is an elaborate technology of preprogrammed authenticity and affectivity – an empowering of the self wholly commensurate with technological manipulation.[3] The therapy which the self receives is that which ensures his or her collusion with the technological imperative and the neutralization of what would animate his or her resistance.

Briefly then, the values vaunted by values education – empowerment, authenticity, adaptability, universality, and creativity – are, in the final instance, wholly at one with the dynamic of modern technological society. Thus, while it is said that with values we have recalled the 'human factor' in the context of wide-scale control and mastery of 'objects,' values education brings the same techniques and expectations to the realm where limits to technology could have been understood. Its discourse is ancillary to, even intertwined in complicity with, the technological discourse.

The conjunction of a relentless technological drive to absorb difference into the sameness of functionality and an inherently nihilistic discourse of 'values' that now operates, quite unabashedly, as a technology of experimental subjugation and population control is finally, to quote Grant, 'the price which modern man had to pay ... for attempting to be absolute sovereign, to become the master and owner of nature, to conquer chance.'[4] The conclusions to which we have come reflect the extreme working out of a logic. Following George Grant, I suggested at the beginning of this study that a logic has a destiny towards which it is bound to unravel. The destiny of values is to reproduce the forms of the will that at the same time wills technology, and to enmesh individuals in the controls and closed scenarios which are its experimental strategies. With values clarification, which represents the ineluctable conclusion of the dynamic which values education releases, we have totally abstract, formalized values, infinitely reactivated, empty of all human content, working in tandem with the equally dehumanized impulse of a disseminated and decentred technological environment. All concrete forms of human existence have vanished, short of those simulated and optimized by a technology that is even capable of turning this operation of simulation wholly transparent. As McLuhan points out, 'with electricity as energizer and synchronizer, all aspects of production, consumption, and organization become incidental to communication.'[5] Efficiency is now losing its anthropocentric, even biocentric, parameters and becoming the expression of the overall effect of efforts to optimize and enhance consumption patterns by an infinitely revolving circuit of scenarios and simulations.

The metaphor through which I have attempted to convey the disentanglement of man from his concrete particularity and from the permanent structure of his political and intellectual existence (as well as his release into a fluidity and perpetual mobility where it has become a question whether the distinctively 'human' still exists) is 'dispossession.' By 'dispossession' I am referring to the losses covered under Arendt's and Voegelin's analyses of 'worldlessness' and 'gnosticism.' In brief, the dissolution of permanent worldly distinctions and the truncation of the amplitude of psychic experience conveyed by these terms constitute a destruction of the coordinates of the forms of life which stabilize and balance the pull of finiteness and infiniteness, motion and rest. I have raised as a dilemma the inanition of the forms of everyday life and the celebration of release from these forms in the 'authenticity' of values education, because values education takes place in a technological environment whose 'fundamental ontology' is inhospitable to the perspective of the human, where what is entails simply what is traversed by the infinite commutability of information signs emanating from myriad anonymous sources. Thus, the spectre which I have wished to raise is that the uniting of values education with the technological environment (to whose motions it uncannily corresponds) produces a situation where the two planes merely modulate with one another, reiterating and confirming each other's dynamism. It is a situation, to recall Arendt and Voegelin, whose danger lies in how it has left humans exposed and vulnerable to 'nonsense and capricious notions' and 'murderous schemes.'

The alternative to 'dispossession' is obviously 'possession,' but a possessive relation to being is not a modality of human life easily retrieved in the contemporary era. Indeed, the history of our attitude to 'possession' is an increasing awareness that our possessive affinity to being is the very form of the pathology impeding us from knowledge and freedom. To see how possession could be denied in this way, and to remind ourselves of how much we have to lose when we abandon the work we undertake in incarnating reality, it is necessary to trace the modern discontent with possession and thereby elevate to a thematic discussion what I have attempted to convey in speaking of values education as an apprenticeship to dispossession.

The Calumny of Possession

In modern thought and social experience possession has come to be viewed through the prism of the peculiarly modern blackmail of the either/or of subjectivity and objectivity – in this case 'being' or 'possession.' Possession is *either* a fetishism of objects, a magical attitude, cathectic sign-objects, and absorption into an in-itself (romantic desire for immediacy), *or* a unidirectional power over something, such as a violation and domination. The dichotomy between these two facets of what constitutes possession is marked: *either* possess *or* be possessed; *either* legitimate the desire for appropriation *or* affirm the detached, free, self-conscious creativity of the authentic human being and refuse the temptation and submission to what is reified and can be fetishized; *either* individual, consumptive appropriation at the expense of others, *or* a respect for men's social function and a full 'human reality'; *either* mechanistic materialism, *or* subjectivity and intentionality.

Underlying all these is the subject/object distinction of modern philosophy. Possession can only be the form of mediation that juxtaposes humans and the world as antagonists. Humankind's ways in the everyday are reduced to mere impediments, obscuring or deforming 'full human reality,' 'fully transparent social relations,' or 'just distribution.' The result of the subject/object division is, finally, the inanition of the experience of possession as a mode of existence that might be of any primary and elementary significance. The contemporary celebration of 'dispossession' is preceded by a long history of disposing of the forms of everyday human existence, of what is 'first and foremost.'

We can find the roots of modern discontent with possession in Rousseau's plea on behalf of a free and sweet 'natural' 'sentiment of existence' against the corruption of property-divided, contentious society. His account is an application of the general enlightenment's turn away from the concrete and external (and thus the conditioning and limiting) to social life. In Rousseau this principle becomes an instrument of historical deconstruction – it allows him to identify the decisive events in human development when open perfectibility was shackled and corrupted. Rousseau's analysis of the historical constitution of humanity as the development of the idea of private property ('clever usurpation') applied to human identity is the starting-point for the identification of possession with an 'effect of force and the right of the first occupier.' Rousseau's thought marks the beginning of the trend which sees other forms of human behaviour as simply repeating a corrupt, possessive desire.

Rousseau's conceptualization of possession as a juridical act is confirmed by Hegel, who identifies it as having 'external power over something,' a right legitimated by the reciprocal recognition of other possessing persons. Henceforth, possession would only be understood in terms of an exclusionary right; it would be a property relation. Marx, accepting the Hegelian equation of possession with the appropriative act sanctioned by law, and recognizing the formative effect of market society on juridical terms, returns to Rousseau's critical perspective and in the process radicalizes it so as to see any possessive relation as object fetishism, as a deformed satisfaction of need and a distortion of true, social relations. Marx highlights the hidden collusion of propriety and property and of production and social performance.[6]

Where Marx critically analyses the social and personal deformations which transpire as a result of the juridical manipulation of possession, Nietzsche takes the deconstruction of possessive relations further into the realm of our moral and intellectual projects. In *The Genealogy of Morals*, Nietzsche shows how all ethical and moral practices of the past operated by an assumption that man was an indebted being and was as a result liable for compensation. Suggesting that our moral terms are founded on a slavish submissiveness to the misconstrued notion that there is something in the order of being which is durative and determinate, Nietzsche attempted to expose the small-mindedness and craven 'account-bookishness' underlying all moral convention. Assuming the permanence and eternal authority of some phenomena – the gods, nature, the past, one's ancestors – is to manifest one's humanness in the form of the petty, niggardly temperament of the ignoble. Running through the ethical and moral conventions of the past, Nietzsche argues, is precisely this contractual language of buying, selling, barter, trade, and traffic of goods. Ethics and morals are organized languages of comportment (how we carry ourselves), conduct (how we collect ourselves), demeanour (how we rule over our own domain), behaviour (how we own ourselves), appropriateness (how we render something our property), justice (how we maintain boundaries), the good (possessing the appropriate), and evil (exceeding due measure). It is a language of owingness, indebtedness, and of having something due on account. To be either ethical or moral is to make appropriation secure and then to be accountable for such security. Accountability guarantees that one will be indemnified and repaid in full. To be prepared so as to be indemnified is to have stood security for one's own future, to have brought forward from a past promise that secured being upon whom recompense can be bestowed. It is a language that has assumed the possibility of a possessing being, of engaging in traffic with that being, and of reproducing that being's permanency in the temporality of human existence.

Nietzsche points out, too, that there is a strange obsessiveness to possession. The perpetual re-enactment of the appropriative act constitutes a desperate desire to achieve the permanence of that towards which the act is directed. Possession is therefore intended to produce self-possession. It indicates a desire for the certain, the rooted, a horizon, and a belonging.[7] But since possession cannot be realized, the infinite task can lead to the deformed relation of debtor to creditor: the incompletable effort to stand security for a debt that cannot be repaid. The result is bad conscience, inordinate fear of punishment, and guilt as the repayment of the debt that cannot be discharged. It can also produce the morality of self-denial. These responses, Nietzsche argues, all arise out of the arbitrary thought that things endure.

Where morality entails such a weighing of allotments and compulsive repetition of indebtedness, Nietzsche counterposes, the vitality and dynamism of life – its pulse towards growth and enhancement of power – is denied and suppressed. Now such restraint, Nietzsche realized, may create the illusion of mastering the contingent, the arbitrary, and the dangerous but not only do the 'values' of such mastery necessarily 'devalue' themselves (that is, are exposed as being just as arbitrary as that which they purport to challenge), but the effort is an attempt to extinguish the source of what is strong and vital in existence itself and thus only leads to torpor, weariness, and denial. 'What if a symptom of regression were inherent in the "good," likewise a danger, a seduction, a poison, a narcotic, through which the present was possibly living *at the expense of the future*? Perhaps more comfortably, less dangerously, but at the same time in a meaner style, more basely? – So that precisely morality would be to blame if the *highest power and splendour* actually possible to the type man was never in fact attained? So that precisely morality was the danger of dangers?'[8]

In the final analysis, Nietzsche suggests, the craven need for a punitive morality is an expression of the unwillingness to accept the truth of the temporality of our existence. The desire for what is durative and determinate is the sign of a weak will that is unable to affirm the sheer transience of life and, in resentment, erects constructs of 'eternal verities' which provide a corrupting surrogate for the healthy expression of life – the experiences of guilt and atonement.

Nietzsche's analysis is more radical than that of his predecessors, for in demanding of us a radical return to primordial genesis he intends the most far-reaching dispossession. Nietzsche argues that to date an arbitrary and life-denying isomorphism characterizes the modalities of our self-interpretation: our possession of the things in the world, our possession of ourselves, our possession of truths which order and adjudicate over our allotments to ourselves and the world we inhabit. Humans, as sentient beings, as ethical beings, and as intellectual beings, he points out, have displayed an inauthentic need to possess reality. The ethically and morally 'proper' phenomena have been about property, about bestowing presence and about insisting on ownership of what is secured. But, Nietzsche challenges, a *healthy* affirmation of life is where being is not taken as a constant, securable, and representable presence.

The desire for possession, which in the final analysis is a desire for presence, is futile, and the obsessive re-enactment of the appropriative act, in the attempt to have being, destroys life. Nietzsche demands a repudiation and destruction of Western metaphysic's possessive affinity for being.

'Futile' is the term Sartre also employs to characterize the everyday relation to being. The everyday is a world where the durable aspect of being is taken as the sole determination of being, and it is this affinity to possess being that for Sartre renders human experience pathological. The individual, for Sartre, is a 'for-itself,' a free project towards an open future. As a 'for-itself,' the individual *is* most fully by not being what has determinate characteristics or properties and by not being what can be reduced to an object-being. The durative and completed is the 'in-itself,' which lies inert and opaque in the everyday and threatens to immobilize life. Where humans adopt closed definitions of their humanness or immerse themselves in material things and thereby stabilize their dynamic mobility, abandoning the open projection of themselves into the future, they have effectively denied themselves and become object-beings. The desire to possess is ultimately a desire for the stationary plenitude of the in-itself. It is an attempt to bestow objective confirmation on one's own subjectivity, to bring that subjectivity to occupy a fixed place within a total determinate context, to grasp and hold the conditions of one's own possibility, and ultimately to be the source and foundation for all that is.

Possession, Sartre argues, is not just intellectual or moral error or blindness, but a pathological phenomenon. To be the for-itself, both intellectual and moral dispossession must occur. Hence his analysis continues as a diagnosis of possession's various pathological twists. In possession, the for-itself wants to both maintain the thing as an externality, as something new, untouched, 'virginal' (as permanent object, durable and impenetrable), and to recognize that thing totally as its own creation (a continuous emanation of itself and thus familiar). Possession will temporarily satisfy the desire to bring an end to the tension of one's existence for it provides the possibility of permanence and stability. The appropriative synthesis of self and thing brings an ideal-totality which pleases, fulfils need, and stills unrest. The possessive act creates a world or totality where the for-itself exists in the mode of the in-itself. But that self is simultaneously a perpetual emanation of creativity. Thus, possession is, in fact, a conflict within the self itself; it is an attempt to be an in-itself–for-itself. There can be no synthesis of familiar continuity with virgin newness. Possession will always manifest this impossibility through the contradictory expectations of perpetual possession and possession which leaves no trace.

Possession then, Sartre writes, is tragically marred by desires issuing in pathological forms: the Actaeon complex, which is the desire to violate purity, and the Jonah complex, which is the wish for a non-destructive assimilation. Possession is the contradictory demand for a perpetual enactment of creation so that the mine-ness of a thing is continually created, and the thing also perpetually renews itself for my enjoyment while remaining independent of me. 'To have' reflects the tension of these contradictory demands of appropriation by creation and appropriation by enjoyment.

Humans cannot reconcile the desires underlying these complexes without finally being subsumed by opacity and inertness. Possession will never bring contentment because whatever satisfaction comes from the bond of possession will always be marred by the fear of being possessed by the possessed thing. Possession finally derails into an engulfment of the for-itself by objects, a taunting persistence of things which have the being that the self is not. Possession and freedom are incompatible, for the former's effort to exist as an indifferent in-itself in relation to itself as a for-itself corrupts the experience of freedom and leads to bad faith and inauthenticity.

Having a primordial relation to things is no longer a possibility for us, according to Sartre. The illusion of a possession which does not entail consuming or being consumed, of an 'indigestible digestible' (Jonah in the stomach of the whale), is merely a sign of self-deception (the magic expectation that the other can become me but still remain the other). Thus, in a decisive way, for Sartre, there can be no belongingness, for humans are not at home in the world. *Things*, and the everyday world in which they are placed, are, in all their dense positivity, the mere 'thereness' of the 'practico-inert.' The self's traffic with them has to be seen as the manifestation of 'inauthentic' passions and interests whose actual impulse is either covetousness or rapacity (possess or be possessed).[9]

The same fearful torment haunts Sartre's depiction of the *practices* within the practico-inert, the motions of which are also deeply inscribed with the tendency of the everyday to ossify life. The for-itself attempts to surge forward towards an open future, but the solid immobility of the everyday in which it is implicated forever encroaches, absorbs, and threatens to engulf it. To affirm one's concrete particularity, for example, is to have imposed on one the logic of possessive affinity. The world wants us to have the consistency and immobility of the in-itself, to participate in the 'thickening' and 'coagulating' of human reality. To accept that being-in-itself that the world calls 'me' is to forsake the project of limitless possibility. 'Facticity' is, for Sartre, a superfluous, overbearing presence – it is what one must come to know oneself not to be. The for-itself, Sartre suggests, must have 'the sense of its complete gratuitousness, it grasps itself as being where it is pointlessly, as being superfluous.' But the 'viscosity' of the world, that is, the forms of the everyday, is always there to violate that purity and innocence.

The everyday, Sartre writes, is deceptive. Unlike things, the practices and forms of the world seem to affirm the transience and fortuitousness of existence and thus offer the conditions for man's project into an indefinite and infinite future. But, in fact, that is not the case. Hence, it has to be recognized for what it is: 'sliminess,' 'melting,' 'stickiness.' The 'gelatinous' of the everyday simply confounds the distinction between solid and fluid and jeopardizes the free project of the self:

What mode of being is symbolized by the slimy? I see first that it is the homogeneity and the imitation of liquidity. A slimy substance like pitch is an aberrant fluid. At first, with the appearance of a fluid it manifests itself to us as a being which is everywhere fleeing and yet everywhere similar to itself, which on all sides escapes yet on which one can float, a being without danger and without memory, which eternally is changed into itself, on which one leaves no mark and which could not leave a mark on us, a being which slides and on which one can slide, which can be possessed by something sliding ... and which never possesses because it rolls over us, a being which is eternity and infinite temporality because it is perpetual change without anything which changes ... But immediately the slimy reveals itself as essentially ambiguous because its fluidity exists in slow motion; there is a sticky thickness in its liquidity.[10]

Sliminess, in short, is 'like a leech sucking me.'[11] The practical world of the everyday turns out, then, to be the same encroaching, absorbing heaviness that characterizes things. Where fluid water 'evokes the image of the constant interpenetration of the parts by a whole and their perpetual dissociation and free movement,' an image which expresses quintessentially our undertaking on behalf of the free projection towards the future, slime is the 'soft clinging' and 'sly solidarity and complicity of all its leechlike parts, a vague, soft effort made by each to individualize itself, followed by a falling back and flattening out that is emptied of the individual, sucked in on all sides by the substance.' The movement of slime entails a gradual sinking, a collapse, a 'fusion with the whole,' a threatening, annihilating, presence which is the precise model of that which we believe to have possessed, but in fact possesses us, a 'surreptitious appropriation of the possessor by the possessed' that compromises us, sucks the human reality out of us. 'To touch the slimy,' Sartre writes, 'is to risk being dissolved in sliminess,' in its 'almost solid permanence.'

Sliminess is the ontological symbol of a being in which the for-itself is swallowed up by the in-itself. The in-itself must ultimately be rejected with nausea. The things and practices of the world cannot be correlated with what we authentically are as pure temporality – they cannot be seen to possess a teleological structure which would break them out of their stultifying positivity. Consciousness confronts an inert world of things and its authenticity is assured only by the project on behalf of a lack of being. Possession, symbolic action, and ritual, indeed all mediating institutions, now take on the spectre of immobilization, ossification, and engulfment.

To avoid the immobility of 'poisonous possession' and to reassert human reality to break free from a slime on which one cannot slide, it becomes necessary to dispossess the self of itself, to dispose not only of tangible, worldly possessions but also of a consciousness that knows only by possessing the other. Dispossession means renouncing the equally pathological desires to immerse oneself in the permanent and to devour and digest the other. What must be activated is the experience of self in a homogeneous and undifferentiated liquidity and fluidity, a 'special relation of appropriation' which Sartre describes in a discussion of the creativity of skiing: as a 'sliding,' as opposed to 'taking root,' it is a continuous creation, marred only by 'that slight disappointment which always seizes us when we see behind us the imprints which our skis have left on the snow ... how much better it would be if the snow re-formed itself as we passed over it.' If the gelatinous is threatening, then it can be overcome by a construct of reality where both oneself and one's environment are entirely non-resistant: a field of indeterminacy, disposability, and fluidity.

Sartre realized, like Nietzsche, that possession has both an ontological and a moral manifestation. Possession's ethic of responsibility and stability, he continues, jaundices human reality by manifesting its congealing character in the very place where vitality and dynamism ought to be evident. 'Thus I am responsible for the existence of my possessions in the human order ... my simple life appears to me as creative exactly because by its continuity it perpetuates the quality of being possessed in each of the objects in my possession. I draw the collection of my surroundings into being along with myself' ('Doing and Having,' p. 723). The pathology of possession, Sartre argues, is what also underlies the realm of 'values.' His answer of mobile dispossession is to be applied to it as well. The final phase of diagnosis of man's pathology is to reveal the centrality of possessiveness in traditional morality. Values, he wants to show, are like inert possessions and, if the self is rendered immobile by binding itself to such inertness, then it loses its authenticity.

The possibility of values, for Sartre, reflects the essential contradiction of human existence: we are the for-itself which seeks the totality of itself by seeking to situate itself in the world, and thus to be in the mode of in-itself, and yet at the same time we are the being whose reality is the 'project' which stipulates that world not to be. The for-itself can never be value and cannot have values as permanent conditions of its existence. For a value to be actualized, to be determinate, is to destroy it as a value. The essence of a value lies in its temporality and its orientation, which extends beyond situation. Yet the for-itself nonetheless seeks desperately to render value determinate and to maintain value in its ontological stability. To be one's possibilities is to refuse that ontological stability to value. Freedom can only make of itself a lack if it can posit and then nihilate values.

Values must resonate with the freedom of moving from a sense of superfluous presence to a being of absence, out of a fixed place and direction in the world into a cyclic process of perpetual transformation. Thus the self must abandon the anticipation that the self projected towards future possibility will meet up with itself: bad faith lies not in the refusal to meet up with oneself but, rather, in the expectation that one will. The self must not refuse the freedom to itself that may entail its being something other than it is once it embarks on its project. The error of the past was to see the control of human behaviour as needing the appropriation of being; to see action as making that appropriation secure; to see 'responsibility' as being accountable for such security.

The self is a for-itself and not an in-itself. Authentic valuing demands the evacuation from situation and determinate finitude: from time as past, present, future and from space as enclosed and exclusive, from time- and space-invested political and intellectual projects of retrieval and recovery. All these manifest the characteristics of inertness and opacity, of stupid contingency. To be is not to be what one is, but to be what one is not. Sartre describes this Nothingness as the endlessly refracting effects of evacuation of situation by a self perpetually engaged in the extrication of itself from itself:

One does not find, one does not discover Nothingness as one might find or uncover a being. Nothingness is always an *elsewhere*. It is the obligation with respect to itself, to exist as a being which is perpetually afflicted with an inconsistency of being. This inconsistency moreover does not refer to another being, it is only a perpetual reference of the self to itself, of the reflection to the reflector, of the reflector to the reflection ... thus nothingness is this hole of being, this fall of the in-itself towards itself by which the for-itself is constituted. But this nothingness can only 'be being' if its borrowed existence is correlated to a nihilating act of being. This perpetual act by which the in-itself degenerates into presence-to-itself we shall call an ontological act. Nothingness is the putting into question of being by being, that is to say exactly consciousness or the for-itself.[12]

The 'putting-into-question' of being by being leads to Sartre's three 'ek-stases' – standing forth in the present – which express the authentic for-itself: not being what is means leaving behind the past of facticity; being what it is not means being the lack of a fixed past or desired future; and being dispersed in the game of mirrors. The for-itself, Sartre sums up, is 'Present, Past, Future – all at the same time – dispersing its being in three dimensions.' Free of precondition and determination, it is a freedom of simultaneity and intensity.

A freedom and a human reality that are like sliding on a surface without leaving a trace, by a self who will harbour no anticipation and no regret, no shame and no boredom, are the only true expressions of authentic existence. A radical dispossession, which triumphs over the concrete, practical world of interests and compromises, and its nascent images of perfection, completion, and achievement, requires a new being. This is a being who presumes no knowledge of the nature and limits of his own existence, who does not need the political world in which to actualize himself, and for whom the question of his being – as a question which, discovering that the origins and ends of his existence are mysteries within the 'in-between' of the *apeiron* and the divine, leads to balance, rather than panic – will ultimately not arise.

Sartre's 'for-itself' is then like Nietzsche's being beyond indebtedness and guilt, beyond defiance and consent. This is the posthumous being who has learned how to die, and how to overcome finitude by becoming a child and affirming life and power in the 'game of creation': 'The child is innocence and forgetting, a new beginning, a game, a self-propelled wheel, a first movement, a sacred "yes." For the game of creation, my brothers, a sacred "yes" is needed: the spirit now wills his own will, and he who had been lost to the world now conquers his own world.'[13]

What is broken here is the possessive affinity of the self for itself – to dispossess is to dispose of the self and the appropriative mode in which it has stood to life, to dissolve the 'sclerosis,' the connectedness and durability bestowed by possession. Values render this disposability into the experience of 'overflowing abundance.' For this reason, as we have already noted, the affirmation of values is dissociable from character formation; such programs of habit formation, exercises of reminiscence to collect together the identity of consciousness, and the production of a total personality are now obsolete.

I wish to argue that this Sartrean dispossession – the unrelenting disentanglement from images of being expressed as completion, finality, and purpose, the ecstatic celebration of relentless negativity, transience, and dispersion – throws its long shadow over the pedagogical principles activating values education. The question is: where does this radical dispossession actually get us? What form will this dream of sliding on a surface without leaving a trace take when it meets the first-order reality where humans love and die, where promises and forgiveness ensure decency and common sense, where the weak suffer injustice at the hands of the stronger, and where, were it not for the intimations of goodness in the beautiful and the true, we would have no meaning in our lives?

Having observed the destiny of 'values' under 'values education,' I am not inspired with much confidence that the collision of the second-order realities with first-order reality will be favourable to the prospect of maintaining human order. To recall, the regulative limits defining the tension within which 'values' traditionally served as prescriptions of conduct – human/divine, immanent/transcendent, vice/virtue, evil/good, desire/reason – no longer enjoy a secure place in the models we surveyed. There is no program of character or personality formation whose aim is to form a political or intellectual being. No idea of habituating a student to certain virtues or excellences, talents or aptitudes, or orienting a student by the distinctions and meanings of the political world can be found in values clarification. No formative experiences which might serve as existential modalities of man's participation in a transcending reality combine to produce a concept of what a human being is which would stabilize the processes to which students are exposed. Freed from these contexts, one would have to say that 'value' is no longer a strictly 'human' phenomenon. Value has withdrawn from man – a human's status as the measure of things has been dispossessed.

Not only is that determinate place where earlier valuation occurred now gone, but that determinate being for whom the valuations were values and hence valuable is now transfigured. Values clarification simply brings out into the open the destiny of the language of values – to break values loose from all regulative criteria and to let them float in an infinite commutability, where the stable relations between signified and referent are abolished by perpetual play. Values become their own referents, not designating any stable ground, but simply referring back to other values. Without representation or referentiality, 'values' merely simulate 'values,' not to say 'morals' or 'ethics.' The non-place of a mere intensity and the non-time of sheer affectivity in which a perpetually self-overcoming will is the relay for the simulacra of values – this is what we have at the end of the history of values.

This is not mere relativism, or its philosophical counterpart, subjectivism, for there is no determinate being for whom the process of affirming, choosing, and deploying of values is any longer meaningful. And since there is no difference between what values have become as simulacra and the infinite number of images and signs processed and reprocessed through every other apparatus of the technological system, values can be substituted one for another and may be disposed of as soon as they falter in their ability to exhibit 'relentless negativity.'

Now, obviously certain images of what a 'human' is do gain ascendancy, as do particular 'values,' just as there are values which decline and vanish. The language of 'proactive' and 'reactive' is precisely an attempt to register such movements. But those evaluative criteria do not derive from an understanding of reality. Neither the transcendent, nor an idea of progress in history, nor the consensus of 'social interest' guides how these values are judged. But if this is so, the swell and retreat of the various images and ideals can only be understood under that most radical concept of analysis, Nietzsche's 'will-to-power.'

We have already noted in an earlier chapter that the will-to-power provides a way of noticing that evaluative criteria measure intensities or modulations rather than determinate locations or continuities. The will-to-power provides a way of explaining how purely formalized, empty syntheses can circulate as if they were substantial. The will-to-power is the idea of an energy field where floating images can play out the simulacrum of totalizing a field of tension, and explains how emptiness becomes the site of endless experimental permutations. The 'will-to-power' moves us away from the mechanical order of distinct phenomena presumed to exist and interact in enclosed space classifiable by a detached observer, and beyond an organic order of developing structures maintained in dynamic equilibrium in sequential time, to a cybernetic play of circuits and radiating intensities (data-patterns, differential equations of motion, exchanges, and pulses) in space-time. In this dream the old order of prescriptive and exclusive places and meaning-endowed histories is dissolved. Intellectual and spiritual order similarly are extinguished.

When values have been separated from meaning and order, value has no value. Value is simply value-in-use, the instrument serving a temporary power configuration. Nietzsche describes the new situation in his characteristic bluntness: 'Value,' he writes, 'is essentially the point of view for the increasing or decreasing of these dominating centers.'[14] Values are simply quanta of power, useful for maintaining and enhancing control over an aspect of reality. These values do not limit the will-to-power, but are its very conditions of possibility. Values cannot be external and unconditional – 'there is nothing outside of being as a whole that might serve as a condition for it. What is lacking is something whereby it [becoming as a whole] might be measured.'[15]

The language of values and the fundamental ontology underlying it makes explicit and, in fact, affirms and celebrates the link between value-positing and the will-to-power. It is a novel situation because values are unabashedly acknowledged to be mere expressions of power. As Heidegger points out, 'This value-positing is new because it makes secure to itself its principle and simultaneously adheres to this securing as a value posited out of its own principle. As the principle of the new value-positing, however, the will-to-power is, in relation to previous values, at the same time the principle of the revaluing of all such values.'[16] Our self-consciousness and our redefinition as the being who wills the will-to-power mean that nothing may remain of the traditional forms of receptivity and obedience. Heidegger concludes:

'The great noon' is the time of the brightest brightness, namely of the consciousness that unconditionally and in every respect has become conscious of itself as that knowing which consists in deliberately willing the will-to-power as the Being of whatever is; and, as such willing, in rebelliously withstanding and subjugating to itself every necessary phase of the objectifying of the world, thus making secure the stable constant reserve of what is for a willing of the greatest possible uniformity and equality. In the willing of this will, however, there comes upon man the necessity that he concomitantly will the conditions, the requirements of such a willing. That means: to posit values. In such a manner does value determine all that is in its Being.[17]

Once we start speaking of 'value rescaling,' 'value redeployment,' 'value restandardization,' 'value implementation retargeting,' 'upgrading/downgrading values,' we are abandoning symbols of human order to a process of circulating and parodic simulacra. Values simply range across the surface, referring and conveying nothing. This is why there can be no conscious investment in values, no rational calculation of their advantage in terms of an essential interest, no participation in a dimension of reality once intimated by heroic models, sublime experiences, divine encounters, sacred rites, or public events. As objects extracted from their contexts and formalized into units of information they no longer permit us the experience of meaning, no longer move us to engage other psyches in speech, or elicit from us the passions and virtues of courage, honour, or trust. They provide no enlargement of our horizon, no testing to alternative vantage points, and no catalyst for a collective memory of a way of life preceding the defiant posture of technological mastery and its infinitely substitutable functional equivalences. Values are a willing of the conditions of dispossession at the heart of technology. The ascendancy of the values of dispossession indicates that conditions of existence, to paraphrase Nietzsche, have been made into predicates of being.

Once values are operationalized and become an object of control, we are left with Nietzsche's insight that values are, 'psychologically considered, the results of certain perspectives of utility designed to maintain and increase constructs of domination.'[18]

'Psychologically considered,' the values education models signify diverse modulations of a vast surface network in which bodies are stimulated, pleasures provoked, speeches extracted, and expertise formed in an organization of controls linking knowledge and power. The models are control sites in which the feelings and desires of the self are sutured to the management of forces throughout the wider technological environment, so that the therapeutic control of the self is at the same time the operational site for global transformation.

The hope of 'a total shift of our society' by way of the new 'mental hygiene' of values education is advanced by three strategies. First, questions of 'morality' have to become psychological problems which can be managed. Erich Fromm offers the quintessential manifesto: 'Neurosis itself is, in the last analysis, a symptom of moral failure ... a neurotic symptom is the specific expression of moral conflict, and the success of the therapeutic effort depends on the understanding and solution of the person's moral problem.'[19] The next step is to link values education with the other processes of transformation occurring in society. A radical pedagogy, Paulo Freire writes in *Education as the Practice of Freedom*, must renounce the view that knowledge is a gift merely confirming a static and compartmentalized reality. Students must see themselves as 'transformers of that world,' their own self-overcoming activity stimulating a world whose reality is also 'a process, undergoing constant transformation.'[20] Counsellors, whose presence throughout the values education field attests, can play a pivotal role, 'operating a feedback system to the school' and working 'to bring about institutional and even, in the long run, societal modification of values and practices in the interests of the personal development and mental health of children.'[21] The final step is to recognize that the school is only one point in the continuum of apparati contributing to the process of global realignment. Proactive values, as a series of provincial health, social studies, and personal life skills curricula intone, arise from a 'total health' concept, whose viability depends on expanding 'the available support systems in the community': 'a team of community health nurses, nutritionists, health educators, dental personnel, speech and pathology personnel, environmental health officers, family planning workers, home care personnel offering services to improve the health of the community.'[22]

Once these linkages are established, values education works to situate students within a whole web of observation techniques, tracking devices, and adjustment technologies and within an entire human-services complex which aims at the therapeutic management of students through values. Values education exploits the personal and social tension created when the human need for possession and the powerful dynamic of indeterminacy and fragmentation collide. Values education pathologizes this tension as 'values stress' and offers a way of managing the anxiety of ontological inadequacy and the enthusiasm of empowered selves which arise as individuals are incited to move from a sense of presence to one of absence, out of a fixed place and direction in the world into a cyclic process of perpetual transformation. Values education has become the privileged point of the technological environment for maintaining the self as a fluid being exuberantly willing the infinite simulations technology can offer, while controlling and optimalizing the self in the process.

The whole series of diagnostic tests and therapeutic interventions, overseen by 'values-facilitators' as 'change-agents,' is a network of power whose result provides the data to substantiate the identification of definite pathologies and remedial therapy – 'type-A personalities' and 'conventional morality,' 'dialogic encounters' and 'proactive thinking.'

'Wellness' is an apt example of how this dispersed network operates because it refers to nothing more than the empty synthesis of effects produced by regulatory devices directed towards the individual from a multiplicity of sources. 'Wellness' is nothing more than a polymorphous excitation. It exhibits no intrinsic or unified principle. 'Wellness' is a pastiche of images and intensities traversing individuals from a multiplicity of sociological, psychological, political, and economic scenarios. These images and intensities are merely inscribed on the exterior of the self. They do not harmonize, but they have the unsavoury effect of ensuring the total control of the individual. 'Wellness' is the technological solution to a technological problem, for it enmeshes the individual within the 'caring-profession' complex, while merely simulating somatic and psychic health.

The management of 'values-stress' should not be interpreted as the emergence of a more 'scientific' understanding of values, or a new progressive understanding of some immutable 'moral substance,' or as the eruption of consensus on the rational principles of human association. What is occurring is the formation of a highly efficient site for subjugating and managing individuals. Its imperatives and protocols have become acceptable to such a majority of people only because of a naive trust that a vast administrative complex within the technological environment is well equipped to solve the problems of contemporary life and ensure freedom and reason. But the project to put in place radically new human relations based on authenticity and empowerment is itself a new regulative deployment of power. Behind 'autonomy' lie the management of the self, behind 'transparency' lie the manipulative techniques of the confessional, behind 'empowerment' and 'authenticity' lie the revolutionary dreams of gnostic activists who are willing to sacrifice freedom and reason for their cause.

Seen in this light, the 'hidden curriculum' was not so hidden after all, because its force was always directly experienced as authoritarian and sovereign, as constrictive and restraining. The current curriculum is much more hidden, its effects subtle and invisible because as its techniques are refined they reach the optimal stage of technological instruments – transparency – where the phenomenon is transformed without a trace of manipulation or intervention. Moreover, whereas the traditional curriculum placed students in a tutelary relation, this was always a temporary relationship, a 'paternalism' justified as the incubating time in which maturity grows. The current ensemble of pedagogical techniques disavows this explicit paternalism, but puts in place a 'fraternalism' whose discourse makes students permanent wards, forever subject to the tutelage of the system of technologically interlocking relations.

As a consequence of the inanition of tension, and its 'hyperreal' simulation as modulations within the communications circuit, there is no mediation and thus neither distinctions nor differentiations. This absence destroys the possibility of a space of politics. The encounter with others, which had been the context for individual action and the commonsensical negotiation of meaning, is no longer a reciprocity through determinate relations. Since there is no relational context and nothing determinate which structures limit and possibility, these transparent encounters – while non-discriminatory and symmetrical – are finally indifferent and chance resonances within the rhythmic cycles of the technological system. They are the resonance of a multiplicity of wills, rather than the plurality of distinct individuals. It is wishful thinking to believe that the emergence of these new encounters reveals the victory of the principle of equality, a sign of its moral superiority to arbitrary authoritarianism. The creation of symmetrical relations is not so much the victory of a new order of justice as the rejection of any principle of discrimination. No permanent relation of tension formed by the space between two poles of reality – which would lead to distinguishing one phenomenon from another, the higher from the lower, the superior from the inferior – remains in the environment of revolving simulations. This means, too, of course, that revivals of 'authoritarianism' are equally possible (the new fundamentalisms, the back-to-basics nostalgia) though these too, unlike their 'original,' have no substantive basis.

Lack of tension between the poles of existence also eradicates the conditions under which the existential modalities of the psyche acquire the tonality that sustains its questioning. In the absence of a permanent structure in which unrest is experienced as movement in a transcending reality, there can only be an 'idolatry of the actual' in its instantiation within the ascending scenario, or the indecisive motions from profile to profile. In either case, the questioning psyche has lost its distinctive rhythms.

Thus, freed from the spectacular forms of domination of the past, we now face the possibility of a total control in which, all 'stress' having been operationalized and managed, and all relations having been made totally efficient, politics and the intellect can no longer serve as resistance points to the global effect. The unrest and rhythms of existence, once taken to be the sources of political and intellectual activity, no longer constitute the tension in which these distinctive modalities of mediation arise.

To recall our earlier discussion, it is precisely this immediate reactivity to the dynamic forces of perpetual innovation and alteration that causes even the inveterate champion of the new technological age, Marshall McLuhan, to hesitate. Reflecting on the process of 'retribalization' in which the Newtonian-Cartesian space and time coordinates are relinquished, and in which we come to interpret ourselves as co-opted within a 'multisensual and multidimensional' field of electric tension empowered by efficient performance, he perceived implications which would unsettle our traditional and moderate political and moral conceptions. 'Terror,' he reminds us, 'is the normal state of any oral society, for in it everything affects everything all the time.'[23] The neo-primitivism of the technological environment has the tonality of constant panic.

The loss of all enclaves and resistance points, enduring enough to provide assurance in the face of transience and to constitute the meaningful structure in which the tension of human existence is given direction and purpose, leads Hannah Arendt to perceive an even greater threat. Let us recall the point she made to which we referred in chapter 2. Examining the processes preceding and underlying the exercise of totalitarian power, she maintains that it was precisely the destruction of public space and common sense which made possible the agitation and mobilization of masses of lonely people to murderous acts. 'Total domination, which strives to organize the infinite plurality and differentiation of human beings as if all of humanity were just one individual, is possible only if each and every person can be reduced to a never-changing identity of reactions, so that each of these bundles of reactions can be exchanged at random for any other.'[24]

Under the shadow of the possibility that this domination could be achieved by the perpetual mobility and revolving functionalities of modern technology, rather than terror or violence (as Ellul says, 'nothing useless exists; there is no torture; torture is a wasteful expenditure of psychic energy which destroys salvageable resources without producing useful results'), one could say that values education contributes to an unsettling pattern. The schools advance technology by situating students in a controlled environment where they can be watched and excited, their tensions managed and instrumentalized, their beings empowered within the circulation of scenarios and simulations and thus attuned to the vast global network of revolving deployments and simulated reconfigurations. Their image of the 'human' is nothing more than the empty synthesis of a being given over to constantly shifting 'regulatory mechanisms,' 'scenarios,' and 'profiles.'

Values education operates within the destiny of which our technology is the quintessential expression – the will-to-power. In the endless becoming of the will-to-power towards more power – power existing only as the discharge of power – values, subjects, and their motions are swept up, activated, and deployed. But the valuing subject is now nothing but an exterior surface, activated in the non-time and non-place of the will-to-power, enfolded totally within technology. 'Man's' context is an apparatus that not only now eludes his will but that has dismantled the place which had once conferred his humanity upon him. The move from the 'mechanical,' through the 'organic,' to the 'electric' brings technology to a peak of efficiency where nothing of the human remains. The modern humanist project of solving the 'human problem,' a project which aimed at mastering the Other in nature, in history, in society, and in oneself, finally, having destroyed all mediation and differentiation, culminates in technological nihilism: a relentless resolve of purposiveness without human purpose. As there is neither the possibility of the retrieval of order that comes from the anamnetic recovery of the structure of being, nor hope for redemptive newness (as the future is perpetually cancelled and deferred), all the terror of immediate reactivity in an eternal present draws towards us.

An Ethic of Possession

In opposition to this extreme danger brought on by dispossession, we need to re-examine the experience of possession, to retrieve it from the grip under which modern subjectivism has held it and to recall the experiential structure which makes it an essential human modality within being.[25] Possession, I would propose, is primarily the experience of belongingness. It requires both consent to otherness and participation within an enduring structure into which otherness draws us. When it is not deformed, possession gives rise to the balanced, human response to transience and finitude.

The either/or's of modern philosophy cannot establish the orderly rhythms of common sense, or the openness to primary and elementary experiences of being, through the forms that are 'first and foremost.' Taking the various paths of modern philosophy to their logical conclusion either underwrites a construct of humans as consumers or maximizers of utility, or loses the perspective of the human entirely. To retrieve the core of possession requires going behind the reduction of possession to exclusive proprietary relations between a subject and an object, or representational cognitive relations between a knower and a known, without leaping into the other extreme of immediacy or unreason. We need to return to the experiences of participation and consent to otherness.

Let us recall the etymological root of possession: *possessio*, from *pos-* or *post-sedeo*, which implies the sense of 'sitting, or setting, near or upon,' 'dwelling on,' and 'belonging with.' C. Reinold Noyes proposes that, as a 'classificatory genitive,' possession's principal characteristic is that of *propinquity*: a belonging there, a sense of accustomedness and familiarity, which suggests a localization and a reciprocity between thing and possessor.[26] Belongingness is a tonality of participation in a context which makes of our relation to things and experiences a covenant of stewardship.

I want to consider this tonality of 'belongingness' in possession under two existential aspects, one being the relation of belonging in a political world, the other being the graduated ascent of understanding which lies at the core of human questioning. Politically, 'belongingness' is characterized by two features. First, it assumes that possessions are not objects to be controlled but things which we invest with care and to which we form attachments. These attachments correspond to our memories of significant events, of creativity, of relations with others. Things are extensions of our sense of meaning – tangible instantiations which collect our experiences of admiration, attentiveness to beauty, desire for the good, and expression of taste. We want these experiences to be enduring, for they are transient, and thus we incarnate them in things whose durability can outlast the fleetingness of attention. With the familiarity which comes from such attachments, we form and become part of a contextual totality. That contextual totality is something new and contingent, a creation from our own point of view. As a localized 'cosmogony' in which we create an *imago mundi*, it is always also a 'hierophany': the 'place' of our things is never chosen, it is discovered. It is a place where meaningful circumstances have produced a point of intersection and an order of value.

Looked at from a human point of view, individuals and things do not exist independently prior to this mutual relation of possession. 'To say that mortals are,' Heidegger writes, 'is to say that in dwelling they persist through spaces by virtue of their stay among things and locations.'[27] Things and individuals have a determinate character only because of the contextual totality in which they have a place and direction.

The dwelling which permits enduring attention implies promises of continuing care. Our relations with things in that totality are then 'sacramental' in so far as our relation to them is an enactment of a covenantal pledge to the totality in which the thing is situated. Care is a continual re-enactment of that covenantal pledge, a renewal of the sense of belonging with things together. Where that care breaks down, and the contextual totality in which human meaning has been invested is divided, the result is that possession becomes control and mastery of objects. But this is a distortion of possession, since to possess is a relation of belongingness in which things are ourselves. Yet, such belongingness is also a fragile achievement – the novelty and contingency which exhibit the power of freedom always seek to renew the parameters of that belongingness.

Secondly, 'belongingness' entails differentiation. Possession separates and demarcates this from that, establishing boundaries between things and conferring singular identity upon them. Attachment to things is a personal preference, a setting out by attention. Attention is a preferment of the particular over the general and, in this attention, the particular acquires the depth and focus of care which no generality could have bestowed upon it. In attention, the other is acknowledged as a distinct particular, as a separate pole in a mediation. This is why possession is not primal immediacy, an enchanted experience of being the thing, but a relation structured by human meaning. As a relation, the possessed cannot absorb the possessor, nor can the possessor lose himself or herself in the possessed. The loss of differentiation is a state where consumption or enchantment prevails.

By marking out and differentiating, and by maintaining boundaries between things, we prevent these states where otherness is denied. To distinguish does not mean that we must stand as legislating subjects over and against objects, to divide out and separate things so that they can become objects for consumption. What ensures that differentiation is not mastery is respect. Respect – which comes from receptivity to otherness – cannot occur if the distance between the possessor and the possessed is not maintained.

The tendency is great for the fragile balance within possession to disintegrate. Possession can turn to love, and at least one aspect of love is an overcoming of the separateness of possession, the alienation integral to it, and the achievement of an enchanted union. But the union love forms does not guarantee respect. If there is to be respect in love, there must be a return to the relation within possession – the demarcations and differentiations in which preference and partiality arise. As such, possession is the work of maintaining separateness, and is inextricably bound to the responsibility we assume for what we have so distinguished and with which we have maintained a relation.

Attachment to things, united with awareness of their distinct location, establishes contextual totalities which are experienced as meaningful. But meaning does not arise from solitary activity. The modalities of experience from which attachment and preferment arise – judgment and discrimination grounded on principles of utility, beauty, and appreciation – are those modalities through which the relations of possession are inscribed with worldly meanings.

At the same time, though, meanings are not constant. They must be continually replenished and renewed. The contextual totalities of private possession are, as a reflection of the transient and mutable ways of man, always new beginnings and new negotiations. When they come into the world, they add to the amplitude and richness of public meanings, and renew the tonality by which they are received.

Meanings are the result of negotiation with others concerning how a reality participated in and observed by individuals with different perspectives appears. Without that negotiation with others, meaning will slide back into private connotation, if not private fantasy. But judgments of use, beauty, and appreciation open possession up beyond the contextual totality of the possessor and the possessed into the world. The relation is actually reciprocal, for the fact of personal possession also contributes both to the durability of the meanings in the world and to their renewal. To destroy the world, which stands behind the contextual totalities in which individuals appreciate the possessed and gather the possessed phenomena to belong, is to jeopardize not only the credibility of the standards of judgment by which it is maintained, but also the thing itself. Then the possessed thing is only stuff, that which can become an object to be disposed by a detached subject. As Aristotle notes in his analysis of the architectonic order of the world in *The Politics*, the particular has meaning, and the care towards it is prevented from becoming obsessive by the presence of the world. The general is strengthened by the care devoted to the particular.

Possession, then, is world-building and world-maintaining. Care and the maintaining of boundaries, from the perspective of worldly meanings, invest spaces with human meaning so that they become 'places.' Things are in place and have meaning because of an interactive pledge between the individual and the world. In possession, we enact at the microcosmic level a covenant to the world in return for meaning. Possessions are things held in trust to the world. A thing is for us a cosmion of the world – invested with meaning it situates us within the web of the world. It is our particular investment in the world, and a covenant to the responsibilities and risks of the world. In return for our commitment to its risks, it provides us with meanings whose enduring permanence stabilizes the transient aspect of our existence, giving us the opportunity through the new beginnings to renew the world's meanings.

In so far as the world invests our personal possessions with its meanings and allows those meanings to be renewed, it also provides us with the talent which keeps the relation between possessor and possessed in balance – common sense. To be absorbed in things, or to see them as objects of consumption – the dangers into which personal possession risks derailing – or to refuse to admit that the judgments and discriminations concerning use, beauty, and achievement are subject to renewal is to stand outside of the reciprocity of belongingness and the harmony which belongingness composes between possession and the world. In either consumption or absorption the distinctively human measures with which possession is related to the world are renounced. Common sense and belongingness go together, for common sense is the tonality of balance which comes from the reciprocity of belongingness. When either the world or possession is abstracted, the result is immediacy or deracinated consumption. The belongingness of possession gives to common sense the durable and situated things on which its discriminations are based. Common sense gives to possession the balanced appreciation of the worth of that possession.

Here the law concerning property can play an educative role. On the one hand, possession acquires a second existence by the conferral of legal identity and ownership upon it. The law of private property provides a standard as to what a balanced relation to the possessed is. But, on the other hand, the conferral by the law does not obliterate the existential pledge. A condition of proper legal ownership has to be that property be always held under the auspices of such a pledge. Property is enabled by the pledge to the world in possession. Where there is no covenantal relation or where property is used to destroy the trust and the commons of the world, the law must see to the regulation of property. When possession becomes an instrument to dominate others, or a fetish of private absorption which withdraws responsibility to the world, then the absolute right to property has to be abrogated. In so far as private possession incarnates the general, what is revealed is that possession is never the mere desire for things, nor are things mere instruments for the attainment of private satisfaction. In fact, possession is a desire to covenant with the world.

If there is to be a world which answers to our finitude, and which has a place for the newness we are individually, there must be a possession which stabilizes and balances the pulls of motion and permanence, infiniteness and finality. Possession, speaking politically, composes a threefold ethic: of responsible care, of respect, and of reciprocal fidelity. Through these it evokes a consent to otherness.

The 'belongingness' of possession is matured, however, under the aspect of our intellectual being. From that perspective, belongingness conveys the fact that the totality of our being – personal, social, historical – participates in the process of reality. It means that the experiences associated with our organic and sentient natures, as much as those articulated by our dianoetic and noetic aptitudes, belong to us as long as we remain humans. To belong within the process of reality means that the motions of existence are experienced by us as a process which we experience at multiple levels. For example, the existential modalities of the everyday – love, trust, persuasion, like-mindedness, desire, courage, friendship, loyalty – all contain structures which are continuous from the organic all the way to the noetic level of being. In so far as the process of reality is continuous, each element informs every other. Each, therefore, also defines the limit and possibility of every other. To renounce any one of them would be to truncate the range with which we participate in the process of reality and to destabilize the understanding we may acquire of its nature.

While we essentially 'belong' to a pre-structured process of reality through these modalities, this does not imply that we are merely blindly immersed in the motions of that process. In fact, these modalities are experienced as rhythms whose modulations create gaps permitting of individuation and differentiation. The infinite ranges of heightened to muted sensitivity, weaker to stronger desires, focused to diffuse spiritedness, more to less natural moderation, and intense to slight emotions allow for the differences within which our own unique destiny is formed. The modulations these experiences produce on one another not only form our historical and spiritual singularity, but also imply criteria of discrimination, judgment, and assent. For one, the simple need to survive in order to be at all establishes an imperative of proportionality, unity, and balance which recurs in the desire for sentient contentment, dialectic speech, and finally within understanding itself. In our essential belongingness, then, are all the formative aspects of the distinctively human.

That participation in the process of reality can be experienced as rhythmic, rather than transient motion, and its modulations as implying criteria of order, rather than mere episodic fluctuations, can only be understood, however, because at the same time man's questioning is a movement within a reality that is transcending. Thought is always, to recall the Platonic teaching, the 'uncompletable ascent from *proteron pros hemas* (what is first for us) to *proteron physei* (what is first by nature).'[28] What this means is that there is more to experience than continuous, if modulating, relations. Our experience is not only within a process, but a graduated movement, a spiral of balances, towards transcendent perfection.

Within this aspect of our being, possession obtains a deeper significance. If experience is of graduated movement, then possession is the apprehension of formative events in the process of transcending reality. Consciousness experiences eventful concentrations of the process of reality as images of finality, completion, and perfection, which in turn bestow on its motions the sense of proportionality and unity. Those events also register the imperative of maintaining balance, that is, of keeping these images permeable to the process of reality. Each event is an equilibrated balance, and the movement of understanding, as a whole, is a spiral of such balances. These events are in no way sequential, nor are they irreversible. They only indicate a deepening of the spirituality of intellectual questioning. In short, these events produce a tonality of trust to occur at each point in our experience of reality. While the everyday phenomena that are 'first and foremost' may seem, initially, to be ambiguous and ambivalent, we can trust that the work of understanding which transpires when we remain within them will reveal an implicit graduated structure wherein our longings are cultivated and matured in light of transcendent perfection.

The classic example of the graduated ascent of thought is the Platonic dialogue. The understanding which Plato aims to form in us depends on trust in the everyday and on the anticipation that order and balance will emerge from the experience of perfection towards which he draws us. Socrates begins with the everyday concerns of craftsmen, poets, and politicians, using their evident experiences of living as the basis for his inquiry. Those experiences are never negated or transcended. Instead, the dialectic of the dialogue involves a spiral of balances in understanding that is itself a graduated ascent connecting the everyday form to the transcendent source of being. In the process, various icons are postulated: the forms, the idea of the good, the exit from the cave of opinion, and the construction of the perfect city, any one of which might appear to deny the everyday. These cannot, however, be hypostatized as actualities. They are, instead, the 'truth' of human participation in reality, the formative events within the process of thinking.

What the Platonic dialogue clearly shows is that images of finality and perfection are what we mean by 'truth' in so far as those images are icons of the formative events of the spiral of understanding, that is, of our participation in the rhythms of a transcending reality. They are the forms of the graduated movement whose condensation gives us concrete evidence of the process of perfectibility which our understanding is undergoing. These abbreviated icons of the process of reality, experienced as 'formative' events, offer a legitimate basis for specifying what the 'human' is. Humans, as a legitimate philosophical anthropology will postulate, possess certain faculties, distinct capacities, specific virtues and excellences.

Both the images which consciousness articulates as the icons of its graduated movement and the philosophical anthropology that these icons sanction are meaningful and useful ordering devices which illustrate concrete instantiations of human participation in the process of reality. They serve as 'commonplaces' in the retrieval of the structure of being. In this they have an instrumental and a didactic value, for they serve as benchmarks to the direction and order of movement.

But if they are taken to be more than the icons which they are, the philosophical anthropology and the symbolic articulation of the process of knowing are dogmatized. What is essential to maintain the proper tonality of the questioning psyche is to think the propriative event without closure. Once a doctrine of man (man the rational animal, man the compassionate being, man the being who has self-consciousness of the end of history), or the assumption of certainty of the end of knowledge (the categoricals of reason, the determinate dynamics of time, the laws of human regularity), ossifies the icons, then participation in the process of reality has been sacrificed to doctrine.

The icons of the formative events of consciousness are very vulnerable to misunderstanding. The error occurs when the icons become the exclusive property of the knower, that is, when the icons are abstracted from the process of movement of thought, or when the formative propriative events are taken to be the results of the process of questioning. This closure, where images of finality, completion, and perfection are taken dogmatically to be the conclusion of the process, is what precipitates dogmatism and then scepticism, and finally leads to the 'devaluation of all value.' The decay into doctrine, one might say, is what has led to the contemporary appeal for dispossession and the total abandonment of the traditional curriculum.

But the answer, if the human perspective is not to be lost and all questioning ended, is not to deepen the dispossession by forsaking all measures of perfection and finality, but to restore the tonality of reciprocity which distinguishes belongingness – openness. Openness retrieves the originating experience of participation in a process of reality that is transcending. Since that participation takes its bearing from what is 'first and foremost' it must retrieve the icons and, to use Voegelin's term, make them 'permeable' again to the process of reality.

If there is to be an existence which answers to our mortality, and which has a place for the being who questions, there must be a possession which balances and stabilizes the pulls of finality and motion, perfection and transience. In terms of the aspect of being which speaks to our intellectual and spiritual longings, possession is a movement of perfectibility, a graduated ascent in understanding expressed in the images of finality and perfection. It is only when we 'possess' these, but without closure and certainty, that there can be openness to the full amplitude of human existence in the process of reality and, hence, worth assigned to the distinctive forms in which human life manifests itself. Possession, here, composes a twofold ethos of trust and moderation. As such, it too is a consent to otherness.

Political and intellectual possession come together in the psyche's experience of 'self-possession.' The balance which must constitute 'self-possession' is a mean between the extreme of primal affectivity and that of conclusive knowledge. The 'self-possessed' experience themselves as orderly rhythms, combining the motions of spontaneity with the spiral of equilibrated balances constituting a graduated ascent. They are not 'posthumous' beings, because they realize that their finitude and the transience of existence cannot be transcended. They sense that they must belong, even if there is no ultimate permanence in those relations.

Possession, politically and intellectually, is our fragile and ambiguous posture in the face of the temporality of our existence. It is an effort to postulate a durability which, while hardly permanent, composes what we call a world. Seen from the perspective of all existence, this posture might be seen as futile and as arrogance. Yet, it is what composes a human world by promises of responsibility and loyalty, care and respect, and what preserves decency and good judgment in the world. There is a futility to the human desire for what endures, but it also supplies what dignity there is to being human.

Morality is what emanates from the tonality of this understanding. Unless that tonality is in place, there can be no answer to the question of why one should be moral, no guarantee that we will continue a lifetime of moral conduct, and no limit to moral ardour. The substance of moral phenomena cannot be present if their prescriptions and practices do not preserve the balance of order and genesis, of mystery and practicality, of world-transcendence and world-immanence, of confidence and humility. This balance requires too that the constitutive experiences and goals of morality are concretely grounded on an understanding of an individual's synthetic nature. All of the inconsistencies and contradictions of a human's compounded existence as body/psyche, desire/reason, or material/spiritual being have to be accounted for. Only then are attempts to make morality the locus for acts of self-divinization or for expectations of global transfiguration avoided.

Moral situations are essentially tragic because they are insufficient, but not inappropriate, attempts to give a dignified tone to the human experience of the tension of existence, to human unrest in both its personal and collective dimensions. To act ethically or morally is to make of oneself an icon of the beautiful against all odds.

The ascent to what is *proteron physei* is, as Voegelin notes, 'incompletable.' As a consequence, there will always be inconclusiveness to all human artifices and a need for acceptance of human limit. In their worst forms, however, these have appeared historically, and under ideological forms, as craven submission and enchantment. These extreme forms arise from seeing possession only under the aspect of stability: things as fetishes, thinking as capitulation to doctrine, human existence as social function. Each arises from excessive desire for certainty and assurance.

But to turn away from the ambiguities of inconclusiveness and humility to a fundamental ontology of transience and deferral of closure because the work of human life is imperfect and lends itself to distortions is to have an unfounded optimism that 'letting-be' is a sufficient response in dealing with the reality of power, of abused power, of cruelty, and of evil. In its more vulgar and pragmatic application as the dispossession on behalf of some indeterminate, fluid potentiality in which the 'self' circulates and enjoys the transformative and transfigurative play of a process of signs, that 'fundamental ontology' appears as a type of vegetative or animal existence characterized by immediate reactivity to the environment.

That construct, which is indicative of a total loss of human perspective, not only leads to the politically dangerous state where a mass of vulnerable selves can be agitated and whose emptiness can be filled by any number of fantastical messianic and chiliastic social projects, but it also exhibits an enormous reduction and truncation of human existence. One can only wonder how such a being could be called 'human' in any meaning of that word.

At the end of the day, we are left with the issue: either all is transience and an infinite number of intensities masquerading arbitrarily as signs of what is complete, final, and perfect, or there is a durative structure which, while unknown, nonetheless allows us those rare experiences of the intimation of perfection which give us hope that the unity and beauty we form in our lives have some foundation.

What we experience in human existence is a state of unrest, tensions between finality and novelty, perfection and lack, proportionality and contingency. Much of that tension is inconvenient and disrupting. But this unrest constitutes the basis from which the inevitability of politics arises and which provides the tonality in which our intellectual and spiritual lives move.

The unrest of our existence is a consequence of being pulled between the poles of infinite and indeterminate flux on the one hand and completion and perfection on the other. These poles manifest themselves in our everyday and commonsensical experiences. Our possession of things is a desire for permanence, and the structure of its constitutive rituals is repeated in the icons of our own development as questioning beings. Our rearrangement and reconsecration of things is a desire for renewals and new beginnings. Possession's constitutive rituals, too, are repeated in the dissatisfaction which arises whenever questions are brought to an· end.

When the experiences arising from the pull of these poles are denied, then the result is randomness, fragmentation, and superfluity – in general, a loss of rhythm and the perspective of the human. I have been suggesting that values education operates on the principle that the tension of existence can be managed and that the formative experiences of the everyday can be overcome. It is presumed that a radical dispossession is the means to achieve satisfaction and justice. But annulling one of the poles does not transfigure human reality and provide a simultaneous actualization of the immediacy and completeness of the other pole. Instead, it brings only political disorder and intellectual confusion.

An ethic of possession holds back from gathering up the things, ways of life, and experiences to render them into certain and secure objects, without however denying the concrete dimension of reality. It rejects the perpetually mobilized subjectivity and abstract universality of contemporary times without advocating a restoration of our natural, undeveloped givenness. It is an ethic of responsibility, receptivity to otherness, and openness to the full amplitude of existence. Thus, an ethic of possession is an ethic of coexistence and mutual belonging, open to the finitude of our belonging to the world, but also capable of openness to the transcendent. Neither requiring ultimate certitudes and totalities, nor embracing the total functionality and disposability of our age, it is a middle-way composed of common sense and openness.

Conclusion

The spiritual condition under which I have analysed the values education models is 'loss of balance.' That loss manifests itself particularly in the rejection of the view that what is 'first and foremost' – that is, the forms of the everyday – should inform our judgments. The metaphor I have used to express the disentanglement from the world, and the attitude of disposability and superfluity regarding the facts of the everyday, is 'dispossession.' Arendt and Voegelin warn of the great danger which follows from abstracting questions of human possibilities and limits from the comprehensive reality in which we participate. These thinkers remind us of the political and intellectual contexts for our existence. Remembering that we are the being who acts and who asks questions, who stabilizes those actions in stories, and whose questioning opens us to transcendence supplies the contexts for sound judgment from a human perspective. Neglecting these contexts leads to the excessive presumption that our values, like our technology, have a singular capacity to remake the world and to overcome the tensions of existence. Or, such neglect culminates in the despair that our values are mere ornaments available to us in our frivolous boredom. We need an alternative to such dispossession and a more thoughtful assessment of the scope and aims of a genuine liberal education capable of supplying moral ballast. Linking Arendt's and Voegelin's analyses offers such an assessment revealing that the ladder of virtue is suspended from above and secured at the surface.

Educating a student to a genuine understanding of his or her participation in the process of reality depends on a judicious balance of genesis and order, or motion and finality. What is formed in such an education is a psychic tonality which is neither wholly 'natural' nor entirely the result of 'artifice.' I want to return to Arendt and Voegelin to elaborate the pedagogy which, in my mind, crafts the appropriate contexts in which human possibility and limit can be discussed.

As a first approximation, one could say that Arendt's and Voegelin's thought revitalizes cardinal components of the 'traditional curriculum.' This statement must be qualified with the understanding that both would be radically opposed to the doctrinaire and dogmatic principles by which the spirit of that curriculum has in great part been implemented. Their analyses are meant to make possible again an encounter with the primary and elementary questions of education. To follow Voegelin and Arendt means, though, that one must proceed by a 'thinking without banisters' or by a thinking which resists attaching itself merely to 'the upper stratum of noetic "results."' With their guidance we can divide and separate out the philosophic core of the 'traditional curriculum' and dispense with the historically contingent techniques whose implementation caused opprobrium to be cast on the whole curriculum.

The focal point of Arendt's understanding of education is preparation of the student for entry into the world. This preparation has two aspects to it: the protection of the child from the world and the protection of the world from the new beginning that erupts into it with the entry of the student. Arendt points out that a true education must see itself as 'incubating' the potential world-dweller by authoritatively guiding its natural dispositions and capacities to maturity. The student must be hidden temporarily from the passions, freedoms, and relations of the public world until he or she is able to assume the advantages and responsibilities of public life. Second, a true education teaches the student the reasons for the distinctions which are made in the world, thus giving the student's natural impulses of free, spontaneous, and unique action a form and direction. The structure and forms of the world serve as the student's benchmarks in making judgments. If, as mature beings, students are to play their part in renewing the world with actions that begin new processes, their education must nonetheless be traditional: 'Exactly for the sake of what is new and revolutionary in every child, education must be conservative; it must preserve this newness and introduce it as a new thing into an old world, which, however revolutionary its actions may be, is always, from the standpoint of the next generation, superannuated and close to destruction.'[1]

To understand why these two facets are so important, we must recollect what Arendt most fears: isolated individuals, thrown back onto their own fears and anxieties, embracing constructs of reality merely because of their universality and internal consistency. For Arendt the causes of the worst derailment are believing self-certainty to be the index of truth and believing reason to be most fully actuated when the mind assents to disembodied universals. And, as we have seen, a social environment which is wholly fluid and impermanent is a state in which these two dogmas become easily accepted as self-evident.

Arendt's thought counters this paradoxical image of an education linking boundlessness and rigidity with the more salutary image of reciprocal action between stability and renewing action. Arendt's prescriptions are, in great part, an education to possession, of belongingness and openness. Students must come to appreciate the importance of possessions, especially public artefacts whose durability contributes to the permanence of the world. Only things – reified expressions of human achievement and aspiration – establish the stability on which a public world can rest, and in turn make possible that the public world does not leave in abstraction such terms as 'rights,' 'judgment,' 'principles,' and 'value.' To orient themselves with good judgment among the particulars of culture and history, and to give structure to their spontaneous and novel acts, students must also be sufficiently self-possessed to have a sense of unity, continuity, and purpose, a self-possession formed from the concrete qualities and immediate relationships of embodied existence, and out of particular promises and actual acts of forgiveness. Possession and self-possession work together, giving unity to memory and conferring stability on the reality by which individuals orient themselves. Such a concrete being is very different from the deracinated self, whose memory is limited to episodic recall, underlying the values education models (especially values clarification). 'Without remembrance,' Arendt writes, 'and without the reification which remembrance needs for its own fulfilment ... the living activities of action, speech, and thought would lose their reality at the end of each process, and disappear as though they had never been.'[2]

Remembrance confers permanence by building on the stability of artefacts and human identity, as well as by establishing an anchor for practical judgment. When remembrance and judgment are united, students have the elements of a genuine education of stability and renewal. They have learned to take their bearing from the common reality seen, heard, and debated by all, and have acquired an openness and receptivity to meaning which is not solely of their own making, while also having a distinctive perspective in the public world from which to initiate new processes. The reciprocity of remembrance and judgment in the public world truly grounds human limits and possibilities, thus avoiding the relentless negativity of both destruction and archaism. It is the single most important hedge against the 'tyranny of logicality.'

The preconditions for being appropriately attuned to these forms of possession, and to the forms of initiative by which they are periodically renewed, are the character traits of moderation and courage. These virtues can only be formed and will only endure if students can respond to the transience of existence without despair or presumption. The formation of a balanced consciousness does not arise spontaneously, or from mere logical demonstration by a teacher who abstracts questions of human possibility and limit from the comprehensive process of reality. Students, Arendt advises, must accept the authority of teachers, and teachers must be authoritative. But teachers' authority is only truly such when their knowledge extends beyond the teaching of 'skills.' 'The authority of the educator,' she challenges,

and the qualifications of the teacher are not the same thing. Although a measure of qualification is indispensable for authority, the highest possible qualification can never by itself beget authority. The teacher's qualification consists in knowing the world and being able to instruct others about it, but his authority rests on his assumption of responsibility for that world. Vis-à-vis the child it is as though he were a representative of all adult inhabitants, pointing out the details and saying to the child: This is our world.[3]

The teacher's authority arises from an understanding of the conditions and balances constituting the world. Only if teachers can instil in students the aptitude to understand the distinctions giving unity to the world, thereby supplying structure and direction to their students' freedom, have the purposes of education been truly fulfilled. 'Education,' Arendt concludes in a stirring evocation of genuine liberal education, 'is where we decide whether we love our children enough not to expel them from our world and leave them to their own devices, nor to strike from their hands their chance of undertaking something new, something unforseen by us, but to prepare them in advance for the task of renewing a common world.'[4]

Voegelin's contribution to our discussion starts where Arendt's leaves off. If the 'common world' prevents the dangers of anomie and social atomism, then we must ask: what assures the unity and integrity of community? If the 'common world' is the condition for a balanced sense of reality, then what guarantees that the sense of reality is more than a collective fiction and that consent to it is more than conformism? What virtues, in short, must education cultivate if reason is to become a living force in the consciousness of students and the substance uniting a community?

At the centre of Voegelin's writings is the traditional inquiry which ought to be the *sine qua non* or beginning step of any discussion about human possibility and limit – a philosophical anthropology. Without an account of the human, there can be no criteria of relevance and thus no basis for distinguishing truth from error, justice from injustice, dignity from disgrace. Nothing, then, can be more important than an education which, in exposing the student's complex nature to the process of reality – its motions and its forms – does so from the perspective of what a human is.

There are two components to this education. First, there is a need to draw out and form the modalities of participation in the process of reality – pathos, trust, longing, turning around and turning towards, hope, and wonder. Only then can the phenomena of the world, as they occur in personal, social, and historical life, be anamnetically recovered to display the harmony and proportion of the order of being. Second, there is a need to prevent the emergence of a consciousness inclined to immanentist symbols of the apocalyptic or ideological form. These constructs of reality need to be exposed as phantasms, their underlying principle recognized as an unwillingness to accept the uncertainty and ambiguity of man's existence and a desperate bid for security in a closed system. Closing the questioning psyche in a tensionless, immanent existence has to be recognized for what it is – the prime source of personal and civilizational disorder.

The details of this education emerge less from specific pedagogical and curricular prescriptions that Voegelin puts forward than through the derailments he portrays. Promoting the assertion of an autonomous will, abbreviating the scope of reality, exalting the creativity of the self, permitting the desires and passions unrestrained expression, arresting the questioning of origins and ends – all these represent a closing down of the psyche to reality. Hence, an education which disavows a criterion of order, which hesitates over establishing hierarchy among opinions, passions, and habits, and which holds back from instilling the confidence to discriminate will be defective. Similarly, an education which allows reason to merely be a faculty of cleverness and technical expertise, and thus an instrument through which human beings maximize their desires, will deform human consciousness. As well, practices which deny the irreducibility of the tension of existence, and which fail to recognize the permanent precariousness of our existence by attempting to overcome stress or reduce ambiguity to controllable psychological forces, will bring about derailment in the psyche's participation in reality. And an education which abandons individuals to their several private worlds of experience, rather than advancing the substance of the one and common world, will contribute to existential disorder. The values education we have been investigating, it hardly needs to be said, displays many of the worst symptoms of the disordered consciousness Voegelin analyses.

Voegelin's *via negativa*, it needs to be added, does offer guidelines to a genuine education. Availing himself of a striking image in Plato's *Laws*, Voegelin explains how a human being can be educated to order experiences. Plato's metaphor is thinking of humans as 'puppets of the gods,' pulled by the strands of various metal cords. The measure of a human's life lies in whether the puppet-player has pulled the iron cords of the passions or the gold cord of reason. Obedience to the pull of the gold cord, as the life of reflective thought or assent to the laws and ways of the community, means a life of order. If the iron cord is pulled, individuals will exhibit truculence and irascibility, despair and presumption, and all the personal and social agitations associated with disorder.

The educator in this image is in the position of *locus deus* having to judiciously pull one cord and then the other. Order in the young is not spontaneous, nor can young souls be persuaded by logical demonstration: 'And the child is the hardest to handle of all beasts, because insofar as it has within it, to a high degree, a not yet disciplined source of thought, it becomes treacherous, sharp, and the most insolent of beasts. That's why it's necessary to fetter it with many sorts of bridles.'[5] If the 'gold cord' is to predominate, habit and discipline must prevail before reason can be activated. It is the height of irresponsibility to allow the desires to proliferate like a 'many-headed beast' or to believe that from private vices arise public benefits.

But Voegelin does not believe that the meaning of the image of the puppet-player is primarily a moral lesson. He suggests that Plato intends three further implications of the myth to be noted. First, the cords should not be understood as immanent forces in social or historical existence. The pulling of the cords takes place within a 'cosmic drama.' Thus, 'the reason why man should follow one pull rather than another is not to be found in the "psychodynamics" of the puppet play, nor in some standards of "morality," but in the potential immortality offered by the divine presence in the *metaxy*.[6] Second, as Voegelin points out, while humans will ask 'why should the gods have made man their puppet?,' because our consciousness of existence in restricted to the *metaxy* we cannot know why humans are the battleground between the forces of truth and untruth, life and death. 'Behind the truth of the discord lies the mystery of the reality in which the discord becomes luminous as its truth.'[7] Third, while humans are 'puppets' they are not passive – 'life to be gained requires the cooperation of man.' Suffering and obeying the experiences of order are not submission. An active seeking and responding constitute genuine participation.

The image of the puppet-player, then, sets out the source of an educator's authority, the proper tonality of a psyche aware of its existence in the *metaxy*, and the twin aim of sound pedagogy: openness to reality and attunement to its transcendent pull. This image of education, balancing humility with hope, is furthest from the image we have observed in the values education models, where unbending righteousness is perversely linked with metaphysical timidity.

Failure to achieve the balance and receptivity prescribed by the image of the puppet-player leads to what Voegelin describes as 'pneumopathological disorder.' Voegelin often recalls Cicero's list of surprisingly modern-sounding syndromes: 'restless money-making, status-seeking, womanizing, overeating, addiction to delicacies and snacks, wine-tippling, irascibility, anxiety, desire for fame, stubbornness, rigidity of attitude, and such fears of contact with other human beings as misogyny and misanthropy.'[8] The enumeration is not intended to focus exclusively on moral behaviour or to imply that the educator should assume a moralistic stance against the passions. Rather, when these 'syndromes' become chronic, Voegelin contends, participation in reality has come to be at stake.

Finally, Voegelin offers an interpretation of another Platonic dialogue pertinent to our inquiry. Plato's *Gorgias*, the dialogue which concerns itself generally with the consequence of dreaming that humans are not 'puppets of the gods' but self-creating and self-defining beings. The dialogue depicts the consequences of believing there is no intelligible meaning to collective existence, but the dialogue also sets out the manner in which a communion of psyches can be formed to counter this breakdown. In other words, justice is shown as something more than a social act performed for conventional reasons or out of shrewdness. The *Gorgias*, as the dialogue ostensibly about sophistry, is about communication and how it is distorted when speech-acts are no longer tied to the reality of our experiences of the world.

In the *Gorgias*, Voegelin contends, Socrates confronts the results of an education which neglects to provide substance in the psyche and society. Gorgias, like so many of the values education proponents, is a teacher who supplies his students with skills. He believes these skills to be neutral and he shirks taking any responsibility for establishing a substantive context in which these skills will be used. And like so many of the values education designers, Gorgias is a respectable human being, but unwilling to examine the conditions required to endow respectability with substance.

Not surprisingly, his student Polus is boorish and, like so many of the values education designers, holds the debased principle that while reason itself is good, or useful, or necessary, reason cannot tell us what is good. Having thus broken partnership with the *logos*, the unifying principle of reason, it comes as no surprise that when Socrates seeks to establish some common basis of civic friendship with him, Polus meets the suggestion that 'It is worse to do injustice than to suffer it and worst of all is to do injustice and not be punished' (472e) with cynical incredulity. Those who praise reason, but refuse to acknowledge that it is the conduit for our experience of divine order, are, like Polus, revealed in the final instance to admire only shrewd calculation and to secretly envy the power of the unjust who can enjoy total power with impunity.

The *Gorgias* ends with Socrates attempting the same bid of *pathos* with Callicles. For Callicles, as in the values education models we examined, traditional morality is a façade, for, without warrant, it affirms a cosmic order where human virtue is an irreducible phenomenon. Contrary to this image of reality, Callicles believes that social existence is little more than the contention of forces arising from self-interested individuals driven by a desire for more and more. Justice is simply a necessary evil, devised by the strongest to protect what they have acquired. The best life, Callicles believes, is pursuing luxury and having power. Socrates' counter-argument that these desires finally end in meaninglessness, and that a meaningful life is one where humans are bound together as friends who desire the good, is ridiculed by Callicles, leading to one last Socratic attempt to invite Callicles to re-enter the comity of humankind. Using an analogy from music, he proposes that Callicles is out of harmony with himself, indeed is spiritually mad, and thus has no genuine reason to live.

If we recall, this is exactly the impasse which Kohlberg felt he had reached at stage 6 before his discovery of stage 7, an impasse because the declaration that the imperatives of morality are acts of reason is not persuasive to the person 'who says in his heart there is no God.' Kohlberg, unlike the proponents of the other values education programs, is more honest at this point and turns to 'the perspective of the infinite,' a perspective which genuinely answers the question 'why be moral?'

Socrates does the same at the end of the *Gorgias*. Taking the last, but most important, option open to him, Socrates tells Callicles a myth of death and final judgment. He explains how those who pursued in life what appeared to bring power and luxury are now stripped of their adorned bodies that covered the state of their souls, and are judged to have committed the greatest of crimes and are condemned. Voegelin interprets this myth as Socrates' bid to have Callicles' life assessed from the widest possible perspective. The story has to be translated so that its mythical elements are recognizable as forces of the human soul. Life and death are symbols of the meaning and non-meaning of existence. Callicles had praised the life of luxury, licence, and excess as virtue and happiness. Socrates says that in this state one's body is a tomb. To escape the reality of death, Callicles had entombed himself in his passions, but the reality of death cannot be escaped. A truly satisfying life is life free of the tomb of the body. Living such a life can be done imaginatively – living as if the body were not the only datum of existence. Fearing death, as the ultimate sign of boundlessness, we want to make the best of ourselves and we want to make it last, to make the good continuous. Undertaking the cathartic purging of 'life' by 'death' and thus experiencing a transcendence towards divine perfection reconsecrates reason's partnership with reality. We realize that meaninglessness is even a greater fear than fear of death. We have become aware of our participation in a dimension of existence from whose perspective mortality seems insignificant, and this dimension appears, Voegelin suggests, whenever the noetic capacity of reason is active. Virtues, excellences, and practical judgment are not primary data, but forms of our participation in reality. They acquire their direction and substance from the 'cosmic-divine movement.' The more comprehensive Platonic teaching is superior to Kohlberg's because not only does it answer the question 'why be moral?' but it ensures the persistence of moral understanding and prevents moral irascibility and divisiveness by reuniting us at a higher stage of our humanity.

Arendt's and Voegelin's thought can be seen as giving new life to the traditional curriculum, confirming its spirit but divesting us of much of its letter. We should be able to see again the value of using the lives of exemplary humans as models of excellence; of using myth, legend, and fable as compact versions of the drama of existence; of illustrating the actions and judgments of the mature human being as the focal point of the student's lesson in ordering desires and passions; of promoting imitation and emulation as modalities of retrieval of the *arche* of ethical action; of disposing the psyche to obedience; of forming human desire and directing it in response to a drawing beyond; of evoking the sense of mystery as a vehicle for the anamnetic recovery of the order of being; of using habit-formation, instilling a hierarchy of virtues, and training memory to discipline and sublimate the forces of the psyche; of encouraging the sense of humility and imperfection; of establishing the necessity of respect and tolerance as a consequence of our ineluctable imperfection; and of seeing the problem of justice in the political order from the perspective of the harmony of the psyche.

The revolutionaries behind values education identified our current malaise as stemming from rigidity, apathy, uncertainty, and lack of relevant skills. Significant as these issues are, I would point to other syndromes of modern discontent. As we look around us, we can see boredom with the simple goodness of life, cynicism, unfulfilled longings for wholeness, unchannelled political passions, untamed erotic desires, unguided anxiety regarding death, feelings of impotence, despair over the inner divisions of the self, and an unanswered need for respect. Students are not satisfied and they carry the lie of contemporary educational reform in their souls.

Central to the educational prescriptions Arendt and Voegelin offer, which I see as antidotes to these syndromes, are receptivity and balance. Education's double task is to foster true intellectual and moral independent-mindedness, as well as those unifying bonds conferring substance to the human psyche and to communities. That independent-mindedness cannot arise unless students are given an opportunity for transcendence from what J.A. Corry calls 'the clamour of the immediate.' The unifying bonds cannot be formed unless students are acquainted with those symbols of wholeness underlying the forms of our civilizational achievements and sent on that voyage of exploration and discovery which Matthew Arnold identified as 'the pursuit of our total perfection by means of getting to know, on all matters which most concern us, the best which has been thought and said in the world.' Education's double task cannot be fulfilled unless teaching methods and content are coordinated to work at forming that psychic tonality which will lead students to consent to the structures and possibilities revealed in the first data of experience. Only a relatively secure hold on the order of reality can prevent us from being mesmerized by doctrines which, in excluding cardinal features of that order, evoke images of worlds freed from the burdens of existence. Only by preserving the distinctive forms of the political world and the conditions of existence in which intellectual questioning arises can we ensure such a hold on reality. As moral educators undertake the formidable task of re-examining the place of morality in the curriculum for students who will be entering a technological environment with awesome and unprecedented powers and dangers, we can only hope that they are truly open to the process of reality and that they are not lacking in the courage and moderation required to prepare the young for their place in the world.

Epilogue

Intellectual sophistry, in the final instance, rarely prevails over the common-sense and everyday judgments which will exist wherever humans come together and circumstances have not made the environment of such coming together one of total domination. Testing the heady promises and dreams of values education against the concrete particulars of human reality will likely lead students, in their maturity, to wholesale rejection of the ideological programs to which they were exposed.

What is unfortunate, of course, and what will lead to inevitable confusions and disappointments, is how poorly the authorized vocabulary of public life will permit such rejection to be recognized as reasonable, even though that rejection accords with the deepest roots and even experiential sources of that public life. Where students, drawn back to reality by the exigencies and hurly-burly of everyday life, and thus by the balanced judgment which is formed within it, find themselves rejecting the fantasies of values education, they will do so increasingly in a language that is private and unrepresented in the authorized vocabulary of contemporary public existence. Even if today's young people find experiential reserves within themselves which inoculate them from the foolishness of values education, nothing from my observations of the world in great part fashioned by the same foolishness leads me to think that their situation will be anything other than that described by Socrates as the inevitable lot of the psychically mature in a world gone mad:

Then it's a very small group, Adeimantus, ... which remains to keep company with philosophy in a way that's worthy ... Now those who have become members of this small band have tasted how sweet and blessed a possession it is. At the same time, they have seen sufficiently the madness of the many, and that no one who minds the business of the cities does anything healthy, to say it in a word, and that there is no ally with whom one could go to the aid of justice and be preserved. Rather – just like a human being who has fallen in with wild beasts and is neither willing to join them in doing injustice nor sufficient as one man to resist all the savage animals – one would perish before he has been of any use to city or friends and be of no profit to himself or others. Taking all this into the calculation he keeps quiet and minds his own business – as a man in a storm, when dust and rain are blown by the wind, stands aside under a little wall. Seeing others filled full of lawlessness, he is content if somehow he himself can live his life here pure of injustice and unholy deeds, and take his leave from it graciously and cheerfully with fair hope. (*Republic*, 496d–e)

Nevertheless it is always possible for us to re-cultivate what we have allowed to lie fallow. Such a task of renewal is what a genuine liberal education would have to undertake.

Notes

Please note that for those citations that are not complete in the entries below, full citations can be found in the Bibliography.

Introduction

1 Cf. Henry Giroux, *Theory and Resistance in Education*; S. Bowles and H. Gintis, *Schooling in Capitalist America: Educational Reform and the Contradictions of Economic Life* (London: Routledge and Kegan Paul 1976); M.W. Apple, *Ideology and Curriculum*; Stanley Aronowitz, *False Promises* and, with Henry Giroux, *Education under Siege*; Pierre Bourdieu and J.C. Passeron, *Reproduction: Education, Society, and Culture*.
2 Cf. Jean-Paul Sartre, 'Doing and Having: Possession,' in *Being and Nothingness*. See also John R. Wikse, *About Possession*.
3 The enormity of our ethical responsibility in the face of such power is discussed by Hans Jonas in 'Technology and Responsibility.'
4 Grant, 'Knowing and Making.'

Chapter 1: Values and Values Education: Towards a New Regime

1 My debt to Foucault should be obvious, though I agree with his reduction of authority to power only in so far as his genealogies expose the workings of modern society.
2 Cf. Michael Polanyi, *Personal Knowledge: Towards a Post-Critical Philosophy* (Chicago: University of Chicago Press 1958); Hubert Dreyfus, *What Computers Can't Do* and his 'What Is Morality? A Phenomenological Account of the Development of Ethical Expertise' (with Stuart E. Dreyfus) in *Universalism vs. Communitarianism: Contemporary Debates in Ethics*, ed. by David Rasmussen (Cambridge, Mass.: MIT Press 1990); H.G. Gadamer, *Truth and Method*; Alas-

dair MacIntyre, *After Virtue* (Notre Dame, Ind.: Notre Dame University Press 1981).

3 Cf. Eric Voegelin, 'What Is Right by Nature?' in *Anamnesis*, transl. by Gerhart Niemeyer (Notre Dame: University of Notre Dame Press 1978), p. 63.

4 Aristotle's writings on ethics have been revived by many authors in this century, but what he says has been transfigured and distorted to coincide with these authors' own philosophic positions. Thus, at their hands, Aristotle has become a forerunner of existentialism, historicism, conventionalism, or aestheticism and his account of ethics has become a weapon to battle against behaviouralism, rationalism, scientism, and objectivism. Hannah Arendt, for example, finds in Aristotle a concern with displaying one's unique existence which she opposes to the anomie of modern social life; Hans-Georg Gadamer sees in Aristotle's account of judgment a sense of historical appropriateness and cultural sensibility which is truer to human life than the methodism of modern science; Alasdair MacIntyre discovers in Aristotle a recognition of the indeterminacy of social practice which he distinguishes from the rigidity resulting from a search for a 'meta-ethical' language among the grammarians of contemporary analytic philosophy; and Michel Foucault finds a concern to promote a stylized devotion to the beautiful life which he sees can be used to challenge contemporary society's control of the individual by various human sciences.

5 Epictetus, *Enchiridion*, in *The Works of Epictetus*, transl. by Elizabeth Carter (Boston: Little, Brown 1866), i.

6 Cf. Michel Foucault, *History of Sexuality*, vol. 3: *The Care of the Self*, transl. by Robert Hurley (New York: Pantheon Books 1986), esp. part 2, 'The Cultivation of the Self.' Foucault's emphasis on the production of right knowledge about virtue that results from the control of the will corrects Arendt's reading that sees in Epictetus the origin of the will-to-power.

7 Cf. Hannah Arendt, 'Epictetus and the Omnipotence of the Will,' in *Life of the Mind*, vol. 2: *Willing*, pp. 73–84.

8 Epictetus, *Fragments*, in *The Works of Epictetus*, vii.

9 Mircea Eliade, *Myth and Reality*, transl. by Willard R. Trask (New York: Harper and Row 1963), pp. 39–74; see also *Patterns in Comparative Religion*, transl. by Rosemary Sheed (New York: Meridian 1968), pp. 367ff.

10 Cf. Eric Voegelin, 'Reason: The Classic Experience,' in *Anamnesis*, p. 114.

11 Cf. H.I. Marrou, *A History of Education in Antiquity* (New York: Mentor 1956); Hastings Rashdall, *The Universities of Europe in the Middle Ages*, ed. by F.M. Powicke and A.B. Emden (Oxford: Oxford University Press 1942); N. Schachner, *The Medieval Universities* (London: George Allen and Unwin 1938); John Marabon, *Late Medieval Philosophy*, Cambridge Medieval History,

vol. 8 (Cambridge: Cambridge University Press 1989); James Murphy, *Rhetoric in the Middle Ages: A History of Rhetorical Theory from Saint Augustine to the Renaissance* (Berkeley: University of California Press 1974); James Murphy, ed., *Synoptic History of Classical Rhetoric* (Davis, Calif.: Hermagoras Press 1983); Donald Clark, *Rhetoric in Greco-Roman Education* (New York: Columbia University Press 1957); Stanley Bonner, *Education in Ancient Rome from the Elder Cato to the Younger Pliny* (Berkeley: University of California Press 1977); Robert J. Connors, Lisa S. Ede, and Andrea Lunsford, eds., *Essays on Classical Rhetoric and Modern Discourse* (Carbondale: Southern Illinois University Press 1984); and Susan Miller, 'Classical Practice and Contemporary Basics,' in James Murphy, ed., *The Rhetorical Tradition and Modern Writing* (New York: Modern Language Association 1982).

12 For a detailed account of the syllabus, see Clark, *Rhetoric in Greco-Roman Education*.

13 Cf. Cicero, *De partitione oratoria* (Loeb edition).

14 Cf. Sr. Joan Marie Lechner, *Renaissance Concepts of the Commonplaces* (Westport, Conn.: Greenwood Press 1962).

15 Cf. Eric Voegelin, 'Anamnetic Experiments,' in *Anamnesis*, pp. 36–51.

16 Plutarch, *De Virtute Morali* (Cambridge, Mass.: Harvard University Press 1975), 443f.

17 The key writer from the point of view of educational theory is Peter Ramus, whose critiques of Cicero and Quintilian and whose 'methodism' and turn from 'practice' to 'basics' reflect the same animus as is present in Bacon's overthrow of Aristotelianism. Cf. his *Arguments in Rhetoric against Quintilian*, transl. and ed. by Carole Newlands (De Kalb: Northern Illinois University Press 1986).

18 Francis Bacon, *Advancement of Learning and Novum Organon* (New York: Colonial Press 1900), p. xi.

19 Ibid., Aphorism 41, Book I, p. 319.

20 Ibid., Aphorism 42, p. 319.

21 Francis Bacon, 'Letter to Lord Burleigh.' For a thoughtful discussion of Bacon's importance, see Hans Blumenberg, *The Legitimacy of the Modern Age*, transl. by Robert M. Wallace (Cambridge, Mass.: MIT Press 1983), part III, ch. 9.

22 For some of the major positions and issues see 'Moral Education and Secular Humanism: A Symposium with Robert Hall, Lawrence Kohlberg, John Wilson, Howard Kirschenbaum, Edwin Delattre, Kevin Ryan, and Gaston Cogdell,' *The Humanist*, Nov./Dec. 1978, pp. 7–25. See also Superka et al., *Values Education Sourcebook: Conceptual Approaches, Material Analyses, and an Annotated Bibliography*; Beck et al., eds., *Moral Education: Interdisciplinary*

Approaches; and John Wilson, N. Williams, and B. Sugarman, *Introduction to Moral Education* (Baltimore: Penguin 1967).

23 Clive Beck, 'The Reflective Approach to Values Education,' *Ontario College for Leadership and Education*, 21 (Winter 1981): 8.

24 Beck, *Moral Education in the Schools: Some Practical Suggestions*, p. 5.

25 Silver, *Values Education*, pp. 9–10.

26 Beck, *Educational Philosophy and Theory*, p. 69.

27 Freire, *Pedagogy of the Oppressed*; see also his *Cultural Action for Freedom, Education for Critical Consciousness*, and *Pedagogy in Process*.

28 Straughan, *Can We Teach Children To Be Good?* p. 55.

29 Kohlberg, 'The Cognitive-Developmental Approach to Moral Education,' p. 26.

30 Ibid.

31 Hare, *Freedom and Reason*, p. 46.

32 Clive Beck, 'The Reflective, Ultimate Life Goals Approach,' in John R. Meyer, ed., *Reflections on Values Education* (Waterloo: Wilfrid Laurier University Press 1976), p. 152.

33 Beck, *Moral Education in the Schools*, p. 153.

34 Giroux, *Theory and Resistance in Education*, p. 79; see also his *Ideology, Culture, and the Process of Schooling* and, with D. Purple, *The Hidden Curriculum and Moral Education*.

35 Charles Reich, *The Greening of America* (New York: Random House 1969), p. 225.

36 Giroux, *Theory and Resistance in Education*, p. 91.

37 Freire, *Pedagogy of the Oppressed*, p. 41.

38 Giroux, *Theory and Resistance in Education*, p. 68.

39 Bourne and Eisenberg, *Social Issues in the Curriculum*, p. 37.

40 Hare, 'Value Education in a Pluralistic Society,' p. 81.

41 In Beck, Hersh, and Sullivan, *The Moral Education Project: Year 4*, p. 23.

42 In Beck et al., *The Reflective Approach in Values Education: The Moral Education Project, Year 3*, p. 3.

43 Beck, *Ethics: An Introduction*, p. 5.

44 Dewey, 'The Problem of Value'; see also his 'The Meaning of Value,' 'Some Questions about Value,' and 'Theory of Valuation,' *International Encyclopedia of the Social Sciences*, 1939.

45 Beck et al., *The Reflective Approach in Values Education*, p. 5.

46 As quoted in Baier and Rescher, eds., *Values and the Future*, pp. 35–6.

47 Ibid., pp. 38–40.

48 Pepper, *The Sources of Value*, p. 7.

49 McLuhan and Fiore, *The Medium Is the Message*, pp. 94–5.

50 McLuhan, *The Gutenberg Galaxy*, p. 149.
51 Beck, *Moral Education in the Schools*, p. 19. For the same liberal optimism, see his *Educational Philosophy and Theory*, pp. 66–71.
52 Beck et al., *Reflective Approach in Values Education*, p. 10.
53 Fraenkel, *Helping Students Think and Value*, pp. 330–1.
54 Baier and Rescher, *Values and the Future*, p. v.
55 Dewey, *Democracy and Education*, p. 219.
56 Reginald D. Archambault, 'The Continuum of Ends-Means,' in *John Dewey on Education*, p. 104; see also 'Scientific Treatment of Morality,' p. 35.
57 Beck, *Moral Education in the Schools*, p. 5.
58 Ibid.
59 Fromm, *Man for Himself*, p. viii.
60 Beck, *Moral Education in the Schools*.
61 Turner, 'Values and the Social Worker,' p. 201.
62 K. Albrecht, *Stress and the Manager* (Englewood Cliffs, NJ: Prentice Hall 1979); T.A. Beehr and J.E. Newman, 'Job Stress, Employee Health, and Organizational Effectiveness: A Facet Analysis, Model, and Literature Review,' *Personnel Psychology*, 31 (1978); Ketz de Vries, 'Organizational Stress Management Strategies: The Stress Audit,' in A.S. Sethi and R.S. Schuler, eds., *Handbook of Organizational Stress Coping Strategies* (Boston: Ballinger 1984); M. Friedman and R.H. Rosenman, *Type A Behaviour and Your Heart* (New York: Knopf 1974); B.B. Brown, *Stress and the Art of Biofeedback* (New York: Harper and Row 1977).
63 Roszak, *Person/Planet: The Creative Disintegration of Industrial Society*. p. 49. See also Fromm, *The Revolution of Hope*.
64 Roszak, *Person/Planet*, p. 49.
65 Ibid., pp. 124–8.
66 Reich, *The Greening of America*, p. 354.
67 Botkin, Elmandjra, and Malitza, 'The World Problématique as a Human Challenge,' p. 15.
68 Beck, *Educational Philosophy and Theory*, p. 109.
69 *Ethics: An Introduction*, p. 10.
70 Ibid., p. 11.

Chapter 2: The World and Spirit as Possession

1 'Letter from Leo Strauss to Eric Voegelin,' in Peter Emberley and Barry Cooper, eds., *Faith and Political Philosophy: The Correspondence between Leo Strauss and Eric Voegelin 1934–1964* (University Park: Pennsylvania State University Press 1993), p. 75.

2 Martin Heidegger, 'Letter on Humanism,' in *Basic Writings*, ed. by David Krell (London: Harper and Row 1977), p. 210.

3 'The Crisis in Education,' in *Between Past and Future: Eight Exercises in Political Thought* (Harmondsworth: Penguin 1977), p. 194.

4 Arendt, *The Origins of Totalitarianism*, p. 438.

5 Ibid., p. 473.

6 Ibid.

7 Ibid., p. 297.

8 Ibid.

9 Ibid., p. 298.

10 Ibid., p. 373.

11 Hannah Arendt, *Eichmann in Jerusalem* (Harmondsworth: Penguin 1963).

12 Eric Voegelin, 'The Gospel and Culture,' in D. Miller and D.B. Hadidian, eds., *Jesus and Man's Hope*, vol. 2 (Pittsburgh: Pittsburgh Theological Seminary Press 1971), p. 63.

13 Eric Voegelin, *Order and History*, vol. 1: *Israel and Revelation* (Baton Rouge: Louisiana State University Press 1956), p. 3.

14 Eric Voegelin, 'On Classical Studies,' *The Modern Age: A Quarterly Review*, 17 (Winter 1973): 4.

15 Eric Voegelin, 'Immortality: Experience and Symbol,' *Harvard Theological Review*, 60/3 (July 1967): 275.

16 Eric Voegelin, 'Reason: The Classical Experience,' in *Anamnesis* (Notre Dame: Notre Dame University Press 1978), p. 103.

17 For those still captivated by notions of human development, either ontogenetic or phylogenetic, and who anticipate a future solution to human 'disorder' through application of a constructed 'system' that 'explains' all human history, the best study showing the full meaning of those expectations is Eric Voegelin's 'Hegel: A Study in Sorcery,' in *Studium Generale*, 24 (1971): 335–68.

18 Voegelin, 'The Consciousness of the Ground,' in *Anamnesis*, p. 170.

19 As quoted in Voegelin, 'Reason: The Classic Experience,' pp. 99–100.

20 Ibid., p. 105.

21 Just how critical a sense of history and place is can be appreciated by recalling the radical reordering attempted by the French revolutionaries during the reign of terror. The revolutionary government of 1793 initiated a new calendar and formally legislated that all documents mandated from 1 January 1793 would be dated Year II, the second year of the republic. In 1795, the effort was made to rename all streets, villages, towns, and cities, as well as to alter the city-planning schemes. The aim of the transformation was to initiate a general amnesia as the condition in which terror could operate. The expectation was that the climate of enchantment and ecstasy would engender a

new consciousness of permanent revolution. The most effective manner in which this was achieved was by dissolving the traditional social milieu into minute components, atomizing what had previously been a compound, reconstituting each component, and then reconstructing a new milieu of perpetual mobilization. What had to be struck from human experience was the recollection of the past, the memories of the place and history of the *ancien régime*.

22 Hannah Arendt, *Men in Dark Times* (New York: Harcourt, Brace, Jovanovich 1968), p. 104; *The Origins of Totalitarianism*, p. 391.

23 For the importance of space and time, see Kern, *The Culture of Time and Space*.

24 Eric Voegelin, *Science, Politics, and Gnosticism* (Chicago: Henry Regnery 1968), p. 42.

25 Voegelin, 'The Concrete Consciousness,' in *Anamnesis*, p. 201.

Chapter 3: Values Education: Three Models

1 For overviews of values education and critiques of the programs, see John Meyer, *Reflections on Values Education*; A.C. Kazepides, ed., *Yearbook of the Canadian Society for the Study of Education: The Teaching of Values in Canadian Education*, vol. 2; Kathleen Gow, *Yes, Virginia: There Is a Right and Wrong*; Robert Carter, *Dimensions of Moral Education*.

2 For a sense of some of the major controversies, see 'Moral Education and Secular Humanism: A Symposium with Robert Hall, Lawrence Kohlberg, John Wilson, Howard Kirschenbaum, Edwin Delattre, Kevin Ryan, and Gaston Cogdell,' *The Humanist*, Nov./Dec. 1978, pp. 7–25.

3 Bruner, *Toward a Theory of Instruction*, p. 36; see also his *The Process of Education*.

4 A.V.E.R., *Prejudice*, ed. by L. Daniels, L. Douglas, C. Oliver, and I. Wright (Toronto: Value Reasoning Series, Ontario Institute for Studies in Education 1978).

5 John Wilson, *The Assessment of Morality* (Slough, England: National Foundation for Educational Research 1973), *Moral Education and the Curriculum*, and *Introduction to Moral Education*.

6 See the reference to the *Value Analysis Capability Project* in David M. Williams, 'AVER in Surrey: An Approach to Research and Development in Moral Education,' in A.C. Kazepides, ed., *Yearbook of the Canadian Society for the Study of Education: The Teaching of Values in Canadian Education*, vol. 2, 1975, for procedures to develop evaluative skills. For a detailed debate on the various components of a formalist ethics see D. Cochrane, C.M. Hamm, and A.C. Kazepides, *The Domain of Moral Education*. See also Wilson, 'Rationality and

Moral Education,' *Introduction to Moral Education, The Assessment of Morality,* and *Practical Methods of Moral Education.*

7 As quoted in Kurt Baier and Nicholas Rescher, eds., *Values and the Future,* p. 54.

8 For an account of the political dimension Kant finds in judgments of taste, see Hannah Arendt, *Lectures on Kant's Political Philosophy,* ed. by Ronald Beiner (Brighton: Harvester Press 1982).

9 Immanuel Kant, *Foundations of the Metaphysics of Morals,* transl. by Lewis White Beck (Indianapolis: Bobbs-Merrill 1980), p. 83.

10 Hare, *Freedom and Reason;* see also *The Language of Morals* and 'Language and Moral Education.'

11 Hare, *Freedom and Reason;* see also *The Language of Morals* and 'Values Education in a Pluralistic Society.'

12 Hare, 'Language and Moral Education,' p. 164.

13 Taylor, *Normative Discourse.*

14 Hare, 'Language and Moral Education,' p. 90.

15 I am not denying AVER's explicit linking of moral autonomy to the political rights of persons, especially evident in the mutual recognition of the dignity of the person promoted by the reciprocity test. What I am saying is that the traditional grounds of the idea of a person – the Homeric Greek notion of human existence under the dispensations of *moira* (fate), the Greek and Christian notion of the spiritual substance formed in the image of perfection and harmony, the early modern notion of the concrete and embodied being of historical existence whose fear of death or compassion for others gives a person palpable cause to exercise his reason – have all been abandoned. The 'person' is only a logical fiction, and to repeat my earlier point, the self represented by the sign 'person' has no concern for a permanent world whose stability would substantiate its claim to specific, enforceable rights.

16 Cf. Stanley Rosen, *Nihilism: A Philosophical Essay,* esp. chs. 1–3.

17 Friedrich Nietzsche, 'History of an Error: How the "Real World" at Last Became a Myth,' in *Twilight of the Idols,* transl. by R.J. Hollingdale (Harmondsworth: Penguin 1968), pp. 41–2.

18 The following account abstracts from four of the modules: L. Daniels, L. Douglas, C. Oliver, and I. Wright, eds., *Prejudice* (Toronto: Values Reasoning Series, Ontario Institute for Studies in Education 1978); L. Douglas, C. Oliver, and I. Wright, eds., *The Elderly* (Toronto: Values Reasoning Series, Ontario Institute for Studies in Education 1978); L. Douglas, C. Oliver, and I. Wright, *Population Problems* (Toronto: Values Reasoning Series, Ontario Institute for Studies in Education 1979); and L. Douglas, C. Oliver, and I. Wright, *War* (Toronto: Values Reasoning Series, Ontario Institute for Studies in Education

1979). See also A.V.E.R., *Report No. 1: A Study of the Characteristics of Moral Discussion in Vancouver Elementary Schools* (Vancouver: AVER 1972) and *Report No. 5: Interim Report of an Experiment in Moral Education at Surrey, B.C.* (Vancouver: AVER 1974).

19 Association of Values Education and Research, 'Population Problems,' p. 30.

20 Ibid., p. 40.

21 Michel Foucault, 'Governmentality,' in *Ideology and Consciousness*, no. 6 (Autumn 1979): 5–21.

Chapter 4: Values Development: The Hegelian Experiment

1 For the most comprehensive explanation and defence of Kohlberg's proposals see Kohlberg, Levine, and Hewer, *Moral Stages: A Current Formulation and a Response to Critics* (hereafter, *A Current Formulation*).

2 *A Current Formulation*, p. 72.

3 Kohlberg, 'The Adolescent as a Philosopher,' p. 1076.

4 *A Current Formulation*, p. 39.

5 'The Cognitive-Developmental Approach to Moral Education,' p. 27; see also 'Stages of Moral Development as a Basis for Moral Education,' in C. Beck, B. Crittenden, and E. Sullivan, eds., *Moral Education: Interdisciplinary Approaches* (Toronto: University of Toronto Press 1971).

6 Kohlberg, 'From Is to Ought: How to Commit the Naturalistic Fallacy and Get Away with It in the Study of Moral Development,' p. 184 (hereafter, 'From Is to Ought'). For a good introduction to the theory, see 'Stages of Moral Development as a Basis for Moral Education,' esp. pp. 62–6.

7 Kohlberg also sees his program as consistent with the account of justice set out by Plato. Cf. 'Education for Justice: A Modern Statement of the Platonic View.' For his empirical studies, see the *Journal of Moral Education* throughout the 1970s and especially E. Turiel, 'An Experimental Test of the Sequentiality of Developmental Stages in the Child's Moral Judgments' and 'Developmental Processes in the Child's Moral Thinking.'

8 'From Is to Ought,' p. 193.

9 Parenthetically, it should be mentioned that 'reciprocity' has a noble and long-standing pedigree as the principle of justice and of intellectual thought. As different thinkers as Aristotle and Hegel identify reciprocity as the hallmark of politics and reason. Reciprocity entails harmonizing difference by permitting the mutual action of such phenomena as part and whole, freedom and law, or motion and completion to appear within a proportional and unified existence. Kohlberg's idea of reciprocity is akin to, but also distinct from,

this pedigree. For him, reciprocity is essentially a logical operation of the mind.

10 *A Current Formulation*, p. 49.

11 'From Is to Ought,' p. 185.

12 *A Current Formulation*, p. 14.

13 Kohlberg, 'The Adolescent as a Philosopher: The Discovery of the Self in a Postconventional World,' 1061.

14 Ibid., p. 1064.

15 Ibid., p. 1072.

16 'Stages of Moral Development as a Basis for Moral Education,' p. 61.

17 *A Current Formulation*, p. 95.

18 Ibid., p. 107.

19 Kohlberg, 'Moral Development,' in *International Encyclopedia of the Social Sciences* (New York: Crowell and Macmillan 1968), p. 491.

20 Ibid., p. 490.

21 'Development as the Aim of Education,' p. 460.

22 *A Current Formulation*, pp. 87–8.

23 *The Philosophy of Moral Development*, vol. 1, pp. 288–9.

24 Positions to the contrary have been argued by E.L. Simpson in 'Moral Development Research: A Case of Scientific Cultural Bias,' *Human Development*, 17 (1974): 81–106, and Sullivan, *Kohlberg's Structuralism: A Critical Appraisal*. Responding to praise he received in the Ontario McKay Committee Report, 1966, and again in a paper by V.J. Cunningham, 1978, of the Ministry of Education, Research and Evaluation Branch, Kohlberg wrote: 'The fact that my expression of the liberal ideology underlying the American Declaration of Independence and Constitution could communicate across national boundaries helps support my own faith in "The Future of Liberalism as the Dominant Ideology of the Western World,"' in *The Philosophy of Moral Development*, vol. 1, p. 230.

25 'Stages of Moral Development as a Basis for Moral Education,' p. 51.

26 *A Current Formulation*, p. 115, from a response to Simpson, 'Moral Development Research.'

27 Cf. Carol Gilligan, 'Woman's Place in Man's Life Cycle,' in H. Giroux, *The Hidden Curriculum and Moral Education* (Berkeley: McCutcheon 1983), p. 118, and *In a Different Voice: Psychological Theory and Women's Development* (Cambridge: Harvard University Press 1982). Kohlberg wrote that where there remained a clash between the two accounts, the ethic of care simply had to be rejected as outside 'the moral point of view' as 'not well adapted to resolve justice problems,' however central it may be to 'personal decision-making' spheres of 'kinship, love, friendship, and sex.'

28 'From Is to Ought,' pp. 214–15.
29 Kohlberg, 'Stages of Moral Development as a Basis for Moral Education,' in Beck, Sullivan, and Crittenden, *Moral Education*, p. 43.
30 *A Current Formulation*, p. 15.
31 Ibid.
32 Ibid. Cf. Colby et al., *The Measurement of Moral Judgment: A Manual and Its Results* and *A Longitudinal Study of Moral Judgment*.
33 *A Current Formulation*, p. 109.
34 Ibid., pp. 12–13.
35 'The Adolescent as Philosopher,' p. 1069.
36 What follows is a synopsis of the interpretation put forward in Kojeve's *Introduction to the Reading of Hegel*. Cf. Cooper, *The End of History* and Darby, *The Feast: Meditations on Politics and Time*.
37 Oddly enough, Kohlberg believes that his psychological method makes no metaphysical claims, although he never substantiates the denial. Cf. 'Development as the Aim of Education,' in *The Philosophy of Moral Development*, vol. 1, p. 56.
38 *A Current Formulation*, p. 75.
39 The conclusion that Hegel's teaching culminates in a global tyranny is developed in the famous debate between Leo Strauss and Kojève. Cf. Victor Gourevitch and Michael S. Roth, *On Tyranny* (New York: Free Press 1991).
40 'The Cognitive-Developmental Approach,' p. 53.
41 Needless to say, Kohlberg's construction of mutual recognition is nothing like the contextual participation and 'judging with' referred to in an earlier chapter. Instead, this is a hypothesized 'ideal community' which is intended to serve as a regulative ideal. As Gadamer notes in *Truth and Method*, p. 36, proceeding by positing ideal communities is an 'intellectualization of the idea of the sense of the community,' rendering judgment and speech into a type of product, with all the attendant intolerance for nuance, ambivalence, and plurality. While Kohlberg can enlist the notion of 'empathy' to engender consensus, he uses it as a technique whereby private individuals share logical operations and actualize an encounter which is pure form, but without substance. There is no context to the judgment, no horizon of meaning, which supplies content to the process.
42 Kohlberg, *The Psychology of Moral Development*, pp. 308–9.
43 Ibid., p. 309.
44 Ibid., p. 345.
45 Ibid., p. 391.
46 Ibid.
47 Ibid., p. 345.

48 Ibid., p. 385.
49 Ibid., p. 347.
50 Ibid., p. 348.
51 Ibid., p. 351.
52 Ibid.
53 Ibid., pp. 359, 369.
54 *A Current Formulation*, p. 60.
55 Ibid., p. 113.
56 Ibid., p. 61.
57 Ibid., p. 62.
58 Ibid., p. 48.
59 Ibid., pp. 65, 9.
60 This is from a response to R. Schweder, 'Review of Lawrence Kohlberg's *Essays in Moral Development, Volume 2. The Psychology of Moral Development*,' pp. 421–4. See also W. Kurtines and E.B. Greif, 'The Development of Moral Thought: Review and Evaluation of Kohlberg's Approach,' *Psychological Bulletin*, 81/8 (Aug. 1974): 453–69, and J.C. Gibbs, 'Kohlberg's Stages of Moral Development: A Constructive Critique.'

Chapter 5: Values Clarification: The Nietzschean Experiment

1 The standard values-clarification manuals are Raths, Harmin, and Simon, *Values and Teaching* (1966), with a revised edition in 1978 which was meant to address the criticisms of relativism and lack of critical reasoning in the approach; Harmin, Kirschenbaum, and Simon, eds., *Clarifying Values through Subject Matter*; Kirschenbaum, 'Current Research in Value Clarification'; and Larson and Larson, *Values and Faith*. Public education packets have been distributed by VC's research unit, the Sagamore Institute, including tactics on dealing with community conflict and attacks on values clarification by the 'radical right.' The Sagamore Institute lists over 200 books, articles (such as 'How to Sabotage "Teacher Proof" Curricula' and 'VIP Skills Approach to Handling Stress'), films, cassettes, and calendars that sustain values clarification through foreign language programs, coaching, family management, Jewish values, strategies for the energy crises, dinner-table learning, death education, stress management, and religious faith; and provides information on teacher's legal rights, techniques for dealing with attempts to discredit 'humanistic education,' and examples of 'extremist literature' attacking 'secular humanism.' Commonly cited books are Combs, Avila, and Purkey, *Helping Relationships*; and Rogers, *Client-Centered Therapy* and *On Becoming a Person*, as well as Allport, *Becoming*.

2 Raths, Harmin, and Simon, *Values and Teaching*, rev. ed., p. 6.

3 Ibid., pp. 41–2.

4 Ibid., p. 289.

5 Ibid., 27–8.

6 Ibid., p. 45.

7 Ibid., p. 28.

8 Dewey, *Reconstruction in Philosophy*, pp. 162–3.

9 Raths et al., *Values and Teaching*, p. 142.

10 Ibid., p. 37. It is statements of this sort that have created the stir about values clarification. See, for example, Gluck, 'Values Clarification: The Engineering of Consensus.' See also, as representative of the resistance, Kazepides, 'The Logic of Values Clarification'; John Stewart, 'Clarifying Values Clarification: A Critique,' *Phi Delta Kappan*, 56/10 (June 1975): 684–8; Eric Beversluis, 'The Dilemma of Values Clarification,' pp. 417–27; George Harrison, 'Values Clarification and the Construction of the Good,' *Educational Theory*, 30/3 (Summer 1980); Bruce Suttle, 'Moral Education versus Values Clarification,' *Journal of Educational Thought*, 16/1 (April 1982); Ann Colby, 'Review of *Values and Teaching and Values Clarification.*'

11 Kirschenbaum et al., *In Defense of Values Clarification*, p. 4.

12 Ibid., p. 34.

13 Perkins, *Human Development and Learning*, p. 580.

14 See Part III of Raths et al., *Values and Teaching*; Louis Raths, Sidney Simon, Leland Howe, and Howard Kirschenbaum, eds., *Values Clarification: A Handbook of Practical Strategies of Teachers and Students*; and Harmin, Kirschenbaum, and Simon, eds., *Clarifying Values through Subject Matter.*

15 Kirschenbaum et al., *In Defense of Values Clarification*, p. 2.

16 Raths et al., *Values Clarification*, p. 87.

17 Ibid., p. 45.

18 Raths et al., *Values and Teaching*, p. 289.

19 Kirschenbaum et al., *In Defense of Values Clarification*, pp. 2–3.

20 Raths et al., *Values and Teaching*, pp. 28–9.

21 Later versions of the methodological process attempted to systematize these indicators by introducing more states to the valuing process. Kirschenbaum's expanded account of the process establishes five dimensions – thinking, feeling, choosing, communication, and acting – with seventeen subprocesses to incorporate divergent thinking, moral reasoning, discharging distress, effective message communication, conflict resolution, and consistency, among others.

22 Raths et al., *Values and Teaching*, p. 201. Compare with p. 201 in 1st edition.

23 *Values and Teaching*, 1978 ed.

24 Ibid., p. 6.
25 Kirschenbaum et al., *In Defense of Values Clarification*, p. 3.
26 Ibid., p. 45.
27 Ibid., p. 294.
28 Ibid., p. 243.
29 Kirschenbaum et al., *In Defense of Values Clarification*, p. 6.
30 These are empirical tests of the effects of values clarification by population-targeting methods: Ojemann's Social Causality Test (measuring decision-making ability), Nowicki and Strickland Internal-External Control Scale (measuring level of personal control over one's life), the Devereux Elementary School Behaviour Rating Scale (measuring overt self-reliant behaviour), the Cutick Self-Evaluation Form or Sears Self-Concept Scale (measuring self-esteem).
31 Cf. Lockwood, 'The Effects of Values Clarification and Moral Development Curricula on School Age Subjects.' Lockwood's conclusions are that claims that values clarification has a positive impact on self-esteem, self-concept, and personal adjustment are 'not persuasive,' that 'there is no evidence that values clarification has a systematic, demonstrated impact on student's values,' and that the techniques appear 'to positively affect students' classroom behaviour.' See also his 'What's Wrong with Values Clarification,' *Social Education*, 42/2 (May 1977): 399–402, and 'A Critical View of Values Clarification.' In 'Current Research in Value Clarification,' Kirschenbaum examines seventeen empirical studies of the effects of values clarification. A typical statement by Raths et al. characterizes their own understanding of the way to test the method: 'On the one hand would be teachers who were certain that students would be better off if they had clearer values. On the other hand would be teachers who were open about the issue of "betterness" but who believed that students might be able to take advantage of value-clarifying opportunities. The test would be to see which teachers produced greater desired change. Our hypotheses would be that the more open teachers would do so' (Raths et al., *Values and Teaching*, p. 299).
32 Concerning the charge of relativism, Raths et al. wrote in the preface to the 2nd edition of *Values and Teaching* (p. ix): 'We do not believe that any one belief, or purpose, or attitude, is as good as another. We too have preferences; we too have made choices; and while we do not believe that our views are eternal, or that they should be made universal, with some small modicum of doubt we do believe that they are to be preferred.'
33 Fromm, *The Heart of Man*, p. 32; see also *To Have or To Be*.
34 Jean-Paul Sartre, *Being and Nothingness*, esp. part IV.
35 Erich Fromm (*The Heart of Man*, p. 87) sums up precisely what to me reveals

the dangerous state the 'encounter' produces: 'Only in the process of mutually alive relatedness, can the other and I overcome the barriers of separateness, inasmuch as we both participate in the dance of life.' The dance of life destroys the principle of individuation producing the ecstasy and immediacy of a pure Dionysian state.

36 Cf. Raths et al., *Values and Teaching*, p. 8.

37 Maurice Friedman insightfully distinguishes empathy from Buber's 'experiencing the other side': empathy means transposing oneself into the dynamic structure of an object, hence, 'the exclusion of one's own concreteness, the extinguishing of the actual situation of life, the absorption in pure aestheticism of the reality in which one participates.' Inclusion is the opposite of this. 'It is the extension of one's own concreteness, the fulfilment of the actual situation of life, the complete presence of the reality in which one participates.' In inclusion one person, 'without forfeiting anything of the felt reality of his activity, at the same time lives through the common event from the standpoint of the other.' 'Introduction' to Martin Buber, *Daniel: Dialogues on Realization* (New York: McGraw-Hill 1965), p. 33.

38 Robert Bellah et al., *Habits of the Heart: Individualism and Commitment in American Life* (Berkeley: University of California Press 1985); Alasdair MacIntyre, *After Virtue: A Study in Moral Theory* (Notre Dame: University of Notre Dame Press 1981) and 'How Moral Agents Have Become Ghosts,' *Synthèse*, 53 (1982): 295–312; Foot, *Theories of Ethics*.

39 For a discussion of the dangers of such a politics, see Hannah Arendt, *On Revolution* (Harmondsworth: Penguin 1963), esp. ch. 2.

40 I examined how such thinkers as Plato and Augustine identified these potent passions and the education they thought was necessary in Peter Emberley and Waller R. Newell, *Bankrupt Education: The Decline of Liberal Education in Canada* (Toronto: University of Toronto Press 1994).

41 I have explored this in 'Rousseau's Management of the Passions,' *Interpretation*, 13/2 (1985), 151–76.

42 Cf. Nikolas Rose, 'The Psychological Complex.' Raths et al. deny that values clarification is related to Carl Roger's client-centred therapy. 'Clarifying is not therapy,' they say, and they have suggested that there is a difference between symptoms of values confusion and the symptoms of emotional disturbances. However, as Alan Lockwood aptly demonstrates, the distinction cannot be maintained. 'There is significant correspondence between values clarification and client-centred therapy regarding: (1) the conditions which produce a need for treatment; (2) the outcomes of successful treatment; (3) the key aspects of the treatment process; (4) the role of the therapist/teacher in the prescribed treatment,' a correspondence Lockwood shows by lining up

relevant passages from Raths et al., *Values and Teaching*, and Roger's *Client-Centered Therapy*, in 'A Critical View of Values Clarification.'

43 Cf. Horkheimer and Adorno, *The Dialectic of Enlightenment*, and Adorno, *The Jargon of Authenticity*.

44 Raths et al., *Values and Teaching*, p. 280.

45 Ibid., p. 154.

Chapter 6: The Technological Environment

1 A literature spanning three decades disagrees with the technicians and managers. An excellent introduction to the philosophy of technology is Mitcham and Mackey, eds., *Philosophy and Technology*. See also Marx Wartofsky, 'Philosophy of Technology,' in Peter Asquith and Henry Kyburg, Jr., eds., *Current Research in the Philosophy of Science* (East Lansing, Mich.: Philosophy of Science Association 1979), pp. 171–84; Leiss, 'The Social Consequences of Technological Progress'; Borgmann, *Technology and the Character of Contemporary Life*; Barry Cooper, *Action into Nature: An Essay on the Meaning of Technology* (Notre Dame: Notre Dame University Press 1991).

2 Grant, *Technology and Justice*, p. 4.

3 Hannah Arendt, 'The Crisis in Education,' in *Between Past and Future* (Harmondsworth: Penguin 1977), p. 195.

4 George Grant, 'Thinking about Technology,' in *Technology and Justice* (Toronto: Anansi 1987), p. 15.

5 Alexandre Koyré, *From the Closed World to the Infinite Universe* (Baltimore: Johns Hopkins University Press 1957); Hans Blumenberg, *The Legitimacy of the Modern Age* (Cambridge, Mass.: MIT Press 1983); E.A. Burtt, *Metaphysical Foundations of Modern Science* (New York: Anchor 1932).

6 Grant in 'Knowing and Making,' quoting P.B. Medawar.

7 Bacon is commonly considered an 'empiricist.' Following the customary meaning of this term, as a mode of knowing taking its bearing from facts which arise through man's sense-apparatus, Bacon is no empiricist. Even a casual reading of *The New Organon* reveals the 'reconstructive' character of his empiricism. Observation of the world is mediated by a critical technique which rids the world of ambiguity and disorder.

8 For example, a contemporary case: particle-physics scientists use a 'standard model,' a mathematical schema of the world, that is complete and coherent and accounts for all the phenomena they bring forth in their technological apparati. Nonetheless, they also agree that while the standard model is 'successful' no one can explain why. Nonetheless its success validates the intelligibility of the model.

9 Cf. Peter F. Drucker, *The Age of Discontinuity: Guidelines to Our Changing Society* (New York: Harper Torchbooks 1973), ch. 7.

10 Cf. Ihde, *Technics and Praxis*, who writes of the 'idealization' of technology where the transformation of experience made possible by machines, regulative techniques, and ordering devices is rendered invisible.

11 Ellul, *The Technological Society*, p. xxv.

12 Winner, *Autonomous Technology*, p. 229.

13 Ellul, *The Technological Society*, p. 79.

14 Ellul, *The Technological System*, pp. 232–3.

15 Ibid., p. 234.

16 Ibid., p. 275.

17 Ibid., p. 12.

18 This is so far from Ellul's intent that he even explicitly points to the connection between the Hegelian system and technology. 'Philosophy,' he writes, 'has tended to totalize in its search for an intellectual system, a master key to universal reality. Today the same tendency prevails, not in the intellectual spheres ... but in the sphere of reality, all parts of the social body being so conjoined and interconnected as to make that organism all-encompassing and uniform' (*Autopsy of Revolution*, p. 257).

19 An excellent account of the transition from Greek antiquity to Christianity can be found in Charles Cochrane's *Christianity and Classical Culture: A Study of Thought and Action from Augustus to Augustine* (London: Oxford University Press 1957).

20 Arendt, *Willing*, vol. 2 of *The Life of the Mind*, pp. 63ff.

21 As quoted in Hannah Arendt, 'What Is Freedom?' in *Between Past and Future*, p. 161.

22 This is the famous thesis of 'secularization' most clearly articulated by Karl Löwith in his work *Meaning in History: The Theological Presuppositions of the Philosophy of History* (Chicago: University of Chicago Press 1949). The thesis has also been roundly challenged by Hans Blumenberg in his *The Legitimacy of the Modern Age*, especially part I, though he is in agreement that Christian images were functionally adapted to explain modern modes of self-assertion.

23 Eric Voegelin, 'Hegel: A Study in Sorcery,' in *Studium Generale*, 24 (1971): 335–68.

24 One of Canada's greatest educators, Queen's University professor John Watson, adopted Kant's moral philosophy of autonomy and Hegel's philosophy of history, as well as their accompanying teaching of restraint, and through students like George Paxton Young, had a major influence on establishing a balanced and judicious education system in Canada. For Watson, as for Hegel, human historical development was a spiritual odyssey. The aggres-

sive autonomy which had made freedom and technological process a historical accomplishment nonetheless threatened the forms of the 'civilized
community' and healthy social integration into which humankind had
evolved. Moreover, in the absence of an ethics transcending the 'industrial
life of modern times,' Watson feared both a narrow, self-interested pragmatism and a reduction of 'the complex civilization of modern times' to 'a con-
temptible obscurity.' Politically, he warned, such a condition could breed 'a
despotic form of government or [lead] to the direst anarchy and confusion.'
Unless the will, Watson concluded, is 'trained in the proper direction, it inevitably seeks a downward path for itself. If it is not filled with great and enno-
bling thoughts, it will seek to find satisfaction in what is mean, and petty and
evanescent.' The relentless negativity of the will had to be tempered so as to
bring about respect for the forms of genuine political community. John Watson, *Education and Life*, An Address Delivered at the Opening of the Thirty-
Second Session of Queen's University, Published by the Alma Mater Society
of Queen's University, 1872, pp. 5–6.

25 Cf. Nietzsche, *The Use and Abuse of History*, whose demonstration of the
actual meaning of 'monumental,' 'antiquarian,' and 'critical' histories as tes-
timonies to the power of life heralds the end of all residual anthropomorphic
readings of existence.

26 Quoted in Heidegger, *Nietzsche*, vol. 1: *The Will to Power as Art*, p. 267.

27 Alphonso Lingis, 'The Will to Power,' in Allison, ed., *The New Nietzsche*, p. 43.

28 Thomas Altizer, 'Eternal Recurrence and Kingdom of God,' in Allison, ibid.,
p. 242.

29 Nietzsche, *The Gay Science*, Aphorism 125, p. 181.

30 Foucault, 'Two Lectures,' in *Power/Knowledge*, p. 90.

31 Ellul, *Autopsy of Revolution*, p. 257.

32 Cf. Paul Weiss, *Within the Gates of Science and Beyond* (New York: Hafner
1971), who details the complexity of system interaction and the paucity of
Newtonian models.

33 The most extensive account of 'simultaneity' appears in Bergson, *Creative
Evolution*.

34 Max Jammer, quoting from William Clifford, 'On the Space-Theory of Matter,' p. 161, in *Concepts of Space*.

35 McLuhan, *The Gutenberg Galaxy*, p. 41.

36 Representative of the new 'ecological' holism that sees modern man's
improved health linked to far greater integration to 'life's systems' is
Gregory Bateson's *Steps to an Ecology of Mind* (New York: Ballantine 1972).
See also Fritjof Capra, *The Turning Point: Science, Society, and the Rising Culture*
(New York: Bantam 1982).

37 Foucault, *Discipline and Punish*, p. 124.

38 Ibid., p. 26.

39 Foucault, 'Nietzsche, Genealogy, History,' p. 149.

40 Wiener, *The Human Use of Human Beings*, p. 46.

41 Nietzsche, *The Will to Power*, Aphorism 658.

42 Ellul, *The Technological System*, p. 3.

43 McLuhan, *Understanding Media*, p. 355.

44 Ibid., pp. 3–4.

45 McLuhan, *The Gutenberg Galaxy*, p. 30.

46 McLuhan, *Understanding Media*, pp. 3–4.

47 McLuhan, *The Gutenberg Galaxy*, p. 31.

48 McLuhan, *Understanding Media*, p. 80.

49 Jean Baudrillard, 'Forget Foucault,' *Humanities in Society*, 3/1 (Winter 1980): 92.

50 Ibid.

51 Cf. Jameson, 'Postmodernism, or the Cultural Logic of Late Capitalism,' who details the fragmentation of position and the consequences for critical distance, depth, and critique. He concludes: 'So I come finally to my principal point here, that this latest mutation in space – postmodern hyperspace – has finally succeeded in transcending the capacities of the individual human body to locate itself, to organize its immediate surroundings perceptually, and cognitively to map its environment ...'

52 Jean Baudrillard, *In the Shadow of the Silent Majorities, or the End of the Social, and Other Essays*, transl. by Paul Foss, John Johnston, and Paul Patton (New York: Semiotexte 1983), pp. 102–3.

53 Baudrillard, '... Or the End of the Social,' ibid., p. 3.

54 Baudrillard, 'In the Shadow of the Silent Majorities,' ibid., p. 1; Arendt, *The Origins of Totalitarianism*, p. 437ff.

55 Lyotard, *The Post-Modern Condition*, p. 74.

56 In his book *The Use and Abuse of History*, Nietzsche writes about forgetfulness as a 'hygiene for life.'

57 McLuhan, *The Gutenberg Galaxy*, p. 114.

58 When Man is effaced, his concrete existence and the world 'imploded,' the discourse that remains runs like this: 'I do not refer to a succession of moments in time, nor to a diverse plurality of thinking subjects; I refer to a caesura which fragments the moment and disperses the subject into a plurality of possible positions and functions,' a speech that expresses the profoundest alienation of man from the world and reality. Cf. Michel Foucault, 'The Orders of Discourse,' *Social Science Information*, 10/2 (1971): 21.

59 Arendt, 'The Crisis in Education,' p. 195.

Chapter 7: From Dispossession to Possession

1 In many ways this is the quintessential Cartesian self. Cf. Giambattista Vico, *On the Study Methods of our Time*, transl. by Elio Gianturco (New York: Bobbs-Merrill 1965). See also Michael Oakeshott, 'Political Education,' in *Rationalism in Politics and Other Essays* (New York: Basic Books 1972), and Richard Bernstein, *Praxis and Action*.

2 Friedrich Nietzsche, *Daybreak: Thoughts on the Prejudices of Morality*, transl. by R.J. Hollingdale (Cambridge: Cambridge University Press 1982), p. 31.

3 Castel, Castel, and Lovell, *The Psychiatric Society*.

4 Grant, *Time as History*, p. 48.

5 McLuhan, *Understanding Media*, p. 354.

6 C.B. Macpherson provides an exemplary version of this diagnosis in his account of the aetiology of 'possessive' individualism (to 'appreciate' is to establish a price), depicting the historical conditions under which appropriation and the relations of appropriation engendered and implied political relations of oppression, exclusion, and deformation of 'true, human reality' (*The Political Theory of Possessive Individualism: Hobbes to Locke* [Oxford: Clarendon Press 1962]). In this account, the phenomenon of possession is apprehended either as the distorted relations arising from a confusion of 'use-value' and 'exchange-value' or as the hegemonic project of a dominant class to further certain sumptuary values in false consciousness of the true needs. Possession is either the expression of appreciating things as exchange-values rather than use-values (a distortion that arises from the deformed relations of capitalist market society), or the projection of 'alienated essence' where things are 'mystified.' A non-deformed relation to things occurs only where 'use-value' is linked to human desires and human encounters which see things as the vehicles for the subjective enjoyment of needs existing collectively in man's 'species-being.' Marx's analysis suggests that the pathology of possession is a peculiarity of capitalist society; as in Rousseau, man by nature is pure and free – only a society that sanctions private property corrupts the desires and channels them towards deforming surrogates.

7 Charles Reinold Noyes, in *The Institution of Property*, shows how the genitive case in Greek and Latin engendered the relation between possession and belonging, and bestowed on this relation the sense of permanency, the determinate marking of something in location.

8 Nietzsche, *On the Genealogy of Morals*, sec. 6, p. 20.

9 Sartre, *Critique of Dialectical Reason*, vol. 1, p. 169.

10 Sartre, 'Doing and Having: Possession,' in *Being and Nothingness*, p. 579. Sartre uses the example of deciding to stop smoking, for it represented the act of destructively appropriating the entire world. To achieve this release, he had to

destroy the symbolic, ritualistic ties his pipe and his tobacco had with the world by reducing it to only itself, thus making it possible to dispose of it. Yet for all this, Sartre recognizes that possession cannot be relinquished: we choose our being in our possessing: having and being are inseparable. It is Marcel who goes the further route towards our utter disposability before God.

11 Ibid.
12 Sartre, *Being and Nothingness*. pp. 579–80.
13 Nietzsche, *Thus Spoke Zarathustra*, transl. by Walter Kaufmann (New York: Viking Press 1966), p. 139.
14 Ibid.
15 Ibid., no. 708, p. 377.
16 Martin Heidegger, 'The Word of Nietzsche,' in *The Question Concerning Technology and Other Essays*, transl. by William Lovitt (New York: Harper 1977), p. 75.
17 Ibid., p. 102.
18 Nietzsche, *The Will to Power*, p. 380.
19 Fromm, *Man for Himself*, p. viii.
20 Freire, *Education as the Practice of Freedom*, p. 60.
21 Antonouris, 'Review Article: The Roles of Counsellors in Education,' p. 134. Cf. Herman, *Guidance in Canadian Schools*.
22 Ministry of Education, Government of Alberta, *1982 Alberta Health Curriculum* (Edmonton: Government of Alberta Publications 1982), p. 125. See also *1986 Health and Personal Life Skills Curriculum*, *1987 Career and Life Management Curriculum*, and *1981 Social Studies Curriculum*.
23 McLuhan, *The Gutenberg Galaxy*, p. 174.
24 Arendt, *The Origins of Totalitarianism*, p. 438.
25 For an account of the pervasiveness of 'possession' within both our moral categories and our social practices, see Wikse, *About Possession: The Self as Private Property*. Wiske, however, confines his understanding of 'possession' to the multiple privative relations ('self-fetishism') engendered within capitalism, and makes no distinction between 'possession' and 'acquisition/consumption,' and thus fails to recognize the 'durative' element to possession. What he emphasizes, like most modern philosophers since Hegel, is the appropriation and what renders it legitimate, rather than the 'thing' and the existential care with which we invest it.
26 Noyes, *The Institution of Property*, pp. 123–4.
27 Heidegger, 'Building, Dwelling, Thinking,' p. 157. See also 'The Thing,' which sustains similar themes.
28 Peter Emberley and Barry Cooper, eds., *Faith and Political Philosophy: The Correspondence between Leo Strauss and Eric Voegelin 1934–1964* (University Park: Pennsylvania State University Press 1993), p. 75.

Conclusion

1 Hannah Arendt, 'The Crisis in Education,' in *Between Past and Future*, p. 193.
2 Arendt, *The Human Condition*, p. 95.
3 Arendt, 'The Crisis in Education,' p. 191.
4 Ibid., p. 196.
5 Thomas Pangle (transl.), *The Laws of Plato* (New York: Basic Books 1980), Book VII, 808e.
6 Eric Voegelin, 'Reason: The Classic Experience,' in *Anamnesis* (Notre Dame: Notre Dame University Press 1978), p. 105.
7 Eric Voegelin, 'Wisdom and the Magic of the Extreme,' *Southern Review*, 17 (1981): 255–6.
8 Voegelin, 'Reason: The Classic Experience,' p. 100.

Select Bibliography

Adorno, Theodor. *The Jargon of Authenticity*. Evanston, Ill.: Northwestern University Press 1973

Alberta Government, Department of Education. *Experiences in Decision-Making*. 1971

– *Responding to Change: A Handbook for Teachers of Secondary Social Studies*. 1971

– *Responding to Change*. 1974

– *Social Studies Phase II Teaching Unit, Supplement to the 1981 Alberta Social Studies Curriculum*

– Junior High School. *Language Arts Curriculum Guide 1978*. Alberta Education 1978

– Junior High School Curriculum Guide. *Health and Personal Life Skills*. 1986

Alberta Government, Project Unit. *1981 Alberta Social Studies Curriculum*. 1981

Alberta Human Rights Commission. *Human Rights: Respecting Our Differences*. 1978

Allison, David, ed. *The New Nietzsche: Contemporary Styles of Interpretation*. Cambridge, Mass.: MIT Press 1985

Allport, Gordon. *Becoming: Basic Considerations for a Psychology of Personality*. New Haven: Yale University Press 1955

Allport, Gordon W., Philip E. Vernon, and Gardner Lindsey. *A Study of Values*. Boston: Little, Brown 1951

Anders-Richards, Donald. 'Humanistic Psychology and Morality,' *Journal of Moral Education*, 4/2 (1975): 105–10

Andrew, Ed. *Closing the Iron Cage*. Montreal: Black Rose Books 1981

Andrews, B., and D. Hakken. 'Educational Technology: A Theoretical Discussion,' *College English*, 39 (Sept. 1977)

Antonouris, George. 'Review Article: The Roles of Counsellors in Education,' *Journal of Moral Education*, 6/2 (1977): 132–7

Apple, M.W. 'Curricular Form and the Logic of Technical Control,' in *Rethinking*

Curriculum Studies, edited by L. Baron, R. Meighan, and S. Walker. New York: Halsted Press 1981
– 'Curriculum as Ideological Selection,' *Comparative Educational Review*, 20 (June 1975): 210–11
– *Ideology and Curriculum*. London: Routledge and Kegan Paul 1979
Archambault, Reginald D. *John Dewey on Education: Selected Writings*. Chicago: University of Chicago Press 1964
Arendt, Hannah. 'The Conquest of Space and the Stature of Man,' in *Between Past and Future: Eight Exercises in Political Thought*. Harmondsworth: Penguin 1977
– *The Human Condition*. Chicago: University of Chicago Press 1958
– *The Life of the Mind*. 2 vols. London: Secker and Warburg 1978
– *The Origins of Totalitarianism*. New York: Harcourt, Brace, Jovanovich 1973
– 'Thinking and Moral Considerations,' *Social Research*, 38/3 (1971): 440
Aronowitz, Stanley. *False Promises*. New York: McGraw-Hill 1973
Aronowitz, Stanley, and Henry Giroux. *Education under Siege: The Conservative, Liberal, and Radical Debate over Schooling*. South Hadley, Mass.: Bergin and Garvey 1985
– 'Radical Education and Transformative Intellectuals,' *Canadian Journal of Political and Social Theory*, 9/3 (1985): 48–63
Association of Values Education and Research. *First Steps in Practical Reasoning: Student Book and Teacher's Manual*. Vancouver: AVER 1982
– *Practical Reasoning: A Focus for Corrections Education*. Ottawa: Correctional Service of Canada, Education and Training Division 1982
– *Practical Reasoning: Individual and Social Decision-Making*. 1983
Auerbach, J.G., 'Value Changes in Therapy,' *Personality*, 1 (1950): 63–7
Ayres, Clarence E. 'The Value of Economy,' in *Value: A Cooperative Inquiry*, edited by R. Lepley. New York: Columbia University Press 1949
Baier, Kurt. 'Ethical Pluralism and Moral Education,' in *Moral Education*, edited by C.M. Beck, B.S. Crittenden, and E.V. Sullivan. Toronto: University of Toronto Press 1971
– *The Moral Point of View: A Rational Basis of Ethics*. New York: Random House 1965
Baier, Kurt, and Nicholas Rescher, eds. *Values and the Future: The Impact of Technological Change on American Values*. New York: Free Press 1969
Barrs, S., et al., eds. *Values Education: A Resource Booklet*. Toronto: Professional Development Committee of the Ontario Secondary School Teachers' Federation 1975
Barton, L., R. Meighan, and S. Walker. 'Curricular Form and the Logic of Technical Control,' *Rethinking Curriculum Studies*. Lewes, England: Falmer Press 1981

Bates, R. 'New Developments in the New Sociology of Education,' *British Journal of Sociology of Education*, 1/1 (March 1980): 67–80

Baudrillard, Jean. 'Forget Foucault,' *Humanities in Society*, 3/1 (Winter 1980): 92

Beck, Clive. 'The Case for Value Education in the School,' in *Value Education in the Schools: A Report to the Ministry on the OISE Moral Education Project for the Year 1973–4*, Appendix E. Toronto: Ontario Ministry of Education 1974

– *Educational Philosophy and Theory: An Introduction*. Boston: Little, Brown 1974

– *Ethics: An Introduction*. Toronto: McGraw-Hill Ryerson 1972

– *Moral Education in the Schools: Some Practical Suggestions*, Profiles in Practical Education No. 3. Toronto: OISE 1971

– 'A Philosophical View of Values and Value Education,' in *Values and Moral Development*, edited by T. Hennessy. New York: Paulist Press 1976

Beck, Clive, Dwight Boyd, and E. Sullivan. *The Moral Education Year 5 Final Report 1976–77*, Appendix 2. Toronto: Ontario Ministry of Education 1978

Beck, Clive, Norma McCoy, and Jane Bradley-Cameron. *Reflecting on Values: Learning Materials for Grades 1–6*. Toronto: Ontario Institute for Studies in Education 1981

Beck, Clive, Richard Hersh, and Edmund Sullivan. *The Moral Education Project: Year 4, Annual Report 1975–76*. Toronto: OISE 1978

Beck, Clive, E. Sullivan, and B.S. Crittenden, eds. *Moral Education: Interdisciplinary Approaches*. New York: Newman Press 1971

Beck, Clive, E. Sullivan, and N. Taylor. 'Stimulating Transition to Post-Conventional Morality: The Pickering High School Study,' *Interchange*, 3 (1972): 28–37

Beck, Clive, E. Sullivan, et al. *The Reflective Approach in Values Education: The Moral Education Project, Year 3*. Toronto: Ontario Ministry of Education 1976

Beiner, Ronald. *Political Judgment*. Chicago: University of Chicago Press 1983

Benn, S.I., and R.S. Peters. *Social Principles and the Democratic State*. London: George Allen and Unwin 1959

Bennett, William, and Edwin Delattre. 'Moral Education in the Schools,' *The Public Interest*, 50 (Winter 1978): 81–98

Bergson, Henri. *Creative Evolution*, translated by Arthur Mitchell. New York: Random House 1944

– *Matter and Memory*. London: Swan Sonnenschein 1971

Bernstein, Basil. *Class, Codes and Control*. London: Collier-Macmillan 1976

– 'Codes, Modalities and the Process of Cultural Reproduction: A Model,' in *Cultural and Economic Reproduction in Education*, edited by Michael Apple. Boston: Routledge and Kegan Paul 1982

Bernstein, B., and Brian Davies. 'Some Sociological Comments on Plowden,' in *Perspectives on Plowden*. London: Routledge and Kegan Paul 1969

Bernstein, Richard. *Praxis and Action: Contemporary Philosophies of Human Activity*. Philadelphia: University of Pennsylvania Press 1971

Beversluis, Eric. 'The Dilemma of Values Clarification,' in *Philosophy of Education 1978: Proceedings of the 34th Annual Meeting of the Philosophy of Education Society*, edited by Gary Fenstermacher. Champaign, Ill.: The Philosophy of Education Society 1978

Bloom, Allan. *The Closing of the American Mind*. New York: Schuster and Schuster 1987

– 'Commerce and Culture,' *This World*, 1/1 (1982): 5–20

– 'Interpretive Essay,' in *The Republic of Plato*. New York: Basic Books 1964

– 'Our Listless Universities,' *National Review*, 10 Dec. 1982: 537–48

Bloom, Benjamin, et al. *The Taxonomy of Educational Objectives: Handbook I, The Cognitive Domain*. New York: David McKay 1956

Borgmann, Albert. *Technology and the Character of Contemporary Life: A Philosophical Inquiry*. Chicago: University of Chicago Press 1984

Botkin, James, Mahdi Elmandjra, and Mircea Malitza. 'The World Problématique as a Human Challenge,' in *No Limits to Learning: Bridging the Human Gap; a Report to the Club of Rome*. Oxford: Pergamon Press 1979

Bourdieu, P. 'Systems of Education and Systems of Thought,' *International Social Science Journal*, 20/4 (1967): 338–58

Bourdieu, P., and J.C. Passeron. 'Cultural Reproduction and Social Reproduction,' in *Knowledge, Education and Cultural Change*. London: Tavistock Press 1973

– *Distinction: A Social Critique of the Judgement of Taste*. Cambridge, Mass.: Harvard University Press 1986

– *Reproduction in Education, Society and Culture*. London: Sage 1977

Bourdieu, Pierre, and Monique de Saint-Martin. 'The School as a Conservative Force: Scholastic and Cultural Inequalities' and 'Scholastic Excellence and the Values of the Educational System,' in *Contemporary Research in the Sociology of Education*, edited by John Eggleston. New York: Harper and Row 1974

Bourne, Paula, and John Eisenberg. 'The Canadian Public Issues Program: Learning to Deal with Social Controversy,' *Orbit*, 30 (Dec. 1975): 16–18

– *Social Issues in the Curriculum: Theory, Practice and Evaluation*, Curriculum Series/34. Toronto: Ontario Institute for Studies in Education 1978

Bowers, C.A. 'Culture against Itself: Nihilism as an Element in Recent Educational Thought,' *American Journal of Education*, 93/4 (Aug. 1985): 465–90

– 'The Dialectic of Nihilism and the State: Implications for an Emancipatory Theory of Education,' *Educational Theory*, 36/3 (Summer 1986): 225–32

– 'Linguistic Roots of Cultural Invasion in Paulo Freire's Pedagogy,' *Teachers College Record*, 84 (Summer 1983): 935–55

Bowles, S., and H. Gintis. 'Contradiction and Reproduction in Educational Theory,' in *Schooling Ideology, and the Curriculum*, edited by Len Barton et al. Sussex: Falmer Press 1980
- *Schooling in Capitalist America*. New York: Basic Books 1976
Boyd, Dwight, and Deanne Bodgan. '"Something" Clarified, Nothing of "Value": A Rhetorical Critique of Values Clarification,' *Educational Theory*, 34/3 (Summer 1984): 287–300
Broudy, Harry. 'Conflicts in Values,' *Education Administration – Philosophy in Action*. Norman, Okla.: College of Education, University of Oklahoma 1965
Bruner, Jerome S. *The Process of Education*. Cambridge, Mass.: Harvard University Press 1960
- *Toward a Theory of Instruction*. Cambridge, Mass.: Harvard University Press 1966
Buber, Martin. *I and Thou*. New York: Charles Scribner's Sons 1958
Burns, R.B. *The Self Concept in Theory, Measurement, Development and Behaviour*. London/New York: Longman 1979
Butler, Lenora, and Solveiga Miezitis. *Releasing Children from Depression: A Handbook for Elementary Teachers and Consultants*, Profiles in Practical Education/12. Toronto: OISE Press 1980
Butts, R. Freeman, and Donald H. Deckenpaugh. *The School's Role as Moral Authority*. Washington, DC: Association for Supervision and Curriculum Development 1977
Carter, Robert. *Dimensions of Moral Education*. Toronto: University of Toronto Press 1984
Carter, Roye, Jr. 'An Experiment in Value Measurement,' *American Sociological Review*, 21 (1956): 156–63
Castel, Robert, Françoise Castel, and Anne Lovell. *The Psychiatric Society*. New York: Columbia University Press 1982
Catton, William R., Jr. 'Exploring Techniques for Measuring Human Values,' *American Sociological Review*, 19 (1954): 49–55
Cicero. *De Oratore*. Cambridge, Mass.: Harvard University Press 1942
Clagett, Marshall. *The Science of Mechanics in the Middle Ages*. Madison: University of Wisconsin Press 1959
Clarke, Norris. 'Technology and Man: A Christian Vision,' in *Philosophy and Technology*, edited by Carl Mitcham and Robert Mackey. New York: Free Press 1972
Cochrane, Don. *Moral Values Education in Canada: A Bibliography and Directory 1970–77*. Toronto: Publication Division OISE 1978
Cochrane, Don, and Casimir Michael Manley. *Development of Moral Reasoning: Practical Approaches*. New York: Praeger 1980

Cochrane, D., C.M. Hamm, and A.C. Kazepides. *The Domain of Moral Education*. New York: Paulist Press 1979

Cochrane, D., and David Williams. 'The Stances of Provincial Ministries of Education towards Values/Moral Education in Public Schools,' *Canadian Journal of Education*, 3/4 (1978): 1–14

Cohen, Morris. 'Property and Sovereignty,' in *Property: Mainstream and Critical Positions*, edited by C.B. Macpherson. Toronto: University of Toronto Press 1978

Colby, Ann. 'Review of *Values and Teaching* and *Values Clarification: A Handbook of Practical Strategies for Teachers and Students*,' *Harvard Educational Review*, 45/1 (Feb. 1975): 134–43

Colby, A., M. Blatt, and B. Speicher. *Hypothetical Dilemmas for Use in Moral Discussions*. Boston: Center for Moral Education, Harvard University 1973

Colby, Ann, L. Kohlberg, J. Gibbs, and M. Lieberman. *A Longitudinal Study of Moral Judgment*. Boston: Social Research and Child Development 1983

Colby, A., L. Kohlberg, J. Gibbs, D. Candee, B. Speicher-Dubin, K. Kauffman, A. Hewer, and C. Power. *The Measurement of Moral Judgment: A Manual and Its Results*. New York: Cambridge University Press 1983

Combs, A.W., D.L. Avila, and W.W. Purkey. *Helping Relationships: Basic Concepts for the Helping Professions*. Boston: Allyn, and Bacon 1971

Connors, Bryan, et al. 'Reform or Reaction? The New Social Studies Program in Alberta,' *The History and Social Science Teacher*, 15/2 (Winter 1980): 115–18

Coombs, J. 'Concerning the Nature of Moral Competence,' in *The Teaching of Values in Canadian Education*. Edmonton: Canadian Society for the Study of Education 1975

– 'Discipline Maintained,' in *Philosophy of Education: Canadian Perspectives*. Toronto: Collier Macmillan Canada 1982

Cooper, Barry. *The End of History*. Toronto: University of Toronto Press 1984

Cragg, A. Wesley. 'Moral Education in the Schools,' *Canadian Journal of Education*, 4/1 (1979): 28–38

– 'Moral Education in the Schools: The Hidden Values Argument,' *Interchange*, 10/1 (1978–9): 12–25

Crittenden, Brian. *Form and Content in Moral Education*. Toronto: Ontario Institute for Studies in Education 1972

Dallmayr, Fred. *Polis and Praxis: Experience in Contemporary Political Theory*. Cambridge, Mass.: MIT Press 1984

Daniels, L.B. 'Psycho-Normative Concepts and Moral Education Research,' in *Canadian Society for the Study of Education Yearbook*, 2. Edmonton: Canadian Society for the Study of Education 1975

Darby, Tom. *The Feast: Meditations on Politics and Time*. Toronto: University of Toronto Press 1982

Davis, Robert. 'The Advance of Cybernation: 1965–1985,' in *The Guaranteed Income*. New York: Doubleday Anchor Books 1967

DeBeauvoir, Simone. *The Ethics of Ambiguity*, translated by Bernard Frechtman. Secausus, NJ: Citadel Press 1975

DeFaveri, I. 'Moral Education: The Risk of Oversimplification,' *Alberta Journal of Educational Research*, 25/4 (1979): 294–306

Delattre, Edwin J. 'The Straightjacket and the Vacuum in Moral Education,' *The Humanist*, 38/6 (Nov./ Dec. 1978): 19–21

Delattre, E.J., and William Bennett. 'Where the Values Movement Goes Wrong,' *Change*, 11/1 (Feb. 1979): 38–43

Deleuze, G. *Nietzsche and Philosophy*. London: Athlone Press 1983

Descombes, Vincent. *Contemporary French Philosophy*, translation of *Le Même et l'Autre* by L. Scott-Fox and J.M. Harding. Cambridge: Cambridge University Press 1979

Dewey, John. *Democracy and Education: An Introduction to the Philosophy of Education*. New York: Free Press 1966

– *Experience and Education*. New York: Collier 1977

– *Human Nature and Conduct*. New York: Random House 1957

– 'The Meaning of Value,' *The Journal of Philosophy* 23 (1924): 126–33

– *Moral Principles in Education*. New York: Greenwood Press 1969

– 'The Problem of Value,' *The Journal of Philosophy*, 10 (1913): 268–9

– *Reconstruction in Philosophy*. New York: Henry Holt 1920

– 'Some Questions about Value,' *The Journal of Philosophy*, 41 (1944): 449–55

– 'Values, Liking and Thought,' *The Journal of Philosophy*, 20 (1923): 617–22

Dewitt, Parker. 'Value as Any Object of Any Interest,' *Ethics*, 40 (1930): 465–95

Dodd, Stuart A. 'On Classifying Human Values,' *American Sociological Review*, 16 (1951): 645–53

Donzelot, J. *L'Invention du social*. Paris: Fayard 1984

– *The Policing of Families*, translated by Robert Hurley. New York: Pantheon 1980

Dreeben, R. 'Schooling and Authority: Comments on the Unstudied Curriculum,' in *The Unstudied Curriculum: Its Impact on Children*, edited by N. Overly. Washington, DC: Association for Supervision and Curriculum Development 1970

Dreyfus, Hubert. 'Knowledge and Human Values: A Genealogy of Nihilism,' *Teachers College Record*, 82/3 (1981): 507–20

– 'On the Genealogy of Ethics,' in *Michel Foucault: Beyond Structuralism and Hermeneutics*. Chicago: University of Chicago Press 1982

– *What Computers Can't Do*. New York: Harper and Row 1972

Durbin, Marshall. 'Models of Simultaneity and Sequentiality in Human Cognition,' in *Linguistics and Anthropology: In Honor of C.F. Voegelin,* edited by Dale Kinkade, Kenneth Male, and Oswald Werner. Lisse: Peter De Ridder 1975

Durkheim, Emile. *Moral Education.* New York: Free Press 1961

Easton, D., and J. Dennis. 'The Child's Acquisition of Regime Norms; Political Efficacy,' *American Political Science Review,* 61/1 (1967): 25–38

Edwards, Clifford. 'Sensitivity Training and Education: A Critique,' *Educational Leadership,* 28/3 (Dec. 1970): 261

Eliade, Mircea. *The Forge and the Crucible.* New York: Harper and Row 1962

Elliott, Murray. 'Clarity Is Not Enough,' in *Four Papers on Moral Education,* AVER, Report #3. Vancouver: AVER 1974

Ellul, Jacques. *Autopsy of Revolution,* translated by Patricia Wolf. New York: Knopf 1971

– *Political Illusion.* New York: Knopf 1976

– *Propaganda: The Formation of Men's Attitudes.* New York: Knopf 1966

– *The Technological Society.* New York: Knopf 1964

– *The Technological System,* translated by Joachim Neugroschel. New York: Continuum 1980

Ewing, A.C. *Ethics.* London: English Universities Press 1953

Fabian, Johannes. *Time and the Other: How Anthropology Makes Its Object.* New York: Columbia University Press 1983

Featherston, Mike. 'The Body in Consumer Culture,' *Theory, Culture and Society,* 1/3 (1983): 4–9

Foot, Philippa, ed. *Theories of Ethics.* Oxford: Oxford University Press 1967

Foucault, Michel. 'About the Concept of the "Dangerous Individual" in 19th Century Legal Psychiatry,' *International Journal of Law and Psychiatry,* 1 (1978): 1–18

– *The Archeology of Knowledge and the Discourse on Language.* New York: Dorset Press 1972

– *The Birth of the Clinic.* London: Tavistock 1973

– *Discipline and Punish: The Birth of the Prison.* New York: Pantheon 1977

– *The History of Sexuality,* vol. 1. London: Penguin Press 1979

– *Madness and Civilization: A History of Insanity in the Age of Reason.* New York: Vintage Books 1973

– 'Nietzsche, Genealogy, History,' in *Language, Counter-Memory, Practice,* edited by Donald Bouchard. Ithaca: Cornell University Press 1971

– *The Order of Things.* London: Tavistock 1970

– *Power/Knowledge: Selected Interviews and Other Writings 1972–1977,* edited by Colin Gordon. New York: Pantheon 1980

– *Power, Truth and Strategy.* Sydney: Feral Publications 1979

– *The Use of Pleasure*. New York: Random House 1985

Fraenkel, Jack. *Helping Students Think and Value*. Englewood Cliffs, NJ: Prentice-Hall 1973

– *How to Teach about Values: An Analytical Approach*. Toronto: Prentice-Hall 1977

– 'Strategies for Developing Values,' *Today's Education*, Nov./Dec. 1973: 49–55

Frankena, William K. *Ethics*. Englewood Cliffs, NJ: Prentice-Hall 1973

– 'Toward a Philosophy of Moral Education,' reprinted in *Philosophy and Education*, 2nd edition, edited by Israel Scheffer. Boston: Allyn and Bacon 1966

Franklin, B.M. 'Education for Social Control,' *History of Education Quarterly*, 14 (1974): 131–6

– 'Technological Models and the Curriculum Field,' *The Educational Forum*, March 1976: 303–12

Freire, Paulo. 'The Adult Literacy Process as Cultural Action for Freedom,' in *The Politics of Education: Culture, Power, and Liberation*, translated by Donaldo Macedo. South Hadley, Mass.: Bergin and Garvey 1985

– *Cultural Action for Freedom*. Cambridge, Mass.: Harvard Educational Review Monograph 1970

– *Education as the Practice of Freedom*. London: Writers and Readers Publishing Cooperative 1974

– *Education for Critical Consciousness*. New York: Seabury Press 1978

– *Pedagogy in Process*. New York: Seabury Press 1978

– *Pedagogy of the Oppressed*. New York: Herder and Herder 1970

Fromm, Erich. *To Have or to Be*. New York: Harper and Row 1976

– *The Heart of Man*. New York: Harper and Row 1966

– *Man for Himself: An Inquiry into the Psychology of Ethics*. New York: Rinehart 1947

– *The Revolution of Hope: Toward a Humanized Technology*. New York: Harper and Row 1968

Fuller, Buckminster R. *Operating Manual for Spaceship Earth*. New York: Pocket Book 1970

Gadamer, Hans-Georg. *Truth and Method*. New York: Seabury Press 1975

Galbraith, Ronald, and Thomas Jones. *Moral Reasoning: A Teaching Handbook for Adapting Kohlberg to the Classroom*. Minneapolis: Green Haven Press 1976

Gardner, John. *Self-Renewal: The Individual and the Innnovative Society*. New York: Harper and Row 1963

Giambattista, Vico. *On the Study Methods of Our Time*, translated by Elio Gianturco. New York: Bobbs Merill 1965

Gibbs, J.C. 'Kohlberg's Stages of Moral Development: A Constructive Critique,' *Harvard Education Review*, 47/1 (Feb. 1977): 43–61

Gilligan, Carol. *In a Different Voice: Psychological Theory and Women's Development*. Cambridge, Mass.: Harvard University Press 1982

Gilligan, Carol, and L. Kohlberg. 'From Adolescence to Adulthood: The Rediscovery of Reality in a Post-Conventional World,' in *Topics in Cognitive Development*. New York: Plenum Press 1977

Gilligan, C., and J.M. Murphy. 'Moral Development in Late Adolescence and Adulthood: A Critique and Reconstruction of Kohlberg's Theory,' *Human Development*, 23 (1980): 77-104

Giroux, Henri. *Theory and Resistance in Education: A Pedagogy for the Opposition*. South Hadley, Mass.: Bergin and Garvey Publishers 1983

Giroux, H.A. *Ideology, Culture, and the Process of Schooling*. Philadelphia: Temple University Press 1981

– 'Mass Culture and the Rise of the New Illiteracy: Implications for Reading,' *Interchange*, 10/4 (1979–80): 89–98

– 'Schooling and the Culture of Positivism: Notes on the Death of History,' *Educational Theory*, 29/4 (1979): 263–84

Giroux, H.A., and A.N. Penna. 'Social Education in the Classroom: The Dynamics of the Hidden Curriculum,' *Theory and Research in Social Education*, 7/1, (Spring 1979): 21–42

Giroux, H.A., and D. Purple. eds. *The Hidden Curriculum and Moral Education: Illusion or Insight*. Berkeley: McCutchan 1983

Gluck, Phyllis. 'Values Clarification: The Engineering of Consensus,' *Teachers College Record*, 79/2 (1977): 267–74

Gordon, Theodore. 'The Feedback between Technology and Values,' in *Values and the Future: The Impact of Technological Change on American Values*. California Institute for the Future 1969

Gow, Kathleen. *Yes, Virginia: There Is a Right and Wrong*. Toronto: John Wiley and Sons 1980

Grant, George. 'The Computer Does Not Impose upon Us the Way It Should Be Used,' in *Beyond Industrial Growth*, edited by A. Rotstein. Toronto: University of Toronto Press 1976

– *English-Speaking Justice*. Sackville, NB: Mount Allison University Press 1977

– 'Knowing and Making,' *Transactions of the Royal Society of Canada*, 4th Series, 12 (1974): 59–68

– *Philosophy in the Mass Age*. Toronto: Copp Clark 1959

– *Technology and Empire: Perspectives on North America*. Toronto: Anansi Press 1969

– *Technology and Justice*. Toronto: Anansi Press 1987

– *Time as History*. Toronto: Canadian Broadcasting Corporation 1969

Green, T.H. 'The Right of the State in Regard to Property,' in *Lectures on the*

Principles of Political Obligation. Ann Arbor: University of Michigan Press
1967

Griffiths, A.P. 'The Autonomy of Prudence,' *Mind*, 71 (April 1962): 161–80

Habermas, Jurgen. *Communication and the Evolution of Society*, translated by
Thomas McCarthy. Boston: Beacon Press 1979

– *Knowledge and Human Interest*. Boston: Beacon Press 1971

– 'Psychic Thermidor and the Rebirth of Rebellious Subjectivity,' *Berkeley Journal of Sociology*, 25 (1980): 1–12

– 'The Public Sphere: An Encyclopedia Article,' *New German Critique*, 3 (Fall
1974): 49–55

– *Theory and Practice*. Boston: Beacon Press 1973

– *Toward a Rational Society*. Boston: Beacon Press 1971

Hall, Robert. 'Moral Education Today: Progress, Prospects and Problems of a
Field Come of Age,' *The Humanist*, Nov./Dec. 1978: 8–13

Hall, Robert, et al. 'Moral Education and Secular Humanism: A Symposium,'
The Humanist, Nov./Dec. 1978: 8–25

Hamm, C.M. 'The Content of Moral Education "The Bag of Virtues,"' in *The
Teaching of Values in Canadian Education*. Edmonton: Canadian Society for the
Study of Education 1975

Hare, R.M. *Freedom and Reason*. Oxford: Clarendon Press 1963

– 'Language and Moral Education,' in *New Essays in the Philosophy of Education*,
edited by G. Langford and D.J. O'Connor. London: Routledge and Kegan Paul
1973

– *The Language of Morals*. London: Oxford University Press 1952

– 'Values Education in a Pluralistic Society,' *Proceedings of the Philosophy of Education of Great Britain*. Dorchester on Thames: Journals Oxford 1976

Harmin, Merrill, Howard Kirschenbaum, and Sidney Simon. eds. *Clarifying
Values through Subject Matter*. Minneapolis: Winston Press 1973

Hartshorne, H., and M.A. May. *Studies in the Nature of Character*. New York:
Macmillan 1930

Hawley, Robert. *Value Exploration through Role Playing*. New York: Hart 1975

Hegel, G.W.F. *On Christianity: Early Theological Writings*, translated by T.M. Knox.
New York: Harper Torchbooks 1967

Heidegger, Martin. 'Building, Dwelling, Thinking,' in *Poetry, Language, Thought*,
translated by Albert Hofstadter. New York: Harper and Row 1971

– 'The End of Philosophy and the Task of Thinking,' in *Martin Heidegger: Basic
Writings*, edited by David Krell. New York: Harper and Row 1977

– *Nietzsche*, vol. 1: *The Will to Power as Art*. New York: Harper and Row 1979

– *Nietzsche*, vol. 4: *Nihilism*. San Francisco: Harper and Row 1982

– *What Is Called Thinking?* New York: Harper and Row 1968

Herman, Al. *Guidance in Canadian Schools*. Calgary: Detselig Enterprises 1981
Hersch, R., D. Paolitto, and J. Reimer. *Promoting Moral Growth from Piaget to Kohlberg*. New York: Longman 1979
Hirst, Paul. *Moral Education in a Secular Society*. London: University of London Press 1974
– *On Law and Ideology*. London: Macmillan 1979
Holton, Hamilton, and John Meyer. *Aspects and Models of Values Moral Education*. Burlington: Values Education Center 1975
Horkheimer, Max, and Theodore W. Adorno. *The Dialectic of Enlightenment*, translated by John Cumming. New York: Seabury Press 1972
Howe, Leland W., and Mary Martha Howe. *Personalizing Education: Values Clarification and Beyond*. New York: Hart 1975
Ihde, Don. *Existential Technics*. Albany: State University of New York Press 1983
– *Technics and Praxis*. Dordrecht, Holland: D. Reidel 1979
Illich, I. *Deschooling Society*. New York: Harper and Row 1971
Jameson, Frederic. 'Postmodernism, or the Cultural Logic of Late Capitalism,' *New Left Review*, 146 (July/Aug. 1984): 53–92
Jammer, Max. *Concepts of Space: The History of Theories of Space in Physics*. Cambridge, Mass.: Harvard University Press 1954
Jonas, Hans. *The Gnostic Religion*. New York: Harper Torchbooks 1958
– 'Technology and Responsibility: Reflections on the New Tasks of Ethics,' in *Philosophical Essays*. New York: Prentice-Hall 1974
Kazepides, A.C. 'The Logic of Values Clarification,' *Journal of Educational Thought*, 11/2 (1977): 99–111
– 'Toward a Modern Approach to Values: The Valuing Process in the Mature Person,' in *Readings in Values Clarification*, edited by H. Kirschenbaum and S. Simon. Minneapolis: Winston Press 1973
– ed. *Yearbook of the Canadian Society for the Study of Education: The Teaching of Values in Canadian Education*. Edmonton: Canadian Society for the Study of Education 1975
Kern, Stephen. *The Culture of Time and Space, 1880–1918*. Cambridge, Mass.: Harvard University Press 1983
Kirschenbaum, Howard. 'Current Research in Value Clarification,' in *Advanced Values Clarification*. La Jolla, Cal.: University Associates 1977
– 'In Support of Values Clarification,' *Social Education*, 42/2 (1977): 398
Kirschenbaum, H., Merrill Harmin, Leland Howe, and Sidney Simon. *In Defense of Values Clarification: A Position Paper*. Boulder: National Humanistic Education Center 1975
Kluckhohn, Clyde. 'The Study of Values,' in *Values in America*, edited by D.N. Barrett. Notre Dame: University of Notre Dame Press 1961

Kluckhohn, Florence, and Fred L. Strotbeck. *Variations in Value Orientations.* Evanston, Ill.: Row Peterson 1967

Kohlberg, Lawrence. 'The Adolescent as a Philosopher: The Discovery of the Self in a Post-conventional World,' *Daedelus*, 100/4 (1971): 1051–86

- *The Assessment of Moral Judgment: A Standard Form Moral Judgment Scoring Manual.* Cambridge, Mass.: Moral Education Research Foundation 1978–9
- 'The Child as a Moral Philosopher,' *Psychology Today*, 7 (Sept. 1968): 181–6
- 'The Claim to Moral Adequacy of a Highest Stage of Moral Judgment,' *Journal of Philosophy*, 70/18 (1973): 630–45
- 'The Cognitive-Developmental Approach to Moral Education,' in *Values Concepts and Techniques.* Washington, DC: National Education Association 1976
- *Collected Papers on Moral Development and Moral Education.* Cambridge, Mass.: Laboratory of Human Development 1973
- 'Continuities in Childhood and Adult Moral Development Revisited,' in *Life-Span Developmental Psychology: Personality and Socialization*, edited by P.B. Balters and K.W. Schaie. New York: Academic Press 1975
- 'Development as the Aim of Education,' *Harvard Education Review*, 42/4 (1972): 449–96
- *Essays on Moral Development*, vol. 1: *The Philosophy of Moral Development: Moral Stages and the Idea of Justice*, and vol. 2: *The Psychology of Moral Development: The Nature and Validity of Moral Stages.* New York: Harper and Row 1981
- 'Education for Justice: A Modern Statement of the Platonic View,' in *Moral Education: Five Lectures*, edited by Theodor Sizer and Nancy Sizer. Cambridge; Harvard University Press 1970
- 'From Is to Ought: How To Commit the Naturalistic Fallacy and Get Away with It in the Study of Moral Development,' in *Cognitive Development and Epistemology*, edited by Theodore Mischel. New York: Academic Press 1971
- *Justice as Reversibility, Philosophy, Politics and Society.* New Haven: Yale University Press 1979
- 'Moral Development and Moral Education,' in *Psychology and Educational Practice*, edited by G. Lesser. Chicago: Scott Foresman 1971
- 'Moral Education and Moralization: The Cognitive-Developmental Approach,' in *Moral Development and Behaviour.* New York: Holt, Rinehart and Winston 1976
- 'Moral Development and the New Social Studies,' *Social Education*, May 1973: 369–75
- 'Moral Education for a Society in Moral Transition,' *Educational Leadership*, 33/1 (1975): 46–54
- 'Moral Education in the Schools: A Developmental View,' *The School Review*, 74 (Spring 1966): 1–30

– 'Moral Education Reappraised,' *The Humanist*, 38/6 (Nov./Dec. 1978)

Kohlberg, L., Charles Levine, and Alexandra Hewer. *Moral Stages: A Current Formulation and a Response to Critics*. Basel: Karger AG 1983

Kojeve, Alexander. *Introduction to the Reading of Hegel: Lectures on the Phenomenology of Spirit*, translated by James Nichols, Jr. Ithaca: Cornell University Press 1969

Kroker, Arthur, and David Cook. *The Postmodern Scene: Excremental Culture and Hyper-Aesthetics*. Montreal: New World Perspectives 1986

LaCapra, Dominick. 'Habermas and the Grounding of Critical Theory,' *History and Theory*, 16 (1977): 237–64

Larson, Roland, and Doris Larson. *Values and Faith: Value-Clarifying Exercises for Family and Church Groups*. Minneapolis: Winston Press 1976

Leiss, William. *The Domination of Nature*. Boston: Beacon Press 1974

– 'The Social Consequences of Technological Progress: Critical Comments on Recent Theories,' *Canadian Public Administration*, 13 (1970): 248–53

Lockwood, Alan. 'A Critical View of Values Clarification,' *Teachers' College Record*, 77/14 (1975): 35–50

– 'The Effects of Values Clarification and Moral Development Curricula on School-Age Subjects: A Critical Review of Recent Research,' *Review of Educational Research*, 48/3 (1978): 325–64

– *Moral Reasoning: The Value of Life*. Middletown, Conn.: Xerox Education Publishing 1973

Loevinger, J., and R. Wessler. *The Meaning and Measurement of Ego Development*. San Francisco: Jossey-Bass 1970

Lyotard, Jean-François. *The Postmodern Condition: A Report on Knowledge*, translated by Geoff Bennington and Brian Massumi. Minneapolis: University of Minnesota Press 1984

Macpherson, C.B., ed. *Property: Mainstream and Critical Positions*. Toronto: University of Toronto Press 1978

Mandel, Ernest. *Late Capitalism*. London: Verso 1980

Marcel, Gabriel. *Being and Having: An Existentialist Diary*. New York: Harper and Row 1965

Marcuse, Herbert. *One-Dimensional Man: Studies in the Ideology of Advanced Industrial Society*. Boston: Beacon Press 1964

Maslow, Abraham. *New Knowledge in Human Values*. New York: Harper 1959

May, Rollo. 'Toward the Ontological Basis of Psychotherapy,' *Existential Inquiry*, 1 (1969): 5–7

May, Rollo, Ernest Angel, and Henri Ellenberger. *Existence*. New York: Basic Books 1958

McLuhan, Marshall. *The Gutenberg Galaxy: The Making of Typographic Man*.
    Toronto: University of Toronto Press 1962
– *Understanding Media: The Extensions of Man*. New York: McGraw-Hill 1964
McLuhan, Marshall, and Quentin Fiore. *The Medium Is the Message*. New York:
    Random House 1967
– *War and Peace In the Global Village*. Toronto: McGraw-Hill 1968
McPhail, Peter. *Learning to Care: Teacher's Guide to Lifeline Series*. Niles, Ill.: Argus
    Communications 1975
Metcalfe, Lawrence, ed. *Values Education: Rationale, Strategies and Procedures, 41st
    Yearbook*. Washington, DC: National Council for the Social Studies 1971
Meyer, John R., ed. *Reflections on Values Education*. Waterloo, Ont.: Wilfrid Lau-
    rier University Press 1976
Meyer, J., ed. *Values Education: Theory/Practice/Problems/Prospects*. Waterloo, Ont.:
    Wilfrid Laurier University Press 1975
Mitcham, Carl, and Robert Mackey, eds. *Philosophy and Technology: Readings in
    the Philosophical Problems of Technology*. New York: Free Press 1972
Mounier, Immanuel. *Existentialist Philosophies: An Introduction*. London: Rockliff
    1948
Musgrave, P.W. *The Moral Curriculum: A Sociological Analysis*. London: Methuen
    1978
Niblett, William, ed. *Moral Education in a Changing Society*. London: Faber and
    Faber 1963
Nietzsche, Friedrich. *Beyond Good and Evil*, translated by Walter Kaufmann. New
    York: Vintage Books 1964
– *Ecce Homo and the Birth of Tragedy*, translated by Walter Kaufmann. New York:
    Vintage 1965
– *The Gay Science*, translated by Walter Kaufmann. New York: Vintage 1974
– *On the Genealogy of Morals*, translated by Walter Kaufmann and R.J. Holling-
    dale. New York: Vintage 1969
– *Twilight of the Idols*, in *The Portable Nietzsche*, translated by Walter Kaufmann.
    Harmondsworth: Penguin Books 1976
– *The Use and Abuse of History*, translated by Adrian Collins. Indianapolis: Bobbs
    Merrill Educational Publishing 1977
– *The Will to Power*, translated by Walter Kaufmann and R.J. Hollingdale. New
    York: Vintage 1967
Noyes, Charles Reinold. *The Institution of Property*. New York: Longmans, Green
    and Co. 1986
Ontario Institute of Studies in Education. 'The Moral Education Project: Year 5,'
    Final Report; *Year 4, Annual Report 1975–76*; Year 3, 'The Reflective Approach in

Values Education' 1976. Toronto: Ontario Institute for Studies in Education 1972–7

Ontario Teachers' Federation. *The Clouded Crystal: Adaptation to Change: The Role of Ontario's Public Educational System 1985–2000*. Toronto: Ontario Teachers' Federation 1985

– *Effect of Computer/Communications Technology on Education: Synopsis of the Ontario Teachers' Federation Submission to the Cabinet*. Toronto: Ontario Teachers' Federation 1981

– *The School to Work Transition, Submission to the Cabinet*. Toronto: Ontario Teachers' Federation 1983

Overly, N., ed. *The Unstudied Curriculum: Its Impact on Children*. Washington, DC: Association for Supervision and Curriculum Development 1970

Parsons, Talcott. 'The School Class as a Social System: Some of Its Functions in American Society,' *Harvard Educational Review*, 29/4 (Fall 1959): 297–318

– *The Social System*. New York: Free Press 1951

Pepper, Stephen. *The Sources of Value*. Berkeley: University of California Press 1959

Perkins, H.V. *Human Development and Learning*. Belmont, Cal.: Woodsworth 1969

Peters, R.S. *Ethics and Education*. London: Allen and Unwin 1966

– 'Moral Development and Moral Learning,' in *Moral Development and Moral Education*. London: Allen and Unwin 1981

– *Psychology and Ethical Development*. London: Allen and Unwin 1974

– *Reason and Compassion*. London: Routledge and Kegan Paul 1973

– 'Reason and Habit: The Paradox of Moral Education' and 'Moral Education and the Psychology of Character,' in *Philosophy and Education*, edited by Israel Scheffler. Boston: Allyn and Bacon 1966

Piaget, Jean. *The Moral Judgment of the Child*. New York: Free Press 1965

Poulet, Georges. *The Metamorphoses of the Circle*. Baltimore: Johns Hopkins Press 1966

– *Studies in Human Time*. Baltimore: Johns Hopkins Press 1956

Raths, Louis, 'Approaches to the Measurement of Values,' *Educational Research Bulletin*, 19 (1940): 175–282

Raths, Louis, Merrill Harmin, and Sidney Simon. *Values and Teaching: Working with Values in the Classroom*. Columbus, Ohio: Charles E. Merrill 1966 and 1978 (2nd edition)

Raths, Louis, Selma Wasserman, Albert Jonas, and A.M. Rothstein. *Teaching for Thinking*. Columbus, Ohio: Charles E. Merrill 1967

Read, Donald, and Sidney Simon, eds. *Humanistic Education Sourcebook*. Englewood Cliffs, NJ: Prentice-Hall 1975

Rescher, Nicholas. *Introduction to Value Theory*. Englewood Cliffs, NJ: Prentice-Hall 1968

Rogers, Carl. *Client-Centered Therapy*. Boston: Houghton-Mifflin 1951

– *Freedom to Learn*. Columbus, Ohio: Charles E. Merrill 1969

– *On Becoming a Person*. Boston: Houghton-Mifflin 1961

Rose, M.C. 'Value Experience and the Means-Ends Continuum,' *Ethics*, 65 (1954): 44–54

Rose, Nikolas. 'The Psychological Complex: Mental Measurement and Social Administration,' *Ideology and Consciousness*, 5 (1979): 5–68

Rosen, Stanley. *Nihilism: A Philosophical Essay*. New Haven: Yale University Press 1969

Roszak, Theodor. *The Making of a Counter Culture*. New York: Anchor Books 1969

– *Person/Planet: The Creative Disintegration of Industrial Society*. New York: Anchor Press 1978

Sartre, Jean-Paul. *Being and Nothingness: An Essay on Phenomenological Ontology*, translated by Hazel Barnes. New York: Philosophical Library 1956

– *The Critique of Dialectical Reason*, vol. 1: *Theory of Practical Ensembles*, translated by Alan Sheridan-Smith. London: New Left Books 1976

Seiler, Hansjakob. *Possession as an Operational Dimension of Language*. Tubingen: Gunter Narr Verlag 1983

Selman, Robert. 'Social Cognitive Understanding: A Guide to Educational and Clinical Practice,' in *Moral Development and Moral Behaviour*. New York: Holt, Rinehart and Winston 1976

– 'Taking Another's Perspective: Role-Taking Development in Early Childhood,' *Child Development*, 42/6 (1977): 1721–34

Shaftel, Fannie, and G. Shaftel. *Role Playing for Social Values*. Englewood Cliffs, NJ: Prentice-Hall 1967

Shils, Edward. *Tradition*. Chicago: University of Chicago Press 1981

Shorr, J.E. 'The Development of a Test to Measure the Intensity of Values,' *Journal of Educational Psychology*, 44 (1953): 266–74

Silberman, C.E. *Crisis in the Classroom*. New York: Random House 1970

Silver, Michael. *Values Education*. Washington, DC: National Education Association 1976

Simon, Sidney. 'Nourishing Sexuality in the Schools,' *National Elementary Principal*, 50/4 (Feb. 1971): 56–60

Simon, Sidney, Leland W. Howe, and Howard Kirschenbaum. *Values Clarification: A Handbook of Practical Strategies for Teachers and Students*. New York: Hart 1978

Straughan, Roger. *Can We Teach Children to Be Good?* London: George Allen and Unwin 1982

Sullivan, E.V. *Kohlberg's Structuralism: A Critical Appraisal.* Toronto: Ontario Institute for Studies in Education 1977

– 'Medical Nemesis as Moral Education,' *New Catholic World*, 219/5 (1976): 244–7

– *Moral Learning: Some Findings, Issues and Questions.* New York: Paulist Press 1975

– 'A Study of Kohlberg's Structural Theory of Moral Development: A Critique of Liberal Social Science Ideology,' *Human Development*, 20 (1977): 352–76

Superka, Douglas, Christin Ahrens, Judith Hedstrom, Luther Ford, and Patricia Johnson. *Values Education Sourcebook: Conceptual Approaches, Materials Analyses, and an Annotated Bibliography.* Boulder: Social Science Education Consortium and ERIC/Clearinghouse for Social Studies/Social Science Education 1976

Taylor, P.W. *Normative Discourse.* Englewood Cliffs, NJ: Prentice-Hall 1961

Turiel, E. 'Developmental Processes in the Child's Moral Thinking,' in *Trends and Issues in Developmental Psychology*, edited by P.H. Mussen, J. Langer, and M. Covington. New York: Holt, Rinehart and Winston 1969

– 'An Experimental Test of the Sequentiality of Developmental Stages in the Child's Moral Judgments,' *Journal of Personality and Social Psychology* 3 (1966): 611–18

Turner, Francis J. 'Values and the Social Worker,' in *Reflections on Values Education*, edited by John Meyer. Waterloo, Ont.: Wilfrid Laurier University Press 1976

Vallance, E. 'The Hidden Curriculum and Qualitative Inquiry as Stages of Mind,' *Journal of Education*, 162/1 (Winter 1980): 138–51

– 'Hiding the Hidden Curriculum,' *Curriculum Theory Network*, 4/1 (1973): 5–21

Van Dusen, A.C., S. Wimberly, and C.I. Moisier. 'Standardization of a Values Inventory,' *Journal of Educational Psychology*, 30 (1939): 53–62

Voegelin, Eric. *The New Science of Politics.* Chicago: University of Chicago Press 1952

Wiener, Norbert. *The Human Use of Human Beings.* New York: Doubleday 1956

Wikse, John R. *About Possession: The Self as Private Property.* University Park: Pennsylvania State University Press 1977

Wilson, H.T. *The American Ideology: Science, Technology, and Organizations as Modes of Rationality in Advanced Industrial Societies.* London: Routledge and Kegan Paul 1977

Wilson, John. *The Assessment of Morality.* Windsor: NFER Pub. 1973

– *Moral Education and the Curriculum: A Guide for Teachers and Research Workers.* Oxford: Pergamon 1969

– *Practical Methods of Moral Education*. London: Heinemann 1972
– 'Rationality and Moral Education,' *Proceedings of the Philosophy of Education Society of Great Britain*, 11 (1977): 98–112
Wilson, John, N. Williams, and B. Sugarman. *Introduction to Moral Education*. Baltimore: Penguin Books 1967
Winner, Langdon. *Autonomous Technology: Technics-out-of-Control as a Theme in Political Thought*. Cambridge, Mass.: MIT Press 1977
Wright, Ian. 'Value/Moral Education in Canada: The Work of Aver,' *Journal of Moral Education*, 6/13 (1976): 32
Wright, Ian, and Murray Elliott. 'Moral Education: A Reply to DeFaveri,' *The Alberta Journal of Educational Research*, 27/1 (1981): 98
Yates, Francis. *The Art of Memory*. London: Ark Paperbacks 1984

Index